ALSO BY AMY S. GREENBERG

Cause for Alarm:
The Volunteer Fire Department in the Nineteenth-Century City

Manifest Manhood and the Antebellum American Empire

Manifest Destiny and American Territorial Expansion:
A Brief History with Documents

A Wicked War:
Polk, Clay, Lincoln, and the 1846 U.S. Invasion of Mexico

Lady First

Lady First

THE WORLD OF FIRST LADY SARAH POLK

Amy S. Greenberg

Alfred A. Knopf
NEW YORK
2019

THIS IS A BORZOI BOOK
PUBLISHED BY ALFRED A. KNOPF

Copyright © 2019 by Amy S. Greenberg

All rights reserved. Published in the United States by Alfred A. Knopf,
a division of Penguin Random House LLC, New York, and distributed in
Canada by Random House of Canada, a division of Penguin Random
House Canada Limited, Toronto.

www.aaknopf.com

Knopf, Borzoi Books, and the colophon are registered trademarks of
Penguin Random House LLC.

Library of Congress Cataloging-in-Publication Data

Names: Greenberg, Amy S., [date] author.
Title: Lady first : the world of first lady Sarah Polk / by Amy S. Greenberg.
Other titles: World of first lady Sarah Polk
Description: First edition. | New York : Alfred A. Knopf, [2019] |
    Includes bibliographical references and index.
Identifiers: LCCN 2018010748 (print) | LCCN 2018012602 (ebook) |
    ISBN 9780385354134 (hardcover) | ISBN 9780385354141 (ebook)
Subjects: LCSH: Polk, Sarah Childress, 1803–1891. | Presidents' spouses—
    United States—Biography. | Governors' spouses—Tennessee—
    Biography. | United States—Politics and government—1845–1849.
Classification: LCC E417.1 (ebook) | LCC E417.1 .G74 2019 (print) |
    DDC 973.6/1092 [B]—dc23
LC record available at https://lccn.loc.gov/2018010748

Jacket images: *Portrait of Sarah Polk,* 1846, by George Peter Alexander
Healy (detail), The Picture Art Collection/Alamy; (flag detail) James K.
Polk 1844 Campaign ribbon, The Frent Collection/Getty Images
Jacket design by Stephanie Ross

Manufactured in the United States of America
First Edition

For Jane Lee Macintosh Greenberg
and in memory of
Mrs. Paul A. Greene (1922–2016)

"A lady rises above it"

Mrs. Polk was a sweet exemplification of lowliness. She was as retiring, as gentle, as though the public eye had never scanned her conduct, and the public tongue never sounded her praise.

—*Sartain's Union Magazine,* February 28, 1850

As to whom Mrs Polk is, her high character &c I need not write to you, but trust you will give her letter . . . such consideration as it deserves, coming from such respectable source, and relating to a matter of importance . . . to the government, and National troops. —ANDREW JOHNSON, October 30, 1863

Contents

Preface

MRS. POLK'S 1848

History can be capricious, as the following story about two events and one exceptionally powerful woman should make clear. For the twenty-three million residents of the United States and the seven and a half million residents of Mexico, the landmark event of 1848 was the ratification of the Treaty of Guadalupe Hidalgo, which ended a twenty-month-long war between the two countries, and transferred approximately half of Mexico's prewar territory to the United States. Although the war left thirteen thousand Americans and at least twenty-five thousand Mexicans dead, and the contested status of slavery in the newly acquired territories, including California and New Mexico, was already provoking threats of secession in the South, it was recognized at the time as a remarkable victory for both the United States and that exceptionally powerful American woman. Her name was Sarah Childress Polk, and the defeat of Mexico was her reward for years of labor alongside her husband in the name of America's "Manifest Destiny."

President James K. Polk, a taciturn fifty-two-year-old left prematurely aged by compulsive work habits and chronic intestinal complaints, emerged from the war admired by some but loved by very few other than his wife. Humorless and secretive, he lied to members of his own party, to Congress, and to the American people. The war was divisive; antiwar agitators across the country condemned the president for prosecuting an immoral war, and the nation turned against his political party, the Democrats. The opposition party, the Whigs, easily won the presidency that year with a war hero, General Zachary Taylor, as their candidate.

But forty-four-year-old Sarah Polk, a slim, elegantly dressed woman whose vivacity, youthfulness, and ability to charm formed a perfect contrast to her husband, suffered no such backlash from the war that she helped promote. On one hand this is entirely unsurprising. An age-old set of assumptions enforced by both law and custom proclaimed women unfit for public life. They weren't citizens, and they couldn't vote. If they were married, their identities were legally subsumed into those of their husbands. That even rich, well-educated white women like Mrs. James K. Polk were biologically and socially incapable of contemplating matters such as foreign policy was for most Americans an assumption so obvious as to go entirely unquestioned.

Were a woman intellectually capable of engaging with affairs of state, American politics was utterly unwelcoming for the "gentle sex." Americans were justly proud of their democratic institutions, but those institutions were competitive, coercive, and quite liable to turn violent. Men physically fought over political positions, while partisans fueled by free alcohol attacked one another at the polls. The wrong political statement, put into print, could result in a challenge to a duel, or a surprise attack in the streets. Election-day riots were sadly common. This was considered no space for women.

There was little debate over this point because America's men and women agreed that the two sexes were suited to different spheres. Men belonged in the political, competitive, public world of work and elections, and women in the peaceful, religious, domestic realm of children and home. Women who crossed this line and insisted on openly expressing their political views did so at their own peril. The abolitionist Grimké sisters became notorious in the 1830s for insisting on speaking in public, and were threatened with death by angry mobs. This was the reality of women's lives in 1848.

Yet somehow Mrs. James K. Polk managed to stand above the constraints that bound other women. Her views on the Manifest Destiny of the United States were well known, as were her political efforts in support of her husband. Indeed, her dedication to her husband's agenda, and the fact that the two were a seemingly inseparable team, was a large part of her appeal as a First Lady.[1]

In 1848 she was the most powerful woman in America. She controlled access to her husband and helped coordinate the Democratic Party's political agenda. She managed her husband's political campaigns and negotiated on his behalf with men who understood her value as a conduit. No accident, her power was grounded in decades of work as a political spouse, her remarkable powers of innovation, a deep and abiding love of politics, and the unpaid labor of dozens of enslaved people who toiled for her in her home and on a cotton plantation. As a marital partner and her husband's closest advisor, Mrs. James K. Polk (the name she preferred for herself) helped create the office of the First Lady. Her political partnership with her husband and the manner in which she expanded the First Lady's role prefigured the activist First Ladies of our own era.[2]

But Sarah Childress Polk wasn't just powerful, she was popular—remarkably so. Parents who know her only as "Mrs. Polk" searched for her Christian name so they might bestow it on their newborn daughters. Gold Rush travelers passing through Gorgona, Panama, reported seeing her likeness hanging on the wall of the alcalde's office. Although her curly hair remained jet black well into her forties, her popularity had little to do with her appearance. Her prominent nose and sallow complexion diverged from the period's standard of female beauty, and she was understandably self-conscious about her bad teeth. But she had a commanding presence and the ability to put virtually anyone at ease. She skillfully manipulated the press in order to manufacture a public persona as a democratic, approachable "perfect partner" to her husband that both women and men found highly appealing. She laughed easily, and was an engaging conversationalist. Even her husband's enemies liked her.[3]

She was the first politically effective partisan First Lady, in a period when the role of women was strictly circumscribed. She forged and maintained private relationships with men, exchanging information with them for her husband's benefit that he was not privy to, and that in some cases he would not want to know. She broke the rules of Washington society, but made sure to always maintain plausible deniability. She outwardly conformed to the idea that men and women had separate spheres of influence, while herself choosing to remain as much as possible with men rather than with women.

A critic in the 1870s admitted that Sarah presided over the White House "with a wider popularity than has since been obtained by any of her successors." Everyone knew who Mrs. James K. Polk was, or thought they knew who she was, in 1848, and almost everyone loved her. Ten years after leaving office she was "universally conceded to be the most amiable, accomplished and intelligent woman of her time."[4]

The Treaty of Guadalupe Hidalgo was the signature event of 1848 in North America, but in Europe 1848 was the "Year of Revolution," marked by a wave of popular uprisings that spread from Paris through Prussia, the Habsburg Empire, and the Italian states. That wave stopped well short of the United States, but America was not wanting for radicals in the 1840s. Inspired by evangelical fervor, American men and women formed religious sects and utopias, and feverishly pursued reforms designed to banish sin from the land, whether in the form of slavery, alcohol abuse, crime, or inequality. In this revolutionary context, the legal and social subjection of women struck some radicals as intolerable and open to change.

A number of committed reformers, including the abolitionist leader Frederick Douglass, met in Seneca Falls, New York, in July 1848, at a convention to address "the social, civil, and religious condition and rights of woman." Two full days of sessions discussed the role of women in society, the inequality of their condition, and means of reform. Most significantly, a third of the attendees, one hundred in total, signed their names to a resolution written by one of the organizers of the convention, Elizabeth Cady Stanton, demanding the right to vote for American women.

Given the consensus that women and politics were incompatible, it's no surprise that a reporter for the local *Oneida Whig* deemed the Seneca Falls Convention for women's rights "the most shocking and unnatural incident ever recorded in the history of womanity." But beyond upstate New York, few people noticed or cared about what happened in Seneca Falls in 1848. It was not the first time American women had petitioned for the right to vote, nor was it remotely as ambitious as the first National Women's Rights Convention held in 1850 in Worcester, Massachusetts. The Worcester convention brought together reformers from across the country, and had an impact on developments in Britain. Seneca Falls, by contrast, was largely local. Not even the participants there recognized at the time that they were part of a watershed moment.[5]

Sarah Childress Polk had no need for women's rights. Her political power stemmed not from the ability to vote but from her connections, her class position, and the willingness of the men around her to recognize as a façade her public embrace of the idea of separate spheres for men and women. By 1848, Mrs. Polk had perfected the ability to hide her power in plain sight under the mantle of female deference, which can be understood as a pose performed for the good of the social order. To be deferent requires acknowledging the "superior political capabilities" of others through "outward and visible signs."[6] Her explicit deference to men not only obscured her power, but it was also, to a large degree, the *source* of her power. Mrs. James K. Polk had learned, over a decade directing social events to political ends as the wife of a congressman and Speaker of the House of Representatives, through three elections for the governorship, and four years as First Lady of the United States, that female deference not only had its privileges, but could also, under the right circumstances, be mobilized for political ends.

That deference could be a source of strength is counterintuitive. One of the most radical outcomes of the American Revolution was the promise that all white men were equal in rights and dignity, so that none need defer to another. But it was a promise made to white men only. James and Sarah Polk owned scores of enslaved men and women. Some did the hard work of cooking, cleaning, and household maintenance, allowing Sarah the time to focus on politics. Others grew cotton on their plantation, providing the income that financed their political efforts. All of these people understood that deference was a requirement for survival. Slaves who refused to defer were beaten, whipped, and sometimes killed. They also faced the threat of being sold away from loved ones. Deference offered enslaved people their best chance of remaining in the good graces of their master and mistress.[7]

By the 1840s, when Sarah Childress Polk was at the height of her powers in Washington, wealthy white women had a good deal more flexibility when it came to deference than did nonwhite people or poor white women. Although Sarah continued to perform the outward signs of deference, there is no evidence that she considered herself politically inferior to her husband. Nor did he. Private interactions within their powerful partnership strongly suggest that he thought her his equal. She controlled his access to news and directed his communications. He turned to her for political advice, and acted on her suggestions. Sarah practiced deference because she was invested in a traditional social order that she believed ideal for society, one in which a white man stood at the pinnacle of power, in command of his wife and children, and were he lucky enough to own slaves, of those enslaved people as well. She believed this hierarchy was both ordained by God and the best way to organize society, and that attempts to overturn it, through women's rights or abolition, would lead to chaos. At the same time she recognized that her own situation was different from that of other women, and that because of the circumstances of her class position, marriage, and remarkable political access she had the responsibility to surreptitiously amass and exercise political power. At the end of her husband's presidency, *Sartain's Union Magazine* lauded Mrs. Polk as a "sweet exemplification of lowliness" who acted as if "the public eye had never scanned her conduct, and the public tongue never sounded her praise," but there was nothing lowly about Sarah Polk.[8]

Sarah Childress Polk's practice of deference worked in her favor throughout a life that spanned almost the entirety of the nineteenth century. She used it to elevate her husband's political fortunes in Washington in the 1820s and 1830s, when James served as congressman and Speaker of the House of Representatives and she became an expert at combining politics and entertainment, and later in Tennessee, where James was elected governor and she became his communications director. Her most spectacular success was during James's presidential term from 1845 to 1849. After his untimely death three months after leaving office, Sarah claimed that her life was over, withdrew from the public eye, and retreated into deep mourning, but she also came into her own as a businesswoman, successfully managing a Mississippi cotton plantation through a tumultuous decade. During the Civil War, she drew on her reputation as a sweet exemplification of lowliness to gain special treatment from politicians and officers alike, including

Presidents Abraham Lincoln and Andrew Johnson, while repeatedly acting in the interests of the Confederacy.[9]

In the decades after the Civil War, Mrs. James K. Polk embraced her position as role model for a generation of deeply religious female activists who praised her humility, her piety, and her "clinging love and single-hearted devotion" to her husband. Woman's Christian Temperance Union president Frances Willard became a fervent admirer of the First Lady's "deep piety and profound convictions." In the late 1890s she lauded Sarah "as the mistress of the White House," who "set an example of American simplicity that has become one of the traditions of the presidential mansion. Gentle, dignified, courteous, approachable and bright, she was esteemed equally by the high and the lowly. Well-informed, thoughtful, vivacious, her conversation had a charm for all, while she kept strictly within the sphere of a true and noble womanhood." At the close of the nineteenth century, Sarah's partnership with her husband and embodiment of Christian womanhood offered an appealing ideal for the many women who believed their society was rapidly degenerating. They proposed to combat urban and moral disorder, from public drunkenness to the proliferation of saloons, prostitution, and pornography, through female-led, religiously based social reform.[10]

But deference did not serve Mrs. Polk remotely as well in death as it had in life. The very characteristics that endeared Sarah Childress Polk to religious women—her piety, her embrace of the "sphere of a true and noble womanhood," and her womanly reserve left turn-of-the-century Progressive reformers decidedly cold. To be fair, there was a great deal about this pious slaveholding southern woman for Progressives to dislike, including the U.S.-Mexican War, which was demonized as a war for slavery by the Republicans who gained ascendency after the Civil War.

But not all of the Progressive critiques of Mrs. Polk were fair. The year after her death in 1891, the liberal weekly magazine *The Nation* marveled that Sarah was being lauded for having "too much delicacy and reserve" as First Lady to openly "proclaim political opinions." This was precisely her mistake, the magazine insisted. "Delicacy and reserve in political affairs are well-bred virtues that have cost Mrs. Polk's country too dear. It would have been as one who set an example of actively expressing enlightened opinions on public questions that she would have deserved to be held up to admiration."[11] These critics failed to recognize the extent of Mrs. James K. Polk's political influence, or to understand how she practiced it.

Although Sarah Childress Polk was in 1848 the most powerful and beloved woman in America, in the twentieth century her accomplishments were largely forgotten. Residents north of the border with Mexico happily forgot about the Treaty of Guadalupe Hidalgo and the less than noble war it concluded, while the dramatic failures of Prohibition and passage of the Twenty-First Amendment in 1933 badly damaged the historical memory of the Woman's Christian Temperance Union.

That Mrs. Polk's practice of political power faded from view is not, on one hand, surprising, given that it flourished precisely because it was hidden. But there was another factor at work rewriting the narrative of women's political power in 1848: the remarkable success of the women's suffrage movement. In 1876, six years after the Fifteenth Amendment extended voting rights to black men, but not to women, Elizabeth Cady Stanton and Susan B. Anthony wrote a history of the women's rights movement that consecrated Seneca Falls as the start of "the greatest movement for human liberty recorded on the pages of history—a demand for freedom to one-half the entire race." While northerners and southerners battled over the memory of the Civil War, Stanton and Anthony assiduously promoted their struggle to gain the rights that men refused to grant to women. The Seneca Falls origin story was retold countless times over the following decades, as the women's suffrage movement experienced a string of dramatic if limited successes before the Nineteenth Amendment to the U.S. Constitution guaranteed American women the right to vote in 1920. Although not even participants at the Seneca Falls Convention recognized its significance in 1848, the women who were there became retrospectively the most important political women of the era.

One hundred and forty years after Seneca Falls, the Treasury Department canonized five nineteenth-century female political leaders on the redesigned ten-dollar bill. Two of them, Elizabeth Cady Stanton and Lucretia Mott, were present in Seneca Falls in 1848, while another, Susan B. Anthony, was instrumental in creating the Seneca Falls mythology. All five were part of the women's suffrage movement. Mrs. Polk, it goes without saying, was not among them. She had been the most powerful woman in America, so powerful she had no need for women's rights when reformers gathered in Seneca Falls. But Mrs. Polk's 1848 has been lost to historical memory.[12]

Although Sarah Childress Polk helped define the office of First Lady, played a significant role in Civil War Nashville, inspired a generation of Christian female activists, and left behind a legacy that, as this book will reveal, profoundly shaped the postwar South, there has been no biography of her life grounded in archival research. Previous accounts (two short life histories, and countless brief summaries in histories of First Ladies) have been marred by misinterpretation, and a willingness to treat fictionalized accounts of the Polks and their marriage as fact. Barbara Bennett Peterson's brief study, *Sarah Childress Polk: First Lady of Tennessee and Washington,* offers questionable assertions without documentation, including the claim that "the Polks never allowed their slaves to be treated inhumanely . . . and refused to sell any of them even in the harshest economic times." John Reed Bumgarner's *Sarah Childress Polk: A Biography of the Remarkable First Lady* draws liberally from two entertaining but openly fictionalized narratives in order to describe an extended period of Sarah Childress Polk's life for which there are few legitimate historical sources. Accounts of her life in collections about First Ladies have taken similar shortcuts.[13]

No source has been more misused than Jimmie Lou Sparkman Claxton's *Eighty-Eight Years with Sarah Polk,* published in 1972 by what at that time was America's largest vanity press. Claxton's admittedly "romanticized" account of the Polk marriage has proven too appealing for most authors to ignore, and virtually all historical treatments of Sarah written since have drawn liberally from her openly fictionalized account, which includes meetings, conversations, and internal monologues for which there is no evidence.[14]

The willingness of scholars to cite fiction as fact derives from a seemingly crippling lack of sources about Sarah Childress Polk's life. She was born in a time and place without vital records. There is no certificate of her birth, or of her marriage. In sharp contrast, some other nineteenth-century First Ladies, well bred, well educated, and aware of their historical legacy, left behind extensive archives. Louisa Catherine Adams, wife of John Quincy Adams, kept a diary, started two memoirs, and wrote regular letters to a variety of friends and family over the course of her long life, including a remarkable series to her father-in-law, John Adams.[15]

Sarah's surviving letters, by contrast, number in the dozens, not the hundreds. By her own admission, she was "always a poor correspondent." But correspondence written to her (of which there is a great deal) makes clear that the vast majority of Sarah's letters have been lost to posterity. We have not a single letter from her prior to her marriage at age twenty, none to her mother or the sisters whom she loved, and only a handful to her husband. Most of her surviving correspondence is brief and direct. None of it can be described as graceful, literary, or contemplative. She kept no diary and wrote no memoir, although in the final years of her life she entrusted the duty of composing her posthumous biography to her friends Anson and Fanny Nelson. She provided them with open access to her papers, and sat for weekly interviews.[16]

The year after Sarah's death, the couple published their *Memorials of Sarah Childress Polk,* based on those interviews. Like all primary sources, *Memorials* needs to be approached with a critical eye. Sarah was eighty-seven years old when the Nelsons interviewed her, recounting events that took place in some cases over half a century earlier. Her memories of events occasionally proved misleading. Furthermore, both she and the Nelsons were invested in burnishing her historical reputation, and left out important aspects of her life that reflected poorly upon her, including her pro-Confederate actions in the Civil War, her secret purchases of slave children during James's presidency, and her ownership of a Mississippi cotton plantation with a death rate higher even than the brutally high average for the region.

But a comparison of Sarah's memories, as transcribed by the Nelsons, with other documents from the period confirms much of what Sarah believed to be true. As a minimally adulterated transcription of her thoughts, *Memorials* offers the single best source available on her life and her views of the world at the end of that life.[17]

Further complicating the messy business of documenting Sarah Childress Polk's life is her notorious lack of candor about her own history. One frustrated biographer complained in 1870 that "Mrs. Polk, though ever willing to converse, and always enriching the conversation from her ready store of information and observation, is remarkably reticent in regard to her own life. Her most familiar friends fail to persuade an account of incidents relating purely to herself." She claimed not to know her maternal grandmother's maiden name, or the date or place of her own parents' marriage. Throughout her life she repeatedly claimed to be born somewhere that she most certainly was not, most likely because of her later identification with that location. It's difficult not to conclude that her reticence about her own history was self-serving. Deflecting attention from herself simultaneously offered proof of her modesty and deference while providing cover for actions that were often radically subversive of the gender order of the day.[18]

Writing a historically accurate account of Sarah Polk and the remarkable but complicated world in which she lived has required both sleuthing and creativity. With the help of research assistants and generous archivists I spent two years assembling copies of every letter written to, from, and regarding Sarah Childress Polk during her lifetime. Many of these letters, including her correspondence with Dolley Madison, and a remarkable letter written to her by her father when she was a teenager, will be new to scholars. The great historian Charles Sellers generously made a gift of all his notes for the final unwritten volume of his award-winning biography of James K. Polk. Government documents, legal and court records, newspaper articles, and firsthand nineteenth-century narratives about Sarah Childress Polk's family, community, and the larger world in which she rose to power have also proven crucial to telling the story of Sarah and her world.

The element of creativity comes from interpreting those sources, which is the most fulfilling aspect of the historian's craft. A great deal can be derived from letters written to a biographical subject about where that person was, what they said, and what they thought. Descriptions written by friends and strangers are often remarkably revealing. And occasionally, where the sources are thinnest, a historian must embrace the opportunity for conjecture grounded in larger patterns of evidence. Given the sources at our disposal, important questions about Sarah's relationship to her husband and to their enslaved people, her desires, and her fears, can be answered only through speculation. I make these points clear in the narrative, and hope that they enhance a life story that is in some important aspects opaque.[19]

Given her previous obscurity, it will come as little surprise that Mrs. Polk has yet to win her deserved spot in lists of powerful First Ladies. One recent presidential historian casts her in a category labeled "Absent Spouses: Idled by Illness and Death (1817–1869)." He explains, "The first ladies of this period were, as a group, less influential and less active both politically and in terms of social hostessing" than those who came earlier. "The roles and responsibilities of the first lady during this period were not expanded and the institution was much less visible. This appears to parallel the status of the presidency. The first ladies themselves were part of the reason for this inactivity, in that they tended to be of a different temperament and had different approaches to their offices than later, more active first ladies."[20]

This analysis is questionable for three reasons. First, just because the executive branch is weak in relation to other branches of government does not necessarily reflect upon the efforts of the First Lady. Dolley Madison stepped into a power vacuum during her husband's relatively weak presidency precisely because Congress had taken on a new leadership role. One might also note that as president, James Polk was nothing if not strong. He threatened war with Britain, started a war with Mexico, and brought that war to a victorious close despite widespread antiwar sentiment. He also vowed to bring tariff rates down, and then did, in 1846 passing the Walker Tariff that lowered standard rates from 33 percent to 25 percent. From beginning to end he lied to the faces of enemies and allies alike to pursue his goals.[21]

And finally there is the classification of Sarah Polk with those idled spouses. Margaret Taylor simply refused to entertain during her husband's brief term in office. Jane Pierce never recovered from witnessing the decapitation of her eleven-year-old son, Benny, in a train crash. Letitia Tyler died while her husband was in office. The wives of Martin Van Buren and Andrew Jackson didn't live to see their husbands inaugurated.

Far from idled, Sarah labored long hours to keep up with her workaholic husband, and she fully embraced the world of politics while operating largely outside the public view. She also entered office with two rare advantages for a First Lady looking to mobilize power: she was childless and her husband embraced her political abilities. She became his communications director and political sounding board. Her life was long, dramatic, and decidedly public, despite her insistence that she was a lady first.

Everyone knows about Seneca Falls and the women's suffrage movement. It's time to tell a different political story, about Mrs. James K. Polk and the world that created and sustained her. This is a story about families: the black and white men and women who went by the names of Childress and Polk. It's also a story of places: new towns and growing cities in Tennessee, political spaces in Washington, D.C., and a Mississippi cotton plantation where over fifty people owned by Sarah Polk struggled to survive, rose up in armed rebellion, and eventually freed themselves. And it's a story of events: deaths, elections, and wars, the growth of political parties, women's activism, emancipation, and Manifest Destiny. Much of this tale is driven by forces outside any one person's control, but it also narrates one woman's remarkable practice of deferential politics over the course of the nineteenth century.

Although Sarah Childress Polk was the first woman to successfully deploy the political power of female deference on the national stage, she was hardly the last. Indeed, she set a model of conservative female power that grew and flourished in the century after her death, and which actively shapes our current political moment. Phyllis Schlafly, Nancy Reagan, and Ivanka Trump: all are political heirs of Mrs. James K. Polk. Her name may be forgotten, but in many ways her world is not so different from our own.

Lady First

1

BLACKBOARD, MAPS, AND GLOBES

The equal share that every citizen has in the liberty . . . of our country make it necessary that our ladies should be qualified . . . by a peculiar and suitable education, to concur in instructing their sons in the principles of liberty and government. —DR. BENJAMIN RUSH, 1798

S ARAH CHILDRESS was the third of six children of Elizabeth Whitsitt and Joel Childress, prosperous young southerners born during the American Revolution. Joel, the grandson of a Welshman wealthy enough to emigrate to North Carolina with his own ship, came of age intent on capitalizing on American victory against the British and their Indian allies. While still a teenager he determined to become a "planter," by which he meant slavemaster and plantation owner. He looked west across the Appalachians for fertile new land on which to plant himself and grow rich.[1]

There was no great originality to this way of thinking. Western expansion was a way of life for the North American colonists of Britain's empire, and the unwillingness of the British to allow settlement of native land west of the Appalachian Mountains after the conclusion of the French and Indian War in 1763 became a major point of contention between colonists and the imperial government. The British hoped to prevent conflict with the Indian owners of the continental interior. But for many westerners across the colonies, the promise of independence was explicitly territorial.[2]

North Carolina's colonial charter fancifully claimed land "west as far as the south seas," but at the end of the Revolution state leaders ceded that territory to the new federal government. Thousands of North Carolinians and Virginians crossed the Blue Ridge Mountains at the close of the war, despite the fact that Cherokee, Chickamauga, and Creek Indians had long owned the lands claimed by North Carolina.[3]

Elizabeth's father, John Whitsitt, was one such frontiersman, one of the thousands of North Carolinians who received western land grants in return for military service during the Revolution. Most soldiers sold their grants to land speculators, but Whitsitt moved west with his large family "before the Indian troubles of the frontier were settled," as one source euphemistically put it. In 1790 the census recorded him as living on 340 acres in Sumner County, and owning another 640 acres in Davidson County, on Cherokee territory only recently organized by North Carolina. As white settlers invaded native hunting grounds, Indians raided livestock and stole slaves from the initially outnumbered interlopers.[4]

In 1791, younger Cherokees and Chickamaugas ignored the entreaties of tribal elders and went on the attack. At the same time, Creek Indians aligned with the Spanish settlers of the Louisiana Territory made clear their intention to "maintain our lands, or die in the attempt." By the end of 1792, middle Tennessee counted ninety-seven white casualties due to Indian attack. Indians also took prisoners: eighteen in a 1792 attack on Ziegler's Station alone. White militia units burned Cherokee and Creek villages in response. The new federal government offered little military support for the settlers, noting that most of the white invaders killed by Indians were "on lands that never have been sold, or ceded by the Indians; that those people have repeatedly been ordered off by the Indians, but will not go."[5]

As hostilities worsened in 1794, militia units began recruiting men from Kentucky to aid in the fight against the "savages' barbarity." But two events that year convinced the tribes that continued war was untenable. In the Northwest Territory the federal general Anthony Wayne defeated a pan-Indian alliance, revealing the potential power of U.S. forces. Later that year, Spain and the United States signed a treaty that resolved their boundary dispute and led Spain to withdraw its support for the Creeks. Attracted by the fertile soil of middle Tennessee, immigrants swarmed into the region. By 1796 the white population of the "Southwest Territory" had reached seventy-seven thousand, enough to enter the Union as the sixteenth state.[6]

It was the first state formed entirely out of federal territory, and thus a creation of the government of the new United States. While the government forbade slavery in the Northwest Territory, in the Southwest Territory slavery was accepted and protected. The territory's constitutional convention christened their new state Tennessee, after the Cherokee village first recorded by sixteenth-century European explorers to the region. The convention also appointed a twenty-eight-year-old frontier lawyer named Andrew Jackson as its lone representative to the federal Congress. According to the first state census in 1800, there were ninety-two thousand white and fourteen thousand black residents of the state. All but three hundred of the black residents were enslaved.[7]

The Cherokees provided more than a name to the new state. Elizabeth Whitsitt was born in 1781, four years before the Cherokees reluctantly signed over control of a swath of what would become Tennessee in the Treaty of Hopewell, and more than a decade before Indian war in the region ended.[8]

There's no way of knowing if "Indian troubles" figured among Elizabeth's childhood memories. She married young, hopefully in full support of her husband's vision of their lives as planters. They settled near her parents, in Sumner County, and in 1799 Elizabeth gave birth to a boy named Anderson. She was seventeen, and Joel Childress twenty-two, in a state even younger than themselves.[9]

FOR THE NEXT TWELVE YEARS, the "enterprising and industrious" young couple made "good use of all the aids at hand," including their enslaved field hands. Joel's facility for buying and selling land won him the reputation as a man of "uncommon sagacity and rare energy and enterprise." He added 220 acres to his Sumner County holdings in 1800, the year before the birth of his eldest daughter, Susan. And a month after Sarah's birth in 1803 he sold two parcels in Rutherford County for the princely sum of $1,000.* Proceeds from these sales bought more land, and increasing numbers of slaves.[10]

---

* Sarah repeatedly claimed to have been born in in Murfreesboro, and historians have understandably taken her at her word. But given that multiple land records place John Childress firmly in Sumner County at the time of Sarah's birth, there is no evidence of the family moving to the Murfreesboro environs before 1810, and that Murfreesboro did not yet exist in 1803, it's far more likely that she was born in Sumner County.

Elizabeth spent those twelve years engrossed in the biennial cycle of pregnancy, childbirth, and breastfeeding typical of a fertile farm woman without benefit of birth control. Two of her six children died in infancy, which was sad, but not uncommon. Elizabeth was deeply religious, an "Old Side" Presbyterian in a region where there was no Presbyterian church at which to worship, and little religious practice of any sort. Her Calvinist faith taught that God had predestined the fate of all mortals at the time of creation: that some were to be saved, but salvation was entirely outside human control. Her conviction in puritan doctrine and the stain of original sin held firm in the face of evangelicalism and the growth of revivalist sects like the Baptists and Methodists early in the nineteenth century. A surviving portrait of Elizabeth reveals a woman of grim determination, dressed in the simplest and least ostentatious style possible. No doubt she understood the loss of two of her young children as part of God's opaque and often painful plan.[11]

Joel does not appear to have held the same faith in God as his wife. He was part of the vast majority of men and women on the southern frontier who showed little interest in worship, and even less concern about the future of their souls. They were "worldlings," in the parlance of the minority who belonged to churches. How he understood the loss of his children is difficult to say, but no doubt both parents took solace in the fact that their remaining four not only survived but appeared to thrive.[12]

Susan and Sarah were both smart, inquisitive girls who inherited their mother's prominent nose and their father's dark, deep-set eyes. John, born in 1807, two years after a boy who died in infancy, was destined to be the baby of the family. Although only twenty-eight years old in 1809 when she gave birth to another child who died in infancy, a daughter named Elizabeth, Elizabeth's childbearing abruptly stopped.[13]

There is no evidence that Elizabeth's final pregnancy was difficult, or that she suffered any injuries that would have prevented her from

---

Whether she was simply unaware of her birthplace, or reconfigured her own history to reflect deep identification with the town where her father rose to prominence, is impossible to say.

having more children. She was a strong woman, and solidly built. Perhaps Elizabeth took the death of her namesake particularly hard. Or perhaps Joel took a look at his fine brood and determined it was large enough.[14]

In either case, they evidently made the unusual decision to stop bearing children while Elizabeth was still quite young. The United States had a remarkably high fertility rate in 1800, higher than any country in Europe. The average white American woman began having children at age twenty-three, and continued giving birth at two-year intervals until her fertility naturally declined in her early forties. Nowhere in the new United States was the white fertility rate higher than in the rural South. Families of eight or nine children were not uncommon. Elizabeth could have had at least three more pregnancies in the natural course of things.

And why not "be fruitful and multiply"?[15] The frontier appeared endless, food and healthy drink were plentiful, and children provided needed labor on farms. More children equaled more helping hands. Few Americans anywhere spoke out in opposition to large families at the start of the nineteenth century. In Massachusetts, Abigail Adams had declared it "sad slavery" for a woman to have too many children too fast, but on the southern frontier, and almost everywhere else in rural America, fathers held sway over their wives and children in a manner nearly as absolute as the way the wealthy ruled over their slaves. Elizabeth Childress was one of the lucky white women who could force her slaves to cook and clean, sparing her the ceaseless labor that other women somehow negotiated in between the demands of infants and children and the discomfort of pregnancy and childbirth. Slaves could be relied on in other ways as well. Elizabeth may have called on an African American midwife to help with her labor, and if one of her female slaves had recently given birth, that woman may have shared or taken over responsibility for nursing a Childress infant. This was common practice in slave-owning families. The even spacing of Elizabeth's pregnancies, however, suggests that she nursed her children herself.[16]

In the early nineteenth century, whether or not another child was desirable varied, but in almost every case it appeared inevitable. The specifics of conception were not well understood, and contraception remarkably ineffective. The little advice available on preventing pregnancy in the early American republic suggested that a woman was least fertile precisely when she was most likely to get pregnant, exactly midway between menstrual periods. Some mothers passed down recipes for vaginal douches to be used after intercourse, or herbal teas that could prevent or end pregnancy. But beyond abstinence, the primary method for preventing pregnancy in 1800 was the withdrawal method, which was no more effective then than it has been since.[17]

Controlling conception was an unusual choice on the frontier, to be sure, but across the new United States significantly more families made a concerted effort to limit their fertility in the decades immediately following the Revolution than had done so previously. And their reasons were as much ideological as practical.[18]

The Declaration of Independence claimed that all men were created equal, and thus posed a direct threat to the relationship between rulers and those they ruled—not just a British king who claimed to act in the interests of his subjects without their direct representation in Parliament, but also the relationship between slave owners and slaves, and husbands and wives. If all men were created equal, why not wives as well? Under British law, wives were far from equal; indeed, they barely existed as legal subjects. English common law declared that a married woman was a "feme covert"—covered by her husband's identity, which meant that her interests were entirely subsumed into his own. Her property became his at the time of marriage, and she could not make a contract without his permission. "Coverture" denied women a legal existence. And it was the law in the American colonies as well as in Britain.[19]

It was hardly lost on colonial women during the Revolution that a husband's rule resembled that of a king. Abigail Adams famously asked her husband to "remember the ladies" while he and his colleagues in the Continental Congress set about drawing up a governing document for the new republic. "Put it out of the power of our husbands to use us with impunity," she asked him in 1776. "Remember that all men would be tyrants if they could."[20]

The Continental Congress did not remember the ladies. Married white women remained "femes covert" after the Revolution; they gained no legal rights, and no separate legal identity from their husbands. But there was a subtle shift in the public understanding of the role of women in the world of politics. The new government of the United States took the radical form of a republic, one that explicitly depended on the virtue of the governed. The success of a republican form of government depended on the informed commitment of a wide spectrum of citizenry. Acknowledgment of this fact, when combined with public recognition of the very real sacrifices made by women during the Revolution, lent credence to a new ideal of female political engagement, one that may have led couples like the Childresses to limit their family size.

America's political survival through a long, hard war of independence depended on the efforts of its "Republican Mothers," educated and virtuous women who would in turn raise virtuous sons. In the words of the eminent physician Dr. Benjamin Rush, "the attention of our young ladies should be directed as soon as they are prepared for it to the reading of history, travels, poetry, and moral essays," because these are the topics most suited to "the present state of society in America." Hierarchical countries could educate their young women as they wished, but in the United States "the equal share that every citizen has in the liberty and the possible share he may have in the government" require that "our ladies should be qualified to a certain degree, by a peculiar and suitable education, to concur in instructing their sons in the principles of liberty and government."[21]

The concept of Republican Motherhood offered a new case for educating young women in a similar manner as young men. For without education, how could women possibly become mothers worthy of the republic? Only women with the ability to reason could be trusted to raise virtuous sons who could understand the difference between liberty and virtue. In short, the Revolution provided no additional legal or political power to women, but encouraged men who could afford it to educate their daughters as well as their sons, while providing a legitimate source of political authority within the household for wives and mothers. For the first time, women had a political voice in America, although it was a voice constrained within the walls of the home.

The ideal of Republican Motherhood encouraged parents to limit family size for two practical reasons: mothers of overlarge families might have trouble adequately supervising their unruly brood, and children had suddenly become an expensive proposition. Children helping with farm chores were economic assets, but those in school became liabilities. Only Massachusetts offered free public schooling in the decade after the Revolution; everywhere else it necessitated significant investment of family resources. Not surprisingly, in post-Revolutionary families there was an inverse relationship between family size and the educational level of women. Educated women and their husbands generally attempted to limit their fertility, as did women like Elizabeth Whitsitt Childress, who intended to provide their daughters with the education they never had.

WHICH BRINGS US back to the Childresses. Joel and Elizabeth Childress do not, at first glance, seem like the kind of people who would embrace the model of Republican Motherhood. Young frontier settlers from the upper South with "limited advantages for education," the distance between them and the Adamses of Boston was more than physical. Joel Childress, husband, father, slave owner, was by definition a patriarch. Both law and custom entitled him to make all the important decisions for the family: what land to buy and sell, where and when to move, what to plant, and how the children should be raised. As a slave owner he forced men and women to labor against their will for his benefit, and none of their own. There is no evidence that he had any moral qualms about slavery, or that his authority over the life and death of more than a dozen human beings troubled his conscience.[22]

Quite the contrary. Evidence suggests that Joel Childress killed a white man in 1801, the year his daughter Susan was born. During a dispute at Madison Creek in Sumner County, Joel fatally assaulted John Reagan with a four-foot oak plank, hitting him over the left temple with enough ferocity that Reagan died within hours of the assault. Childress was tried for murder, but convicted only of "felonious slaying." He was branded with an "M" on the palm of his hand as punishment. If any man was likely to become a "tyrant" in his own family, the exact brute Abigail Adams hoped to protect "the ladies" from, a convicted killer voluntarily moving his young family and slaves deep into land recently wrested from Indians would seem to be a prime candidate.[23]

In frontier Tennessee, however, it was often necessary to look beyond the appropriation of Indian land and the buying and selling of slaves, beyond even murder trials and branded hands, to see a man as his white neighbors and children saw him. Then a very different Joel Childress comes into focus. Joel's neighbors accepted Indian removal and slavery as the preconditions for prosperity. Many of them accepted violence, even between white men, as natural. We can be fairly certain that the judge in the case of the "State vs. Joel Childress" felt this way, because Judge Andrew Jackson carried these views all the way to the White House. And despite his conviction of Joel Childress, the two men become both political allies and friends over the following decade.[24]

Sarah later insisted that neither of her parents had been formally educated, but her father's fine penmanship and grammar suggest, at the least, a remarkable facility at learning. The volumes of Cicero and Ovid, histories and works of philosophy, as well as a fine collection of atlases in his library, indicate a wide breadth of knowledge, and curiosity about the world around him. Joel liked music, and had a sophisticated understanding of the complexities of the early American republic's banking system. On January 22, 1818, during a trip back to Tennessee from New Orleans, he had $5,000 in U.S. banknotes stolen from him in St. Francisville, Louisiana. By reporting the theft in Philadelphia, where the notes had been issued, he regained his money.[25]

Despite the manslaughter conviction, the Joel Childress known to his family and friends was not only a cosmopolitan gentleman, but also a gentle man. Unlike his neighbors, he did not view children primarily as a labor source. Unlike most fathers, when it came to his own family, he declined the role of family king.

About Elizabeth we know far less. Unlike Abigail Adams, she left no written statements on women, patriarchy, or family size. Her morality was as strict as her Presbyterian faith demanded, and her commitment to slavery unwavering. But nothing about her faith or her actions suggest anything other than veneration for learning. Both Joel Childress and the Whitsitts welcomed the economic opportunities unleashed in the shift from colony to republic. After all, Tennessee was born out of a land rush. Both families would have been keenly aware that their wealth was in large part due to their ability to capitalize on the territorial bounty of the Revolution.[26]

Whether Joel, or Elizabeth, or most likely the two of them together, made the decision, it's clear that they determined to educate all their children, the girls as well as the boys, properly, extensively, and expensively. Although it is impossible to say if they were inspired by the ideals of the Revolution, in their actions they proved as progressive on the subject of women's education as anyone in Boston or Philadelphia. It seems unlikely that their family size was accidental. The Childresses clearly had plans for their children.

IN 1810, Joel and Elizabeth Childress moved their four children and sixteen slaves to a fifty-acre farm on the west side of the west fork of the Stones River.[27] It was an excellent location for growing cotton, a crop that had been introduced to the region by one of the original white settlers, John Donelson (later to become father-in-law to Andrew Jackson). Cotton was initially grown for home consumption, in small patches of an acre or less, planted, tended, and collected by women. Most likely Elizabeth Childress had a cotton patch in the garden of the first home she shared with Joel. Perhaps her own mother had one as well. Separating the cotton from the bolls, or "seeding," was shared work for women and children, black and white alike, on small farms on the frontier.[28]

But almost certainly it was Joel rather than Elizabeth Childress who arranged for the cotton crop at the Stones River property, with slaves solely responsible for the work of growing and harvesting the bolls. Thanks to Eli Whitney's cotton gin, which mechanized seeding and became widely available in middle Tennessee in 1807, it was economically feasible to grow cotton on a scale previously considered impossible. The Childress crop was destined not for home production but for export, and barring any disasters, it would help make Joel's fortune, which, thanks to his luck at land speculation, was already sizable, and on the way to prodigious.[29]

The new property was beautiful, dotted with valuable elm, cedar, and oak, as well as black walnuts, fruiting mulberry, and flowering dogwoods that put on a show in the spring. The neighborhood was legendary. In 1793, U.S. forces under General James Robertson were turned back by their Cherokee foe at a nearby spring. The following year, U.S. Army major James Ore, under directions from territorial governor William Blount, overpowered Cherokee chief Black Fox at the same spot. According to legend, "Black Fox leaped into the spring and emerged from Murfree Spring, three miles away," avoiding capture. Ore went on to burn two Cherokee villages to the ground, while Black Fox became a national leader of his people. The Childress slaves planted an apple orchard and built a large frame house where Cherokee families had recently lived, which the children remembered fondly. It was to be their home until adulthood.[30]

In the fourteen years since statehood the white population of Tennessee had tripled, and the slave population more than quadrupled. A year after Joel bought the Stones River property, the Tennessee legislature placed the seat of newly formed Rutherford County in Murfreesboro, a town just three miles away. Murfreesboro was not then much of a town; it had an aspirational main street of irregular, rough-hewn log buildings; an unattractive tavern where visitors could find a meal or shared lodging for the night; and, most important, a Presbyterian church where Elizabeth could at last worship. But it was destined for greater things.[31]

Despite the "felonious slaying" conviction a decade earlier, Joel was appointed the first postmaster of Murfreesboro. He purchased a second home in town, and opened a "store-house" of provisions for travelers, from shoes and boots to sugar and coffee. In 1812 he purchased yet more land, including another hundred acres adjoining the property. Soon afterward he was buying vast tracts of land in Alabama, on credit, just as prices were beginning a stratospheric rise. Land speculation of this sort was risky, but it was the best way to get rich quick on the American frontier, and almost all wealthy men indulged in the practice. Joel was remarkably lucky in his investments. He never felt the sting of a nationwide financial panic, nor did he, like his friend Andrew Jackson, lose all his profits in the bankruptcy of an investor. Jackson's lifelong aversion to debt was in large part the result of land speculations gone wrong. But Joel Childress's investments almost always turned out well.[32]

By the time Sarah Childress, known to the family as Sally, started school, Joel had become a man of substance in the community, rich and widely admired. The family lived in what their neighbors must have considered uncommon splendor—an ample library, a pianoforte, fine carpets, and complex sets of china and glassware proved physical evidence of their refinement. Given the dozens of wineglasses, dining plates, teacups, and Windsor chairs owned by the Childresses, the neighbors doubtlessly had many occasions to contemplate that splendor firsthand.[33]

As for the children, Anderson, Susan, Sarah, and John were literally raised with silver spoons in their mouths, for the family owned two and a half dozen. Sarah said she never knew, "even in childhood, what it was to be simply clothed, or to long for splendor of raiment, having always possessed it." Her clothes, like the objects that surrounded them, were imported. From her "earliest recollection," she and her sister were "dressed in silks and satins of delicate texture, in beautiful designs and colors." Their home was filled with gilt mirrors in which they could contemplate that finery in detail. Nor were Sarah's and Susan's wardrobes the only ones in middle Tennessee blessed by the largess of the Childress fortune. When Andrew Jackson left for New Orleans in 1814 to fight the British, he carried with him a magnificent dress uniform purchased for him by Joel Childress.[34]

The four young Childresses began their education in a one-room log schoolhouse in the neighborhood but quickly moved on to better things. At age fourteen Anderson enrolled in Samuel Black's Murfreesboro Academy, which occupied a large log building in the center of town. The curriculum at the Murfreesboro Academy was rigorous and diverse, including Greek, Latin, mathematics, philosophy, logic, rhetoric, and "useful and ornamental branches of literature." The institution, the finest in middle Tennessee, attracted pupils from across the region. The star of Anderson's class, James K. Polk, hailed from Columbia, fifty miles away.[35]

Murfreesboro Academy was open to white men only, a policy shared by nearly every other serious educational institution in the United States in the very early nineteenth century. None but the most devoted proponents of the ideal of Republican Motherhood advocated a rigorous education, of the sort offered by Samuel Black, for women.

But Joel Childress was apparently one of those proponents. And as a donor and trustee of the academy, he was in a unique position to do something about it. He reached an arrangement with Samuel

Black, one that perhaps raised eyebrows among his neighbors. Susan and Sally would take lessons from Mr. Black himself at the academy as soon as instruction for the boys was completed in the afternoons. Young Sally most likely made the acquaintance of her future husband one of those afternoons while she and her sister were receiving their unconventional lessons.[36]

James would have seemed ancient to Sally. He began his education late, after an unpromising childhood. Jimmy, as his family called him, was small and sickly as a child, unable to compete with his peers in physical contests, and eventually rendered an invalid by the pain of bladder stones. His enterprising father transported him 230 miles to Kentucky for experimental surgery to remove the stones. The brutal surgery likely left him unable to father children, but the offending stones were removed. Jimmy's recovery struck him as miraculous, and he threw himself into his studies with a feverish intensity that would later characterize his political career. While a fast learner, James was still older than his peers at the Murfreesboro Academy by several years; he was eighteen or nineteen when he first met Sarah. She was only ten or eleven, with a sister two years older.[37]

James Polk was no doubt worthy of notice. He became friends with Sarah and Susan's brother Anderson while in Murfreesboro, and was the star of the school, widely considered brilliant by his classmates. Nor was he unattractive. While small of stature, James had bright eyes, even features, and thick, light-colored hair.

But there's no reason to assume that Sally noted any of this. What she remembered about her time under Samuel Black's tutelage, at least publicly, was that during a period when "there was still found the . . . false and injurious opinion . . . that a girl does not need a thorough education," her parents ensured that she had "blackboard, and maps, and globes." In Murfreesboro, she was "thoroughly drilled in the difficult beginnings of learning."[38]

In 1816, the year when Anderson Childress and James Polk moved on to the University of North Carolina, Joel sent his two daughters to Abercrombie's School in Nashville, the finest academy open to girls in middle Tennessee. Nashville was much more sophisticated than Murfreesboro, and in previous years the girls had taken advantage of opportunities to visit, staying with some of the lawyers, judges, and other "men of reputation" whom Joel counted among his friends, and who stayed with the Childresses while on business in Murfreesboro. Some of those friends spoke highly of Abercrombie's, and sent their own daughters to the academy.[39]

But the contrast to their education under Samuel Black was striking. In place of blackboards and globes, Susan and Sally got a taste of the sort of "higher education" reserved for the wealthiest southern girls, including instruction in piano, needlework, fine arts, and personal deportment. It was hardly a rigorous course of study, and not exactly the ideal education for future Republican Mothers.[40] A decade later, critics of finishing schools like Abercrombie's warned that "the systems by which young ladies are taught" at such schools "are only calculated to keep the degrading idea perpetually present, that they are preparing for the great market of the world. Real elegance of demeanor springs from the mind. Fashionable schools do but teach its imitation."[41]

What these critics failed to understand was that Abercrombie's lessons were not without value for a girl like Sarah. Real elegance of demeanor might spring from the mind, but what the etiquette of refined society quite often demanded was pantomime and performance. Sarah's mind wasn't greatly improved at Abercrombie's, but her manners and confidence were, and this enabled her to make the most of her intelligence. Sarah and Susan had a wonderful time in Nashville. The two Childress girls, just entering their teenage years, were able to see General Jackson, then in the "zenith of his military glory," on a regular basis. They attended "brilliant" parties, including a ball at Jackson's home that Sarah recalled vividly many decades later. Their time there wasn't long, but when she left Sarah carried with her a confidence in her own refinement that she never lost.[42]

WHEN SALLY WAS FOURTEEN and Susan sixteen, Joel pulled both girls from Nashville, put them on horseback, and in the care of Anderson and a family slave sent them on a 350-mile journey, to a very different sort of academy. Salem, North Carolina, was a world away, and their parting was painful, but there was nowhere closer where the girls could access an education equivalent to that offered their brothers. And this was what Joel wanted for his daughters. When they left, Joel handed each girl a gold coin from France, and extracted in return a promise to write daily.

The journey was an adventure. For a girl to travel so far, with only a brother, sister, and family slave for escort, was, in the words of one neighbor, "unthought of" at the time. The possibility of "assault" by the "rude and cruel warriors of the forest," and of the "severest privations and hardship," loomed large in the imaginations of those they left behind. But Sarah and Susan delighted in the topography, the ancient trees, graceful streams, and stir of many kinds of animal life. It was during this extended journey that Sarah first cherished "the indescribable variety and charm which nature bestows in the favored climate of Tennessee and North Carolina."[43]

She also gained a deep and lasting appreciation for her enhanced class position. In Murfreesboro, her identity was largely defined within her family. But the long trip to Salem exposed her to class hierarchy in the southern backcountry for the first time. At the end of each day of travel, she and her companions stopped at a friendly but modest farmhouse, where they were first exposed to the domestic life of white settlers of modest means.[44]

The contrast with the world Sarah knew in Murfreesboro was stark. There were no mirrors, silver spoons, libraries, or mahogany chests in these farmhouses. Nor did the farmers own slaves. Most residents of the southern backcountry lived in simple one-room plank or log homes of less than four hundred square feet, the size of an average American living room today. In 1850, 35 percent of the white population west of the Appalachians owned no property at all. The rural poor struggled to live off land to which they had no title, moved frequently, and were unable to provide anything beyond the most rudimentary formal education to their children.[45]

Wealthy planters like Joel Childress called them "crackers" and "squatters." They inspired anxiety among privileged and educated people, but proved to be superb Indian fighters, and thus crucial to Indian displacement and American territorial expansion. Andrew Jackson and his Democratic Party celebrated these "common men" and vowed to represent their interests, rather than those of "aristocrats," by which they meant the wealthy and well connected who were outsiders to the region. Even the wealthiest planters in Tennessee and Kentucky were able to pose as popular tribunes against aristocrats who were conveniently external to Tennessee. Eventually this would become Sarah's political stance as well. But not before she received an education that rendered her even less common than when she started her journey.[46]

The Salem Female Academy of North Carolina was the oldest institution of higher education for women in the country, exceptional both for its prestige and its curriculum. With an emphasis on practical subjects, including history, arithmetic, grammar, and geography, the founding Moravians intended to turn out thoroughly educated women, suited for more than lives of domestic decoration. The course of study prepared students for a life of social leadership, and many graduates went on to teaching careers. The long school day offered little time for recreation. Sarah slept, dined, and studied in a single building on campus with a group of other girls in her "room company." During the brief periods set aside for outdoor recreation between classes, pupils were expected to "avoid noise and rudeness." Morning chapel and extended Sunday religious instruction in English was required of all students.[47]

At Salem, Sarah forgot the frivolities of her Nashville school. Pupils dressed in the simplest style: given that the Moravian sisters who ran the school did all the laundry, there was little opportunity for fancy dress. The students wore simple caps of pink or white. School rules emphasized "economy and frugality" as "an essential requisite of your sex in housekeeping," banned servants, slave or otherwise, and required permission of the tutoresses to leave campus.[48]

The curriculum encouraged students to attend to their sewing and knitting as diligently as their classes (Sarah produced one very fine piece of needlework at Salem, a scene of a marble crypt worked in chenille on a white satin ground that she cherished for her entire life), but her peers primarily wrote home about their challenging workload. Sarah's curriculum included reading, cyphering, arithmetic, geography, history, grammar, music, and possibly German.[49] One of her classmates reported that she had read several very good books in recent weeks, noting in particular that she was very much pleased by a history of Bonaparte's Waterloo campaign written by Helen Maria Williams.[50]

The contents of the academy library might have struck Sarah as familiar; most of the philosophical and historical works in her father's library were in evidence, along with French classics by Rousseau and Montesquieu, as well as travel writings and histories, many of which were written by women. Sarah may have enjoyed Mary Hays's *Female Biography; or, Memoirs of Illustrious and Celebrated Women, of All Ages and Countries*, published in 1807, or Francis Augustus Cox's *Female Scripture Biography: Including an Essay on What Christ Has Done for Women*, published the year Sarah arrived at school. Dr. Isaac Watts's classic work of logic and moral reasoning, *The Improvement of the Mind*, was required reading at Salem Academy, as it was at many men's academies and colleges. One of Sarah's classmates admitted struggling with it, but was sure she would "obtain much instruction from an attentive perusal."[51] Wherever Sarah turned in the library, she would have seen evidence of the significant role women had played in the past and should, with the proper education, play in the future.[52]

Students recognized their good fortune to receive such a high-quality education. An older cousin wrote to one of Sarah's classmates that the previous generation had "in a great measure [been] excluded from intelligent company," forced by ignorance to "set like statues, or whenever they opened their mouths, said something foolish." But a Salem education rendered a woman capable of contributing "sensible remarks on science and literature" in the most august company.[53]

Her time at Salem Academy profoundly shaped Sarah Childress. She took to heart the lesson that books held the key to the active participation in "intelligent company," and made sure in future years to educate herself to the same level as the men in her life. Rarely without a book, she set a clear example for younger women that reading held the key to female self-improvement, and that education was a lifelong process. She would be sensible rather than decorative.[54]

For years wealthy Nashville parents had occasionally sent their daughters over the mountains for a Moravian education, but it wasn't a universally accepted practice. The Moravians "are as far removed from the graces, as the north pole is from the south," fumed one local newspaper. An education of the sort offered in Salem, warned the *Nashville Whig*, would render young ladies unfitted for the higher "circles of society." Sarah later remembered that many of their neighbors believed that all learning beyond "reading, writing, and the first principles of arithmetic, was absolutely hurtful, disqualifying her for the obvious duties of her station."[55]

But Joel Childress had a different sense of the society in which his daughters would move than did his neighbors. In 1818 Murfreesboro became Tennessee's state capital, replacing Knoxville, which was no longer convenient to the rapidly expanding western population. Suddenly the postmaster of Murfreesboro was at the very center of things. Joel had great expectations for his daughters, for he had an unusually generous view of the relationship between parents and children.

A LETTER between Joel and "Sally," written in 1818 while she was away at school, reveals the affectionate relationship between the two. Like other fathers, Joel encouraged Sally to "be industrious and learn all you can" and warned her of the dangers of physical overexertion. Looking forward to her return from school at the end of her first year, he cautioned her not to "ride far" the first few days on the road home from school, "or you will get sick."[56]

Joel offered explicit expressions of affection. Most letters from fathers to children in the early nineteenth century were formulaic and consistent in tone. Obliged to instill discipline in his children, a father usually offered practical advice and moral admonition. The work of providing a strict example left little room in most cases for emotional warmth. Frontier planters were especially likely to adopt an explicitly authoritative relationship with their children. Yet the relationship between Joel and Sally Childress was openly affectionate. After assuring his daughter that all members of the family "are wanting to see you very much," he left no doubt about his own deep regard for his daughter. "You know my love is with you," he wrote.[57]

Also notable is Joel's unusual discussion of business and finances with his fifteen-year-old daughter, providing information about the recovery of the money stolen from him in Louisiana without preface or condescension ("I understand $5000 of my money is got in the Lower Country and will be sent me"). The letter suggests her familiarity with matters of family business and that Joel thought this information would interest her.

But perhaps the most telling line of the single-page letter is the last. Most parents closed their letters to their children in a formal manner, signing themselves "your father" or "your mother." By contrast, Joel Childress closed his letter to Sally, "your father and friend, Joel Childress."[58]

What Sally Childress indeed had was a father who was also a friend, who treated her as a partner, if not an equal, who allowed her access to his political and business world, and felt no qualms about openly expressing his affection and respect for her. What a gift that must have been for Sally Childress. No wonder she adored him.

But in 1819, a month before Sally's sixteenth birthday, Joel fell sick and died. He was only forty-two. Newspapers reported the early death of the "Tennessee Postmaster" as far away as Massachusetts. Sally's education came to an abrupt end. It was not because her mother could no longer afford Salem Academy. Joel had left her and the children a sizable fortune: $20,000, thirty-four enslaved people, multiple lots in Murfreesboro town, and hundreds of acres in Tennessee and Alabama. Determined to treat his daughters as the equals to his sons, he left all four of his children equal portions of the bulk of his fortune.[59]

Sally could have returned to school, but she did not. Although she had three siblings, her mother needed her. Thirty-eight-year-old Elizabeth was utterly unprepared for widowhood, and fell into shock after Joel's death. And Susan was suddenly unavailable. Within three months of her father's death she married Dr. William Rucker, a veteran of the War of 1812 (he served as an assistant surgeon under General Andrew Jackson), nine years her senior, and soon to be elected mayor of Murfreesboro. Anderson married less than a year later. And Sarah's younger brother, John, was still a child.

There is no evidence that Sarah viewed her obligation to her mother as anything other than a "sacred charge." She and her mother mourned together, both finding solace in the Presbyterian catechism and conviction that Joel's salvation was predestined. Baptists and Methodists disagreed with this position. They believed in free will, and professed that divine grace could be accessed by the low as easily as by the high. They also taught that baptism washed away sin, but that further sinful acts, even after salvation, could cost someone the chance at everlasting life.[60]

Old School Presbyterians knew otherwise. The mind of the Lord was unknowable. All one could do was keep the Sabbath holy, avoid evils like gambling, dancing, or hunting, and trust in the Lord. The comfort that Sarah and Elizabeth's Presbyterian faith provided lay not in the hope of being "born again," but in its rituals and traditions. While evangelical sects invited former sinners to preach, provided they were filled with the spirit of the Lord, Old School Presbyterians had no use for uneducated ministers. Theirs was a religion of hierarchy and order. It was a deeply conservative worldview that made sense to Sarah in her time of crisis.[61]

SARAH EMBRACED her mother's religion, but also entered into the political life her father left behind. In the year since Murfreesboro became the state capital, the Stones River property had become a hub of activity, frequented by politicians on their way to or from state business. Among the Childresses' houseguests were Governor Joseph McMinn and the famed orator Felix Grundy, who left Congress in order to pursue a lucrative legal career in Nashville. Starting in 1822, after the Murfreesboro courthouse burned down (some said by rivals hoping to see Nashville become the state capital), the legislature moved into the Presbyterian church. Elizabeth and Sarah's weekly trips to church were also therefore visits to the meeting place of the state government, a fact that reveals how tenuous the split between church and state was in 1820s Tennessee.[62]

Sarah knew many of her father's political friends from childhood, and particularly after her time in Salem, she found their conversation to her liking. Elizabeth Childress's comfortable home, just three miles outside town, continued as a social center after Joel's death, but with interest increasingly swirling around their highly eligible teenage daughter. Among the guests to the Childress home was James K. Polk of Columbia. After his graduation from the University of North Carolina in 1818, James moved to Nashville to study law under Felix Grundy. The following year, under Grundy's mentorship, Polk started a legal practice and became chief clerk for the upper house of the Tennessee state legislature. James and Sarah may have first become reacquainted at the May 1819 wedding of Grundy's eldest daughter to the clerk of the Davidson County circuit court. The wedding took place at the Grundys' imposing Nashville mansion, and fifteen-year-old Sarah served as a bridesmaid.[63]

James soon acquired a reputation as "a young man of mark." Sarah was happy to fire his ambition. He was by no means an easy conversationalist, but Sarah admired his quiet reserve, and thought that his "unswerving rectitude" revealed a sterling character. She respected his work ethic as well as his ambition, and no doubt thought his smile lovely. That the two young people shared an interest in politics should go without mention given the setting in which they met, surrounded by politicians, on the outskirts of the state capital.[64]

Beginning around 1822, Polk's visits to the Childresses' became increasingly frequent. Allegedly Andrew Jackson encouraged James to court the teenaged Sarah, but it seems unlikely that James needed persuading by another man. After all, Sarah Childress was rich, educated, and politically well connected, important considerations for a young man with political aspirations and no great fortune. The similarities between their families would have been comforting: James's mother was as committed a Presbyterian as Sarah and Elizabeth Childress. Both families owned slaves, speculated in land, and had moved to Tennessee from North Carolina at the end of the eighteenth century. Sarah Childress was not a great beauty according to the standards of the day, for her nose was too large, her lips too thin, and her teeth bad. Her sister Susan's features were both more traditionally feminine and more symmetrical. But Sarah's dark hair and eyes were fine, and she possessed an angularity that could easily be read as elegance. James was also won over by a personality that formed a perfect contrast to his own. Sarah was vivacious, with a ready wit and ease of conversation that must have struck the reserved young man as rather miraculous.

In 1823, James ran for the Maury County seat in the state legislature, likely at the prompting of Sarah. He faced a veteran incumbent. The race was hard, and expensive, for voters expected candidates to treat them to free food and drink. Polk paid for twenty-three gallons of cider and hard liquor in his home county. After two days of voting, he emerged the winner. The other freshmen legislators in the Tennessee legislature that year included the populist and bear killer Davy Crockett of newly settled western Tennessee.[65]

James had also won Sarah Childress's hand. During the final months of 1823, Sarah purchased yards of the finest silks and satins, "Circassion" plaid, lace, and ribbon to be turned into finery for her bridal trousseau. She bought new gloves, and shoes, and lace handkerchiefs. She loved beautiful things, and there was no reason to economize. She was rich, and if anything justified extravagance in matters of appearance, it was a wedding. Nor did her religious faith frown upon ostentation in dress, as more upstart evangelical faiths did.[66]

The couple married in "a large country wedding" at Sarah's home on New Year's Day 1824, with the pastor of the Murfreesboro Presbyterian Church performing the ceremony. Among James's attendants was state senator Aaron V. Brown, his law partner and college classmate, another frequent visitor to the Childress home. In time Aaron would become one of Sarah's most intimate friends. She had plenty of opportunities to show off her wedding finery, including a particularly luminous blue embroidered silk dress, in the four nights of festivities around the capital that followed. Among her hosts were Susan Childress Rucker, whose young family already included two nieces for Sarah, three-year-old Elizabeth and year-old Joanna. Sarah's older brother, Anderson, also had a daughter, two-year-old Mary. The three little girls made a lively addition to the Childress family celebrations.[67]

On Tuesday, January 6, Sarah and James declined a sixth day of wedding festivities in Murfreesboro in order to depart for their new life in James's hometown of Columbia. Midwinter high waters required extra care to cross. The couple spent two days making the fifty-mile journey, but still arrived with time to spare before the Polk family and friends began celebrating. Sarah's "affable manner charmed all the guest[s]." One admirer noted that "her eyes looked as if she had a great deal of spice."[68]

The sheer size of the Polk clan might have overwhelmed anyone from a small family. James was the eldest of ten children, seven of whom, not counting James, were living at home. A younger sister, Naomi, was a student at the Nashville Female Academy, where Sarah and her sister had once done very little studying. James's two married sisters lived close by. Jane Walker, who was already the mother of five children of her own, was literally next door. None of the Polk siblings had escaped the influence of their pious and hardworking mother, Jane Polk.[69]

Nor were all the Polk children as reserved as James. The outsized personalities included Jane, the oldest, who immediately expressed her affection for her new sister-in-law, and Franklin, who, after following his older brother to the University of North Carolina, was well on the way to an early death from alcoholism. Eighteen-year-old Marshall was an open and friendly young man with the potential of matching his eldest brother's accomplishments.[70]

James's parents embraced their new daughter-in-law. Clearly Sam and Jane Polk intended to incorporate Sarah into their world. They arranged for the newlyweds to rent a cottage within easy walking distance of their home. Family meals and important entertaining took place in Jane Polk's home, and Jane expected Sarah to follow along with the rest of the Polk brood. Sarah also joined her mother-in-law in worship at the newly constructed wood-framed building housing the Columbia Presbyterian church. (Had Sarah arrived in Columbia just a bit earlier she would have again found herself worshipping in a courthouse, the previous home of Columbia's Presbyterians.)[71]

And so Sarah found herself, at age twenty, with a new home, surrounded by a new family. Her transition was eased by the many similarities between Columbia and Murfreesboro, two similarly sized county seats with majority white populations, surrounded by fertile farmland worked by slave labor. The two towns were founded just three years apart and incorporated the same year, allowing town residents to elect a mayor, pass laws, and levy taxes without first consulting the state legislature. They shared a similar streetscape of brick, sawn board, and log buildings, laid out in an orderly grid surrounding a courthouse square anchored by a fine two-story brick courthouse that served a wide variety of civic functions. Columbia offered a slightly wider variety of shops and businesses than did Sarah's hometown, but both were growing, prosperous places that their white residents were inordinately proud of.[72]

Nor was Sarah alone in her new world. She inherited nine slaves when her father died, including a young mother named Matilda (Milly) and her three-year-old son, Harbert, as well as several other young children. Sarah chose to bring one of them, twelve-year-old Mariah, with her to Columbia to serve as a lady's maid.[73] It was a difficult job. As lady's maid, Mariah was responsible for dressing Sarah and doing her hair, attending to her personal needs, and caring for her heavy, valuable dresses and delicate underclothes. She had to master an exacting code of behavior emphasizing loyalty and discretion, to learn how to anticipate demands without intruding, while simultaneously appearing deaf to confidential conversations and blind to private acts. This was a lot to ask of a twelve-year-old girl, but most lady's maids started their extensive training as children.[74]

Mariah was not the only young slave in Sarah's new home. Not long after the wedding, a teenager named Elias drove to the door with a new cart and said, "'Old Marster' told me to come here." The young man was a wedding present from Sam Polk, and he came complete with a cart and water barrel, so that he could haul water to the house from White's Springs.[75]

Both Sarah and Mariah benefited from Elias's knowledge of Columbia. Columbia's sizable black population, like Murfreesboro's, was composed almost entirely of domestic servants, with very few free black residents and no segregated black neighborhood. In large cities and on plantations black people could find anonymity and privacy, but neither of these was available to Elias or Mariah. They lived on the property of the family they served, as did most small-town enslaved people. As the abolitionist Harriet Jacobs described it, a town was a place where "all the inhabitants knew each other." She credited her survival under slavery to living in a place where a lack of anonymity restrained the worst behavior of some slaveowners, including her own, although that was of little comfort to the many tortured and murdered town slaves whose owners felt no such constraint. One-third of Columbia's residents were enslaved (approximately three hundred people), and Elias knew virtually all of them. They shared household duties across rear lots, casual exchanges in the street, and card games in the back of storehouses. Elias introduced Mariah to Columbia's black community and helped her to find her place within it.[76]

Elias knew almost as much about Columbia's six or seven hundred white residents, information gained, in large part, through his labors as the Polk family's water hauler. A town's well also functioned as its informal "news depot." Each morning between thirty and forty enslaved men met at White's Springs to collect the household's water for the day, and while there exchanged news about what transpired during the night. In the words of one town resident, "by breakfast time every family was familiar" with the events of the previous evening.[77]

Sarah quickly came to depend on this information, which Elias, like other water haulers, could shape as he saw fit. James campaigned aggressively, and work took him away from home on a regular basis. Left in the company of her in-laws, Sarah quickly learned that the life of a politician's wife was a lonely one. Because the state capital was in Murfreesboro, James ironically spent a great deal of time in his wife's hometown without her.[78]

Sarah and James moved the following year, but Elias didn't have to change his water hauling route. The young couple moved into a modest two-story structure with an unfinished second floor down the street from the Polk family home. They remained neighbors with the Walkers as well. Neither of Sam and Jane's two oldest children wished to be far from their parents.[79]

THE CRUSH of Polk family members might have been overwhelming. But perhaps Sarah understood her current condition as temporary. It's impossible to know the extent to which James and Sarah understood each other at the outset of their relationship. Surely James recognized that Sarah's upbringing was significantly different from that of most women. Since a very early age she had access to spaces that were otherwise limited to men: at the Murfreesboro Academy, in a home where politicians congregated, and in her own church, which was also the meetinghouse of the legislature. Her education, while cut short by her father's death, was so far superior to that available to most other women that critics worried it would leave female students unsuited for the roles of wife and mother. Even the arduous horseback trip to and from Salem, North Carolina, accompanied only by her brother, sister, and a family slave, set her apart from other women.

Most significantly, she had had the great privilege of a loving father who treated her as an intellectual equal, and spoke of himself as her friend. He died much too young, and so could only remain perfect in her memory. James knew his new wife was ambitious, and spirited, and unusually interested in politics. Did he promise to be her friend as well, to treat her as an equal? Was an implicit promise of this sort, gleaned through their early interactions, part of his appeal to her?

And what did Sarah understand about James? Did she know that what he wanted from a wife was a partner in work as well as life? Did

she know that the price of his youthful surgery would be their childlessness? Did she perhaps tell James that the life she imagined for herself
was different from that of other women? Was the implicit suggestion
that this might be a part of her appeal to him?

The extent of their accord is opaque, but there is no question that
some sort of understanding between James and Sarah Polk existed.
Sarah was destined for greater things than the Polk cottage. She
recognized James's political promise and pushed him forward. She
shared his passion for small government and continued territorial
expansion. She saw what he could do, and what they could do together.
James quipped that "had he remained the clerk of the legislature,"
Sarah "would never have consented to marry him."[80]

A year after their wedding, James ran for Congress—and he won.

2

A woman here, as in Paris, can learn more than a man—greatly more.

—JOHN CATRON TO SARAH CHILDRESS POLK, January 7, 1840

As a general rule, congressmen did not bring their wives to Washington. Sarah celebrated her twenty-second birthday in the fall of 1825 with her newly elected husband, and then, following convention, James left her behind in Columbia and departed by horseback for Washington.

James and Sarah Polk were in some respects deeply conservative young people. They so venerated their parents that they voluntarily purchased a home across the street. They owned slaves, which is to say that they embraced authority and hierarchy. While James himself was not particularly religious, he lived and worshipped with women whose Old School Presbyterianism was at war with an internal enemy: upstart evangelicals attempting to overthrow centuries of tradition in favor of the dangerous proposal that salvation was open to all, be they sinners, lowly, or enslaved. Inspired by the Second Great Awakening, young people across America dreamed of the possibilities of individual and social reform. But Sarah and James were not among them. Both were committed territorial expansionists by upbringing and inclination, enthusiastic supporters of Andrew Jackson, and Thomas Jefferson before him, men suspicious of centralized government who spoke loudly about restoring the values of the past and fighting the corruption of moneylenders, bankers, and aristocrats. Late in her life Sarah wondered why "men are not governed by the upright stern principles of former days" and expressed nostalgia for a time when "men of sound principles and integrity" ran the country. But nostalgia was a key component of her political philosophy from the outset. In short, in a period of unprecedented economic, social, and cultural change, Sarah and James Polk were committed, both politically and socially, to the values of an older generation.[1]

Suddenly they were faced with a convention, a lengthy separation so James could fulfill the duties of his office, that did not sit well with either of them. The six months that James spent in Washington were torture to Sarah. Without him by her side she was at wit's end, and was drawn into a family controversy that revealed both her growing independence from the Childress family and her emerging sense of herself in relationship to her slave property.

When James and Sarah got married, Sarah's dowry included nine slaves, five of whom were later sold to pay off debts incurred by her older brother Anderson's mismanagement of their father's estate. Mariah, now a teenager, was one of those people. She was forcibly returned to Murfreesboro for sale, but she showed no interest in being separated from the community she had formed in Columbia. Nor did she keep her displeasure with being relocated a secret. She told the other enslaved people in Murfreesboro that she would follow Sarah back to Columbia and "that she would take a horse" if need be.[2]

Mariah kept her word, and ran away from Murfreesboro just before Christmas in 1825. Both of Sarah's brothers wrote her about it. Anderson Childress warned her to be on the lookout for Mariah, who "does not intend that you shall see her . . . she told the negroes she would stay at one of Major Polk's [slave] quarters . . . where she perhaps has a husband, or intends to have one."[3]

Writing a week later, her brother John's view of the situation was somewhat different. Although he informed Sarah that Mariah had fled with new clothes to wear to a Christmas dance held by Polk family slaves in Columbia, and that she intended (as she told the Childress slaves) to be "at the frolick all evening," it was clear to him that Mariah had fled *to* Sarah. Why Mariah fled to Sarah is unclear, but Sarah was loath to hand her over. "She may not want to come" home, John wrote his sister, "but Mah says you must send her, and you would act prudently to secure her in some way. . . . You must send her up by all means."[4]

Sarah did not send Mariah back, and there was nothing her mother could do about it. Sarah, in common with other southern girls of her race and class, had been taught how to manage and discipline slaves, but her freedom to do so was curtailed before her marriage by her mother. Elizabeth Childress was an exacting slavemistress. She banished Caroline, a fifteen-year-old seamstress and house slave, to labor in Mississippi cotton fields after the girl was raped by a white man, despite appeals on her behalf made by both black and white members of the household, and a great deal of evidence that Caroline was not at fault. Elizabeth would never have allowed Mariah's behavior to go unpunished. But Mariah was in a different home now. Under the legal doctrine of coverture, Sarah's mother had no claim over her married daughter. James was now legally responsible for Sarah's actions, and James was in Washington. Mariah may very well have fled to Sarah in order to escape Elizabeth. And Sarah may have sheltered Mariah to prove her independence from her mother.[5]

Without any record of what passed between Sarah and Mariah, it's exceedingly difficult to fully explain either woman's motivation. Quite likely Mariah encouraged Sarah's sense of obligation by flattering her. Sarah was vulnerable to such an appeal. She was stuck in Columbia, without her husband, and Mariah offered a human link to her previous life in Murfreesboro. White women enjoyed imagining themselves a benign presence in the lives of their slaves, despite the coercive reality of forced labor. By "protecting" Mariah, Sarah not only gained the fruits of Mariah's labor, but she was also able to conform to the myth of the "benevolent" slavemistress, while exerting her power as a slave-owning adult woman. Slaves understood how to manipulate the fantasies of white people. It's quite possible that Mariah encouraged Sarah to imagine herself a kind mistress.[6]

Mariah's flight from Murfreesboro did not hurt her in the long run, and may have worked to her advantage. Not long after Mariah's Christmas journey to Columbia, Sarah insisted that James purchase her for $350 from the Childress creditors. Years later Sarah also insisted that James purchase Mariah's husband from his owners, and eventually their son, Henry, became a valued servant in Sarah's household.[7]

THE SIX-MONTH SEPARATION may not have been any better for James than it was for Sarah, despite the fact that his fellow citizens had elected him to a position of such eminence, and by and large, he acquitted himself well. He had proven himself a strong voice in favor of "the people" and their hero, Andrew Jackson, against the "special interests" who controlled the Adams White House, particularly Secretary of State Henry Clay and his banker friends. In a short six months he had already proven himself a pure Jacksonian, and a radical voice in favor of democracy.

But James was very much alone in Washington. Since boyhood he had worked to overcome his natural reserve, and had succeeded in his efforts to such a degree that he was now considered one of the "finest fellows" in middle Tennessee. In truth he had no intimate friends, and no one to confide in besides his new wife. Sarah was blunt with James. She wanted to come with him to Washington.[8]

So what exactly was stopping her?

Well, a number of things. Where to live, for one. Congressmen did not rent houses—their political terms were too brief, their salaries too small. James had spent the first six-month session of the Nineteenth Congress in the cheap, sprawling Capitol Hill boardinghouse owned by Captain Benjamin Burch, along with the five other members from middle Tennessee and assorted other congressmen too green or undiscerning to find somewhere better to live. Each man had a small room for sleeping and correspondence, but took his meals at a long table in common with his "messmates." Evenings were devoted to conversation and cards. It was noisy, convivial, and men only.

Captain Burch's house would not do for Sarah, clearly, but not all boardinghouses in Washington were quite as primitive. Nor were they all single-sex. Boardinghouse life was practically impossible for couples with children, about this everyone agreed. Most wives of congressmen had to make a difficult choice if they wanted to join their husbands. The experience of the Polks' close family friend Caroline Nicholson offered a cautionary tale. When her husband, Alfred O. P.

Nicholson, talked her into accompanying him to an extra May session of Congress, she left three young children with relatives in Columbia. The session was only supposed to last a few weeks, but it dragged on until September. When Caroline and Alfred finally returned to Tennessee, "with hopes high at the thoughts of so soon seeing . . . our dear little children," their close friend James Polk met them as they entered town and had to break the news that their "little four year old girl was dead."[9]

What happened to the Nicholsons was tragic, but not something Sarah had to worry about. Whether or not she knew at the time of her marriage that James would never father a child, two years later, with nary a rumor of pregnancy, it must have been obvious that they would remain a unit of two. James gave his word that he was "not dissatisfied" with their childlessness, but close friends found it hard to believe that Sarah felt the same. "I've been married long enough to know that however indifferent ma[n]y Gentlemen may appear, as to this privation," one of James's friends wrote, "their 'better part,' are on this point, much more sensitive."[10]

Was Sarah "sensitive" about not having children? If so, she did an excellent job hiding it. None of her friends or family members suggested at that time or later that she longed for children of her own. On the contrary, the decisions she made in her later life make it clear that Sarah delighted in her life with James as a couple.

And childlessness was by no means uncommon. In every city in the United States there were "genteel" boardinghouses that catered to young, childless couples who "welcomed the friendly bustle of public abodes." Boardinghouse life was stigmatized by a larger culture that venerated the privacy and domestic virtues of a growing brood in a single-family home, but it also offered certain virtues for a couple without children: freedom from housework, access to like-minded couples, and ease of entertaining.[11]

Of course, no Washington, D.C., boardinghouse could possibly be as comfortable as the cottage in Columbia. But as Sarah had already learned, that comfort came at a price. Despite occupying her own home in Columbia, she was still to all intents and purposes living with her mother-in-law. Jane Polk managed the household and fed Sarah most of her meals. None of this was likely to change unless Sarah changed it; childless southern couples of the Polks' race and class generally continued living with the husband's parents, sometimes for decades. Sarah loved Jane Polk, and their shared devotions to the Presbyterian Church and to James bound them tightly together. Sarah entered into the life of the Polk family with an open heart. She enjoyed family and comfort, but they weren't her top priority.[12]

Can we blame Sarah if she was bored in Columbia? Another childless and politically active woman of Sarah's class, Mary Boykin Chesnut of South Carolina, could hardly have been alone when she dismissed life without her husband at his family's plantation as a "social desert of Sahara." Moreover, Washington, D.C., was the epicenter of political life. Surely many politicians' wives, women with far less interest in the theory and exercise of politics than Sarah, yearned for the excitement and freedom their husbands experienced in the nation's capital.[13]

SARAH KNEW WHAT SHE WANTED. When James left for the second session of the Nineteenth Congress in November 1826, she traveled with him in their private carriage accompanied by two slaves: a lady's maid for her, most likely Mariah, and Elias, who was already established as James's valet, as well as two of Tennessee's most esteemed Democratic politicians, Senator Hugh L. White and Congressman Sam Houston.

It was not an easy trip. How best to reach Washington from middle Tennessee was a topic of heated discussion among those forced to make the multiday, seven-hundred-mile journey. There were the Appalachian Mountains and multiple rivers to negotiate, vast tracts of forest won from the Creek Indians in the War of 1812, and not a single decent road south of Ohio. Men traveled "heavily armed, for it was not unusual for robbers to hold up a coach."[14]

Rural taverns were primitive, and if overnight lodging was available, it often entailed (for a single man, anyhow) sharing a bed with a stranger. Nor was there an excess of taverns. Portions of Kentucky and Virginia were barely settled; sometimes the best one could hope for was space in the home of a generous farmer. Travelers had to weigh all these considerations, factor in the unpredictable weather, and try not to think about the relative likelihood of a stagecoach overturning on a road or capsizing in a river (Sarah would experience both over the course of time), or a steamboat exploding (which happened with surprising regularity). Not even a president with the stature and omnipotence of the great Andrew Jackson could be sure what to do when faced with the task to traveling to Washington. Jackson's route from his Tennessee estate, the Hermitage, to Washington, D.C., in 1829, at the start of his presidential term, was subject to repeated inquiries and "many conjectures" in Washington. The only thing all who had made the trip agreed on was that it should start as early as possible.[15]

The most direct route was the least comfortable: a stagecoach over dirt roads through the mountains of eastern Tennessee and western Virginia. It was also possible to travel by carriage over equally uncomfortable dirt roads north to Lexington, Kentucky, and from there along a much better road to the Ohio River, where a steamboat could take a traveler to Wheeling. Travel became much easier at that point: Wheeling was a stop on the graded and surfaced "National Road" connecting Columbus to Baltimore. It was also possible to head north from Tennessee by carriage to Ohio and catch the National Road near its western terminus. Given how far east Washington, D.C., was relative to middle Tennessee, going north to Ohio seemed counterintuitive, but the National Road was so luxuriously smooth, so wide (two carriages could pass each other with no danger of either overturning), and so efficient that few westerners could resist its allure. It was the federal government's signature "highway," indeed the only interstate road financed by the federal government, and for many Americans it was a revelation. Its success provided a strong rationale for federal funding of "internal improvements"—roads, bridges, canals—and did a great deal to boost the reputation of western politicians aligned with Henry Clay, the nation's preeminent supporter of internal improvements.[16]

James was, on principle, firmly opposed to federal expenditures on internal improvements. Indeed, from the moment that the new Democratic Party coalesced around Andrew Jackson in the 1820s, Democrats opposed public monies being devoted to anything that might favor one group of citizens over another, with their opponents, who by the 1830s would be known as the Whigs, enthusiastically supporting internal improvements. It was scripture among the Democracy (as the Democratic Party called their followers) that the best government was a small government. Many Democrats, Polk included, were fairly certain that without the explicit consent of the states concerned, federal improvements were unconstitutional.

But the people of middle Tennessee didn't necessarily agree with him. They wanted their own National Road, or any dependable road, to get their produce to market. Had James not held his nose and offered his support to "a judicious system of Internal Improvements" by the federal government, he would never have been elected. Nor did his scruples prevent him from taking the National Road on his first trip to Washington.[17]

But even with the help of the National Road, the route was uncomfortable at best, perilous at worst. Sarah had every reason to suffer from the physical hardship and wretched accommodations, yet she found "neither care nor trouble" on the journey. This was November in the Appalachians. Autumn's leaves had fallen, and a bleak landscape promised a long winter.

But instead of complaining, Sarah conversed with the eminent Democrats in her carriage about their shared conviction that the nation was moving in the wrong direction under the sway of the secretary of state, Henry Clay. Clay's party wanted protective tariffs to help develop American industry, and a strong central bank to provide credit for businessmen. They were comfortable with the elite of America's cities, and seemingly unconcerned about the dangers posed to American democracy by urban aristocrats.

Sarah and her Democratic colleagues agreed that nothing was more likely to lead to the destruction of the American experiment than a consolidation of power among the aristocrats of Boston and Philadelphia. Life in frontier Tennessee had taught them that American virtue lay in the hands of yeoman farmers, that "special interests" needed to be brought down by the people, and that cities were, as Thomas Jefferson put it, "great sores on the body politic." Bankers, they believed, were particularly corrupt, interested only in their own aggrandizement, while tariffs would inevitably enrich the aristocrats at the expense of the common man. And they were all disturbed by the growing opposition to the expansion of slavery, which was already an issue of national contention. The passengers in the Polks' carriage, slave owners all, believed that slave labor was necessary to grow staple crops, the main route to agrarian wealth.[18]

What America needed, Democrats agreed, was not industry, but more land, which meant moving Indians off territory that rightfully belonged in the hands of white farmers. They traveled to Washington in order to enact their vision of society, convinced that the power of the federal government should be limited, that territorial expansion was God's plan, that the ownership of slaves was a matter of private property and deserving of government protection, and that ordinary white American men should be empowered to make their own decisions.

In the close confines of her own carriage, buoyed by high spirits, political talk with important men, and the knowledge that "a wider life and a more extended prospect now stretched its dim outline before her," it was easy for Sarah "to make light of the toils by the way." It was a fitting odyssey from one life to another.[19]

When they reached Washington, James and Sarah found lodgings at Williamson's Hotel on Pennsylvania Avenue. It was a step up from Captain Burch's—more spacious, and with other couples in residence. But it was by no means a place they intended to put down roots. Prior to the adoption of the Twentieth Amendment to the Constitution in 1933, congressional sessions always began in the first week of December. Sessions ending in odd-numbered years ran into the summer, while those ending in even-numbered years ended on March 4. This, James's second session, was an even-numbered one, which made for a short second session of three months. James and Sarah determined to make the best of their quarter year at Williamson's and, should James have the good luck of reelection, find somewhere better the following December.[20]

Sarah's decision to leave Columbia for Washington understandably raised eyebrows back home. What could account for it? Might Sarah be pregnant, and if not, was the couple at work on the project? One of James's friends in Columbia wrote him not long after they settled into Williamson's to offer entirely unnecessary congratulations to "yourself and Mrs Polk . . . with my sincere wishes that a residence at the City may prove felicitous in more ways than one."[21]

But Sarah's mind was not occupied with babies. Washington, D.C., was a work in progress; the spacious avenues of Pierre Charles L'Enfant's plan were marked by empty lots, and pigs roamed unfinished streets. It was also hot, swampy, and unsophisticated. Its physical deficiencies were obvious to transplants from America's cultural centers: Boston, New York, and Philadelphia. Louisa Catherine Adams, raised in Europe, declared Washington's streets "dreadful beyond anything you can conceive."[22]

But they bothered Sarah no more than had the discomforts of her journey there. Having been "immediately introduced to the gay and interesting life which high public office bequeaths," she became a frequent visitor to the "ladies' galleries" in Congress, and took as much pleasure in the political debates as any representative. Surrounded by "learning, refinement, and activity" far beyond anything she had ever known, she immediately declared it a "delightful" city. Could the "capital of the nation" be any less than delightful for a woman already in love with politics?[23]

IF SARAH DIDN'T KNOW when she reached Washington, she soon learned that there were more opportunities for women to make their mark there than in any other American city. Women were an active presence in the capital from its earliest establishment; they were present at all public gatherings, were spectators at Supreme Court hearings, and witnessed all the most significant ceremonial occasions. Women were given preference for seats in the cushioned front row of the gallery of the House of Representatives. On the final evening of short sessions of Congress, the entire gallery was reserved exclusively for female visitors. Elite Washington women read the newspapers, were familiar with political debates, and socialized with the male leadership of the new federal government. Friendships between elite men and women, nourished by politics, thrived. Although they could neither vote nor (with the exception of widows) own property, women's presence in Washington helped to legitimize politics. By the time of the Madison administration, they were doing more than simply listening.[24]

No one played a greater role in integrating women into Washington, D.C., politics than Dolley Madison. Dolley Payne Todd was a twenty-six-year-old widow when she married the forty-three-year-old bachelor James Madison in 1794, a year after a yellow fever epidemic killed five thousand people in Philadelphia in four months, including Dolley's first husband and her infant son. Already famous as the "father of the Constitution," the introspective Madison was particularly attracted by Dolley's vivacious personality, so different from his own. He adopted Dolley's two-year-old surviving son, John Payne Todd. Dolley's first three years of marriage were spent as the wife of a congressman in Philadelphia. Madison retired from office in 1797, but it was a short retirement. When Thomas Jefferson became president, he called on his old friend to serve as his secretary of state.[25]

Jefferson was elected president in 1800, the year that the federal government moved permanently to Washington. Dolley insisted on renting a large house, fit for entertaining. It was one of the best decisions either Madison ever made. Jefferson's eight years as president were tense, marked by internal dissent, international crisis, and an extremely fractious Congress. Under Dolley Madison's guidance, the "Ladies of Washington" played a crucial role structuring the extraofficial events necessary for the smooth functioning of government. By carefully orchestrating social events where political allies and foes could meet outside the confines of Congress, the wives, daughters, and sisters of leading politicians used the private sphere to advance public policy. In this way Washington women became avid participants in the "family business" of politics. In an era when even elected politicians were supposed to act as if they were above politics, and political parties were considered suspect by most of the population, Washington's women, by doing a great deal of dirty political work behind the scenes, allowed male politicians to appear virtuous, honest, and nonpolitical. Women determined who would or would not be invited to a dinner when important legislation was about to be introduced, or whether a reception would be held that could detract from the actions of political enemies.[26]

When James Madison was elected president in 1808, Dolley Madison embraced her role as First Lady, which is neither elected nor defined by the Constitution. To say that she defined the office broadly given the time and place is to understate the case. Dolley skillfully deployed rules of etiquette to her husband's benefit, personally calling on every member of Congress at the start of his term, thus setting into effect a series of "visits" that bound the men to the first couple. The social relationship between the president, Congress, and the Supreme Court is also undefined in the Constitution. Dolley's carefully selected guest lists established a precedent of cordiality between the three branches of government that was not self-evident at the birth of the nation.

As First Lady, Madison not only seated herself at the head of the table, but also created the most important social institution of the early republic, her Wednesday night drawing room. These weekly soirees, which began in March 1809 and lasted through both of her husband's terms in office, "created a new kind of political space" that offered access to politically powerful men, and integrated women into the practice of politics.[27]

Dolley's Wednesday night gatherings were "open house" events, unusual in that all guests remained standing for the entirety of the evening. They were carefully managed by Dolley, who cajoled guests into attending and made sure to offer necessary introductions. To a large degree they enabled the practice of politics for a famously fractious Congress, offering a space for the formation of alliances and structures in a period when official channels failed to operate. Under her skillful orchestration, these gatherings established Dolley's White House as the "focal center" of Washington. She made use of them to secure posts for family and friends, but above all else to bind people to her husband. It was commonly understood that the social efforts of the "Lady Presidentess" secured a second term for her husband.[28]

In 1817 the couple returned to their Virginia plantation, and James and Elizabeth Monroe took their place. The eight years the Monroes spent in the White House were known as the "Era of Good Feelings," primarily because James ran unopposed for reelection in 1820. But there was nothing particularly good about the feelings inspired in Washington by the "President's lady."

Parlor politics atrophied with Dolley's absence. Elizabeth Monroe believed the prestige of the office of president would increase if she limited social access to herself and her husband. Her reserve was in part due to her Francophilia (the Monroes chose to converse exclusively in French when alone), but Elizabeth also suffered from a serious and debilitating medical condition, one she felt necessary to hide from the public. Most likely she had epilepsy, which was mistakenly considered a mental illness at the time.[29]

Elizabeth announced that she would entertain only visiting dignitaries and canceled Dolley's weekly drawing rooms, known as "squeezes" for the crush of visitors. In their place the Monroes hosted irregular, very formal dinners for a select few guests. European etiquette ruled. On one occasion, dinner guests were greeted at the door of the White House by six liveried footmen.[30]

This was such a radical shift from the way things had been done under Dolley Madison that President Monroe felt obliged to call a meeting with his cabinet to explain the new White House rules of protocol. Washington society was forced to accept the new rules, but they were accepted with resentment, and a new appreciation arose for Dolley's regime. The extent of Elizabeth Monroe's disdain for Washington society became clear when her younger sister was married in the White House, the first ever White House wedding. The Monroes invited only forty-two guests and even refused to accept presents from outsiders to their very small circle.[31]

John Quincy Adams's wife, Louisa, born and bred in Europe, showed early promise at what historian Catherine Allgor has called "parlor politics." While John Quincy was Monroe's secretary of state, Louisa threw genteel and politically savvy weekly drawing-room gatherings. That Louisa intended to follow in Dolley's footsteps was made obvious when she purchased the Madisons' original Washington home and immediately undertook a series of renovations that doubled the space for entertaining. She threw costly balls, including one for Andrew Jackson that a thousand people attended, and worked hard to ensure that other women's entertainments did not upstage her own. She understood the business of politicking better than John Quincy did, not only arranging dinners in his support, but encouraging him to meet with supporters, and even lobbying editors on his behalf. Despite her suffering from occasional "depression of spirits," her efforts on his behalf while he was secretary of state were heroic and largely successful.[32]

But John Quincy never seemed to recognize the efforts his wife made to advance his political career. Nor did he deign to discuss political issues with her. Perhaps his inability to acknowledge his wife's political value and abilities contributed to her loss of interest in the whole business. In any case, the election of 1824 was bitter and ugly, full of mudslinging. Andrew Jackson received more popular votes than Adams in the four-way race, which was eventually decided in the House of Representatives when Speaker of the House Henry Clay threw his votes to Adams in return for the position of secretary of state. Jackson's partisans denounced the election results as a "corrupt bargain."[33]

Louisa's health and spirits failed under the combined stresses of the campaign and family crises; she felt "very unequal to labor in my fatiguing vocation."[34] Tellingly, she was too ill to attend her husband's inauguration. She found she had lost interest in the work of parlor politics. Well before the election she noted, with some equanimity, "My Constellation is in eclipse," and that she would "shine a faint satellite" amid a "brilliant" social season. John Quincy, hardly a social man, began throwing his own dinner parties. Louisa, increasingly reclusive and depressed, took to raising silkworms, and for a time bemoaned marrying into the Adams family.[35]

By the time James and Sarah arrived in Washington, two years into the Adams presidency, Louisa was no longer an active social presence. Her receptions were as tasteful as ever, but infrequent and notably subdued. The time had come for a change.

WHETHER OR NOT twenty-three-year-old Sarah realized it, she had arrived in Washington at the perfect moment to capitalize on Washington, D.C.'s domestic power vacuum. James's mentor Andrew Jackson defeated Adams when he ran for reelection in 1828. The rise to power of "Old Hickory" lifted all his followers, but none more so than James. Jackson, the first president from west of the Appalachians, brought new attention to Tennessee.

Not that Jackson's arrival in Washington was a moment of unmitigated happiness. Jackson's beloved wife, Rachel, did not live to see his inauguration. She had been the subject of slander during the election campaign because her first marriage had not been legally voided before she married Andrew, making her a bigamist before the divorce could be secured. Some said that she died from shame after hearing the worst of the slander. Certainly Andrew Jackson held his political foes responsible for her death. It left the president bereft, and the White House lacking a First Lady. Andrew's niece stepped in, but she lacked the authority to command Washington society.[36]

The lull in parlor politics would not last; as Washington grew in population, the need for informal socializing became increasingly evident to members of both parties. An 1829 etiquette guide attributed Washington society's love of private parties ("everyone aims at them") to a lack of "regular theater" or any "other public amusement." But socializing was serious business. The magnificent Capitol Building, burned to the ground by the British in 1814, was reborn between 1819 and 1826 with a soaring copper dome, and acoustics so wretched that congressmen found it literally impossible to hear one another speak in the House chamber. The many women who packed the ladies' galleries often heard more than did the representatives in the chamber. Both chambers had trouble consistently maintaining a quorum. Because so little real negotiation was possible on the floor of Congress, many representatives skipped daily sessions or napped at their desks. Anyone hoping to find consensus or influence opinion needed to look beyond congressional chambers.[37]

Sarah Childress Polk was the ideal person to take charge of Washington parlor politics. She had known Andrew Jackson her entire life, and was the public recipient of both his affection and his respect. Jackson was her husband's mentor; James's enthusiasm for Old Hickory's vision of territorial expansion, small federal government, and political power for the common man had already earned him the nickname Young Hickory. Sarah was also young and energetic, if somewhat less so after a case of the measles kept her in bed for most of the month of August. When she and James returned to Washington that winter, an observer noted that "she looks as if grown 45 years older and seems awkward and distrait."[38]

Surrounded by friendly faces, she bounced back quickly from her illness, and was soon as vibrant as ever. New Yorker Gulian Verplanck, a wealthy widowed congressman of exacting tastes, described Sarah as a "Tennessee Belle" when he accompanied her to an 1829 New Year's reception at the Adams White House. He and Sarah enjoyed the lame duck's discomfort when faced with Jackson partisans. "Cannot say we were received with any particular pleasure either by Mr. A or Mrs.," Verplanck wrote a fellow Democrat. "But there was a tremendous mob with whom we mixed very amusingly for an hour." It was a marker of both Verplanck's and Sarah's populism that they, unlike the elitist Adams family, embraced the opportunity to mix with the common people, even when those people formed a disorderly "mob."[39]

Sarah's political connections were matched by something equally important: her refinement. As one Washington etiquette guide noted, the nation's capital was a city where different social sets practiced "customs peculiar to their own clique, and all who do not conform exactly to their methods are looked upon as vulgar persons, ignorant of good-breeding." Many women, raised in households less opulent than Sarah's, found the formal etiquette in Washington intimidating, so much so that some refused to accompany their husbands on the grounds that they were unprepared to meet such society. Even women prepared for the challenge concluded that "a dinner, well performed by all the actors in it, is very fatiguing." Louisa Catherine Adams noted that "to entertain well you must forget that you are so engaged. . . . This like most things is easier in theory than in practice."[40]

But Sarah's refined upbringing, including the time she spent at Abercrombie's Nashville Female Academy studying manners rather than books, left her amply prepared to meet the exacting standards of Washington high society. "Much etiquette and form was observed, especially at the grand dinners, which were of frequent occurrence," she later remembered. "To me it was delightful." With the implicit sanction and ear of the president, Sarah had no problem making important female friends among the Washington, D.C., political class, none more so than Floride Calhoun, wife of South Carolina senator John C. Calhoun. When her husband was appointed secretary of war in 1817, Floride moved to Washington from the family's plantation in South Carolina. Her great wealth and commanding personality provided her with social power even before her husband was elected vice president under Andrew Jackson in 1828. Until 1832, when Floride returned to South Carolina, she played an outsized role in Washington society. By entertaining the Calhouns, and in turn being entertained by them, Sarah proved herself able to navigate the female culture of gossip and social hierarchy that reigned in tight-knit Washington.[41]

Sarah was able to direct politically expedient socializing among Washington's Democrats, even though she lived in a boardinghouse rather than the White House. The lack of facilities and privacy in boardinghouses drove many women away—Mary Todd Lincoln lasted less than three months in a Washington boardinghouse with a baby and toddler in 1847 when Abraham first took a seat in the House of Representatives—but Sarah was different.[42]

The lack of privacy in her Washington lodgings didn't bother her. (Given that her domestic married life had thus far been under the control of her mother-in-law, she may not even have noticed its absence.) And she loved the company of men. Francis Scott Key, author of the national anthem, enjoyed visiting with the Polks at their boarding-house. He was something of a celebrity, and many women wished to meet him. But the tedium of the drawing room was too much for them. "I get tired of staying in the parlor so long, but I wish very much to see 'Star-Spangled Banner,'" they told her. "Do please let me know in some way when he comes." Sarah never seemed to tire of staying in the parlor. The bustle of the boardinghouse drawing room may have reminded her of her family home at Murfreesboro, where public spaces resounded with the gossip and politics of men in town on government business.[43]

Indeed, the boardinghouse, far from being a liability, actually facilitated Sarah's entertainments. While Dolley Madison's power had derived in large part from her mastery of female-centered communica-tion, from the first, Sarah's entertainments were, like the spaces of the boardinghouse itself, dominated by men. Social doyenne and longtime resident Margaret Bayard Smith declared that manners in Washington were "different from those in other places," in large part because in the cramped spaces where socializing proceeded, women enjoyed "more ease, freedom and equality" than in traditional settings where they waited for men to approach them. Congressmen in boardinghouses were well aware that meals could easily turn into lobbying sessions, and that if the boardinghouse was coed, the lobbying could come from women as well as men. In 1812, Catherine Mitchill, the wife of a New York congressman, used her boardinghouse to successfully lobby both branches of Congress for a pension for a war veteran and his wife. Three years later, Margaret Bayard Smith herself considered lobbying President Madison for a position for her brother-in-law.[44]

Sarah made the most of these opportunities. She was a superb lis-tener, with what contemporaries described as "charming" manners. She kept herself informed about political issues, and since her school days she had followed a course of "systematic reading." She made it a policy to try to read every book given to her, as well as books writ-ten by the authors invited to her entertainments. Men who visited the boardinghouse found it easy to discuss the business of politics with her. Remarkably easy. Supreme Court justice Joseph Story praised her "playful mind" in a poem he composed in her honor. Sarah's success at mixing politics and pleasure was palpable, and "her entertainments left many pleasant memories." But pleasure was always mixed with business in the Polk household. Sarah's skill at gaining the confidences of men and women alike provided James with useful information to which he might not otherwise have been privy.[45]

JAMES WAS REELECTED TWICE. He and Sarah fell into a routine; summers in Columbia, the fall and spring in Washington. But in 1830, something happened that disrupted their happy equilibrium. President Andrew Jackson's cabinet was torn apart in an explosive debate over Peggy Eaton, the wife of Jackson's secretary of war. Many Washington wives refused to speak to Eaton, whom they believed to be sexually promiscuous. Some men also accused her of meddling in politics, a serious charge, and one that cast into high relief the danger that women faced when venturing into the realm of men.[46]

Andrew Jackson believed Peggy innocent of the aspersions cast upon her, and threatened members of his party with retribution if their wives did not treat the Eatons with respect. Sarah Polk was caught in the middle of the debate. She herself later recounted that she had sided with her husband, publicly acknowledged Peggy Eaton, and asserted to other wives the necessity of putting "country" above her personal scruples. Eaton long remembered that Sarah Polk "had always treated me with consideration—perhaps I ought to use the warmer word of kindness." Yet at the time, one of James's congressional colleagues, New York representative Rudolph Bunner, observed that Sarah would "sooner suffer" a pirate to "set at Table with her than be [on] any familiarity" with Eaton. Bunner's perception may have been colored by his own wife's views. Elizabeth Bunner, the granddaughter of Revolutionary War hero Philip Schuyler and niece of Alexander Hamilton, would never have acknowledged Eaton.[47]

The Peggy Eaton affair made the power of Washington women clear; their ability not only to assist men, but also to derail their careers. Sarah suddenly became a political liability for James. Remaining in Washington offered her the untenable choice of either infuriating Jackson by shunning Peggy along with the other influential Jacksonian wives, or alienating the wives of the other powerful Democrats.

The dilemma cast into relief the striking similarities between herself and Peggy. Both Peggy and Sarah were young and vivacious. Both were favorites of Andrew Jackson's. And most notably, like Peggy, Sarah developed close and confidential relationships with men she wasn't married to, relationships that brought her both information and power. Sarah and Aaron V. Brown maintained an intimate correspondence for decades. His political rise echoed that of his former law partner, James, and in the years since he attended the Polks' wedding he also made the move from the Tennessee House of Representatives to serving in the nation's Congress. Supreme Court justice John Catron was another intimate confidant who moved from Tennessee to Washington and wrote Sarah letters that he did not intend for James to read. Both Brown and Catron passed information about James to Sarah, and addressed her as a political equal. While Sarah's relationships with Brown and Catron were not, strictly speaking, flirtatious, they had more in common with the flirtations of Peggy Eaton than most outsiders were aware. Given what was at stake, the Polks' joint decision that Sarah should return to Tennessee for the 1830–31 congressional session was not particularly surprising.

Back in Columbia, Sarah found that she suddenly had plenty of time to think, and to read. Since her school days she had loved historical literature; now she began to amass a collection of fashionable literature, including Laurence Sterne's novels, *Don Quixote*, and Washington Irving's *Sketchbook*. And she indulged her lifelong love of clothing and fashion when she subscribed to a new magazine, *Godey's Lady's Book*, the year after it began publication.[48]

No woman with an interest in fashion could afford to ignore L. A. Godey's *Lady's Book: A Monthly Magazine of Belles-Lettres and the Arts. Containing a choice and multifarious variety of original and selected Literary Compositions. Embellished with several Hundred different Engravings. Designed and executed by the most Eminent Artists, with beautiful illustrations of the prevailing Fashions, splendidly colored, and various patterns for ornamental embroidery. In addition to which its Contents embrace a number of the most Popular Melodies, set to music and arranged for the Piano Forte.* It was something entirely new, a large, lavish, and expensive (the three-dollar-a-year subscription, at a time when three hundred dollars a year was considered a decent income for a laboring man, put it out of the reach of the majority of Americans) monthly women's magazine that offered the latest fashion news from Philadelphia, London, and Paris, including colored plates of demure-looking women in elaborate outfits.

Godey invented the American fashion magazine, and helped create demand for a growing market in cloth and clothing produced in British and American factories in a period when both men and women wore the same few valuable outfits of heavy cloth year in and year out. By profiling the latest fashions, *Godey's* encouraged American women to use changing fashions as a way to express their refinement, taste, and wealth. Sarah's neighbor in Columbia, Caroline Nicholson, was an avid subscriber. She considered it a "household treasure in the way of literature," and carefully saved every issue.[49]

But the magazine simultaneously maintained that a woman's virtue had little to do with her wealth or the cost of her outfits. Which is not to say that appearance was unimportant. On the contrary, "the character of a woman may be known by the internal appearance of her house, and the dress and manners of her children," the magazine asserted. "If the ornaments of her house, however splendid they may be, are badly arranged . . . it is a 'proof strong as holy writ,' that she is deficient both in taste and neatness." And if her children "are dirty or carelessly dressed . . . the mother will most generally prove to be both ignorant and indolent, or which is worse, wholly indifferent to the well-being of her children." But *Godey's* had little time for vain or decorative women. The ideal woman, countless articles asserted, was a selfless wife and mother who "ennobled" even "menial" tasks with "a spirit of love and kindness—anxiety for the comfort of others, and forgetfulness of her own."[50]

This was a magazine that catered to domestic women and helped create an ideology of domesticity in which "the true key to the universe is love," and pure, selfless women held that key. If a woman wished to learn how to clean silk stockings, or achieve "happiness in the marriage state," *Godey's* had an answer. In addition to the sheet music for popular ditties such as "She weeps over the trinkets he gave her," and embroidery patterns suitable for framing, readers knew to count on monthly news of the "language of flowers," historical fiction full of romance, and poems to women's beauty and chastity.[51]

Sarah could easily skip over articles about proper parenting, but there was a great deal more than just fashion to interest her here. Not politics—with the exception of an occasional antislavery aside, *Godey's* resolutely avoided references to contemporary politics, out of a widely shared conviction that such material was inappropriate for a female audience. But the magazine offered a clear model of the useful wife. The ideal wife was a "help-mate . . . designed by providence" to make up for her husband's "deficiencies," and that "her influence over him was unbounded" but she "had no ambition to rule, and never interposed but where the general good required it." As a "help-mate" a woman could gain and exercise power. Sarah may have envisioned herself alongside the "Distinguished Females" *Godey's* profiled in February 1831. Calpurnia, the wife of Julius Caesar, was so "anxious to promote the happiness of her people" that "she in fact became their idol." Agrippina, wife of Germanicus, "united great talents, exalted virtues, and refined delicacy." Thomas More's oldest daughter was a "wise and amiable lady" whose "learning was almost eclipsed by her virtues," and who devoted herself to her father's cause and memory. But perhaps most inspiring was Plotina, wife to Emperor Trajan, who was "as much celebrated for the sweetness of her manners as she was for the solidity of her judgement. . . . So thoroughly was the emperor acquainted with the capability of her intellectual powers, that he always consulted her upon affairs of importance . . . and so great was the ascendancy she obtained over the emperor, that historians ascribe many of his noble acts to the influence of her virtue." Catherine, the wife of Peter the Great, profiled in 1834, offered another model to emulate. Catherine was Peter's "companion in all his wars and expeditions," and her "influence . . . was unbounded; not from the solidity of her judgement, or the brilliance of her wit; but from the sweetness, pliability, and equanimity of her temper." Sarah had read similar accounts of female heroism while a student at Salem Academy, many penned by women.[52]

SARAH CONTINUED her subscription when she returned to Washington in December 1831, after nineteen months in Tennessee. Their gamble proved a wise one: James emerged from the Eaton controversy unscathed, and with Jackson's support defeated a rival Tennessee politician, John Bell, as Speaker of the House in 1835. Although Bell was not distinguished either "for his brilliance or his knowledge," he was wildly popular in middle Tennessee. But his public disapproval of Jackson's opposition to the Bank of the United States drove a wedge between Bell and the Democrats, and henceforth he and James would be political opponents. "The speaker," Sarah noted, "if the proper person, and with a correct idea of his position, has even more power and influence over legislation, and directing the policy of parties, than the president or any other public officer."[53]

James was clearly the right person, and both he and Sarah had a correct idea of his position. According to a contemporary report, "the responsibilities which this position imposed upon" Sarah "were fulfilled by her with ease and dignity," in large part because she took extra rooms in the boardinghouse explicitly for the purposes of political entertaining. She threw herself into twice-weekly dinner parties, happily and successfully presiding over social engagements for the colleagues, allies, and potential allies of Young and Old Hickory alike. The meals were catered, the guests rising Democrats or established men in James's party. These events required little organization on Sarah's part—what she was called upon to do was arrange the guest list, provide an ample spread of food and wine, listen, and facilitate discussion. The cramped quarters encouraged mingling and listening. "Making her apartments elastic and expansible at her pleasure, she could receive a large party of guests at any time, without the care of an extensive establishment."[54]

So successful was this initial investment in a housework-free "private" political space that the Polks expanded their entertaining area when they moved to a second boardinghouse. They took a suite of rooms in a large house on Pennsylvania Avenue, known as Elliot's Building, where most of the rooms were appropriated by the Supreme Court. Sarah's neighbors now included the most powerful justices in the nation.[55]

Sarah used this expanded set of entertaining rooms as a conduit between James and the Supreme Court. She became "famous friends" with all their wives, and "her drawing room was always crowded." Despite Presbyterian scruples that kept both her and James away from the theater, horse races, dancing, and hard liquor, the Polks ran up a wine bill of $138 during a single session of Congress (the equivalent of $4,400 today). It's safe to say that neither Sarah nor James were drinking that wine themselves. "Mrs. Polk frequently met the judges and members of the court, and became so well known to them that upon her departure many of them sent letters expressing regret at her departure." She also sent out several hundred invitations for a party that even the acidulous journalist Anne Royall, who specialized in mocking the pretentions of the elite, admitted was "the genteelest party that has been given this winter by far."[56]

What Sarah unintentionally created in her boardinghouse was an American version of the Enlightenment salon. These salons, which flourished in Paris in the eighteenth century, were a central institution of French upper-class life. They encouraged socializing between men and women and offered opportunities for intellectual debate. They also, in the years before the French Revolution, provided opportunities for women to shape politics through their command of social conversation. Philosophers celebrated female-directed salons as the basis of order in their republic and happily submitted to the rules of polite discourse enforced by the "female governors" of the salons. The Scottish essayist David Hume admiringly noted in 1742 that in neighboring Paris, "the Ladies, are, in a Manner, the Sovereigns of the learned World, as well as of the conversible."[57]

While salons went into eclipse in Paris during the French Revolution and the reign of Napoleon, by the 1820s they were once again at the heart of "elite political networking and discussion." Along with more familiar institutions of modern political life—mass-circulation newspapers, political parties, and voluntary societies—salons run by powerful women helped structure the practice of politics there. In 1834, British intellectual Edward Bulwer-Lytton proclaimed that "woman is queen in France" because she "reigned by a power greater than laws." British travel writer Frances Trollope agreed that France was "le paradis des femmes" and bemoaned that British women lacked the "power" and "influence" of their otherwise inferior neighbors.[58]

Washington, D.C., was no Paris. But in both cities, women took on an outsized importance as conduits of information and mediating forces in political environments that were growing ever more polarized. As insular and parochial as was the capital, the similarity to Paris was not lost on all its residents. John Catron, previously chief justice of the Tennessee Supreme Court, was appointed to the U.S. Supreme Court by Andrew Jackson in 1837. He had married into the Childress family when Sarah was very young, and over time became one of her closest friends. He marveled at the power women held in Washington. "A woman here, as in Paris, can learn more than a man—greatly more," he wrote Sarah two years after arriving. Nor was he alone. James's associate Samuel H. Laughlin offered his congratulations to Sarah after one election "on her being again a membress of Congress-elect."[59]

Sarah's success at entertaining was only possible because her husband was suddenly at the center of power, but it's also true that James remained at the center of power because of Sarah's success at entertaining. "It was incumbent upon the Speaker to entertain a great deal, and Mr. Polk was not remiss upon this obligation," noted a journalist. "These entertainments of the Speaker were very elegant, and at them Mrs. Polk always appeared, attired in the most elegant manner, and was always the recipient of a great deal of admiration and attention." James was remarkably successful and was easily returned to office.[60]

POLITICAL ADVANCEMENT wasn't the only change of fortune for the Polks in the early 1830s. In 1827, James inherited a large tract of West Tennessee land, and in 1831 he moved the majority of his and Sarah's slaves, including Mariah, onto the unimproved property in order to grow cotton in his first foray into plantation ownership. This was an unwelcome move for the Polks' enslaved people, who were forced to leave loved ones for the hard labor of cotton planting. In the place of family members left behind, they were joined by four strangers, slaves whom James purchased for plantation labor. Three of them were teenagers, all torn from their families. The youngest, Giles, was just thirteen years old. Sarah had once taken pride in serving as Mariah's "protector," but her sending Mariah to the plantation proved her benevolence a sham.[61]

But worse was yet to come. Three years later James sold out and invested in a potentially much more lucrative plantation on Mississippi land recently taken from the Choctaws. The 920 acres southwest of Coffeeville, Mississippi, were uncleared, but in close proximity to the

Yalobusha tributary of the Yazoo River, allowing for easy access to New Orleans. There was no fate, besides death and separation from family, that slaves feared more than being sold to the Mississippi Delta, where climate and labor conspired to end too many black lives. But as James explained to Sarah, he was "determined to make more money or loose [sic] more," to win big with this new plantation or to lose big. In short, he hoped the plantation would make him rich.[62]

James purchased eight additional young slaves from strangers and shipped them to Mississippi. Some were only children. The Polk slaves were welcoming, but conditions on the plantation were not the sort that allowed for the happiness of children. Eighteen-year-old Caroline, daughter of the enslaved plantation midwife, remembered one little girl's arrival well. Dafney "was a child of 10 years when she was bought and come to the place." Within two years, at the age of twelve, the new arrival had started a family with Giles, who had been just a year older when he arrived at the first Polk plantation. "About the time she was grown she got in a delicate state," Caroline explained, "it was laid to Giles, a man on the place, the higher powers made them claim one another, and this was all the wedding they had." Dafney admitted that "we were neither of us hardly grown when we were married," but she didn't know any better. She was just "a little girl" when she "come to the Polk Place."[63]

Two years after purchasing the plantation, Polk successfully ushered through the House a congressional resolution tabling, without discussion, any petition regarding slavery, despite the fact that the right to petition is enshrined in the Constitution. Most of those petitions were signed by northern white women, and directly addressed the expansion of slavery as immoral. Petitioning was a new foray for women into the political realm, and their political involvement made antislavery petitions doubly odious to many southerners. Passing the "gag rule" was James's signature accomplishment as Speaker of the House, and a singularly appropriate resolution for the master of a cotton plantation intent on becoming rich off the labor of enslaved people. It was no coincidence that he would make territorial expansion into lands fit for slave labor his main issue. Although indebted to his wife's work on his behalf, as Speaker of the House, James K. Polk proved himself a master in more ways than one.[64]

———

LIKE OTHER AMERICANS who left home in order to pursue opportunity, Sarah discovered that mobility, whether social or geographic, came at the cost of community. Both she and James had grown up in small, tightly knit towns, and as much as they might wish it otherwise, life in Columbia and Murfreesboro continued in their absence. Her family in Columbia and Murfreesboro had suffered traumatic losses while she was in Washington. Her father-in-law, Sam, suffered through a long illness, and died in 1827. While Sam was on his deathbed, her elder brother, twenty-seven-year-old Anderson Childress, fell off a horse and also died, leaving behind an orphaned daughter who moved in with her grandmother. Four years later, in 1831, Jane Polk suffered through the tragic early deaths of three of her sons.[65]

Sarah's losses were insignificant in comparison, but one day in January 1832 she picked up a copy of the *Courier* and discovered that her brother John had gotten married. Neither of her siblings had bothered to tell her. Her twelve-year-old niece, Mary, who had lived with her grandmother Elizabeth Childress since the death of both her parents, sent Sarah a piece of wedding cake, along with an account of a wedding neither of them had attended (Mary wasn't invited either).

Sarah wrote to young Mary, unable to hide her hurt feelings. "Your Aunt Susan nor Uncle John has not thought worth while to write me one word about the wedding," she fumed. "I think that it is a little as some of them could do to write me, and I also think they treated you very badly not to let you go to the wedding. If I had been there . . . you should have gone." Then she lashed out at poor Mary herself. "I was very sorry to hear that you are not going to school this season, for you are very backward for a girl of your age and not to loose any time from school. Tell Ma you ought to go to school." Sarah's solicitude for Mary's welfare was clearly sincere. In the future she adopted the role of patron to several of her nieces, encouraging them to better themselves through education, as she had. But her mind quickly flew from Mary's misfortune to her own. She asked Mary to "tell your uncle John he might have waited until I came home before he got married."[66]

Physical distance wasn't the only source of friction. Jane Walker, James's oldest sister and their neighbor in Columbia, was a frequent correspondent. Sarah loved "Sister Jane," as she and James called her, as much as her own sister, or more so, if one can judge such things by the number of gifts sent from the privileged aunt to her nieces and nephews on each side of the family. Eleven-year-old Joanna Rucker, her sister Susan's daughter, jealously noted the beautiful new dresses worn by her Walker cousins, and wondered if "perhaps I am not a great favorite of my dear Aunt?" Jane Walker may in fact have been Sarah's closest female friend.[67]

But as Jane's family grew, so too did the distance between their experiences. Staying in touch was a priority for Jane. When her "scolding" about "nobody" in the extended Polk clan writing to James and Sarah fell on deaf ears, it was Jane who pulled herself out of bed just days after giving birth to "the finest little girl" to update Sarah about the goings-on in Tennessee. Her first priority was news about the children born to the "prolific lot" of Polks—not only her own daughter, but Sam's second girl, born "two weeks since," and two enslaved members of the family, Malinda and Mariann, each of whom had "increased their families"—followed by news of housework (starch bags and baby caps), two recent parties to which "everybody was invited," including the recently married Charlie and Mary, "the most pleasing looking couple there," a mutual acquaintance's romance after a recent depression ("he went to a ball with Jane, and to a party, and rides with her"), and her general annoyance that her husband had missed the birth of his daughter and had yet to return. Jane looked for him "daily" and was "right vexed that he stays so long" away. She was particularly impatient because she left it to her husband to name the baby. "She has no name and I am at a loss for one," she sighed to Sarah.

Jane's experiences of childbirth, housework, and a husband at both a physical and a psychological distance from his wife were shared by most of the women in the Polk clan, indeed by most adult women of her age and class. It was a world idealized as a domestic idyll within the pages of *Godey's Lady's Book* and women's novels.

But it was not Sarah's world. Jane was dead tired, but she was not a stupid woman. Perhaps at some point near the close of her narration of babies, housework, and parties, she realized that these events might be less engaging for a childless congressman's wife, living in a boarding-house seven hundred miles away, than they were for her. Because on

the second page of her letter, Jane announced, "I have political news."
She began to explain: "I have not seen Andrew May but once since
M. Walker left home—"

Jane's narration broke off as suddenly as it began. One of her children had clumsily stumbled into her, and in the process "blotted" her
letter, which was now a mess.

Jane's frustration, and her deep exhaustion, ooze from the letter.
Political discourse, even gossip, were too much for her to undertake
given the chaos of her household. And so she gave up writing before
conveying her promised political news. "It is too hard work for me to
write it over," she explained to her sister-in-law. "My eyes are weak,"
and she could "hear the babies crying all around." She begged Sarah to
"excuse this short letter" and closed with one final bit of family news,
about her youngest son. "I forgot to tell you that Andrew Jackson can
walk and is as fat as a little pig."[68]

Jane Walker's Andrew Jackson was no doubt every bit as demanding as Sarah Polk's, most likely more so. But the differences between
the two sets of demands were not easily overcome. And both women
knew it.

3

Holingsworth is a candidate, and Mrs. Walker (from whom you know that I
get a good deal of news) says it makes some sensation among the whigs. Dr.
McNairy will vote for him, & Joe Norvell thinks he will be elected. This of
course is womens gossip and not worth much.

—SARAH CHILDRESS POLK TO JAMES K. POLK, Nashville, June 18, 1841

WHEN JAMES AND SARAH returned to Columbia in the late
summer of 1838 for the Twenty-Fifth Congress's summer recess,
they had some decisions to make. Foremost among them was whether
James should keep his congressional seat or run for governor. Running
Tennessee was an alluring proposition in many ways: it would raise
his profile nationally and put him in a strong position for a future vice
presidential nomination. The state party was floundering, and James
represented the Democrats' best hope for ending a six-year slide into
the hands of Henry Clay's Whig Party, a slide that had become decidedly more precipitous in the wake of the Panic of 1837, also known as
"Van Buren's Ruin," in honor of the Democratic president with the
bad fortune to preside over the national economic collapse caused by
economic policies of his predecessor, Andrew Jackson. And perhaps
after thirteen years in Congress, James was ready for a new challenge.

But the life they had built in Washington wasn't easy to leave
behind. Sarah in particular had carved out a uniquely powerful space
of influence as wife of the Speaker of the House. They both loved their
life in the capital. So James publicly backed former governor William
Carroll for chief executive of the state, and settled into his summer

vacation. Matters appeared to be set. They would return to Washington at the end of the summer for the second session of Congress, and hope the national wave of enthusiasm for the Whigs and economic reform would crest before it cost him his speakership. Or at least this appeared to be their plan before the Murfreesboro dinner.

One advantage of spending vacation in middle Tennessee was the relatively easy access to the extended Polk and Childress families. James didn't hesitate when invited to address a large crowd at a "public dinner" in Murfreesboro at the end of August 1838, despite the fact that the event required writing an extensive new speech. Murfreesboro was Sarah's hometown, after all. Not that James would have hesitated in any case; he rarely turned down a request to speak. No successful politician in the 1830s could afford to. The ability to speak with eloquence, and at great length, was crucial to political success in the Democratic politics of the Jacksonian Era. Both men and women were accustomed to listening to political addresses of two or more hours in length, while the greatest speakers of the era, including Senators Henry Clay of Kentucky and Daniel Webster of Massachusetts, were renowned for their ability to bring listeners to tears in orations that lasted entire afternoons. In return for their patience, political parties in the 1830s treated voters well, offering up entertainment, food, and copious quantities of alcohol at political rallies like the one set for Murfreesboro. James and Sarah happily made the fifty-mile trip from Columbia so that James could address the public on subjects close to his heart and Sarah could visit with her mother.

The event organizers expected between three and four hundred guests, but over two thousand turned out at noon on a Tuesday in a beautiful grove a quarter mile from Murfreesboro. Whether the main draw was the free meal and drinks or a two-hour address by Speaker of the House James K. Polk on the evil of banks and the glories of small government, James's "masterly exposition of the present state of parties" held the audience enchanted, according to a friendly Democratic account. As James delivered the final lines of his stirring address, assuring the public that "though others had deserted their principles . . . he would fall, if fall he must, with his flag flying and his face to the foe," the crowd moved on to a banquet composed "of the plain substantials of life," including "forty fat sheep, forty fine shoats, six beeves, three hundred pounds of fine ham, and bread and vegetables without limit. Nor was the generous juice of the grape, whisky, and old cogniac, wanting to give life and animation to the scene." The weather was as fine as the libations. It was shaping up into a splendid party.

Then the Democratic candidate for governor, William Carroll, arrived. It was an unexpected honor, and the arrangements committee called for a toast to his election prospects. But Carroll rose to the podium and made a shocking announcement. Due to health considerations, he could not and would not be able to stand for governor.

A murmur ran through the crowd, men laid down their whiskey, and all eyes turned to James. The arrangements committee called on Polk to take Carroll's place at the head of the state ticket. Would he run? James rose, expressed his surprise and dismay at such an unexpected turn of events, and then immediately announced that he "had reflected on his duty, and his mind was made up." According to press reports, he automatically answered the call to duty, agreeing without need for contemplation or consultation to become the party's candidate for governor of Tennessee.[1]

How spontaneous and decisive! James K. Polk's manly response was exactly the sort of confident and independent leadership that followers of Andrew Jackson expected of their political candidates. Whigs mocked Polk as a "little Jackson," but he demonstrated at the Murfreesboro dinner that he was bound by no debts to party leaders, not even to Jackson himself, before assuming his rightful place as party leader. Nor, it goes without saying, did he need to consult with his wife.[2]

And where was Sarah, exactly? She's not mentioned in any account of the event, but this proves very little. Women regularly attended political rallies, speeches, and dinners in the 1830s, but were only infrequently noted by reporters. Sarah enjoyed listening to James speak, and wasn't too delicate for a plate of mutton and ham. She might, of course, have been present when James accepted nomination as the Democratic candidate for governor of Tennessee. But Sarah hadn't seen her brother or sister, her nieces and nephews, or her mother in months. Elizabeth had always been demanding of Sarah's time, and she wouldn't have easily agreed to her attending a political event immediately after such an extended absence. It seems likely that Sarah skipped the beeves and shoats in favor of dinner with her Childress relatives. In which case, if we are to believe the press coverage, the wife of the Speaker of the House of Representatives didn't learn the fate of her carefully constructed Washington political salon until after James's return from the dinner.

This account, while highly flattering to a candidate who hoped to personify the Democratic ideal of manly independence, was almost certainly wrong. While William Carroll may not have formally agreed to withdraw from the race before springing the news in Murfrees-boro, Democratic leaders had been attempting to ease him out for two weeks. And for exactly as long the same Democrats had encouraged James "to be ready to step into the breach." James was not a man who liked surprises; his quick and gracious acceptance of the nomination suggests he was well prepared and forewarned about what was going to happen.[3]

Nor does it seem possible that James made a decision of such enormous consequence to Sarah without consulting with her. However potent the idea of separate spheres might have been in shaping the ideal of men and women in the 1830s, the Washington, D.C., political class understood that a politician's wife was never separate from politics. Even Andrew Jackson, the party's ideal of patriarchal independence, consulted with his wife, Rachel, before committing to political campaigns.[4]

And Sarah was no ordinary wife. In addition to running her political salon, she had become adept at managing James's correspondence over his seven congressional campaigns. Those campaigns had been relatively straightforward affairs in recent years. Although Jacksonian democracy promised voters a previously unimagined degree of contact with their elected officials and those who hoped to be elected, a politician of James's stature faced few challenges to reelection to the House of Representatives.

A gubernatorial campaign, by contrast, was far from straightforward. There may have been no more strenuous campaign that a politician could run in the 1830s than that for state governor. Presidential candidates rarely campaigned openly, in order to maintain the fiction that they stood above the fray of party politics. Congressmen need only canvass their districts. Senators were elected by state legislatures.

But a gubernatorial candidate was expected to travel the entire state and to meet with the voters in every county. Not even the Speaker of the House of Representative could rest on his laurels when running for governor in the 1830s.

And Tennessee was no ordinary state. It was geographically and politically divided into three distinct regions, united by a widespread distrust of residents of the other districts. Middle Tennessee, characterized by fertile farmland, was Polk and Childress territory. Eastern Tennessee was a Whig stronghold where James knew full well he had "but a very limited personal acquaintance." The river town of Knoxville dominated this mountainous region, which was unsuited to the staple-crop agriculture that dominated the rest of the state. Few families in the east owned slaves. The newly settled lowlands of western Tennessee had a very different topography, but just as much enthusiasm for the Whig platform. Western Tennessee residents looked west to the Mississippi River to make their fortunes. Internal improvements, easy credit, and increased trade were appealing positions in this developing region.[5]

James had signed on to a tremendous amount of campaigning. And whether Sarah knew it or not, her burden would be almost as taxing. Left alone in Columbia, with none of her Washington friends to support her, she faced ever-increasing burdens to manage correspondence and communication across the 440-mile-long state. This campaign would place singular challenges on their relationship. James's nomination as Democratic candidate for governor came as no surprise to Sarah. The surprise would come later, during a political campaign that would stretch Sarah's capacities and redefine the work of the political wife.

JAMES ENTERED the 1839 gubernatorial race with several advantages. He was Tennessee's most popular Democrat, and his opponent, the "sluggish" sitting governor, Newton Cannon, had alienated many in his own party by not being Whiggish enough: his endorsement of crucial Whig legislation in support of new roads and a railroad line had been halfhearted. The Democrats were far more enthusiastic about their candidate than the Whigs were about Cannon. Indeed, the "whole Democracy," a fellow Democrat wrote, was "firm and erect" in James's support. But this only made the stakes higher. A loss would be a disaster not only for the state, but also for Polk personally. Nor was James the only person to see it that way. "You are too valuable a man to the County and the party," one correspondent wrote him, "to be lost" with this election.[6]

Despite their mediocre candidate, James knew the Whigs were dangerous. Tennesseans were proving to be as enthusiastic about the Whig financial platform as their Kentucky neighbors to the north. Many, remarkably enough, had a soft spot for the Kentucky politician who led the party, Henry Clay, despite Clay having earned Andrew Jackson's passionate enmity. Nashville's Democratic newspaper, the *Union*, ran advertisements for gilt frame portraits of Henry Clay available for purchase at the city bookstore. Congressman John Bell, middle Tennessee's leading Whig politician and James's most formidable opponent both at home and in Washington, wasn't at all worried about James's return to their home state. He wrote Clay at the beginning of the summer that the state party expected a Whig victory by "15000 votes at least."[7]

James determined to campaign his way to victory. As he and Sarah traveled home at the close of what would be their final term in Congress, he informed her that he intended to devote himself to the goal of "meet[ing] the people as generally as possible" prior to the August 1 election. That meant four months of near-constant separation, the most they had spent apart since the 1830–31 congressional session. After directing Sarah to forward his letters to him and "fill" the county lists by sending campaign literature to voters on each stop of his tour, James took leave of his wife on April 7. The campaign had officially begun.[8]

The very next day an anxious James wrote home for help. He had left papers behind, papers that he now imagined he "might need"— including the voting results from the previous two gubernatorial elections. Wasting no time in chitchat, he asked Sarah to locate the missing papers (he had a fair idea where they were, but was not totally confident). He closed not with expressions of love or hopes that their time apart would pass quickly, but with a reminder about the county lists she had promised to fill.[9]

This first written communication of the gubernatorial candidate set the tone and the terms for many to come. James was always prepared, often overprepared, but only because of Sarah's daily focused involvement in the campaign, involvement he insisted upon. It was up to Sarah to make sure that he had everything he could possibly need, and his needs were vast. After requesting the entire run of a newspaper, he explained to Sarah that he would meet his opponent "under great disadvantages. I shall be fatigued and almost worn down by my long tour, and will not have a single day at home, to select the documents I may need. Not knowing upon what points he may touch I should be prepared upon all." And so Sarah sent them all.[10]

Might not someone else have done this? James's campaign had an official director: his close friend General Robert Armstrong, who despite fighting under Jackson at the Battle of New Orleans had been unsuccessful in his own run for governor two years earlier. But Armstrong appears to have been manager in name only. There is little evidence that the two men communicated directly with any great regularity. Rather, it was Sarah who was responsible from the start for delivering both messages and material to Armstrong. And as the campaign progressed, responsibilities increasingly fell on her rather than on the general.

Whatever trepidation James felt at the start of the campaign was considerably alleviated as he toured the state that spring. In Nashville he addressed "an immense crowd" and successfully talked down his opponent. "So clearly was he put in the wrong & so complete was the victory over him, that, the shouts of applause were long and tremendous," James crowed to Sarah. "The day was clearly ours & our opponents knew it." He was in "good health and spirits." Matters on the campaign trail looked good.

James's celebratory tone lasted a single paragraph before he began issuing orders. Sarah needed to secure copies of two speeches he had delivered as Speaker of the House and send those copies to three different men for distribution among the Tennessee electorate. He wasn't exactly sure where the speeches were, but was confident Sarah could locate them and send at least six thousand copies immediately, as "their early circulation is important." He closed his letter, "You know where I will be from day to day. Do write me often."[11]

It's a curious letter: intimate insofar as James, a notoriously reserved man, was willing to brag about his successful oration in a manner he would hardly adopt with anyone else. But his letter is also, to our ears, detached, demanding, and more than a bit supercilious. He never said please. He didn't ask how Sarah was, how things at home were progressing. His statement "you know where I will be from day to day" suggests that he also knew where Sarah would be from day to day—at home, managing the logistics that would make his election possible. He never suggested that she had any responsibilities to compare or interfere with her work as unofficial campaign manager.

And indeed she didn't. Besides the house. And the management of the enslaved people who labored in their home. No one would argue that this work was remotely comparable to that of running a gubernatorial campaign. Women's work in the home was largely invisible to men; it had been "pastoralized" over the previous decades, as an ideology of separate spheres imagined the home as a refuge from the competition and strain of the business world.[12]

If Sarah was hoping James might ask for her help, rather than take it for granted, or write her about something other than his political needs, his letters over the coming months would hardly reassure. As he traveled east, into potentially hostile territory, he kept Sarah informed about the day-to-day minutiae of what quickly turned into a grueling campaign. Riding up to forty-five miles in a single day, James addressed "large assemblages" virtually every day, with "most encouraging" results. On April 21, he crossed the mountains into eastern Tennessee, a stronghold of Whig support. Attendance at the events was light, but perhaps that was because these were thinly populated counties. His friends informed him that he was gaining ground, and he wished Sarah to spread the word in middle Tennessee that he was "much pleased" with his prospects thus far.[13]

This was far from all he asked of Sarah. Not only was she to forward important correspondence that arrived at the house, to locate relevant materials in his files, and to sort and address enormous numbers of handbills and publications to supporters around the state, but she was also responsible for conveying directions to male relatives and close friends who were working on his behalf. When the desired materials failed to arrive, which happened more than once, James politely

restated his request. He never admonished Sarah for missing correspondence, but often insisted that she do her work "without delay" or
"immediately." Surely he recognized that given the less-than-reliable
nature of the post and his constant travel, complex political correspondence might not always be within her control. But neither did he thank
her for successfully locating and posting scores of documents, letters,
publications, and handbills. It was clear what James expected of her,
and his expectations expanded as his tour took him farther from home.
Soon he began directing other politicians to write directly to Sarah for
useful information.[14]

"I promised Col. R. M. Burton of Lebanon to write to you to forward to him some documents," he warned her, before listing his own
requests. He wished her to go through his pamphlet collection, locate
every speech made by his Whig archrival John Bell, and send them to
one supporter, and to send an unspecified number of copies of one of
his own congressional speeches to a different supporter. He warned
her not to fail to send a box of a third supporter's material in her possession to a fourth man. And he asked Sarah, rather than local political
supporters, to have notices of his appearances printed and forwarded
to his future destinations.[15]

Sarah became, in effect, the campaign's communications director,
although the extent of her responsibilities were neither made public
nor openly acknowledged within Nashville's political class. Although
women were an established presence in Washington, D.C., their role
in Tennessee state politics was comparatively slight. This is not to say
that James kept Sarah's work secret. Given that he directed men to
write her directly for information, it would hardly have been possible
for him to do so. One correspondent, recognizing that Sarah reviewed
and forwarded James's mail, spoke directly to her in a letter to her
husband. "If Mrs. Polk or some other friend at Columbia should in
the absence of Col Polk open this & should the Col. be very distant
& not conveniently reached by Mail no extra effort need be made to
forward it."[16]

At least one frequent correspondent, Sarah's brother John, had a
clear understanding of her position. Parents like Joel and Elizabeth
Childress encouraged "sibling devotion" among their children, and
Sarah and John, the two youngest Childresses, developed what was

for the most part a caring and egalitarian relationship. Whether Sarah was in Columbia or in Washington, John wrote to share local news and complain about family members (he wasn't the only Childress to find Susan's husband, Dr. William Rucker, occasionally exasperating).[17]

But mostly he wrote Sarah in search of political information. When "a rumor" reached Murfreesboro that James's nemesis John Bell "has lost his whole estate gaming and an agent has come to take possession," he turned to Sarah, and asked, "Is it true?" Sadly, it was not. John asked Sarah to "write me soon and give all the news, for Col. Polk will not." The two of them openly discussed the political campaign during visits, and John turned to Sarah for information when other channels proved dry. After hearing rumors of unexpected Whig strength in local Maury County in June, John wrote Sarah for confirmation. He asked her directly, "If there is any foundation for the report, and as you are as likely to know as anyone else I write to you."[18]

But in recognizing Sarah's power, John was the exception even within their families. James Walker, Jane Polk Walker's husband, hoped to see James elected, and put a great deal of his own money toward that cause. In mid-July he advised the candidate to direct a series of letters to prominent men in East Tennessee. Recognizing that James was "too much fatigued to write those letters yourself," he recommended that James enlist their brother William and Walker's son Knox to do the work. At no point did Walker suggest that Sarah might help with this project.[19]

Clearly Sarah could have mailed those letters. She did little but mail things for James, a fact her husband's brother-in-law must have realized. But could she have written, or even "copied," the letters? Certainly. James and Sarah had very different handwriting, and a perusal of James's official correspondence makes clear that Sarah wrote some of his letters. That summer she acknowledged receipt of an invitation to a dinner, and regretfully declined, signing the letter with James's signature. James Walker was far from alone in his inability to see Sarah on the front line of the 1839 gubernatorial campaign. But this was the last time she would be so invisible.[20]

Less than a month into James's tour, events arose that required an important shift in Sarah's position. In addition to the usual laundry list of documents to be located and posted (as always, with the reminder,

"Do not fail to attend to this immediately"), James decided he could no longer trust the editor of the local party journal, *The Democrat*. He "has treated me badly, by delaying the publication of my Addresses," he admitted to Sarah. "I fear he will not, at last publish the numbers (10,000) which I ordered." Because his addresses were in great demand, it was up to Sarah to make things right. Not only must she ensure that ten thousand copies of the address were copied and forwarded for distribution, but he also asked her to locate a copy of *The Democrat* from June 18, 1837. If she couldn't find the issue in his papers, he directed her to go to the office of the offending paper and retrieve a copy herself.[21]

Up until this point, Sarah conducted the vast majority of her political work from the confines of her own home. While the work itself might have been unusual for a woman (and only possible for a woman without young children), the space within which her actions took place was wholly appropriate. Daily trips to the Columbia post office to mail heavy packages, all "put up in strong brown paper, bound with tape and well marked," as James directed, were possibly completed by a Polk slave rather than by Sarah herself. But there would have been nothing unusual about a woman visiting a small-town post office. Before the advent of free home mail delivery in 1863, the post office was one of the few public spaces open to women in big cities. Some even established separate counters just for female patrons.[22]

Women in small towns had a great deal more freedom in public spaces than they did in cities. They were particularly prominent in the streets of Columbia since the completion of the town's magnificent Female Institute, staffed by unmarried female graduates of northern women's colleges. Rising like a medieval castle on a hill at the edge of town, the Columbia Female Institute's 120-foot brick façade, complete with turrets and a crenellated roof line, lent the town a decided gravitas. The curriculum, designed to train women for careers as teachers, was just as ambitious as the building. That such a grand institution existed in middle Tennessee offered proof that female higher education was no longer restricted to privileged daughters of enlightened parents, as it had been in Sarah's youth.[23]

But there were limits to female-friendly public spaces, even in Columbia. What James now requested was Sarah's invasion of a particularly masculine public space, the office of a newspaper publisher, on a mission explicitly political. A woman in public space during an election campaign might face real danger. Letter writers and newspapers reported fistfights between Whigs and Democrats in the streets of Tennessee. One congressional candidate carried pistols to his public appearances. Sarah had not only to traverse this territory, but she was also directed do so on the way to an encounter with a publisher whose allegiances were far from clear. There could be no mistaking Sarah's role in this potentially combative encounter. By directing her to the office of *The Democrat,* James announced his wife as a political actor.[24]

WHILE SARAH AND JAMES understood in an abstract way that the 1839 gubernatorial campaign would pose new challenges, they had no way of predicting the strain it would place on James's health. According to his own account, between May 12 and May 18, he met and addressed no fewer than eleven thousand people in a heavily Whig district of eastern Tennessee, including "all the ladies" of two separate villages. In two months of campaigning he visited over half the counties in the state, and rode more than thirteen hundred miles, including a last-minute trip to East Tennessee three days before the election where he confronted the governor in the streets, and then broke open a barrel of whiskey for his followers.[25]

Although James increasingly admitted to being "much fatigued," he generally maintained a positive tone in his daily letters to Sarah. Both crowds and polling results spoke to the success of their efforts. James's requests to Sarah continued to multiply. Admitting that he had waited until the last moment to learn where his opponent would be, and that he had no time to write letters for distribution to the counties he was scheduled to visit, he asked his wife and brother to reach out to politicians to schedule campaign events. He wanted, in particular, "a fine barbecue" to "bring all the people out." He was relying "upon brother William and yourself," he wrote Sarah. "Have this attended to, without fail." Given William's marginal role in James's gubernatorial campaign (no letters between the two from this period are known to exist), it seems likely that James asked Sarah to include William in the process of setting campaign appearances because voters expected to see a man's name at the close of a request for political support, and not that of a woman. James concluded his letter with one last request, that Sarah inform all his "friends" that he would defeat his opponent in previously hostile East Tennessee.[26]

James was home for a single day, in mid-June, as he passed from east to west. In early July he had warned Sarah not to expect him "at home" until the day of the election. Not that his definition of home was necessarily the same as Sarah's. "Where I will be on that day I do not certainly know." If his "friends" in a neighboring town wished it, "I will be there." Any hopes Sarah had of James returning to Columbia for election day were dashed a week later. All his information was cheering, he told her, except he would not return home until after the election. He immediately followed this news with the request that "you must not fail to send my letters to me."[27]

On August 1, the long agony was at last over, and Tennessee "redeemed and regenerated by the universal genius of democracy." James K. Polk was elected governor of Tennessee by 2,500 votes out of just over 105,000 total. It was a close election with a "glorious" result, one that validated his move from Washington. "The great [Democratic] Party of this Nation owe to you higher obligations than to any other man (now acting) in the Union," one supporter wrote James. Sarah received letters as well. A Democratic congressman wrote her from Washington, D.C., "All who know you personally, & the ladies particularly, take part in your pleasure on this occasion." James was unquestionably "a distinguished favorite of the whole democracy of the country."[28] Her confidant Aaron Brown addressed her as "Mrs. Governor."[29]

It's telling that James spent election day without "the lady of the next Governor of Tennessee" by his side. A couple that had once been inseparable had endured months apart, both engrossed in the common goal of his election. During those four months James never once told Sarah he missed her, at least not in writing, although he missed his "Sulky horse" enough to write Sarah repeatedly about him.[30]

It's difficult to determine how Sarah felt about any of this. Although she wrote James almost as frequently as he wrote her, only one of her letters from the 1839 gubernatorial campaign has survived. On June 25, Sarah complained to her "Dear Husband" that he had failed to provide her with his current address, forcing her to forward letters "I thought might be useful to you" to a third party who knew his whereabouts. "There is nothing occurred since you left of importance," she assured him. "I have only heard from you by Genl. Pillow since you left. . . . I am anxious to hear from you, not political prospects only, but your health."[31]

With the exception of its final phrase, asking about James's health, Sarah's brief letter is as impersonal and single-minded as any of his own. She provided no personal information about herself, nor open expressions of affection. It's possible that the request for news of his health represented a longing for personal connection with her absent husband, but it seems just as likely that she was as consumed by the campaign as James was. Being apart from her husband on election day probably didn't come as a great surprise, and hopefully not much of a disappointment either. Sarah had risen to the challenges James set for her.

The governor-elect and First Lady of the state of Tennessee celebrated their victory with Andrew Jackson, James's political mentor and law tutor Senator Felix Grundy, and a few other leading Democrats at Tyree's celebrated mineral springs, twenty miles north of Nashville. For several days they enjoyed the clear air, commanding views, and sulfurous waters, amusing themselves for hours on end with a mock court in which the gentlemen were fined for "every trivial offense conceivable," such as "failing to bow when passing a lady." Fruit and flowers were purchased with the proceeds and distributed to the supposedly aggrieved ladies in the party.[32]

It's highly unlikely that James offered Sarah a flower for any of his trivial offenses against the privileges of womanhood, such as leaving her at home on election day or suggesting she visit the offices of a hostile newspaper editor. Nor does it seem likely that they followed the rule that all political talk be forbidden during their "Democratic lovefeast" at the springs. They had too much to discuss. "You have probably in your position more power than any man in the South," a South Carolina congressman wrote James after the election. It was time for the Polks to start a new chapter of their life, and to exercise that power. The experience would prove instructive to them both.[33]

———

Ralph E. W. Earl painted the earliest surviving image of Sarah Childress Polk when she was twenty-six, had been married for five years, and was living in Washington, D.C. *Courtesy of the James K. Polk Memorial Association, Columbia, Tennessee.*

Elizabeth Whitsitt Childress. *Courtesy of the James K. Polk Memorial Association, Columbia, Tennessee.*

Sarah's closest female friend, and James's eldest sister, Jane Polk Walker. *Courtesy of the James K. Polk Memorial Association, Columbia, Tennessee.*

Sarah's only surviving needlework from her tenure at the Salem Academy: a marble crypt worked in chenille on white satin, ca. 1818. *Courtesy of the James K. Polk Memorial Association, Columbia, Tennessee.*

James as Speaker of the House of Representatives, 1838. *Lithograph by P. S. Duval, Library of Congress Prints and Photographs Division.*

Supreme Court Justice John Catron, photographed here by Mathew Brady, was Sarah's confidant for decades. *Library of Congress Prints and Photographs Division.*

The unfinished city of Washington, D.C., as it appeared in 1834, when Sarah was first honing her political skills. *Library of Congress Prints and Photographs Division.*

James's onetime law partner, Aaron V. Brown, was another confidant of Sarah's. *Painting by Washington B. Cooper, courtesy of the Tennessee State Museum.*

Matilda Childress Catron, the "female politician" about whom Martin Van Buren was warned. *Painting by Washington B. Cooper, courtesy of the Tennessee State Museum.*

Sarah's display of the "Presidential Fan" at James's inauguration in March 1845 received wide notice. *Courtesy of the James K. Polk Memorial Association, Columbia, Tennessee.*

Sarah Childress Polk, painted by George Healy, 1846. The simple design and rich fabric of this claret-colored velvet gown, worn with a matching turban, exemplified Sarah's "republican" style. Sarah's niece Elizabeth Childress Brown, who believed herself to closely resemble her aunt, coveted this painting. *Courtesy of the James K. Polk Memorial Association, Columbia, Tennessee. Photograph by Lisa Childs.*

America's leading printmaker, Nathaniel Currier, produced this 1846 lithograph of Sarah Polk at the height of her popularity. Her penetrating gaze, oddly bulky velvet dress, and simple background surrounded by stars and red-striped cloth all emphasize her gravitas and stature. This is no decorative First Lady. *"Mrs. J. K. Polk, from a daguerreotype by Plumbe." Courtesy of the James K. Polk Memorial Association, Columbia, Tennessee. Photograph by Lisa Childs.*

Sarah and James Polk, 1849. This daguerreotype portrait of the Polks, taken near the end of their tenure in the White House, reflects both their conviction and their close personal bond. Sarah wears the brooch featuring James's portrait. *Courtesy of the James K. Polk Memorial Association, Columbia, Tennessee.*

IN 1826, Tennessee's capital moved from Murfreesboro to Nashville, much to the chagrin of the residents of Sarah's hometown. The two cities were only thirty miles apart, but as the state's population continued to move west, Nashville's access to rivers proved more alluring than Murfreesboro. The statehouse still had a transitory character when James was inaugurated Tennessee's ninth governor in 1839. It had moved before, and many residents hoped to see it move again. Perhaps because the people of Tennessee were far from united on Nashville, they failed to provide the governor with a mansion, or any lodging at all.

James and Sarah were on their own, which was less of a problem than it might have been, given how many supporters in the capital hoped to curry favor with the new governor. The couple chose to rent a "well-finished" brick two-story on one of Nashville's best streets, for five hundred dollars a year. The first floor featured two parlors with folding doors, as well as a family room, and there were four rooms above. Outdoors were stables and kitchens, as well as a garden. John Catron, who negotiated the rental of the property for the Polks, described it as "a very tasty house." Less invested friends described it as "modest." James's primary concern was the lack of an office, but after the owner assured him that a spacious upstairs room with its own staircase "will be found more convenient than an office under another roof," he was satisfied.[34]

Negotiations over the rental of the property took place between men, but both parties recognized that furnishings were the responsibility and business of women. "If Mrs Polk could come in it is highly probabl[e] that she and my wife could drive a trade in some articles of furniture that would be mutually advantageous," the owner wrote James. Referring to his own wife, he informed the new governor, "I can at least assure you that Mrs. C will be content with a moderate price for any furniture she is disposed to part with."[35]

Sarah was, by this point in their marriage, used to handling money and making decisions about expenses. Which was helpful, given that at the very moment she was being asked to negotiate over the price of furniture, the couple was for all intents and purposes broke. Sarah declined to purchase any furniture from Mrs. C. However advantageous a price she might have negotiated, it wasn't as economical as moving her own furniture from Columbia to the rental house. She traveled with Sister Jane from Nashville up to Columbia at the end of October to arrange the move.[36]

Neither the postage and printing nor the whiskey and barbecue came for free. James had gone into debt during the election, and the governor's salary of $2,000 a year didn't even cover their living expenses. Had they no reputation to uphold, no doubt they would have chosen a less "tasty" house, but a governor couldn't live just anywhere. So, like gentlemen across the United States in the late 1830s, he borrowed money to make ends meet: $6,000 from a bank, and thousands more from close friends Archibald Yell and Judge Catron.[37]

He also still carried debt from the 1834 purchase of cotton planting land in Mississippi. James had hoped his plantation would make him rich, but thus far it had caused him little but trouble. His onetime partner in that endeavor, his younger brother William, had frittered away early profits through mismanagement and gambling. James bought William out in 1838, but almost immediately the market for both cotton and slaves plummeted. James remained sanguine that land speculation and slavery would work out as well for him as it had for his father, and so many other southern white men of his generation, but in 1839 matters looked bleak. He considered selling some of the slaves, but Sarah refused to hear of it. Her vision of herself as a caring slave owner with a responsibility for "her people" precluded selling them. This became a point of contention between the couple. In order to increase his cash flow and keep his creditors at bay, James instead hired some of their enslaved people out to other cotton planters. Sarah reluctantly agreed that one of their neighbors, Gideon Pillow, could hire Harbert, who she inherited from her father, provided she could reclaim Harbert upon demand.[38]

And then she turned to the business of serving as First Lady of Tennessee. Sarah's Washington, D.C., receptions had gained her acclaim, and her husband needed votes. The layout of their new house in Tennessee, particularly the parlors and "good" outdoor kitchens, held great promise for the sort of political entertainments that she had mastered as wife of the Speaker of the House. But those festivities never materialized. There were no great parties, intimate lobbying events, or elaborate dinners in their rented Nashville house. During their years in

Nashville, the Polks rarely entertained beyond immediate family and old friends.[39]

The only explanation for Sarah's failure to entertain is financial. Clearly one or both of them believed it impossible to entertain in the style to which they were accustomed given the pittance of a salary James received as governor. This did not stop Sarah from throwing herself into the social life of the city. She became an active presence in Nashville, happily accepting dinner invitations she was unable to reciprocate. She usually attended these dinners alone, as her requests that James accompany her were generally met with dismissal. He claimed to be too busy, that he "could not lose half a day just to go and dine."[40]

It's true the governor was busy. James's work ethic had always been exemplary. But in truth the governor's office in Tennessee was little more than a "distinguished clerkship," with few meaningful responsibilities. The real power lay in the statehouse. Which is why both of his choices, to skip dinner in favor of work and to economize in the realm of entertainment, ended up costing him far more than the entertainment would have.[41]

Since the governorship translated into very little real power, James had to rely on personal influence to guide and control a fractious Democratic majority. His experience as Speaker of the House should have prepared him for this role. Yet in Tennessee he met with only limited political success. More often than not the legislature disregarded his proposals, and the two-year term raced right by the governor. Why was he so much less successful in Nashville than he had been in Washington? Where was his famous tact when he needed it?

Sarah was at dinner, without him, breaking down both social and political barriers. One family she became friendly with was her Whig neighbors the Morgans. Colonel Samuel D. Morgan was an active leader in the Whig Party, but Morgan's wife and daughters became so close to Sarah that they blew out the candles Samuel lit to celebrate Whig president William Henry Harrison's election in 1840. Colonel Morgan "bore this opposition patiently for a little while," and relit the candles, but ultimately lost his temper when the women in his family continued to side with their Democratic friend.[42]

Another neighbor whom Sarah befriended was sister to the publisher of the *Nashville Whig*, the leading opposition newspaper. This woman became so attached to Sarah that she protested the paper's "onslaughts" against James, telling Sarah, "I haven't opened my brother's paper to-day, for I dislike so much to read what he says against your husband." That their neighborhood was full of politically powerful people did not escape Sarah, and she made the best of it, considering that she was unable herself to lobby for James from her own front parlor.[43]

James's economy and unwillingness to dine out cost him the opportunity for his wife to build coalitions for him. Sarah did a poor job hiding her annoyance. James warned her against losing her temper when she heard that a politician intended to vote against him. He tried to soothe her with the view that "every man had a right to his own opinion." But what he didn't recognize was that Sarah's bad temper was at least in part born of the fact that James deprived her of the opportunity to change those opinions. Ironically the same man who during the 1839 campaign pushed his wife into the male world of partisan politics failed to recognize the political value of her abilities in the private sphere. It was the last time he would make such a mistake.[44]

GIVEN THE FRUSTRATIONS she faced as First Lady of Tennessee, Sarah had good reason to miss Washington. Washington certainly pined for her. "I miss you more here than any person living, and profited more by your information in regard to most things," Supreme Court justice John Catron wrote Sarah in January 1840, before launching into a four-page detailed analysis of how things had changed since she left, for her eyes only. The nomination of war hero William Henry Harrison as the Whig Party's presidential candidate left Democrats in shock, particularly given the national appeal of the Whig economic platform in the aftermath of the Panic of 1837. Catron thought that James's pet project of a subtreasury, in the place of the national banking system that Whigs lobbied for, was "too feeble for any good to come of it." This opinion, he underlined, "is between you & I."

Catron assumed the Whigs would prevail in November, and was already looking forward to 1844. Martin Van Buren might try for the nomination again, but he was "unpopular with all classes." As for alternative candidates, Missouri senator Thomas Hart Benton was "too extreme" to win the nomination, and James Buchanan had lit-tle to recommend him except that he was from Pennsylvania, a state that had never had a Democratic presidential candidate despite voting reliably Democratic. All told, Catron believed Buchanan the best of a poor pool, but until "Gen Jackson" weighed in, nothing was set. It was an enticing letter for someone with Sarah's ambitions, particularly given Andrew Jackson's favorable view of her husband. But without a parlor there was little she could do to promote James as a candidate for the vice presidency, or perhaps even the presidency.[45]

Although Sarah's parlor politics atrophied during James's two years as governor, her role as communications director blossomed. Men wrote her directly for papers and political news when the governor was unavailable, and communicated freely with James about her role in his communication network. Sarah regularly met with a fairly large circle of Democratic insiders, including Robert Armstrong, Alfred O. P. Nicholson, and J. George Harris, in order to directly gather "news," which in her letters to James never meant anything but politics. After meeting with John Catron she wrote James, "Judge Catron told me he had in a few instances in his tour in the District intimated to some of the Whigs, that Judge Green would be a more suitable candidate for the Senate than [former Whig senator Ephraim] Foster, a broken down hackneyed politician and it took well."[46]

By 1840 she and James were composing lengthy political letters together. Given the complexity of the arguments, it seems likely that either James dictated the contents to Sarah, or she worked from a draft previously composed by him. In one case, the majority of a lengthy attack on a petition charging Polk with abandoning his duties as gov-ernor, written in Sarah's hand, closed with four sentences and a post-script in James's hand.[47]

And whenever possible, Sarah accompanied James on his political travels. When Andrew Jackson summoned James to visit him at the Hermitage a month after Harrison's election as president, Jackson directed the governor to "bring Mrs. Poke with you." Sarah enjoyed traveling with James, flattering herself that she "would not be in the way," as she demurely put it on one occasion. But the responsibilities of running the house often interfered with her political travel. After waiting on a delivery of meat for longer than she wanted to, she made a joke in a letter to James about prioritizing politics over their house-hold. She promised him she would join him "on Saturday, I think, meat or no meat. Though I do not know that it will make a man think any more of this wife for her to neglect the domestic duties of the house hold, I will risk it at all events."[48]

There was little risk that James blamed his wife for neglecting her "domestic duties," given his increasing dependence on her political advice. In July 1840 she warned her husband that opposition newspapers were critiquing him as the "traveling Executive," because of his "long absence[s]" traveling the state. "I think you had better go home without talking to many places on your circuit." James soon returned home "to catch up with his executive business."[49]

Six months later the state was abuzz with rumors of a special session to elect a senator after Polk's mentor, Senator Felix Grundy, died. Before the Seventeenth Amendment to the Constitution in 1913, state legislatures, rather than voters, appointed U.S. senators. Given the extent of the Whig victory in 1840 (William Henry Harrison defeated Martin Van Buren by fifteen thousand votes in Tennessee), James realized that his chances for reelection were slim. His supporters in Washington knew it too. They suggested that he allow the legislature to appoint him senator for the remainder of Grundy's term.

Sarah did not approve. James's reputation as a man of the people would suffer were he to manage his own appointment to the Senate. "Brown & Turney both write that you should be the person to be elected," she wrote him. "I have given you their views written to you privately in as few words as I could express the intention. I do not understand matters sufficiently well to form an opinion yet," she demurred, but nonetheless expressed her opinion, firmly: "It does not strike me that it is the right thing for you to do." James followed her advice.[50]

AND SUDDENLY it was time to start another summer election tour. Matters from the start looked bleak. Not only were the Whigs in the ascendency, but James's opponent was young, energetic, and charismatic in a manner that James would never be. And his nemesis John Bell, who was now serving as President Harrison's secretary of war, was canvassing for the Whig candidate. Sarah was worried, not only about the outcome of the election, but also about its toll on her husband's fragile health. But she maintained an upbeat tone with James. "I do not think it likely that the Democrats will get out any candidates in this county. There seems to be no prospects of doing so," she reassured him in April 1841. Whig "attacks amount to but little and only proves to me they are uneasy," she wrote him a few days later. After Harrison's shocking death just thirty days into his presidential term, she didn't hesitate before sharing her judgment that nothing would change. "The same powers will [remain in] control, Clay, &c.," she wrote him.[51]

The best place she could be was by his side. But Sarah was needed at home. Unlike two years earlier, she was front and center in the political campaign, and facing demands not only from her husband but from a wide range of Tennessee Democrats as well. After a short visit to see her mother, Sarah returned home to find "Dr. Young anxious to learn some thing about the Bonds sent to you," she wrote James, a request she dealt with as well as she could while simultaneously gaining an "account of the prospects in E. Tennessee" from General Anderson, visiting from Knoxville.[52]

By 1841, information gathering had become an integral part of her duties as communications manager. James expected her to meet with important men and convey their views to him by writing while he canvassed the state. When, as often happened, she could "not gather much news as I see but few persons to talk to," she apologized. "I see so few Gentlemen that I do not have much chance to pick up news," she told James on one occasion, expressing exasperation that meetings weren't more fruitful. She wrote dismissively about two meetings in one letter to James, one with a gentleman who "does not seem to know much about any thing," and the other with a man whom James asked her to deliver letters to. In return all she got was old news, and "speculation . . . which is to be seen in the papers now and before you left." James repeatedly asked her to work on his behalf, convincing men of the importance of the campaign, and taking for granted that she would read and deliver letters for him.[53]

One thing James did not do was ask Sarah to gather information from women. Given their years in Washington, where political women were openly acknowledged, this is perhaps surprising. Sarah's role as communications director made it abundantly clear that women could distribute political information. But the news that men had to share was understood as more valuable than that carried by women. Nor was it only men who thought so. Sarah's own letters make clear that she perceived information gathered from men as separate from and superior to information gathered from women, a peculiar distinction to make when she herself was both gathering and distributing information. After conveying some useful details about potential Whig candidates and their supporters, information identical to political news obtained from men, but in this case taken from "Mrs. Walker (from whom you know that I get a good deal of news)," Sarah apologized: "This of course is womens gossip and not worth much."[54]

The only thing that made political information gained from a woman "women's gossip" was that it originated with a woman rather than a man. In Sarah's definition, a rumor was "news" if it came from men, and "gossip" if it came from women. At least this was the way she chose to present the distinction when speaking to a man. Since her time at the Salem Female Academy, she had been versed in the dangers of "evil communication" and taught not to "communicate bad things." Her fashion magazine, *Godey's Lady's Book,* warned readers about the female "propensity for tattling, gossiping, and slandering, which so often manifests itself to the annoyance of whole neighborhoods."[55]

In labeling Jane Walker's information "gossip," was Sarah casting aspersions on Sister Jane? Or was she suggesting she, Sarah, was immune from the accusations made against gossiping women generally? Perhaps it was an inside joke between James and herself (although given James's profound and sustained lack of humor, this last option seems rather unlikely).

In point of fact, without considering the sex of the storyteller, there is no possible way to distinguish between gossip and news in the information Sarah gathered. Consider three "political" letters she received from men while in Tennessee. Joshua Martin, a former Alabama congressman, wrote her a letter soon after James's 1839 election. After congratulating her on James's victory, and reporting that "the town is very dull at the moment" since so many of their Washington friends had left for "some fashionable watering place," he launched into an

enthusiastic narrative of the attempted seduction, for political purposes, of President Van Buren by a Mrs. Clinton: "The lady, who is
from all accounts, a very abused person, was put up to it, & placed
herself conspicuously in the way of the President, for the very purpose" of seducing him. "She was an old maid when Mr. Clinton married her & [Clinton] is not the father of her children." Fortunately, this
"ridiculous plot" came to nothing.

A narrative of an attempted seduction containing an unsubstantiated
report of mistaken paternity seems to meet the definition of gossip. Yet
this was gossip with clear political importance, since the letter writer
claimed that Henry Clay's reported involvement in the "scene" had
badly damaged the Whig leader's chance of winning his party's presidential nomination in 1844. As a result of his supposed involvement,
Clay "will scarcely be the candidate," Martin (incorrectly) predicted.[56]

Sarah's brother-in-law William Rucker also sent her a letter containing politically powerful gossip, or as Rucker called it, "rumor." In
May 1839 he wrote her about the "considerable state of excitement" in
Murfreesboro "on the count of politicking," including slander "against
our cause" in "the filthy Telegraph" and a detailed report of accusations that nearly led to a duel between political opponents. Rucker
made it clear that gossip was a powerful tool. "Men are slandered by
rumor," he wrote, "but it is the first time I ever heard of a man's being
challenged [to a duel] by rumor."[57]

Sarah's brother John wrote her the same week as Rucker. He
repeated the story of the potential duel. But that wasn't the only rumor
he shared with his sister. He wanted her to know all about "one not
yet in the papers." John claimed that a particular Whig candidate was
"boasting that he wheedled the [Polk] Gov[ernment] out of the State
Bonds before any work had been done on the road & bought him a
stack of goods with the proceeds." He told Sarah his rumor about
Whig graft precisely because she not only understood the power of
gossip, but had the connections and abilities to mobilize it politically. "I
mention these things to you," John admitted, "that you may suggest, if
you choose to those who manage [the party newspaper] the Democrat,
the prospect of considering the effect an issue of this kind may have."
In other words, not only was the boundary between political news and
gossip remarkably permeable in the political world of the 1830s and

1840s, but part of Sarah's power lay in her ability to exploit gossip for political ends.[58]

Unfortunately, this power didn't carry James K. Polk far in 1841. His tone remained upbeat during the summer campaign. "In regard to my prospects, in East Tennessee, I think them as good as they were in 1839, as far as I have gone, if not better," he wrote Sarah early in the campaign, and a month later still maintained that his chances were good. But Sarah's repeated reassurances suggest that she recognized the likelihood of a defeat before he did. When newspapers in Nashville complained that the governor was spending more time campaigning than working, she reassured him that the "all prevailing topic of today," a major bank robbery, had "swallowed up" his bad press, "so you need not think that your absence will make any impression as they have something else to talk about." A month later she struck the same tone: "I do not believe any thing they put in the papers will have any affect, so you need not be uneasy. I am not troubled at any thing that has yet appeared." Negative press, she assured him a third time, "can not hurt you any where."[59]

What worried Sarah was James's increasingly fragile health. Riding great distances and sometimes addressing multiple audiences in a single day, he was again campaigning himself into exhaustion. "I am not at all discouraged at any thing I see in the papers or hear from any quarter," she wrote him in April, "but when I think of the labour and fatigue you have to undergo, I feel sad and melancholy, and conclude that success is not worth the labour." A week later, having "felt some uneasiness since you wrote me from Jasper that you were not well, and seeing in the papers that you declined speaking on some occasion because you were unwell," she was increasingly ambivalent about the campaign. "I hope to hear from you tomorrow and hear that you are well again. Success is not worth the trouble, much less ruining ones health by it and do take care of yourself."[60]

Sarah fulfilled James's directives to lobby men, gather information, and make sure "every thing which may require my official action to be in a state of preparation & forwardness." But she began to express doubts that the campaign was worth it, for either of them. "It makes me unhappy to think of what you must suffer, and for what? You can not be honoured by success, nor dishonoured by defeat, so I have not much to stimulate me." When James admitted his exhaustion, Sarah prayed "that you may have health which is more than success." By early July, his fatigue was compounded by "an affection of the bowels, such as frequently happens with me," he wrote. But in this case, the attack was "rather more violent than usual." Medication (most likely opium) prescribed for the diarrhea left him considerably debilitated. He canceled a speaking engagement, and asked Sarah to coordinate a writing campaign among his political allies in order to turn out Democrats across the state.[61]

Sometimes James's political needs conflicted with Sarah's household responsibilities. A visit from Sister Jane dragged on far longer than Sarah expected. On June 25, Sarah wrote James that his sister intended to leave for Tyree's mineral springs, but on July 5 she was still there. Sarah chafed at the visit: "Sister Walker being here has confined me at home for the last two weeks," she complained to James. As a result, she'd had but "a poor opportunity of learning any thing . . . and I know but little that is going on." As an excuse for hearing "so much less of Politics here than I ever did before," she offered not only Jane Walker's visit, but also a dinner party. "You need not be alarmed when I inform you that there is an addition of ten to our family this evening: Mr. & Mrs. Walker, Majr. Bills, Mr. McDowel, Jane, Sally, Andrew &c. &c. Do you think I am lonesome"?[62]

Three weeks later, Sarah had lost her sense of humor about the houseguests. "The house full of kin that I have had ever since you left, and indeed all the summer has made me nothing more than a servant and a senseless round in my house keeps me at home and keeps away such company as I might gather some information from," she complained to James. "So you can perceive that I have no means to learn anything."[63]

Despite Sarah's blindness to the difference between herself and the slaves who labored on her behalf, when it came to politics she knew more than she let on. She could see that the enthusiasm of the Democracy was not what it had been in 1839. James's allies were deserting him. A publisher he was counting on was "of no account," a fact she attributed to the man's sudden "crazed" passion for a rich widow. Sarah was reassuring: "In my opinion you do not loose much from the inefficiency of his paper." But by midsummer she was editing the information she sent James in order to ease his mind. "I am at a loss what to think of prospects. Let the result be what it may, so you do not destroy your health or kill yourself with fatigue; I shall not grieve, but be thankful," she told him.[64]

By the end of July, she was blunt. Although she was resolved to "hope for the best in all things," James's reelection was looking unlikely. Always his greatest cheerleader, she reassured him that "you have now character enough in the country to stand a defeat, temporary as it must be, without injury to your future prospects." And as for herself, "I shall have philosophy to stand it, and think that I can be as happy with my husband at home, defeated candidate, as to have a successful one always from me. . . . If you can get through the canvass, health unimpaired and at home safely once more, I will be content."[65]

James remained sanguine to the end. Just days before the election he composed a letter to a colleague complaining that the Democrats in East Tennessee "have lost confidence of our success," but still predicted a strong showing. "If I maintain my old strength in the West I will be re-elected," he asserted. He left it to Sarah to copy the letter in her own handwriting and send it along, out of concern that his own "hand-writing is known" and "correspondence . . . closely watched." It was the last letter the two of them composed together before the election. Once again the vote was close, but this time the final result favored the Whig by a little over three thousand votes, or 3 percent of the total electorate. Sarah had the misfortune of collecting the official results as they arrived in Nashville and distributing the bad news to James's friends and supporters. James and Sarah had been "for the first time, defeated and by a decided vote."[66]

IT WAS ALSO the first time in their married life that James was out of office, indeed unemployed. It was a strange state of affairs, and not perhaps one that Sarah anticipated when she first encouraged him to run for Congress in 1824. In a letter of condolence, Samuel H. Laughlin asked James to assure Sarah "that a wife never gives up the ship where her husband or his friends are concerned." Less than two weeks later he asked James to remind "Madam" again "that a lady never gives up the ship when her husband is on board." Which is somewhat odd, because that's precisely what a woman does when the ship is going down.[67]

Of course, Sarah did not give up the ship; she was first mate. They left Nashville for their plantation in Mississippi, and two months later returned to Columbia, where they met with a warm reception among the extend Polk clan. James halfheartedly formed a law partnership with his brother William, but devoted the bulk of his energy to writing political letters. They fell into a peaceful routine of socializing with family and friends, trips to Murfreesboro, and visits in the spring and the fall to the Yalobusha plantation.[68]

Many couples would have treasured such an idyll. But Sarah's boredom was palpable. Writing James, who was away from home on legal business, she offered what little political information she could glean from the papers, including a sharp analysis of "the tone of the Whig papers." But she had little else to report. "I have heard very little individual conversation since you left. Weddings, examinations &c. seem to occupy the whole attention of every one here at present. No politics, no party feeling but every thing quiet as far as I know." She felt "more anxious than usual to hear from" him, and would "be thankful even for one line from you."[69]

In August 1842, a year into their postgubernatorial slump, John Catron sent Sarah a letter that sharpened her desire to be back in the action. It was a long, gossipy letter about "crafty men . . . behind the scenes" of state and national politics who were "moving the wires of the puppet," unnoticed by less astute observers than Catron and Sarah. The Whigs were at sea, but so, it seemed, were the Democrats. "Our people will follow Men, almost regardless of principle," Catron concluded. "We need new names to head our ticket." No need to be more specific when writing Sarah Polk. Yet she could do nothing but wait.[70]

James recognized his wife's frustration. His letters to Sarah were never more affectionate than the ones he wrote in the years immediately following his 1841 election defeat. One Sunday morning that fall, he picked up a pen and apologized that he had "no news—not even town gossip" to share with her, and declared himself "your affectionate husband."[71] And he fought against her boredom the best way he knew how: by sharing his work. When Sarah found him up late reading newspapers and writing to political colleagues, she admonished him, "You work too much." Instead of protesting, James handed her some newspapers and quietly replied, "Sarah, here is something I wish you to read." In this way, "he set me to work too," she recalled, and "in giving him sympathy and assistance in many wifely ways" she "found no time for loneliness."[72]

With no campaign to run, Sarah was free to travel, and James encouraged her to join him on his political jaunts. "Sarah, wouldn't you like to go to Nashville?" he asked her. "Why should you stay at home? To take care of the house?" He knew she had no interest in taking care of the house, and rather than think less of her for it, as she had once joked he might, he told her, "Why, if the house burns down, we can live without it."[73]

James's decision to run for governor a third time, in 1843, was driven at least in part by the assurances of his friends that success in redeeming Tennessee for the Democrats a second time would "lead on certainly to your elevation to the Presidency." But although Sarah clearly yearned for something more than her sedate life in Columbia, she had soured on state politics. Her brother John should have received a clerkship in the Murfreesboro court, but was passed over in favor of someone with better connections. John vowed to his sister that he would "pay back" the men who "ought to have helped," and would do so "with interest." Both of them at least suspected that had James's star been shining brighter, his brother-in-law would have received the office.[74]

Sarah openly expressed her ambivalence about a third gubernatorial run. In March she warned James that "the Nashville papers are attacking you" about the position he had taken against a popular Democratic platform, relief for debtors. "From the tenor of these articles they hope to prejudice all the Democrats who have taken benefit of the Bankrupt law . . . and I fear they may effect something with some persons." Nor was she only speaking freely to James. After reading a letter published by a fellow Democrat that she "didn't like," she bemoaned the fact that "I have not seen any one to talk with since the paper came out."[75]

But her primary concern was with his health. She didn't believe James was physically ready for a third political campaign. "I must confess that I feel sad & melancholy at the prospect before me, or I should say before you," she wrote him on the eve of his election campaign:

The fatigue exposure and absence for four months can not present to me a bright prospect. I have not the assurance that the body and constitution can keep up under such labours as you have to go through, and it is only the hope that you can live through it that gives me a prospect of enjoyment. Let me beg and pray that you will take care of yourself, and do not become to[o] much excited.

After this singular expression of emotion, she backed up a bit. "Don't think that I am down in the <u>celler</u>, for as soon as I am done writing I am going to dress and go out visiting."[76]

Hopefully James's high spirits over some initial successes reassured her. "I suppose it will not be immodest for me to say to my wife, that my speech was perhaps the happiest effort of my life," he wrote Sarah after a debate with the current governor. Not only had he destroyed the argument of his opponent, but he had made the audience laugh—a remarkable achievement. "As in his speech he had made a great effort to turn the occasion into frolic, I concluded to close my speech by fighting the old boy with fire, and accordingly I turned the laugh upon him—& almost laughed him out of the Court-House," he crowed to Sarah. "Without going into further details the result is, that my victory is the most triumphant I have ever achieved."[77]

But the euphoria was short-lived. Within a week they were back to their usual campaign routine: James wearing himself down, Sarah attempting to meet his exacting standards, which now extended to persuading men to act in his best interests. He asked Sarah to impress upon one man "the vast importance of having perfect harmony in the County of my residence," and a week later demanded that Sarah immediately send for a second man and "urge him, for my sake, and the sake of the party" to "induce" three or four important Democrats to give up their objections to his campaign. Were Sarah to speak to enough men, James was certain "the trouble can be prevented."[78]

Sarah met with four men, but had nothing good to report. "The truth is they are all at sea without a compass, no one to guide, all leaders, none with judgment and all controlled by personal feelings or interest. . . . I do not wish to make you uneasy, and I do not think you could do any good by writing now, to any one." Where was the party discipline? Sarah made her views of the relative value of the individual and the party clear when she complained to James, "Every one pulls his own way and according to his liking, <u>not principles</u>. Such is the state of things." She was trying her hardest to influence, but needed her husband to know the truth: "I have not much to opperate on."[79]

Sarah refused to give up, and determined to take matters into her own hands. "Campbell promised to come to see me in the morning," she reassured James. "And I will try to get a talk with Jack Johnson tomorrow and I assure that if I can do any thing by urging them to union and harmony and getting our own sort of a man I will try. There is no excitement here on the subject of politicks. Only this jarring among our folks."[80]

Clearly Sarah was astounded that they were putting themselves through this routine a third time. "All my fears are you can not stand the hard labour of the canvass. I am not patriotic enough to make sacrifices for my country. I love myself (I mean my Husband) better or more than my country," she admitted. James's responses to her moods were gentle. Perhaps he remembered how low she became during his first congressional term. "It pains me that you write so despondingly," he told her. "You must cheer up. It is now but 7 weeks until the election. The worst of the canvass is over. I am blessed with fine health, and am in good spirits." A week later he struck the same note. "You continue to write despondingly, and it distresses me that you are in such low spirits. If I could be with you, you know I would be. It is however impossible for the next six weeks, and I hope you will endeavor to recover your former cheerfulness and good spirits." He reassured her, "I am still blessed with fine health & am in fine spirits. I shall be elected, as I think."[81]

But Sarah needed more than paper reassurance from her husband, and suddenly he appeared not only able but willing to provide it. "You have rather tantalized me in making appointments so near home and yet giving me no opportunity of seeing you," she wrote him, sounding very much like a lonely wife. A month later her appeals were more brazen. "All I hear is good, but that does not reconcile me, to a separation from you under such circumstances and I never wanted to see you more in my life than now. And as I hope to see you soon I will write no more."[82]

James received the message, and reciprocated the feeling. There was so little in this campaign to distract a man, or a woman, from the misery of separation. He wanted his wife; she wanted him. This was worth making a sacrifice for. James was neither a poet nor a romantic, but he rose to the occasion. "In less than a week I hope to be at home," he wrote her. "Be sure to send the Buggy to Centerville. Let two come down in it, so that one can ride my horse & the other drive me. The moon will shine & in this way I think I can get home on Saturday night."[83]

James's moonlit homecoming was a warm one. A week after their reunion, Sarah's mood was still playful. "I was pleased to find that you had time to play the beaux in receiving flowers from young ladies," she teased him. But she was also annoyed that he was again away from her side. By leaving he proved, she wrote, "that you did not act the beaux towards your wife when at home."[84]

ULTIMATELY THE SOLACE of marital affection could not obscure a failing campaign. In August 1843, James Polk was once again defeated, by a slightly larger margin than in 1841. John Bell, who had again campaigned for Polk's Whig opponent, was giddy. James asked former president and presumptive 1844 Democratic Party nominee Martin Van Buren to "not give up Tennessee as lost to the Democracy." He assured his friends, "So far from surrendering my sword is still unsheathed & I am still ready to do battle for our principles." But in truth it was the darkest time in his life.[85]

Sarah had repeatedly stated that she could stand a loss, if it meant having James at home. But it was unclear to James what he had to look forward to. Not only did his political career appear to be over, but he was in serious financial straits. The Mississippi plantation continued to operate at a substantial capital loss, and his efforts to find a new investor had proven futile, in part because of Sarah's insistence that they retain ownership of all of their enslaved people. James warned her that he might have to sell the plantation outright, a plan that she also deemed unacceptable.[86]

And the Polk relatives were becoming an increasing burden. The death of three of James's brothers in the same year a decade earlier had left him with the difficult job of managing all three of their estates.

Emotionally, it was the death of Marshall Polk, at age twenty-three, that hit him the hardest. Marshall had always stood out in the family for his sense of humor and clear intelligence. Some in their circle even believed that he was "the most talented Polk."[87]

Marshall left behind a two-year-old daughter and newborn son. As the eldest and most successful brother, James was expected to financially support the family and take charge of the children's education. This he was happy to do. But Marshall's widow, Laura, also expected that her son, Marshall Jr., would eventually live with James and Sarah. "When he is of a proper age for you to take him under your care," Laura wrote James, "I hope he will even then be an honor to the uncle his father so devotedly loved."[88]

The leading Polk biographer has argued that James pushed to adopt Marshall's two children after his second gubernatorial defeat because "James as well as Sarah began to feel ever more poignantly their failure to have children." Visits from nieces and nephews, writes Charles Sellers, were "no real substitute for children of their own."[89]

But there's good reason to question whether either of them felt their childlessness as a lack. Nowhere in the voluminous James K. Polk correspondence does he express regret over not having children. Nor is there any evidence, in Sarah's limited correspondence, of her wishing to be a mother. Indeed, their decades of happy coexistence argues for mutual contentment as a unit of two.[90]

Furthermore, the letters James wrote in the eleven years following Marshall's death offer to pay for the education of his niece and nephew, but say nothing about adopting them into his family. It wasn't until 1843 that he first suggested that his nephew might come live with him and Sarah. While that date corresponds with his second gubernatorial defeat, another circumstance was likely the deciding factor in his change of heart. In 1842, Marshall's twelve-year-old daughter, Eunice, died tragically. She had just started studying Latin, a fact her mother proudly reported to James and Sarah.

Eunice's younger brother, eleven-year-old Marshall Jr., was sent away to school. In September 1843 he wrote his uncle James from the drafty school, asking to come live with him and his aunt Sarah. He complained of cold: "We haven't much fire in the schoolhouse." Although his sister-in-law made it clear in 1835, when Marshall was four years old, that she expected him to eventually live with James and Sarah, James only agreed to take Marshall in after the now twelve-year-old asked directly. In the spring of 1844, Sarah and James welcomed Marshall Tate Polk Jr. into their home. But even then, the welcome was incomplete. Marshall arrived as a ward rather than as an adopted son.[91]

This was hardly an obvious choice for the Polks to make. Americans, particularly in the South, had been adopting orphaned relatives since the late eighteenth century. Visiting Europeans considered adoption to be a particularly "American" habit, and an admirable one. Ten years after Charles Dickens highlighted the shame of England's orphanages with a hungry protagonist named Oliver Twist, Englishwoman Sarah Mytton Maury praised "one blessed custom they have in America, resulting from the abundance which they enjoy. . . . The mother dies—her orphans find a home among her friends and relatives." Wealthy childless couples regularly adopted young relatives, oftentimes to gain an heir. Andrew and Rachel Jackson adopted one of the twin sons of her brother, Severn Donelson, and renamed him Andrew Jackson Donelson. They adopted a grandson of Rachel's sister, also named Andrew Jackson. Their most famous adopted child was a Creek (Muskogee/Red Stick) infant named Lyncoya, who had been orphaned by Jackson's troops at the Battle of Tallushatchee. Andrew and Rachel did not rename their Indian son Andrew Jackson.[92]

But James and Sarah did not adopt Marshall in 1844, or at any point in the future. Nor did they adopt any other children, despite the sense of responsibility James clearly felt for Marshall, or the pleasure he took in the company of his many nieces and nephews. One Polk acquaintance blamed the decision on Sarah. "Mrs. P. never would consent to adopting children," she claimed.[93]

It seems highly unlikely that Sarah, who never denied James anything of importance, would refuse to adopt Marshall if he desperately wanted a son. There was good reason for her to hesitate before adopting a child. She knew herself to be remarkably fortunate. The "gay and interesting life which high public office bequeaths" was "delightful" to her, and even though James was out of office, she had faith it wouldn't be for long. If we assume that she was content to remain childless, there was little reason for her to exchange the parties, elections, and political gossip that had absorbed her life since her marriage for the domestic responsibilities that consumed other women. She need only have looked at Jane Walker's life to see the crippling effects of motherhood on a woman's freedom. Jane had given birth to her first child at age sixteen, and was now in her forties, still bearing children. She had given birth eleven times, surpassing even her remarkably fertile mother. The first nine children were still living. But Jane's two youngest, Ophelia and Leonidas, hadn't survived long. Neither reached the age of three. Jane's home was chaotic, someone was always sick, and her husband was rarely there.[94]

But given that there is no more evidence that James wanted a child than that Sarah did, why should we assume that refusing to adopt Marshall was her decision? Or even her idea? James had no more reason to change the status quo of his political partnership with his wife than she did. They had every reason to treasure their childless life. Thirteen-year-old Marshall entered their household, and then directly left for a less drafty boarding school than the one he had attended before joining his aunt and uncle. They kept their responsibility for him as limited as his presence in their home.

For nearly a month after his defeat in 1843, James didn't receive a single letter from Washington or Nashville. He would not have overlooked the clipped tone of those friends who resumed writing that fall. They may not have deserted him, but James K. Polk was no longer a sure bet. Even Aaron Brown seemed guarded. He devoted half of his first postelection letter to President John Tyler's proposition to annex Texas, and most of the rest to peripheral issues of patronage and committee memberships in Washington, issues that had nothing to do with James. Only once did Brown mention James, a secondhand assertion that Senator Thomas Hart Benton and the Ohio Democrats were opposed to potential vice presidential candidate Richard Johnson, "and would be for you against any body" when it came to the vice presidential seat that November. Brown promised to do everything possible to encourage his prospects before returning to his discussion of patronage.[95]

James pleaded for more information, and then excoriated his friend for not writing more frequently. Brown, in turn, directed James to talk to his wife. Sarah could tell him "every thing that has occurred not likely to reach you through the papers."[96]

Aaron Brown preferred writing to Sarah. As did John Catron. And there's no mystery as to why. She didn't berate either man. She made no demands. And she was happy to be the recipient of gossip, both political and personal, of a kind James did not tolerate. Sarah, for instance, appreciated Brown's homophobic jibes about James Buchanan and the man he lived with, Senator William Rufus King. Brown compared King to a strumpet and referred to him in correspondence with Sarah as "Aunt Nancy" and Buchanan's "better half." Sarah was interested in the details of social events. James was not. Sarah understood that Washington was a "theater" and could be "excruciatingly dull." James was concerned with little beyond policies and elections. He received two-page fact-filled letters from Brown. Sarah received four-page flights of fancy, which Brown trusted that Sarah would edit before reading out loud to James. "Of course you will not show him this letter," he wrote Sarah, but he also knew that she would deliver the information that James needed—including the following attack on James Buchanan, and the man all of Washington believed to be "his wife," William King (or Mrs. B, as Brown preferred to call him):

> I was amused to day at hearing of a little incident affecting our friend Gen. Saunders. He is a warm Calhoun man you know & in the presence of Mr. Buchanon & his wife & some others advanced the opinion that neither Mr Calhoun nor Mr Van Buren had any chance to be elected, & being asked by some one "who that can be," he forgot himself & said that Colo. Polk could run better than any other man in the nation. This of course was highly indecorous toward Mrs B. to whom the Genl. found much difficulty in making the necessary apology. I am exactly of that opinion. That is to say Colo. Polk is now encountering the very identical difficulties as to the Vice that he would have to do for the first office of the government & if he can overcome the one he could have done the other.

In other words, Brown found Buchanan's sexuality ridiculous, and was convinced by the exchange that James had a shot at the presidency. Indeed he was now convinced that James should set aside thoughts of the vice presidency in favor of the greater goal, since they appeared equally within his grasp. James wouldn't care to hear about Buchanan's "wife," of course, because that was gossip. Unkind gossip. But he would certainly like to hear North Carolina Democratic congressman Romulus Saunders's endorsement of his chances. This, he told Sarah, she could convey to "our friend," James.[97]

The communications director did so. And she was never happier weeding political news from gossip.

4

Throughout this state I have seen only two of your old friends who are not for you more warmly than ever, and those two are John Catron and his wife. She has no children and therefore has become a great politician. These women you know who do not breed must always be busy either in making matches or making and unmaking Statesmen.

—ALFRED BALCH TO MARTIN VAN BUREN, Nashville, November 22, 1842

ALFRED BALCH was a Nashville political strategist with a devotion to the Tennessee Democratic Party that dwarfed both his legal practice and his personal ambition. He loved Andrew Jackson, was faithful to Jackson's political heir, Martin Van Buren, and like so many other men of his type, gained a respect for James Polk that never evolved into friendship.

Appointed by Van Buren to a federal judgeship in the Florida Territory four years into a war between the U.S. Army and Seminole Indians the government was trying to eject from their ancestral homelands, Judge Balch found the climate, including the political climate, "deplorable." Central Florida was a lawless frontier. "The leading men are divided into bitter parties, and violence is the order of the day," he complained to Van Buren. Tales of Seminole atrocities against white women had become popular fodder in urban penny newspapers. Those stories helped justify the ongoing war against the Seminoles, but also prevented the kind of family settlement that might have stabilized the territory.[1]

As for the single white men who hoped to profit from the final act of Andrew Jackson's 1830 Indian Removal Act, they had proven ungovernable. They routinely demanded the protection of U.S. authorities while ignoring U.S. law. Squatting on land that didn't belong to them, they committed depredations against Seminoles and their runaway slave allies. Army officers questioned both the purpose and possibility of vanquishing the Seminoles from what they saw as worthless Florida swampland. Some officers found the Indians more sympathetic than the poor white settlers occupying their land.

In short, Balch was out of his element. With an important presidential election on the horizon, he decided the Tennessee Democratic Party had more need for him than did the territory of Florida. He quit his judgeship and moved home to Nashville. Balch's political instincts were usually infallible.[2]

Despite Van Buren's embarrassing defeat by William Henry Harrison in 1840, and the fact that his opponents still referred to him as "Martin Van Ruin" for presiding over the Panic of 1837, at the close of 1842 he remained the Democratic Party's presumptive presidential nominee. Balch thought Van Buren's chances in 1844 excellent. Nashville's leading Democrats, with only two exceptions, were firmly behind Van Buren. But the holdouts were significant. One of them, Supreme Court justice John Catron, was a close Jackson ally who had run Van Buren's first presidential campaign in Tennessee. And then there was the "great politician," Catron's wife, Matilda. She held no office, nor could she (or any other American woman) vote. Balch was hardly alone in finding her an object of scorn, but he nonetheless understood that Matilda was a force to be reckoned with. It was said that John Catron owed his Supreme Court seat to his wife, that when she read that a vacancy had opened up on the court, she went straight to Washington without consulting John. Arriving early in the morning, she burst in on President Jackson, "his gown and slippers on, and long stem cob pipe in his mouth." Fortunately, the president, who had known Matilda since she was a child, "was glad as surprised to see her." Matilda "asked if the vacancy on the Supreme Court had been filled, and when answered in the negative said, 'I ask the appointment for Judge Catron.'" Catron was appointed "before the sun set."[3]

Whether true or not, the story of Matilda Catron's ambition suggested the power that "female politicians" might exercise. Nor was Matilda alone. She was a type, one the long-widowed Van Buren would recognize: a wealthy childless woman with political influence.

"Provided they have money enough to buy fine clothes and ride in their own carriages," Balch complained, "these women you know who do not breed must always be busy either in making matches or making and unmaking Statesmen."[4]

Van Buren was not one to underestimate the power of female politicians. While a young widowed congressman in Washington, he realized that his political advancement depended on women. He threw card parties for the wives and daughters of his political allies and gained a particular reputation for female courtesy. Sarah was not alone in admiring his "pleasing address." But his critics noted that the politician often "used" ladies for political purposes, in particular "for the advancement of his schemes" to gain Andrew Jackson's trust, and to succeed him as president. No less than Peggy Eaton had lobbied Jackson on Van Buren's behalf.[5]

If Van Buren hadn't learned the power of women in politics in 1836, he certainly did in 1840. Eighty percent of the men eligible to vote in 1840 did so, the highest voter turnout in American history. The 1840 election was also, and not coincidentally, the first in which women played a major role. The Panic of 1837 hit American families hard; in some locations unemployment was as high as 25 percent, and the Whig Party was prepared to capitalize on bad times by emphasizing both their economic and moral superiority to the stagnant Democracy. William Henry Harrison's "Log Cabin" campaign drew on the techniques of popular religious revivals to energize supporters across the country.

One of the most radical innovations in the campaign was its inclusion of women. They sewed banners for Harrison, lobbied men in their families, and sang Harrison songs. But the Harrison campaign also encouraged women to take their support out in public, to attend campaign rallies, to march at the front of their parades, and to deliver speeches in his honor. The Whigs paid tribute to their female supporters at every opportunity. "The ladies are coming to the rescue," reported a Connecticut newspaper on the eve of the election. "The Whig ladies . . . have taken the election of General Harrison in hand" and "are determined to give the cause all the assistance in their power." After Harrison's landslide victory, Van Buren was unlikely to question Balch's implication that Matilda, or any other woman, might influence the outcome in 1844.[6]

However worrying Matilda Catron might be, Balch confidently

predicted Van Buren's nomination and election in 1844, in large part because he also predicted a Polk victory in 1843. "Polk is already in the field," with a "commanding position," he wrote Van Buren. "He is untiring in his efforts. . . . As Ten[nessee] goes in the Governor's election next August so she will go in the Presidential election of 44."[7]

Of course, Balch was wrong about the 1843 gubernatorial election. Polk's work ethic was not enough to overcome the ascendancy of the Whig Party in Tennessee, leaving him twice defeated by the same popular opponent. But Balch was right about at least one thing: Matilda Catron was worth counting. She was prescient in recognizing that Van Buren's fortunes were on the wane, and that there was a better man in the field, one with a wife who had proven her aptitude at "making Statesmen" in Washington, D.C., and Tennessee—a woman who also happened to be Matilda's cousin, and one of her best friends. Before the 1843 gubernatorial race was over, Matilda Childress Catron was hard at work making another statesman.

WHEN ANDREW JACKSON left office in 1837, he promised Sarah Polk that "the scepter shall come back to Tennessee before very long, and your own fair self shall be the queen."[8] It was Texas that made it possible. The Republic of Texas declared independence from Mexico in 1836 after a revolution fought largely by slave-owning American men drawn to Mexico by the opportunity to grow cotton. Mexico never accepted Texas's independence, and rejected its claims to territory far to the south and west of its former state boundaries in Mexico. Newly independent Texians (as the Anglo residents referred to themselves) clamored for American statehood, but as president, Martin Van Buren refused to consider annexation, agreeing with his predecessor, Andrew Jackson, and successor, Harrison, that Texas annexation was unwise both because it would likely lead to war with Mexico and because the admission of a new slave state would upset the sectional balance of power in the Senate.

But when President John Tyler negotiated a secret treaty to annex Texas in 1844, Van Buren, as the presumptive Democratic nominee, was forced to take a stand. His assertion that annexation was both unwise and unethical was identical to that of his Whig opponent, Henry Clay, and it destroyed his credibility with expansionist Democrats throughout the South. A new man was needed to lead the Democrats: an expansionist who would not only bring Texas into the Union but fight for more American territory to the west and south under the banner of Manifest Destiny. As Andrew Jackson himself informed James, "The candidate for the first office should be an annexation man and from the Southwest." James K. Polk, a lifelong proponent of expansionism, was clearly "the most available man."[9]

When the delegates to the Democratic National Convention gathered in Baltimore in May 1844, the majority intended to cast their votes for Martin Van Buren. But at the start of the convention, a minority group committed to the annexation of Texas seized the floor and changed the convention rules so that a winning nominee required two-thirds of all votes. The annexationists supported Lewis Cass of Michigan, a stolid, serious man with a pronounced sympathy for the South. Van Buren's supporters derided the Michigan senator's supporters as "Jack Casses," but the man's expansionist credentials were above reproach. Cass had been instrumental in the Indian removal of the 1830s, arguing loudly and repeatedly that the "savage" Cherokee were undeserving of their lands, despite the tribe's wholesale acceptance of the norms of their white neighbors. His views could not have been further from Van Buren's: he would annex Texas, just as he hoped to annex Canada, Cuba, and any other territory in the Western Hemisphere that might be available.[10]

To the astonishment of Van Buren's many supporters, Cass quickly began to gain on the front-runner. By the seventh ballot he was firmly in the lead. At that point, however, the Jack Casses were faced with the unpleasant reality that their man was no more likely than Van Buren to win the votes of two-thirds of the assembled delegates, particularly given that most of Van Buren's delegates would sooner vote for Whig candidate Henry Clay than allow "the *damned rotten corrupt venal* Cass" the victory of the nomination. Tempers flared, and the Van Buren delegates threatened to return home. The convention deadlocked.[11]

That night Democratic operatives cloistered themselves in a nearby hotel room and hammered out a solution to the deadlock between Van Buren and Cass. By dawn they had settled on a candidate who had the power not only to unify the fractured and angry delegate pool, but perhaps also pull out a victory against Henry Clay in November. He hadn't received a single vote on the first day of the convention, and his reputation was shaky even in his home state. But he had no enemies, and was a true believer in annexation. The following morning, on the ninth ballot, James K. Polk was unanimously proclaimed the Democratic nominee for president in 1844. With undistinguished Pennsylvania senator George M. Dallas offering sectional balance as his vice president, and a platform calling for "the re-occupation of Oregon and the re-annexation of Texas at the earliest practicable period," James prepared for the election of his life.[12]

Polk was the first "dark horse" candidate in American political history, a fact that might not have surprised Matilda Catron, but certainly did a great many other people. His nomination was so unexpected that when Samuel Morse's new "wonder working telegraph" transmitted the nomination to Washington, "it was heard by all the faithful with speechless amazement." Listeners assumed the device had erred. Even close friends of the Polk family were surprised. When news made it to Columbia, James's friend and political ally Alfred O. P. Nicholson exclaimed to his wife, Caroline, "Well guess who's nominated for President—but you can't in a month. James K. Polk."[13]

The Whig Party was delighted. "Of the nomination of Mr. Polk we hardly know how to speak seriously," the *New York Herald* reported. "A more ridiculous, contemptible and forlorn candidate, was never put forth by any party. . . . Mr. Polk is a sort of fourth or rather fortieth-rate lawyer and small politician in Tennessee, who by accident was once speaker of the House of Representatives. He was rejected even by his own state as governor—and now he comes forward as candidate of the great democracy of the United States." Henry Clay was the founder of the Whig Party and possibly the greatest orator of his era. He had already run for president twice, and he was as charming and charismatic as he was accomplished, with a magnetic personality that endeared him to men and women alike. Who was Polk in comparison? Clay's supporters were so confident in their candidate's victory that they commissioned an enormous suite of solid rosewood bedroom furniture for his use in the White House. The thirteen-foot crimson-topped bed cost more than a modest house, and was accompanied by a set of similarly imposing chairs, a dressing table, an armoire, two marble-topped washstands, and a standing mirror.[14]

But the Whigs badly underestimated both their opponent and the appeal of Manifest Destiny. Young men and women in 1844, particularly in the old Southwest, had seen their parents and in some cases their grandparents profit from western migration, getting rich off lands taken from Indians. Sarah's family wealth derived in large part from land speculation, as did James's. Texas, and Mexico's lands farther to the west, were the next step in a march to the Pacific that most Americans believed had been preordained by a deity who smiled on the young and thriving republic. James was a true believer in Manifest Destiny, and made territorial expansion—including the annexation of Texas and all of the Oregon Country, which was jointly occupied with Britain—key elements in his platform.

For many voters that was plenty. Two Whigs traveling on horseback through Kentucky immediately after Polk was nominated learned this firsthand when they met "a Kentucky citizen horseman" crossing a stream. He naturally "inquired who had been nominated by the Democrats for President." When the two Whigs informed him, the Kentuckian asked, "Who the h-ll is this here Polk, anyhow? I never heard of him." The Whigs told the man about James's platform, and soon thereafter the three of them met up with a second Kentucky "citizen horseman," who also asked about the nomination. The first Kentuckian responded, "Governor Jeems K Polk, sah." "Who's Polk?" asked the newcomer. "Polk! Why you durned old gumphead! Jeems K Polk, the greatest man in America."[15]

BUT WAS MANIFEST DESTINY ENOUGH? Those who knew the Polks best recognized Sarah's value in the coming campaign. Soon after James's nomination, John and Matilda Catron offered him some unsolicited advice: Sarah should campaign for him. "She ought to be seen also by those from abroad," John wrote. "The _wife_ of a man aspiring to the White house is no minor circumstance. Few have passed muster there." There was no precedent for a woman to campaign for her husband, for the presidency. Indeed, it was hardly acceptable for presidential candidates to campaign on their own behalf. Candidates were expected to stay out of the public eye during nominating conventions and general elections.

But the Catrons had a solution: Sarah and James could stay at the

Catron home in Nashville, where Sarah could work on James's behalf from the safe confines of a family home. The presence of James in their home "would afford the excuse to have it open to all suitable visitors," John noted, "and I very much desire this. I desire that Mrs. Polk should be visited by Whigs and democrats of her own sex—& so she will, as the ladies of the other side uniformly speak well, and generally highly of her."

John Catron was dead serious. "This may look like a small matter. I think otherwise." Nor were John and Matilda alone in seeing Sarah as a crucial advantage in the coming campaign. "The matter was mentioned to Mrs. Catron by Doct[o]r Eselman, & she consulted me," John asserted. "On the subject I have no doubt, nor has Mrs. Catron," who thought Sarah would be particularly effective with "gentlemen from abroad."

Catron reminded James that while serving on Andrew Jackson's "Whitewashing Committee," tasked with refuting slander against Old Hickory during his presidential campaigns, John learned the true value of a wife. Had Rachel survived, she might have worked on Jackson's behalf, but instead the widowed Jackson had to turn to friends to vouch for his character. They "had more trouble . . . on the wife head, than with all else," he admitted. "More public men have received potent help from the wife in this country than in any in the world, not excepting France. The working, anxious, and troubled husband, has no time and tact, to conciliate and please the women, the young men, or the vain old ones. This is the very business of the wife, and one not fit for it, is a dead weight." Sarah could conciliate in a way her introverted and anxious husband was unable to do. The Catrons knew full well that Sarah Polk had the power to soothe their allies and put their opponents on guard. That Sarah "is fit in high places," John assured James, "should be well known to friends and opponents."[16]

Sarah did not openly campaign for James. Either one or both of them recognized that their political partnership was too radical for the rank and file of the Democratic Party. That she was "fit for high places" was never in doubt, but the Polks chose to conform to their party's patriarchal vision of the household by celebrating her deference, instead of her political acumen. Both would agree they made the right decision.

Sarah resumed her role as communications director from their home in Columbia, handling correspondence and the press. Because James was intent on maintaining the façade that "he never sought the distinguished office for which the democratic party have nominated him," he also, unusually for him, refrained from campaigning. The party press bragged that "he probably has not been five miles from home since his nomination. The democrats had a mass meeting in his own town, and begged him to attend, if only for one moment . . . but this kind request he most modestly declined."[17]

Although Sarah would not campaign, her fitness for "high places," as interpreted by the Democratic Party, was made known through campaign propaganda. "She is a very worthy and a very well-looking lady," a Washington letter writer to the *New York Express* assured her readers. "She is not highly accomplished, either in a literary point of view or in those blandishments which now-a-days make up so much of fashionable life. Nevertheless she makes a charming housewife, and knows enough of 'good society' to make the balls and visits of her guests both easy and agreeable."[18] A capable housewife with easy social skills and no pretentions to intellectual superiority: this was the ideal of a deferential wife.

And she was, moreover, well loved. "There is no lady in Tennessee more respected and beloved than Mrs. James K. Polk," the *New York Herald* reported. Her "intellectual, regular and beautiful features . . . beam intelligence, kindness and benevolence. She is a professing and consistent Christian."[19] The *New York Journal of Commerce* added that Colonel Polk's "lady is both beautiful and accomplished. . . . There is not a human being living that is enemy of her."[20]

What more did the country need from a First Lady? The question of character was, in 1844, as in most presidential elections, a concern of voters. The Whigs were the party of religious reform, loud advocates in favor of temperance, and enthusiastic supporters of putting government to work improving society. But the party's leader and presidential candidate was a good deal less temperate, and less reformed, than many religious Americans wished. Democrats accused Henry Clay of drunkenness, debauchery, foul language, gambling, and dueling. There was a grain of truth to most of these claims, but Clay's worst indiscretions had taken place decades before, when he was a very young man in very high office.

James Polk's character, by contrast, was "pure and without reproach." He was Henry Clay's opposite. "During his whole life he has been strictly a temperance man in every thing, in liquor, tobacco, in eating, and in all respects," newspapers reported. "He never gambled. In all his life he never gave or accepted a challenge to fight a duel . . . and has the moral courage to put in practice the moral principles he professes." Not even Columbia's Whig "clique" could say differently. A Democratic reporter quizzed James's "most violent opposers in Columbia . . . if there was anything wrong in his whole private life." They all, "with one voice, to a man, declared that Col. Polk's whole private life was one of the most unspotted purity."[21]

Democrats credited a great deal of her husband's virtue to Sarah. Happily married to the same woman for twenty years, James in his "private life . . . has ever been upright and pure." And Sarah's Sabbatarianism was suddenly a great advantage. The fact that James kept the Sabbath holy thanks to the "auspicious domestic influence" of his wife helped counter the presence of Theodore Frelinghuysen, the "Christian Statesman," on the Clay ticket. Clay's vice presidential pick was a Sabbatarian and president of the American Bible Society.[22]

But was the influence of a vice president comparable to that of a wife? Most Americans in the 1840s, particularly middle-class Americans who idealized women as moral exemplars, thought not. Moral suasion was the job of a wife. Henry Clay's wife, Lucretia, was the adoring mother of eleven children, well known for her domestic prowess: her cured hams were said to be some of the best in Fayette County. But her domestic influence was confined to their Kentucky estate. She avoided Washington, leaving her husband to face the demons of temptation alone.[23]

Sarah's energies, in contrast, were entirely focused on James. Democrats were quick to promote her as his "guardian angel," a woman so devout and pure that she could be safely trusted to guide a president "amid the perils and darkness" of political life. And that influence extended beyond her own household. Sarah's insistence that her husband attend church with her each Sunday was well known. If he was "engaged in the company of men who, either from indifference or carelessness, forgot the Sabbath and its universal obligation," Sarah would enter the room "shawled and bonneted" and "ask her husband and his friends to go with her to church, saying that she did not wish to go alone." It made for a good campaign story, and it also happened to be true. Sarah took the sanctity of the Sabbath seriously. The only time she ever denied James a request for political work on his behalf was when he asked her to work on a Sunday.[24]

Sarah embraced her moralizing image, but made no effort to conform to the ideal of the good housewife during the presidential campaign. In the fall of 1844, a "lady remarked to a friend of Mrs. Polk's that she hoped Mr. Clay would be elected to the presidency, because Lucretia Clay was a good housekeeper, and made fine butter." When Sarah heard this story she proudly replied, "If I should be so fortunate as to reach the White House, I expect to live on twenty-five thousand dollars a year, and I will neither keep house nor make butter."[25]

This was a fairly radical claim given the pride that elite white women took in their domestic virtues. Whig women had proudly prepared "Harrison Cakes" in 1840, confections designed to promote his presidency, and they were prepared to go further in 1844. After the success of the Log Cabin campaign, the Whigs knew the power of their female supporters. The party publicly celebrated women's moral power in the household and in society. Whig men knew women mattered; they were proud to admit it, to declare their wives and sisters their moral superiors, and to support female-led moral reform efforts. As for the party's candidate, Henry Clay, his charm with women was legendary; they positively "idolize[d] their favorite *Harry*." They were ready to work on his behalf.[26]

Whig men recognized the power of women not only to uplift their husbands and sons, but also to turn out votes. In 1844 the Whigs gave their female supporters unprecedented authority in the elaborate ceremonies that structured presidential campaigns. Women around the country paraded, attended Whig meetings and conventions, and proudly announced their support for "Harry of the West." The wife of the president of the Democratic National Convention, Hendrick B. Wright, made her Pennsylvania home a meeting place for Clay women, and proudly told her husband's Democratic friends that "though my husband is a *Polk* man, I am a *Clay* man; in fact the ladies are all Clay men."[27]

Tennessee's female Whigs were particularly emboldened. In 1840, 350 Whig women signed a letter inviting Henry Clay to speak in Nashville, after two invitations from the men of the city had been turned down. The women were successful, and Clay spoke to a mixed audience of, reportedly, thirty thousand people. Women in the audience swooned. In 1844, Tennessee Whigs resolved that "the ladies . . . be specifically invited to attend" their rallies. And female Whigs did so, with passion. In July, Whig women were bold enough to host a "sumptuous barbecue" in Sarah's hometown, "to which all sexes and all parties were invited." Nashville's Whig paper reported five to seven thousand present at the barbecue, including fifteen hundred ladies. "What cause can fail to triumph when women is its advance?" the paper asked.[28]

Nor were the Whigs afraid to critique James's masculinity. After the barbecue a veteran of the War of 1812 gave a rousing speech critiquing his military credentials. Polk might be called "a young hickory," but, asked the speaker, "what great deeds of heroism bestowed upon him this title"? Where was James during the "late war—when our country demanded the help of all her sons. . . . Where was this hero? Was he in the army defending his country? Far from it. He was by his cheerful fireside, in Grundy's law office." The attack no doubt stung. Appointed colonel of the state militia by a friendly Democratic Senator, James was one of the few Democratic politicians of his generation who had never fought in a battle. His early ill health kept him from military service.[29]

Sarah couldn't have helped but hear about the great Whig meeting a month later in nearby Shelbyville: perhaps twenty thousand Whigs gathered in a town of a thousand for two days of Henry Clay celebration, with single women prominent among the celebrants. A grand parade on the first day of the festivities featured a "Union Company" of twenty-six women, "arrayed in pure white, with sashes of blue, and handsome caps ornamented with white feathers," each of whom carried a banner suggesting they would have a "Whig" husband or "no husband" at all. John Shofner, a local Whig, was thrilled by the sight. "That was about as nise a site as men ginerley sees, 26 young ladys all drest in uniform marching and each carriing a banner." And women marched at the head of a procession the following day to the grandstand on the edge of town, where Tennessee Whigs, including the governor who had twice beaten James, spoke in Clay's support.[30]

Similar scenes played out around the country, much to the shock and dismay of Democrats. "Though popular opinion is against female politicians," one female supporter wrote Sarah from Virginia soon after the election, "that was not the principle advocated here, by gentlemen politicians who used the influence of the ladies—every device in the way of flags banners, and all their ingenuity was exercised in the handiwork of our political ladies—and the attendance and cheers of their nocturnal club meetings." Picking up on a favored slogan of the Whigs, Virginia's "female politicians . . . foolishly inquired—Who is James K. Polk?"[31]

In the meantime, where were the Democratic women? The influence of Whig ladies on the partisan politics of the 1840s was so pronounced that it was easy to assume, as had the wife of the president of the Democratic National Convention, that "the ladies are all Clay men." But this was not the case. While Democratic women weren't as prominent as Whig women in the campaign itself, the heated issue of Texas annexation brought them out in public. Three months before the election, Nashville's female Democrats sewed a tremendous banner, "handsomely wrought and embellished," which they presented to a battalion of soldiers back from Texas. "The lovely young lady who presented it pronounced her address in a remarkably graceful and spirited manner," the Whig *Republican Banner* reported. Noting "a large attendance of Ladies" at the rally and meeting in favor of the annexation of Texas, the writer for the *Banner* sighed, "it is only doing the *fair* democrats justice to say that *their* part in the proceedings was distinguished by so much taste and elegance that we cannot help wishing they were all *Whigs*."[32]

Democrats could easily have capitalized on this nationalist enthusiasm. One of Polk's supporters suggested that "the influence and ingenuity of our ladies can now be of service if they are properly Called . . . to action." Some Tennessee Democrats took a step in that direction when they invited men to bring their wives to parades.[33]

But a deep antipathy to the specter of "female politicians" was, like much of the Democratic Party's appeal, grounded in nostalgia and a yearning for values that seemed to have been lost in the dramatic changes of the nineteenth century. The Democratic *Nashville Union* expressed its ambivalence about the prominence of women in the Whig campaign with an appeal for female support that remained firmly in the private sphere. "To THE RESCUE, then, in your own lovely sphere; embroider the LONE STAR on every national flag you can find; offer prize banners to promote vigilance; and by winning votes for James K. Polk, you may consummate immediate annexation." Embroidering stars, donating handmade banners to men, even "consummating" annexation, depending on your definition of annexation: these were all indoor activities, none of which threatened male control over public space. Democrats recognized the value of women in electoral politics, but fully capitalizing on that potential would have meant embracing change. This the party was unwilling to do.[34]

But just because Democratic women were less visible than Whig women doesn't mean they were less plentiful. The father of the party, Andrew Jackson, had female partisans. James's college roommate voted against Jackson in 1828, after "mature deliberation," he admitted to James, because he "did not think" Old Hickory "would make a safe President of these United States." But his wife, Susan, was "a real Jacksonian," and "as an evidence of it" had one of Jackson's speeches "printed on satin, suspended in a large gilt frame."[35]

Polk had his female supporters as well. Elizabeth Bosworth, of Carroll County, Louisiana, considered herself very much a part of "The Democracy," and proudly sent Sarah the "flag of the Democratic Association of Carroll" County when James won the nomination. "I consider his nomination as victory already achieved," she wrote. "This is the feeling that animates the whole Democracy and will lead us to a glorious victory." Another Louisiana Democrat, Mrs. McGimsey, challenged a female Whig to bet her house slave on the outcome of the election. Cincinnati resident Jane Frindlay's apology for her lack of partisan effort suggests how normal she viewed female partisanship. "You are aware that I am too far advanced in life to pay much attention to most party politics," she wrote Sarah Polk, although she admitted that "one can never be too old to take an interest in their country."[36]

Most of the Democratic ladies believed that their Whig sisters had crossed a line of decorum with their political activism. But a conservative understanding of the proper spheres for men and women did not lessen the political passion of Democratic women. "A patriotic zeal for the cause of Democratic principles" has been "coeval with my existence," one wrote to Sarah, and she was not afraid to let those views be known, even when surrounded by "adverse female partisans . . . who respect me, though not my principles of politics." Matilda Catron, Caroline Nicholson, and Sarah Polk were exceptional not because they espoused the principles of the Democratic Party, but because their wealth and power provided them with a large sphere of influence. Democratic women were quieter about their politics than their Whig sisters, but no less committed.[37]

And their efforts were no less crucial to the functioning of high politics, on the state and national level, than were the efforts of Whig women. As Sarah's experiences made clear, political success in Washington might have been possible without female help, but it wasn't easy. The etiquette of Washington's "official society" required skill to navigate, skill cultivated by women, and success was dependent on relationships forged outside official work hours. From the earliest establishment of the nation's capital in Washington, D.C., politics was a family business, one in which wives, sons, and daughters played a role.

It's no wonder that so many sons of politicians followed their fathers into politics and that so many of their daughters married politicians, or helped husbands forge political careers. Jessie Benton, the daughter of the powerful Missouri Democratic senator Thomas Hart Benton, married explorer John C. Frémont in 1841. His increasing involvement in politics over the following decades occurred in close tandem with his wife, who lobbied on his behalf and helped manage his campaigns. Although Jessie was likely the only wife of a presidential candidate in the antebellum era to write her husband's campaign literature, few found anything strange about the son-in-law of a powerful senator entering politics, or the daughter of a senator drawing on political skills learned and political connections forged in her own childhood family home. It took the efforts of an entire family to cultivate the relationships necessary to succeed politically.[38]

Nor was the role of women in politics limited to Washington. Etiquette in Nashville was nowhere near as exacting as in the nation's capital, but Sarah learned the hard way that the social exertions of the wife of the governor were just as crucial to political success as they had been for the wife of the Speaker of the House of Representatives. Men might complain about female politicians, but they ignored them at their own risk. The nation was about to learn that the true value of a political wife had little to do with making butter.[39]

THE 1844 PRESIDENTIAL CONTEST was remarkably close, a difference of just 38,000 votes out of more than 2.7 million votes cast. Polk carried the Deep South, but proved Alfred Balch correct on a second point: Tennessee swung the same direction in 1843 as it did in 1844. Polk not only lost Tennessee, but even his hometown of Columbia.[40]

Nevertheless, just like that, Sarah Childress Polk was elevated to First Lady. When the Polks first heard the news, hours before it was reported in the press, they kept it private, remaining quietly at home. If Sarah hadn't thought through the implications of her new status before the election, she did so during those final hours before the news broke in Columbia.

When it did, she was prepared. A boisterous crowd gathered at their home. "A gentleman" reportedly entered the Polk parlor. "Mrs. Polk," he said, "some of your husband's friends wish to come in to the house, but we will not let the crowd in, because the street is muddy and your carpets and furniture will be spoiled." Sarah responded, "The house is thrown open to everybody. Let them all come in; they will not hurt the carpets." Although she reported that "this decision was exactly in accord with Mr. Polk's wishes and preferences," it was wholly her innovation to bring mass democracy into her own parlor, stamping her domain with the party's vaunted egalitarianism as surely as dirt was stamped on her carpets.[41] Of course, she wasn't the one who would be cleaning them.

This grand gesture was excellent preparation for the White House. After almost two decades of political experience in Washington and Tennessee, Sarah was in an ideal position to transform the office of the First Lady. Given the public association of "political" women with the Whig Party, there's an irony to the fact that the first serious female politician elevated to the office of First Lady was a Democrat. Her Democratic supporters surely celebrated when Congress passed a joint resolution to admit Texas as a state at the close of John Tyler's presidency.

Perhaps because the Whigs were the party of "female politicians,"

Sarah's elevation provided very little critiquing of her political partnership with James among the politicians who knew them best. Although deferential Democratic wives like Sarah did an excellent job pretending to be apolitical, well-connected and wealthy political wives had been making use of their access to politicians since the earliest days of the republic. A wealthy woman had the ability to make a generous donation to a political campaign, or to influence powerful men in her orbit. At the state and local level, women of high social status had easy access to politicians. They entered state legislatures "as if they assumed their welcome" and successfully lobbied politicians for friendly laws and corporate status. Or, in Matilda Catron's case, with a Supreme Court judgeship for her husband. Sarah was not alone in making use of her political access while disavowing the reformist sensibilities of Whig women. Her privilege justified her actions at the same time that her politics obscured those actions.[42]

A month before the president's inauguration, Vice President–Elect George M. Dallas, who had neither the president's trust nor his friendship, expressed his disapproval to his wife, Sophia, of the power "political" women held over their husbands. Mrs. Polk, he told her, "is certainly mistress of herself, and I suspect of somebody else too." But Sophia Dallas made her priorities clear when she chose to remain in Philadelphia during her husband's term as vice president. Their marriage was very different from Sarah and James's partnership. Fellow Philadelphian Henry Gilpin did not share Dallas's concern. "If I am not mistaken," he wrote Martin Van Buren about Sarah soon after the election, "she has both sagacity and decision that will make her a good counsellor in some emergencies." Sarah Preston Hale of Massachusetts, a forty-eight-year-old supporter of Henry Clay, found hope in Sarah's elevation. She wondered if "perhaps Mr. and Mrs. Polk together will make a very good President."[43]

Sarah never forgot her trip to Washington with the president-elect. The travails of 1826 were long forgotten; although the Cumberland River was too shallow to navigate, once they reached Kentucky, technology smoothed their way. In Louisville they were able to board a steamboat heading up the Ohio River, and railroad tracks extended as far west as Cumberland, Maryland. They spent two leisurely weeks, traveling only during the day, fending off the "manifestation of the people" in support of the new president, and meeting with committees of "prominent gentlemen."[44]

They arrived in Cincinnati on a Sunday, and were met by Democrats serenading them with a band. Sarah offered a preview of her administration when she broke up the impromptu concert. There was to be no music on the Sabbath. James accepted her decision, and apologized to his supporters, quipping, "Sarah directs all domestic affairs, and she thinks that is domestic." Had he a sense of humor, it might have been meant as a joke. Instead it was an accurate statement about both their relationship and Sarah's approach to politics. He conceded command of "domestic affairs" to his wife, and allowed for a remarkably elastic definition of the term. But he also demanded her participation in his political and economic affairs. The Polks gave lip service to the ideology of gendered spheres of influence, but Sarah's own sphere was copious, and never separate from that of men.[45]

The letters she received just after the election suggest that her supporters recognized that having "no children to occupy her time," she could serve as a "valuable assistant" to her husband. Sending his best wishes for "her" administration, Leonard Jones of Shelby County, Kentucky, offered, "May all your actions be original. . . . Hope the characteristics of your administration may be to feed the hungry, clothe the naked, visit sick & in Prison, & Take the *Stranger in*." Another recognized that she would be a "helpmeet, in the best sense, to your Husband."[46]

But mostly they wrote about religion. Sarah's strict morality was a great comfort to a great many. One aged professor of religion, who wrote not long after the Polks arrived in Washington, prayed that Sarah would "let all the nation see—that in the house & family of the President of the United States, the Lord's day is sacred." He hoped she realized the extent of her power to influence others. "Do not forget how much is, humanly speaking, in your power to promote the good of all around you, how great an influence a bright Christian example in the family of the President, may exert . . . on the whole country." Her influence and example could be "the means of drawing down blessings on his administration." Sarah loved getting letters like these. "A good letter from a Christian friend," she marked on the envelope.[47]

Of course, moral suasion didn't stop at the White House front door. It was "common cant," one male admirer wrote, "that the world is governed by men, and that men are governed by women," but "age and experience have taught me . . . that women govern both, and it is a fortunate interposition of Providence that it is so. . . . At home they have all the turmoil, anxiety and care. Abroad they are the ministers of comfort, of peace, and consolation."[48]

The many women active in reform movements during the period made it clear that domestic ideology sanctioned a broad array of public activities in the name of benevolence, from charity work, to moral reform, to temperance, and even abolition. Men wrote letters to Sarah waxing enthusiastic about women's "generous hearts, and hands . . . kindly contributing to the wants, and necessities of the orphan, and the widow." Although most reform societies attempted to conform to standards of female propriety by asking men to chair meetings and address public gatherings, it was not a great secret that behind the scenes women wielded most of the authority. Leonard Jones's letter jokingly referred to the "favorite doctrine of female supremacy" to justify writing to the new First Lady, but cautioned her that he felt certain that "women's intuitive powers will be called forth in this trying season" in order to "fix the principles of the succeeding administration, & practically carry out" the responsibilities of high office.[49]

Jones recognized that Sarah would play a role in carrying out the responsibilities of high office. But in what way? Although partisan politics was largely considered off-limits to women, and both women and men held differing opinions about the propriety of women petitioning Congress, thousands of women nonetheless did so in opposition to slavery. They pressed their congressional representatives for legislation to improve the lives of women, children, the weak, and the vulnerable. In the name of benevolence they lobbied men in power. No one was more successful in this regard than Dorothea Dix, who the year before Polk's election gained national attention by successfully advocating for state-funded insane asylums. In order to secure an insane asylum in New Jersey she stayed up late into the night cajoling votes from elected officials. "You cannot imagine the labor of converting and convincing," she wrote.[50]

Only a few of the letters Sarah received from strangers were explicitly political. A Virginia Episcopalian wrote her to warn that some

Presbyterian ladies lobbying her for funds for a new church were in fact firm Clay supporters. Those women were "foremost in having public meetings" on Clay's behalf during the election, including one "in the church they solicit your aid in decorating." She wrote not to "influence you against these Presbyterians," but "if you aid them let them know you are doing good for evil, that you know they used all their influence against your honored and distinguished husband." This news may not have surprised Sarah, since Whig women were far more likely to belong to benevolent associations pushing for social reform than were Democratic women. She declined their request.[51]

GIVEN SARAH's well-known church membership, her Sabbatarianism, and the widespread view of middle-class women as the keepers of moral virtue in society, it's hardly surprising that her constituents assumed that Sarah would guide her husband's behavior by setting a moral example. But in fact James and Sarah's relationship bore little resemblance to what the public imagined. It was James, not Sarah, who was the moral influence in the household. Sarah attributed her own moral standards to the "strict" moral "school" run by her husband. She made sure James attended church, and did her best to keep the Sabbath holy. But his "ideas of propriety" were far stricter than hers, and in private he was not above admonishing her for failing to conform to what she described as his "delicate conception of the fitness of things."[52]

There's little doubt that Sarah was a gossip. Indeed, her intimate friendships with Aaron Brown and John Catron were in large part fueled by a shared love of political gossip. Her willingness to engage in what James would certainly have considered unfair conjecture opened up a space for communication with men clearly distinct from the manner in which those men communicated with her husband. Aaron Brown warned Sarah against sharing with James their cruel jibes about James Buchanan's "marriage" to William King. But Brown wasn't the only recipient of Sarah's indelicate gossip. When Sarah's niece learned "something amusing about Mr. Buchanan," she immediately told her aunt, despite the gentleman who spread the news promising "to tell me more if I should not say anything about it." Sarah didn't need to be warned, because if James heard her joke unkindly about another person, he rebuked her. "Sarah, I wish you would not say that. I understand you, but others might not, and a wrong impression might be made."[53]

But disagreements about morality were a minor blot in a remarkably harmonious relationship between the First Lady and her husband. Sarah and James had a truly companionate marriage, one characterized by mutual respect, deep affection, and a recognition of their dependence upon each other. Wife and husband, they were above all else a team of two, in politics as in life. As they moved into the White House it was with a shared mission that would transform not only the office of the First Lady, but the entire North American continent.

5

MRS. PRESIDENTESS

Mrs. Presidentess is quite a courtier, desirous, as is natural & proper, of winning favour wherever she can. —WILLIAM WOODBRIDGE, January 7, 1846

On TUESDAY, March 4, 1845, the soon-to-be eleventh president of the United States took the oath of office in the pouring rain, in front of a record crowd. First Lady Sarah Childress Polk, dressed in a gray-and-red-striped satin gown, carried an elaborate ivory-handled fan, featuring on one side portraits of the eleven presidents, including James, and on the other a picture of the signing of the Declaration of Independence. It was a gift from James. The rain didn't bother her any more than had that first dangerous trip to Washington. Her homecoming returned her to the center of power.[1]

When James K. Polk entered office he was only forty-nine years old, the nation's youngest president. Admirers described him as "a short, slender and pleasant looking gentleman," with excellent manners. He and Sarah had been married twenty-one years. She was now forty-two, a full eighteen years older than outgoing First Lady Julia Tyler, who the previous year had married a president thirty years her senior.[2]

Although Sarah was much older than Julia Tyler, she was not particularly old. When she entered the White House, the average age of First Ladies upon inauguration was a full decade older than she was at that time. With thick, curly jet-black hair, excellent posture, and a slim figure suited to the fashions of the day, Sarah Polk struck many in their circle as relatively youthful, perhaps, some intimated, because she was childless. Acquaintances plausibly described her as tall, in part because she carried herself so well, and because James was himself short. But based on her surviving clothes and shoes, she was no taller than five foot two, weighed less than a hundred pounds, and wore a size 3 shoe. "Time has dealt kindly with her charms," noted one male acquaintance in a private letter. "She dresses with taste. . . . If she is not handsome she is at least very prepossessing and graceful."[3]

Compared to the luminous Julia Tyler, very few women could hope to pass as "handsome." With her pale skin, translucent complexion, and feminine features, Julia personified the 1840s ideal of white female beauty. Sarah's deep-set eyes, prominent nose, and sallow coloring, by contrast, were decidedly unfashionable. One observer described her as "a little too much the color of 'refined gold' in the day time, but lovely at night, in a scarlet cashmere turban trimmed in gold." If it weren't for her prominent teeth, one friendly observer suggested, she "would be a very handsome woman." But if no one (other than James) considered her a great beauty, many admirers thought her beautiful. And almost everyone agreed that she was elegant and personable. One typical commentator described Sarah as "a woman of striking presence, stately and tall, perhaps a little too formal and cold, yet none the less an ornament and example."[4]

She returned to a Washington badly in need of her example. It had been nearly two decades since there was a steady spousal presence in the White House. Both Jackson and Van Buren were widowers. William Henry Harrison's wife declined to accompany her husband to his inauguration, which mattered less than it might have because he died just a month later. John Tyler became the first vice president elevated to office by the death of his predecessor, and was thereafter known as "His Accidency." Tyler's first wife, Letitia, was incapacitated by a stroke, and died at age fifty-one just five months into her husband's presidency. And his second wife, Julia, was as jejune as she was lovely.[5]

Julia's eight months as First Lady were not successful. Determined to have what she identified as a "Court interesting in youth and beauty," she surrounded herself with young women, none as beautiful as she.

"Wherever I go they form my train," she reported proudly. She bought a greyhound, because she thought the Italian dog lent her an air of sophistication. She spent her mornings in bed, and afternoons distracting her husband. "Let your husband work during business hours," her mother scolded. "Business should take the precedence of caressing." Directing her daughter's attention toward the filthy White House, her mother suggested alternative work. "You know how I detest a dirty house. Commence at once to look around and see that all things are orderly and tidy. This will amuse and occupy you."[6]

Julia instead made Texas annexation her pet project, promising to secure votes in favor of the bill through ballroom lobbying. She invited at least fifty members of Congress to a reception at the White House, and, once they assembled, regally entered the room, as if "votes might be influenced by awe alone." On another occasion she passed a note to a male guest at dinner that read "Texas and John Tyler." But she was a latecomer to politics, and her efforts to win votes were clumsy, further evidence that she was not ultimately a serious person.[7]

Sarah was nothing if not serious, and experienced enough to blanch at Julia's awkward political attempts. She was old enough to be Julia's mother and happy to act her age. In contrast to the lively Julia, who loved parties and dancing, and wore opulent jewelry, Sarah might have seemed a bit dour. Soon after the election, the new First Lady let it be known that she would ban dancing, cards, and hard liquor from the White House. She and James were conspicuously absent from the Tylers' "Grand Finale," a going-away ball, where a reported three thousand guests drank cases of champagne, several barrels of wine, and innumerable large bowls of whiskey punch.

Sarah claimed to be unwell, but the Tylers were not alone in taking the absence of the Polks at their last party as a slight. "Imagine," John scoffed to his wife, "the idea of her being able to follow you." Newspaper reports did nothing to mend the rift. One admirer wrote "Mrs. President Polk" that he had read that her absence from "the large dancing party at the President's" was "caused by indisposition." But he wasn't fooled. "In an instant a thought flashed through my mind," that Sarah was not in fact ill, but rather "you have determined to abstain altogether from attending these parties, thus setting an example to the American people, worthy of the high station you occupy."[8]

This was precisely her idea. When Sarah invited the muddy guests into her Columbia parlor the day Tennessee learned the result of the 1844 election, she did so with the intention of becoming an entirely new kind of First Lady. And when she forbade the Cincinnati band from playing on their route to Washington, she gave public notice that her administration would diverge from those of the past. She offered her ban on White House frivolity as evidence of her respect for high office. "Why *I* wouldn't dance in the *President's* house," she told a company of ladies who inquired. "Would you?" Dancing was "undignified" and "respectful neither to the house nor to the office. How indecorous it would seem for dancing to be going on in one apartment, while in another we were conversing with dignitaries of the republic or ministers of the gospel. This unseemly juxtaposition would be likely to occur at any time, were such amusements permitted."[9]

Her ban on dancing in the White House did not prevent Sarah from attending her husband's inaugural ball at the National Theatre, dressed in an "elegant white brocaded silk" gown. The dress, a souvenir of Commodore Lawrence Kearny's recent China expedition, provided evidence of America's growing global reach and power. But she did not dance. And this, too, was intentional. She would set an example to the American people worthy of the high station she occupied.[10]

As her choice of inaugural gown made clear, Sarah Polk understood the symbolic power of her position in a manner that her predecessors had not. She entered the White House determined to use that power to promote not only her husband's administration, but also the ideals of the Democratic Party. James's inaugural speech left no doubt about his allegiance to Andrew Jackson's principles and policies. He decried the evils of banks, federal spending on national infrastructure, tariffs to support American manufacturing, and governmental interference in state matters. He warned abolitionists against interfering with slavery, and offered a grand vision of territorial expansion that he would bring to fruition during his four years in office. In this Polk was one of a generation of politicians who emulated Andrew Jackson. Men who had fought with or under Jackson later rode on his coattails into high offices across the Southwest, proudly asserting their allegiance to the father of the Democratic Party. Archibald Yell had become governor of Arkansas, Sam Houston the president of the Republic of Texas, Thomas Hart Benton the senior senator from Missouri.

But James most clearly proved his fealty to Old Hickory when he spoke about the newfound power of the common man. "All distinctions of birth or of rank have been abolished," he claimed, clearly oblivious to the distinctions of birth that enslaved two and a half million African Americans. "All citizens, whether native or adopted, are placed upon terms of precise equality. All are entitled to equal rights and equal protection." As president, James promised to put the common man first.[11]

The First Lady delivered no inaugural address, of course, but her actions at the start of her husband's presidency prove that she was just as committed to Jacksonian principles as her husband. Sarah's innovation was to demonstrate Jacksonian principles as a woman. She would be anti-elitist, democratic, and thrifty, "easy without familiarity, and dignified without restraint." This was a fairly radical change from recent precedent. Julia Tyler spoke freely about her "court." Elizabeth Monroe and Louisa Adams embraced the aristocratic potential of the office. None of these women were particularly religious. But piety was one of Sarah Polk's defining features. While the common man, and woman, might enjoy dancing, they would never begrudge a First Lady whose moral code was stricter than their own. Soon after Sarah arrived in Washington she joined the First Presbyterian Church, paying twenty-six dollars to rent pew 7 for a year.[12]

Sarah had no model to guide her on the path to embodying the female virtues of the Democracy. But she nonetheless determined to make "herself popular with all classes," and thus a worthy partner to Young Hickory. Her attempts to revive the Jackson legacy were not lost on the public. Jackson received significant evangelical support in 1828, and many of those supporters felt cheered by the Polk election. "Gen. Jackson had the honor of having abolished the use of brandy & wine at the President's levee," one admirer wrote her, incorrectly. "Now let the wife of another Tennessee President have the honor of abolishing the sinful practice of dancing parties."[13] What better way to prove to the world that James was Jackson's rightful political heir than to give that legacy female form?

There was a great deal at stake in this presidency, but twenty years in politics had left Sarah Childress Polk singularly prepared for the challenges that awaited her as First Lady. She had mastered the art of the political salon as wife of the Speaker of the House. She knew how receptions and dinners could be used to build political coalitions.

As wife of the governor of Tennessee, and communications director through three gubernatorial elections, she learned the importance of "news," and how to obtain it. Those elections had deepened the personal and political bonds between her and James and taught him the value of her advice. Now was the time to put all those skills to work in support of an agenda that would transform the nation, and the continent.

In order for that to happen, Sarah needed to reestablish her political salon, and with it a space to influence men and policy. She needed to insulate herself from routine social obligations so that she could return to her real work as James's political partner. She had to insulate her husband from the constant demands of job seekers who plagued every president in an era when average citizens believed they had a right to enter the "people's house" at will. And she needed to establish a public image as a woman of the people that was in many respects a complete fabrication. Only then could she fulfill both her destiny and the nation's.

It was a tall order, but Sarah had a plan.

BUT FIRST CAME THE REDECORATING. The "Grand Finale" ball, and all the other balls only slightly less grand, left their mark on the president's house. The Tylers vacated a White House in serious disrepair. Particularly in the staterooms, the carpets were worn bare, the wallpaper was filthy, and floorboards were stained by the errant spit of tobacco-chewing guests. When the great British author Charles Dickens visited the Tyler White House in 1842, he was horrified to find "gentlemen . . . so persevering and energetic" at "spitting" that he could only hope that "the Presidential housemaids" were particularly highly paid. As for the White House furniture, some of it was so badly damaged that a reporter for the *New York Herald* declared it "a contemptable disgrace to the nation." He claimed the furniture was so wretched it "would be kicked out of a brothel." The Tylers bought some new pieces to replace the worst of it, but then took their new furniture with them when they left Washington.[14]

It would be easy to blame Julia for not listening to her mother, or to blame champagne and whiskey punch. But true responsibility for the sad state of the White House lay with a hostile Congress, which refused to appropriate renovation funds to the "accidental" president, John Tyler, out of pure spite after he proved himself less committed to Whig ideals than either his predecessor Harrison or the Whig-controlled Congress. But after Democrats regained both the presidency and Congress in 1845, legislators happily granted $14,900 toward renovations, an enormous sum at the time. And because, as James liked to say, "Sarah directs all domestic affairs," here, as in Nashville, decisions regarding renovations were Sarah's to make alone.[15]

The new First Lady recognized a public relations opportunity when she saw one, and a chance to evince her Democratic bona fides. Her party was the party of small government, intent on limiting the scope and expense of federal intervention in the economy. Sarah could also economize. She announced that they would use only half of the appropriation Congress granted, and would refurbish only the staterooms. What better way to demonstrate her thrift and good sense? The *New York Journal of Commerce* reported that upholsterers left the White House "with very reduced expectations" after "the President's lady" told them that "if the private apartments had been satisfactory to Mrs. Tyler, they would be so to herself."[16]

As "new mistress of the White House," Sarah was lauded for her simplicity and moderation in her renovations, but in fact leaving the White House in its current somewhat dilapidated shape spared her a great deal of tedious work. The Tyler family, who clearly wished they still occupied the executive mansion, declared the Polks "monstrously small people" when they heard the news.[17]

Another woman would have embraced the opportunity to spend the country's money on interior decoration, particularly given the financial straits the Polks found themselves in at the start of 1845. The Polks were not rich, and James had again gone into debt during the election. Now they were faced with enormous expenditures. The president's salary was $25,000 a year. Economists have estimated that a dollar in 1845 is worth $28 today, so the president's annual salary was equal to $700,000. This would have been a fortune had not the president been responsible for almost all the expenses of the White House. The president paid the staff, he paid for his own meals, and he paid the expenses of guests, even at official dinners.[18]

The guests were never-ending. One visitor described the Polk White House as "quiet . . . no young people, and no children." But there were always Polk or Childress relatives in residence. They stayed for weeks or months at a time, and Sarah made sure they were well fed. "We have the finest peaches, nectarines, grapes, melons and in great abundance," one guest wrote home. "They grow twice as large here as they do in Tennessee."[19]

But the costs incurred by visiting Polk and Childress relatives were insignificant compared to the vast sums the Polk White House devoted to political entertaining. If Sarah's two years as First Lady of Tennessee had taught her anything, it was the value of her political salon. Early in the Polk presidency, she established a schedule of dinners and receptions that revealed how seriously she took this aspect of her job. By the middle of the second year of the Polk presidency there was a social event almost every night of the week, with the exception of Sundays. "The 'Presidentess,' as she is known here," and her husband "made themselves socially accessible to an incredible degree," wrote one admirer. They received visitors "without ceremony and without invitation" every Tuesday and Friday evening at events that attracted between twenty and two hundred guests. On Wednesday evenings the Marine Band played on the grounds of the White House, and twice a month Sarah followed those concerts with a large formal reception.[20]

Sarah received little help from her husband in any of this. She charmed. Visitors described her as "affable, full of conversation, easy in her address, & quite disposed to make others so." But James's social skills were limited. And the best that could be said for the president at such events was that he generally "preserved his equanimity, courtesy, and patience." Given that James "was in the habit of cutting off from his sleep the hours lost" to such entertainment, it was little wonder that he was often cranky at events that frequently carried on until close to midnight.[21]

Indeed, Sarah's passion for entertaining tested the stamina of the most extroverted. Less than three months after her teenaged niece Joanna Rucker arrived in Washington, Joanna admitted to a cousin that she stayed upstairs in her room during "a dinner party here last evening . . . as I have been to so many that I have tired." A visiting doctor who had the pleasure of spending twenty minutes speaking to

Sarah at a Tuesday afternoon "levee" found her "exceedingly affable, and agreeable in her manners, and well calculated to adorn the high station that she fills." But he felt no need to attend her evening levee a few hours later.[22]

James hoped that his informal Tuesday and Friday events would spare him the necessity of further entertaining, but Sarah instituted an additional two or three dinners when Congress was in session, with the explicit purpose of "cultivat[ing] congressional support for the administration's measures." Mrs. Polk "presided at all state dinners" whether or not James was present, and frequently he was not.[23]

Nineteen-year-old Varina Davis, wife of newly elected congressman Jefferson Davis of Mississippi, found that she preferred the events hosted by Sarah. "Polk is an insignificant looking man, I don't like his manners or anything else," she wrote her mother after attending a dinner party for "members of Congress and the ladies of their families, numbering between 30 & 40 persons" in January 1846. She was not initially impressed by Sarah, who while "a very handsome woman is too entertaining for my liking—talks too much a la President's wife, is too anxious to please." But three months later she attended one of Sarah's levees and "had quite a long chat" with the First Lady. She noted that no one at the party seemed to want to leave.[24]

Whether deliberately or by accident, Sarah appeared to make no pretensions to caring about the details of household management. "She said the servants knew their duties, and she did not undertake the needless task of directing them." But her focus on conversation led to some awkwardness at the table. She once presided over a dinner with no napkins on the table, and failed to notice. On another occasion, dinner guests, including one of James's most important allies, Senator Thomas Hart Benton, waited far too long to be fed. Benton asked Sarah if he had come at the right time. "Colonel Benton," she responded, "have you not lived in Washington long enough to know that the cooks fix the hour for dinner?"[25]

Nor did she particularly care about the food. Not that it was bad; Sarah's standards were high. Even the most exacting guests declared "her entertainment (for I believe she takes credit to herself, as indeed she has right to do, for whatever of good taste distinguishes her parties;) . . . elegant as well as luxurious." The wife of one wealthy southern congressman was flabbergasted by the dinner party she attended at the White House: "We had about fifty courses it seems to me." Guests at the Polk White House described elaborate multicourse dinners "in the French style" featuring upward of twenty separate dishes and six different wines. Sarah brought her Tennessee cook with her when she came to Washington, but paid a French chef, the son of Jefferson's chef, eleven dollars a day to cater the dinners. She rarely ate anything herself at these receptions. Nor did James, who preferred foods he was "accustomed to" such as "corn-bread & broiled ham."[26]

These formal events were expensive, and even the informal receptions required food and drink. In two weeks in January 1846, the Polk White House ran through five and a half gallons of oysters. And Sarah's decision to ban hard liquor from the White House turned out to be a costly one. Washington, D.C., had a far more liberal attitude toward intoxicating spirits than did rural or small-town America. Whiskey was remarkably cheap in the 1840s, rum not much more expensive. Punch made from one or the other was ubiquitous at the receptions and parties of earlier administrations. (Dolley Madison won acclaim for her potent "Roman Punch" composed of rum, brandy, sugar, and lemons.) Alcoholic punch was enjoyed by both male and female guests to a degree that would have shocked most Americans.[27]

Sarah never touched alcohol, but realized that for most people, socializing benefited from lubrication. Wine was not only less intoxicating than whiskey, it was more decorous, and because it was an established complement to fine dining in the European style even in the 1840s, it was nonnegotiable at state dinners. One White House guest described "a rainbow" of wineglasses around each plate at a dinner held for the Supreme Court and members of the House Judiciary Committee, "pink champagne, gold sherry, green hock, madeira, the ruby port, and sauterne." When James toasted to the health of the guests at the table, she joked about how drunk they already were: "We looked in pretty good [shape] just then." Even the exceptionally temperate James admitted to raising a glass from time to time.[28]

Unfortunately, wine was a great deal more expensive than hard liquor. There was no domestic wine production in the 1840s, meaning all of it was imported, and with the exception of the distilled spirit brandy, and fortified wines like Madeira, it spoiled easily. Although the

Polks hoped to economize, it would not be on beverages. Sarah never threw a party as elaborate as Julia Tyler's "Grand Finale" ball, but the Polk White House nonetheless consumed more table wines with dinner, more champagne with dessert, and more after-dinner brandy than did any previous administration, including that of Thomas Jefferson, whose passion for wine was equaled only by his inability to economize on household expenses despite the small size of his frequent dinner parties. The Polks bought table wines by the barrel.[29]

In an attempt to economize, Sarah cut the White House staff. She let the baker and the chef go, along with a steward who had worked at the White House for twenty years and a handful of other experienced domestic workers. She hired Paul Jennings, a slave who became familiar with White House protocol when he served in the Madison White House, from Dolley Madison, and hired a new white steward as well. She employed at least two of her own slaves, who moved into slave quarters in the White House basement, and contracted with free African Americans, whom she chose herself, to provide additional help when needed. And she made do with less staff by reorganizing their duties. In the process she won praise as an "admirable housekeeper," a title that may have come as a surprise to a woman who had spent the formative years of her adult life in the orbit of her mother-in-law and in Washington boardinghouses. Bringing "order into the domestic managements" of the White House may have been gratifying, but it was also "a great deal to add to all her other duties."[30]

WINNING OVER and maintaining potential allies for James was high on the list of those duties. Within months of the inauguration, Sarah started meeting privately with congressmen when they called at the White House. One of James's first challenges in office was appeasing the different factions of the Democratic Party with his appointments. Few Democrats were more powerful than John C. Calhoun of South Carolina. Calhoun had served as secretary of state under Tyler, and hoped to continue in that position, at least until his pet project, the annexation of Texas, was consummated.[31]

But James had no intention of keeping Calhoun in the most powerful office in his cabinet, so he offered him the position of minister to the

Court of St. James's, in London. A disappointed and angry Calhoun declined. Sarah, who had been close friends with Floride Calhoun during the Jackson administration, encouraged John to accept the post, but to no avail. The resentment John Calhoun felt toward James was tempered by his "cordial friendship" with Sarah, and he made sure to call on her before leaving Washington once out of office. Calhoun may not have been happy with James, but thanks to Sarah, he had been at least temporarily appeased.[32]

Not all of the Democrats James offended during his first months in office were as easy to pacify. Before his inauguration, James made his independence from "any of the cliques" in the Democratic Party abundantly clear by disregarding advice about appointments from Martin Van Buren and other party leaders. "I do not intend, if I can avoid it, that my counsels shall be distracted by the supposed or not conflicting intents of those cliques," he wrote to his friend Cave Johnson. "I intend to be myself President of the U.S."[33] In the month before inauguration day, he made promises to Thomas Hart Benton and other Democrats regarding Texas annexation that he appeared to have no intention of fulfilling. "He had no confid[a]nts except from calculation and for a purpose," one contemporary noted. "His secretiveness was large, and few men could better keep their own secrets." From the perspective of party unity, it was an inauspicious beginning.[34]

Sarah needed an ally of her own, a woman who understood the challenges of her position and could provide advice on the trials to come. Someone unconnected to any of the cliques James was busy alienating. Someone with social authority of her own. There was only one woman in Washington with these qualifications: Dolley Madison, the doyenne of parlor politics.

Seventy-seven-year-old Dolley Madison was still a fixture in Washington, long after the demise of her husband and the First Party System within which he operated. Madison's successors in the White House were expected to call on the "Dowager Queen," as she was known, and they did. Everyone of importance who came to Washington paid their "respects to one whom every body delights to honor." But almost no one did so as quickly, or as sincerely, as Sarah Polk.[35]

The Polks called on Madison as soon as they arrived in Washington for James's inauguration, and let it be known that Dolley had a

standing invitation to all cabinet dinners and "entertainments" held at
the Polk White House. She was a regular guest as well at presidential
outings. Two months after entering office, James and Sarah requested
"Mrs. Madison's company on a visit to Mount Vernon on tomorrow.
Will Mrs. M. take a seat in their carriage? The party will consist of half
a dozen friends."[36]

Even had she been wealthy, instead of nearly destitute after repeatedly paying the debts of a ne'er-do-well son, Dolley Madison would
have been unlikely to dismiss the Polks' hospitality. She became a frequent visitor to the White House, and could depend on James escort-
ing her to the table, in a sign of his particular respect. Previous First
Ladies might have been miffed by this arrangement, but Sarah understood the political importance of ceremony, and followed behind them,
not the least upset.[37]

It was certainly good public relations to pay homage to Madison, but the relationship wasn't only for show. Despite a thirty-five-
year age difference, Madison became First Lady Sarah Polk's closest
female companion in Washington. They made a natural team. Dolley was about the same age as Sarah's mother, and happy to relive her
White House glory days. Dolley, like Sarah, had served for a time as
her husband's private secretary, although in Dolley's case it was long
after James Madison left the White House. Sarah found her a valuable and discreet confidante. The two women exchanged small favors:
Dolley supplied Sarah with her autograph when a Polk acquaintance
expressed interest in a memento from the founding generation, and
Sarah was happy to meet friends and relations of Dolley's who wished
an introduction to the current First Lady. Sarah helped relieve Dolley's
financial distress when she hired Paul Jennings, with Jennings's wages
paid directly to Dolley. When Jennings almost immediately thereafter
left Washington, D.C., for several weeks without leave, Dolley worried that he would lose his position, and she would lose his wages. But
Sarah made no complaint about the absence, or the transaction.[38]

They exchanged gifts as well. Dolley assured Sarah that her "gratitude for" a "magnificent present" from Sarah was "comeensurate with
its size—& my taste." As soon as Dolley was freed from "an acking
head" she would meet her and tell her in person "how highly I estimate the prize from your kindness & how affectionately I am always

yours." Not that Sarah likely needed evidence. Dolley was remarkably affectionate with the younger woman, playfully referring to Sarah in front of other people as "a lover as we all know of the fine Arts & every thing else that is good." She considered Sarah Polk her "sweet friend."[39]

Sarah in turn made her adoration of Madison publicly visible by adopting the older woman's signature headwear, the turban, and by appearing in public with Madison as frequently as possible. Many of these appearances were charitable in nature. As First Lady, Sarah might not make butter, but it was nonetheless the hope of her constituents that she would "feed the poor and clothe the naked," as Leonard Jones of Kentucky had suggested. Four months after inauguration day the two First Ladies were scheduled to meet with "many little children," for which Dolley believed Sarah "entitled to a premium of unlulling breezes for the delight you will occasion."[40]

It has been Mrs. Madison's personal goal for decades to construct a monument blending "stupendousness with elegance, and . . . of such magnitude and beauty as to be an object of pride to the American people." Under Madison's leadership, the nation would honor George Washington with a monument "like him in whose honor it is to be constructed, unparalleled in the world." But political infighting and debt thwarted the project until Sarah Childress Polk became the monument's salvation. With the fund-raising abilities of a popular First Lady behind it, the dream of the great marble obelisk to Washington at last found physical form. President Polk laid the monument's cornerstone in a media event orchestrated by Sarah, designed to link the current president to the father of the country.[41]

Sarah made Dolley's Washington Monument a reality, but what Dolley provided Sarah with was far more valuable. Few obligations for the wife of a Washington politician were more time-consuming than that of "calling" on other women. The practice, a bedrock of English upper-class etiquette, prescribed a series of brief visits during which individuals would leave cards engraved with their names at the homes of those they wished to become acquainted with. Those receiving the cards had three options. They could ignore the overture. They could return the visit, and leave their own card, complete with specific times during which they were willing to receive the caller. Or they could make a personal visit, which was never to last more than fifteen minutes or to diverge from a few set topics. The practice of leaving calling cards was designed to separate desirable from undesirable companions.[42]

In Washington, D.C., calling was a political act. Both women and men established communication, opened up lines of dialogue, and pursed job opportunities through the etiquette of the call. The only person immune from the requirement to return a call was the president.[43]

His wife, however, was not so lucky. Since no one was more in demand than the president's lady, or more liable to ruffle feathers by a gaffe, the pressure of making visits and returning calls was intense. Dolley Madison, who called on every new congressman upon his arrival in Washington, regretted that she had instituted the practice. It became, according to one observer, a "torture, which she felt very severely, but from which, having begun the practice, she never found an opportunity of receding." Louisa Adams described the etiquette of leaving and returning calling cards as a "perpetual slavery to which I seem to be doomed." She marveled that "all the ladies appear to think that they must visit me about once a week so that I have no sooner got through [making return calls] than I am compelled to begin again."[44]

Sarah knew the burdens of Washington etiquette better than most women in her position, and she understood that James could hardly be the independent president he desired without her constant assistance. So she conceived of a radical solution. She would invite teenage nieces to visit for as long as they wished, and leave the work of returning an endless round of social calls to them. Joanna Rucker, Susan Childress Rucker's daughter and Sarah's eldest niece, arrived in 1845 and stayed two years. Sister Jane's daughter Sally Walker kept Joanna company for five months in 1846. Joanna's sister, Sarah Polk Rucker, took Joanna's place in the summer of 1848, along with Virginia Hays, the daughter of James's sister Ophelia. These last two nieces stayed with James and Sarah until the close of the Polk presidential term.[45]

One historian has suggested that Sarah "seemed to relish . . . prolonged visits by nieces—doubtless to compensate for the lack of children of her own." But Sarah had spent two childless decades engrossed in politics, without revealing any need to compensate. Having finally reached the pinnacle of political success, is it likely she would start expressing remorse for the very condition that enabled her to get there? Indeed, Sarah's closest friends recognized that children were peripheral to her world. John Catron, who Sarah admitted was "well acquainted with my tastes," said to her that "you are not the one, Madame, to have the charge of a little child; you, who have always been absorbed in political and social affairs."[46]

Sarah loved her nieces, lavished them with gifts, and was generally indulgent of their whims. They, in turn, adored her. They shared stories with one another about her. They wrote to her for advice. They asked her to send them things. Aunt Sarah was no doubt the most fabulous, cosmopolitan, powerful woman any of them would ever know. The nieces who had the good fortune to visit her in Washington realized how lucky they were. "Aunt Sarah has just left my room she is fat and well," Joanna wrote fondly to her grandmother Elizabeth Childress, a year into the Polk presidency. True, Aunt Sarah's ban on dancing left her niece "more conspicuous than any young lady at a party on account of not dancing, as this is a dancing community." But Joanna otherwise declared her time in the White House "the happiest of my life. . . . My uncle and Aunt have acted the part of parents and I sometimes fear they have been too indulgent," she confessed at the close of her almost two-year stay.[47]

But Sarah also needed them in the White House. She had no time for visiting with ladies. So when women called on her, they were frequently met by "two or three sallow Tennessee nieces." And it was virtually always Joanna Rucker, or Sally, or Virginia, or Sarah Polk Rucker who returned their visit in Sarah's stead. "I sometimes get homesick," Joanna wrote a cousin back in Tennessee in the fall of 1845, "but I have not had much time to remain so long. I am kept busy returning calls as Aunt Sarah never visits." Oftentimes Joanna spent the entire afternoon returning "visits for the house as well as those made on ourselves." She left the house at noon and did not expect to get home before dinner.[48]

While this practice was certainly better than leaving a social debt unpaid, no one believed the First Lady's niece was her legitimate social surrogate. The ladies of Washington turned to Dolley for vindication. They asked her, "Now Mrs. Madison, we leave it to you; don't you think so young a lady as Mrs. Polk ought to return visits, and come to see us as she used to do" when James was in Congress? "Did you not return calls and make visits when you were in the White House"? But Dolley's allegiance to Sarah trumped the rules of etiquette. "Yes, my children, I did," she told them. "But one parlor would then contain all who came to my receptions. . . . Now there are so many people in the city that is an impossibility to return the calls that are made on the President's household."[49]

SARAH MADE GOOD USE of the time that might have gone to calls as she resumed her accustomed role as James's unofficial communications director and secretary. Before entering office, James had hired Sister Jane's twenty-nine-year-old son, Knox Walker, as his personal secretary: Knox held this post for all four years of the presidency. James paid Knox out of his own pocket, clerical help being yet another unreimbursed expense of the presidency. He also paid for the upkeep, including food, for Knox's wife, Augusta, the two children who moved with them into the White House, and the two additional children Augusta gave birth to while Polk was in office. They were a happy addition to White House family life. Sarah cared enough about the family to make a christening gown, using extraordinarily fine lace, for one of the new babies.[50]

Knox had a nice hand, but his work ethic left something to be desired, and far too often his absences left James responsible for "having to perform the duties of secretary as well as President." Sarah's experience makes clear just how difficult it was to meet James's standards. The president was tireless, incredibly exacting, and rarely if ever offered thanks. When Knox left town on a "thoughtless & inexcusable" pleasure trip to Annapolis, James vented to his diary. "In truth he is too fond of spending his time in fashionable & light society, and does not give that close & systematic attention to business which is necessary to give himself reputation and high standing in the estimation of the more solid & better part of the community. This I have observed for some months with great regret."[51]

So it is not surprising that, as with the Tennessee gubernatorial campaigns, it was Sarah and not Knox whom James preferred to turn to for assistance. When the Polks moved into the White House they set up a shared office in the upstairs oval room, in the family quarters. After the business of the soirees and dinners concluded, they transitioned to the quieter but no less taxing labors of the office. Sarah worked her way through the day's newspapers, marking the articles James needed to read, while James answered correspondence and reviewed the productions of secretaries, clerks, and diplomats.[52]

The work, for both of them, was relentless. Andrew Jackson established the precedent of replacing officeholders at the start of a new presidency. The spoils system provided a marvelous way to reward the party faithful, but left a new president inundated with requests for employment. Supplicants appeared at the White House by the dozens, confident that as American citizens they had a right to walk into the White House, the "people's house," and ask the people's president directly for a job. And remarkably enough, most of them were able to do exactly that. During the first months of his presidency, James spent most of the day turning away job seekers.

Sarah ran interference in the best way she could, greeting visitors at the base of the grand staircase, listening to their concerns, and, when possible, informing them that the president was not available. Those who did not appear in person sent plaintive inquiries by mail. They wrote to James, of course, in great numbers. But they also wrote to Sarah. John Grigg, a former chaplain of the navy, came directly to the White House to ask for a job, but after being introduced to Sarah felt it was "too delicate" a matter to ask her for another chaplaincy in front of the other visitors to the White House. So he wrote her to ask in a letter.[53]

The men who wrote Sarah inevitably excused their appeal on the grounds of shared Christianity. Out-of-work "faithful" Christians with large families claimed that their Democratic beliefs prevented them from gaining employment.[54] A fellow Presbyterian involved in building a new church hoped for "the collectorship of Washington City, worth 7 or 800 dollars per Annum" for himself or his son. An employee of the New York customhouse worried about being replaced "felt almost tempted to tear up" his letter to the First Lady, because he was "fearful you might find it intrusive, but remembering that we are bound by the same faith & united in the same communion, I am encouraged to address you." They were generally wise enough to assert their Democratic bona fides as well. A candidate for washing the White House linens was "a good Democrat, which is the best recommendation any one can possess."[55]

Many more letters came from women. Some requested "charity" from Sarah, for a position in "her" sphere. Widowed and deserted women hoped to become seamstresses or dressmakers in order to support themselves. Some wrote simply asking for money. But women wrote in greater numbers for jobs for their husbands, brothers, and sons. They addressed Sarah, in many cases, because they believed that an appeal by a woman was less likely to transcend "female delicacy or discretion" when addressed to the First Lady than to her husband. Mary Houston of Indiana appealed to "those fine feelings which can alone be found in the female heart," and lobbied for a position for her husband without his knowledge, "because his proud spirit could ill brook" it. It's unclear if she knew how much Sarah valued her own education when she added that a clerkship would not only repay her husband's devotion to the Indiana Democratic Party, but also put it in her "power to give an only Daughter the parents best blessing; a good education."[56]

Mary Throckmorton addressed the First Lady as "My dear Mrs. Polk," but seemed to conflate the president and his wife. "I apply to you my dear friend feeling confident our dear President will provide for us," she wrote. The widowed C. C. came to the White House hoping to secure a naval position for her son. She listened "with much pleasure" to Sarah's "just and liberal comments upon patronage" and "female influence," but Sarah turned her away before she could speak to the president in person due to "arrangements necessary to" James's "comfort and recreation." Writing directly to Sarah, she asked "too whom can a female go with so much propriety, as to a Wife for interception with her husband"?[57]

Sylvia Glover of Roxbury, Connecticut, excused her imposition on the grounds of democracy. It was "the freedom which our political institutions give to all" that explained why a "poor cottage girl" felt free to write to the First Lady. Caroline Brewerton dismissed her "overstep" when she wrote Sarah to gain admission to West Point for her son. She recognized that letters of appeal were a "social privilege of friendship," but argued, rather eloquently, that the president and

First Lady were, by virtue of their position, friends of the people. "The characters of the Rulers of our land, and of those closely connected to them, soon become the property of the nation," she wrote. The public nature of Sarah's position allowed Caroline Brewerton not only to imagine herself friends with Sarah, but to treat her as such.[58]

What many of these letters made clear was that Americans were suffering, and they believed the Polks could help them. Although the economy had supposedly fully recovered from the Panic of 1837 by the time James took office, there were a great many men, still out of work, who would be hard pressed to believe it. Sarah's charitable contributions, including headlining a "Ball for the Benefit of the Poor" at Carusi's Hall and donating liberally to religious organizations, were widely praised. But the public imagined she might do more, for the nation, but also, perhaps, for individuals.[59]

HAD SARAH BEEN IGNORANT of the sufferings of women and families before entering office, she could hardly remain so after reading the day's mail. Few of the letters she received were more moving than the neatly penned three-page appeal from E. Ellicott, of Lewistown, Pennsylvania. Her husband, Lewistown's postmaster, was a "good man," a member of the Methodist Church, and a Democrat, but in danger of losing his position to two "warm politicians, with warm adherents," one of whom was rich, the other without a family to support, and neither of whom "stand high, in point of Christian character." Her family, by contrast, was large, poor, and totally dependent on income derived from her husband's position as postmaster. Ellicott clearly had wavered over whether to write Sarah, adding an addendum that "if you are not inclined to favor my suit I pray you . . . let not this attempt to serve my poor husband be injurious to his interests." But she also suspected that the "trials and difficulties of a particular nature" she faced entitled her to Sarah's sympathy, as well as "the sympathy, of every female, that can feel."

I have had fourteen children—have been nursing thirty years—as I still have a babe a few months old—and I am now forty seven—with a family of nine children still to provide for daily—surely dear

lady I may claim your sympathy and friendship. Every woman preserves influence in her own sphere, and as the great God, in his infi-
nite wisdom, has in his providence, located you to your present high
station—no doubt it is, that you may have it in your favor to do the
most good.

Her husband had no idea she had written to the White House. "He
would think it a vain and romantic effort, but lady I am not romantic,"
she assured Sarah. "I have seen to much of the sober realities of life to
be so." Like many women, including Jane Walker, E. Ellicott had been
blessed with more children than she could handle. But Jane was rich,
and E. Ellicott destitute, and that made all the difference. Virtuous,
hardworking Americans without "special" connections: these were the
people that the Democratic Party claimed to represent and fight for.[60]

Both the men and the women who wrote to Sarah seemed to assume
that she either had the power to employ help herself or that she had
"influence" enough over James to secure employment for the virtuous.
John Childress, who never underestimated his sister's power (in 1839
he had suggested that she plant a story in a Democratic paper about a
corrupt Whig politician), wrote her requesting a clerkship for a party
stalwart from Murfreesboro. He had no doubt that she could procure
the position, and wrote that "although it may be considered as [out-
side] the range of your duties, I think you can without much impropriety interfere in his behalf with the head of some of the Departments,
for so small a favor."[61]

There's a good deal of evidence that office seekers were correct
about Sarah's power. James gave Sarah's cousin Thomas a place in the
Mobile customhouse, noting in his letter to Thomas that the appointment was "most gratifying" to Sarah. After Sarah lobbied for a position for the husband of a good friend, James complied, adding in his
letter to the lucky recipient that he had "informed Mrs. Polk of the
assignment, who is much delighted with it." Nor was Sarah's power to
influence appointments limited to the president. She wrote Secretary
of the Navy George Bancroft to request the appointment of a friend's
son as midshipman. Bancroft made the appointment, and did so, he
told her, with "pleasure."[62]

———

First Lady Sarah Polk's calling card. Sarah was able to serve as the political partner of her husband because her nieces assumed responsibility for the elaborate and time-consuming etiquette of "calling" on friends and acquaintances. Sarah's nieces left her card at the homes of women who had "called" on her and expected a visit in return. *Courtesy of the James K. Polk Memorial Association, Columbia, Tennessee.*

As a teenager, Sarah was so taken by the military march "Hail to the Chief" that she copied the music into her Salem Academy copybook. *"Hail to the Chief," from Sarah Childress's Salem Academy copybook, ca. 1818. Courtesy of the James K. Polk Memorial Association, Columbia, Tennessee.*

The earliest known photograph of the White House, taken during the Polk presidency. *Library of Congress Prints and Photographs Division.*

Sarah's favorite cameo pin of her husband. *Courtesy of the James K. Polk Memorial Association, Columbia, Tennessee. Photograph by Lisa Childs.*

Mathew Brady retouched his 1849 presidential portrait of James in order to make the president look softer. *Library of Congress Prints and Photographs Division.*

The White House family in 1848. President and Mrs. James K. Polk with, from left, Secretary of State James Buchanan, Harriett Lane, Sarah Polk Rucker, Cave Johnson, John Y. Mason, Dolley Madison, and Mrs. Cave Johnson. *Courtesy of the George Eastman Museum.*

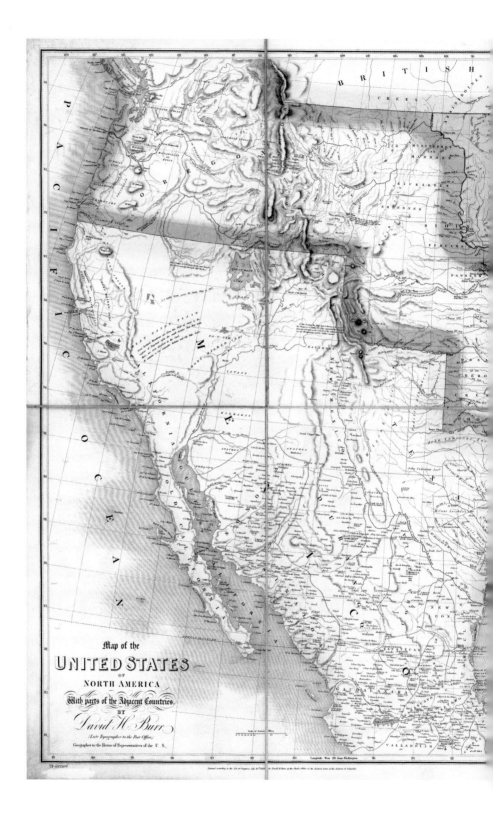

Map of the
UNITED STATES
OF
NORTH AMERICA
With parts of the Adjacent Countries.
BY
David H. Burr
(Late Topographer to the Post Office;)
Geographer to the House of Representatives of the U.S.

The United States as it appeared prior to the Polk presidency. *1839 Map of the United States of North America with parts of the adjacent countries. David H. Burr,* The American Atlas *(London: J. Arrowsmith, 1839). Library of Congress Geography and Map Division.*

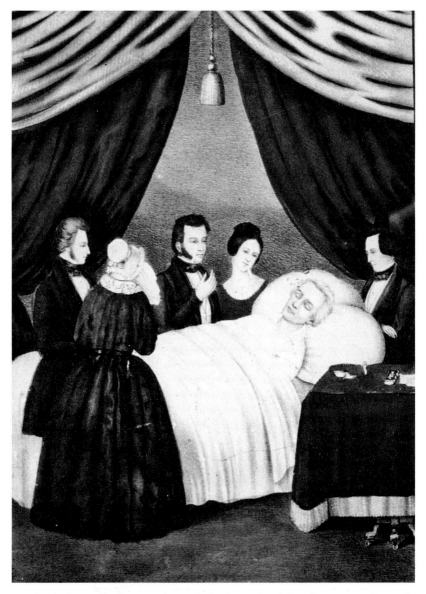

A clearly fictionalized image of James's death, produced for sale in 1849. *Library of Congress Prints and Photographs Division.*

Above: Polk Place, with James's tomb in the foreground. *Courtesy of the James K. Polk Memorial Association, Columbia, Tennessee.*

Right: Portrait of Hernán Cortés looted from Mexico and presented to Sarah by General William Worth, 1849. *Courtesy of the James K. Polk Memorial Association, Columbia, Tennessee. Photograph by Lisa Childs.*

Sallie Jetton and Sarah Polk at Polk Place not long after Sallie's arrival. *Courtesy of the James K. Polk Memorial Association, Columbia, Tennessee.*

DURING THE FIRST YEAR of the Polk presidency, Sarah established a grueling social schedule designed to advance James's agenda, employed resident nieces and the social authority of Dolley Madison to free herself from the tyranny of social calls, helped James negotiate the demands of office seekers, and successfully sidestepped the labor of properly redecorating the White House in a manner that supported the Democratic values of thrift and simplicity. She faced one final challenge in 1845: establishing a public image as the female incarnation of Jacksonian principles, despite having had an upbringing, education, and marriage that were anything but common.

Late in her life, Sarah Polk claimed never to have known what it was like to go without beautiful things. From her "earliest recollection she had been dressed in silks and satins of delicate texture, in beautiful designs and colors." Her many years in Washington, where social women were expected to be properly turned out for every occasion, had done nothing to tame her love of shopping. "I imagine you are all getting ready for Congress," an envious Tennessee relative wrote her. "How many bonnets, dresses, & etc. are made and ordered for Congress"? Another correctly took it "for granted that you like to hear about the fashions, tis said to be a natural failing of our sex."[63]

As a representative of the common man, and common woman, Sarah could hardly dress like an aristocrat, though as a First Lady she couldn't risk being seen as common. In keeping with her Democratic persona, she made sure that her dress was always "simple, chaste and elegant." Noted a British visitor to the White House, "She has excellent taste in dress, and both in the morning and the evening preserves the subdued but elegant costume which characterizes the Lady."[64] Another described her as "very handsome, very dignified," and "quietly gracious."[65]

But few fashion statements are as exacting as to be always "modest, yet commanding in appearance," and in walking this line Sarah spent outrageous sums on her clothing.[66] She made regular purchases from a variety of merchants, a few for single items, like the $30 black cloth coat ($840 today) she purchased in August 1845, or the two pairs of boots she bought from separate shoemakers in October 1845 (one with cork soles, one without). Other merchants took elaborate orders from Mrs. Polk. Clagett and Company, who billed by the month, provided a regular supply of white kid gloves and new scarves (one described as "silver blonde"). In six months Clagett billed her $122 ($3,416 today). James was also well turned out. Tucker and Sons, tailors, billed him $100 for a black French cloth and doeskin coat, a satin vest, and two $25 beaver hats with cases.

The president's hats may have been of the finest quality, but both their cost and their magnificence were dwarfed by the extravagant fabric Sarah regularly purchased for her gowns. She loved rich colors: royal blue, emerald green, and claret. She spent $25 for fourteen yards of "changeable" Chinese silk in February 1845, $24 for nineteen yards of less expensive changeable silk, and $22 for fifteen yards of black lace in September 1845. In December 1845 alone, she spent $41 for fifteen yards of velvet, $25 for embroidered silk, $22 on ten yards of plain silk, another $20 for two headdresses, a tassel, a satin scarf, and a very expensive feather ($4.50). That same month she paid her free black maid and seamstress, Teresa, $22 to convert those precious fabrics into dresses and capes with simple, elegant cuts that impressed wealthy and discerning women as "handsome and tastefull." During a single month, in which the White House heating bill came to less than $6, and the two gallons of oysters they served the day after Christmas cost only $3, Sarah Polk spent $132 (the equivalent of $3,700 today) on her personal wardrobe.[67]

Her tastes were decidedly European. In the summer of 1847 she spent nearly $450 ($12,600 today) on one order of dresses from Paris, made-to-order extravagances by one of the best-known couturieres of the day, while also keeping Teresa busy making more dresses. News that Sarah had "sent to Paris for your wardrobe" made it all the way back to Tennessee. She ordered hats from the purveyor to the queen of France, and had American diplomats in Europe send her items from Paris, billed to James.[68]

Monday was shopping day, the day that, as Sarah jokingly referred to it, her "purse" took "the consumption." She, Teresa, and any young female relatives in residence took a tour of Washington's fashionable specialty stores, lingering over the cashmere and silks at Pennsylvania Avenue's Walter Harper & Co. "The Spring fashions are beginning to be the topic with the ladies, and the Avenue is filled with ladies in their new hats and robes," her niece wrote after one outing. Things Sarah wanted but could not find in Washington, she asked William Corcoran, a Washington banker and art collector who was a close Polk family friend, to buy for her in New York City. "He is very rich," Sarah's niece wrote, "has all of Uncle Sam's money." A wealthy Polk sister-in-law in New York supplemented Corcoran's purchases. They were reimbursed for their purchases.[69]

Sarah's most obvious fashion concession to Democratic simplicity was her jewelry. In the place of gems, which were considered too ostentatious and aristocratic for the First Lady of the world's great democracy, Sarah wore cameos and jewelry of coral and paste, "giant stone breastpins," in the opinion of those with more refined tastes. And she made sure her nieces were adorned likewise. She wound long strings of cut jet around the waist of her dress and around her neck. Julia Tyler loved showing off her "full set of diamonds" in the evening, but was outshone by the wife of the Russian minister, a frequent dinner guest at the Polk White House, who sported "fifty-thousand dollars worth of diamonds . . . head-dress and necklace and bracelets of immense magnitude."[70]

Sarah's favorite piece of jewelry couldn't be more different. At public occasions she favored a cameo portrait of her husband. James had the piece made by a New York jeweler for $12. Wearing that cameo allowed Sarah to demonstrate her fidelity to both her husband and to the country he led. Long before the advent of the campaign button, Sarah found the opportunity to make personal decoration a political statement.[71]

Sarah found other opportunities to promote the values of her party and establish her Democratic credentials. She made a public effort to acknowledge common citizens at the weekly receptions she opened to the public, particularly if they were elderly. On the Fourth of July 1846, she approached an "old man, supported by a long cane, and dressed in humble garb." After speaking to him with her trademark "kindly sympathy," she directed that the "venerable visitor should be treated with special respect." She also requested that the White House gardener stop cutting roses for her because "the public did not have the privilege of plucking the flowers" and "I did not desire this distinction to be made between myself and others."[72]

Taken as a whole, Sarah's attempts to mold both White House entertaining and her public image to conform with the ideals of Jacksonian democracy were remarkably successful. "We have seen few women that have developed more of the genuine republican characteristics of the American lady," wrote one visitor. "She has her admirers not only in the highest, but in the humblest walks of life. The poor know her for her benevolence; the rich for the plainness of her equipage, the church for her consistency; the unfortunate for her charities."[73]

And the public loved her. Admirers sent her oranges from Florida and grapes from the Cape Fear River. An Ohio man wrote the president in order to learn the First Lady's "Christian" name, "as I have a daughter whom I wish to name after her." The *Nashville Union* noted that although politicians differed about the "merit of Mr. Polk's administration, there can be no difference as respects that of his lady, in her department of the Presidential mansion." John Catron agreed. "All sides seem to vie in vaunting you," he wrote a few months after they entered office. "If this keeps on through the four years, [it] will stilt you up to so giddy a height that you may incure more danger in getting down than in climbing up." Three months after the Polks entered office, "a female in the Lunatic Asylum on Blackwell's Island" made the news with a particular form of flattery. She "fancies herself Mrs. James K. Polk. She has erected herself a throne, seated upon which she graciously receives visitors, when assured they do not seek for office."[74]

This is not to say that everyone approved of Sarah's Democratic pretensions, or the elevated tenor of her gatherings. Some in Washington missed the wild entertainments of the Tyler presidency, the rum punches, dancing, and parties that left the White House worse for wear. Less than a year into her retirement, Julia Tyler noted, with ill-disguised pleasure, "I don't see or hear that Mrs. Polk is making any sensation in Washington." But Julia and Sarah had very different understandings of sensation. Author Lydia Sigourney, who dined with the Polks at the White House, had a good sense of Sarah's ambition. "Intelligent, refined, unaffected, affable, courteous, and above all, pious," she wrote admiringly, "thou art not for the fashions of these times."[75]

Sarah's success creating a unique and appealing public persona was not her only innovation as First Lady. Political salons, whether in Paris or Washington, were defined by elevated conversation between men and women. But increasingly in the middle decades of the nineteenth century, wealthy Anglo-Americans declared that men and women should have space apart after dinner, so that women would not be bothered with cigar smoke, brandy drinking, or the coarse language that might ensue as a result of the cigars and brandy. A safe space for women to gather offered a physical manifestation of the ideal of separate spheres, and in time became one of the hallmarks of Victorian socializing. Sarah was the first to establish such a space for White House dinner guests, in the Red Room. She outfitted it with a "marvelous" piano built expressly for the room. Sarah did not herself play the instrument. She had every intention of taking lessons when she and James first moved to Washington in the 1820s, but given the demands of her social schedule, she never seemed to find the time. Guests said that she liked to invite visitors to gather around the piano and sing Methodist hymns.[76]

This was highly decorous of the First Lady. But according to at least one report, Sarah was likely to leave her female guests to their own devices and to disappear into the parlor. "Knowing much of political affairs she found pleasure in the society of gentlemen." And preferring to converse with men, "she was always in the parlor with Mr. Polk." This was not the only time Sarah Childress Polk would pay homage to female difference while flouting that difference herself. With her political salon and Democratic public persona established, Mrs. Presidentess turned her attention to matters that were better accomplished in the parlor with Mr. Polk than in the room with the piano.[77]

6

I . . . cannot other than discern the face of the times, for God writes them in legible characters to be read and known by all men, that is, the extension of our wide spreading Empire.

—JOHN REES TO SARAH CHILDRESS POLK, May 28, 1845

JAMES K. POLK rode to office on a Texas platform, but his inaugural address looked well beyond the Lone Star State. A Polk administration would wrest the Oregon Country from joint control with Britain—"Fifty-Four Forty or Fight!" as their enthusiastic northern supporters cried—and deliver Mexican land to hardworking American settlers who would put the land to use the way God intended: by farming and developing it. "Our title to the country of Oregon is clear and unquestionable" he asserted, and he lyrically extolled the millions of pioneers who "have filled the eastern valley of the Mississippi, adventurously ascended the Missouri to its headsprings, and are already engaged in establishing the blessings of self-government in valleys of which the rivers flow to the Pacific." God ordained that the magnificent experiment of democratic governance and free enterprise known as the United States would spread its blessings across the continent. This was America's Manifest Destiny, and James K. Polk was its apostle.[1]

So what did that make Sarah? After two decades assisting her husband with lobbying, campaigns, and the press, she had become a master of the family business of politics. A Democrat since childhood, she asserted that American principles were driving the "marvelous growth of our country . . . holding forth the radiant light of a new era." Her faith that America's "mighty genius is building home of peace and content for the poor and oppressed of every land" never wavered. She was every bit as much of a true believer in Manifest Destiny as her husband.[2]

But she was also a woman, in a period when middle-class Americans promoted the idea that there were two spheres of influence. It's true that from the establishment of Washington, D.C., women were an active presence in public, that their actions had both legitimated national politics and enabled the functioning of party politics. It's also true that by the 1840s the Whig Party embraced its female partisans, and female Democrats were avid supporters of their own party and its platform of territorial expansion. But most educated men and women nonetheless accepted that the natural terrain of women was the domestic sphere.

The definition of the "domestic" could be, and was, interpreted flexibly. Female reformers in the North used their authority over domestic matters to justify lobbying for social reform—from public education, to helping the poor, to abolishing slavery. James was open about the fact that Sarah defined the boundaries of the domestic sphere as she chose. But if there was any division between the domestic realm and the realm of men, surely the domestic was constrained by the boundaries of the nation. It could not, by definition, include the foreign.

Or maybe it could. The former consul to Trinidad and Cuba, Edmund C. Watmough of Philadelphia, sent Sarah a copy of his *Scribblings and Sketches: Diplomatic, Piscatory, and Oceanic* not long after the election, because "the President's Lady should be familiar with *Diplomacy,* some of the forms and principles of that abstruse science." Sarah no doubt found Watmough's volume, dedicated to the emperor of China, a bit odd. In addition to a curious collection of diplomatic correspondence both serious and humorous, the bulk of the volume alternated between engaging descriptions of foreign lands visited by the author and an argument in favor of increasing the size of the navy, grounded in accounts of significant naval battles.[3]

But she would not have missed the pro-expansion message underlying the whole, which justified female engagement with diplomacy:

that territorial expansion was God's work. "Send your unbeliever out of your crowded cities into God's holy temples upon the mountain's side or teeming valley . . . and he will bow down . . . humbled in spirit and elevated in sentiment," Watmough declared. And God's work was women's work. Catharine Beecher, one of the era's leading reformers, declared in her 1841 *Treatise on Domestic Economy* that God designed that America "shall go forth as the cynosure of nations, to guide them to the light," a "great moral enterprise" that would be "enacted by American women."[4]

Nor was Beecher the only popular writer to suggest that women who chose to go forth and "civilize" foreign lands were especially patriotic. The ability of women to domesticate the wilderness was celebrated on every American frontier, from the Southwest to the Great Lakes. In Florida, the need for the army to protect female settlers became a prime justification for violence against the Seminoles, and helped drag out the Second Seminole War for six long years. Women provided a convenient cover story that Manifest Destiny was in fact a religious mission.[5]

Now there was a committed expansionist in the White House, and by his side a passionate and powerful Christian woman, one who in her first year in office had gained the love and trust of the public as a pious, down-to-earth Democrat, while reconfiguring the work of the First Lady in a radically new manner. By freeing herself of the tedium of returning calls, she gained the time to share in her husband's work. It was her labor, paradoxically, that enabled James to claim independence from clique or faction and to become "himself, president." Her days were spent assisting him with correspondence and job seekers, and limiting access to him in the White House. Most of her evenings consisted of entertainment for political purposes. And her nights included working with her husband in their shared office.

For Catharine Beecher, who was traveling through the Northeast championing "a special role for women" in a series of well-attended speaking tours, Sarah's elevation appeared a remarkable opportunity to expand the sphere of female influence, both on the frontier and throughout society. "It is a matter of great satisfaction," she wrote Sarah in September 1845, "that the distinguished lady whom Providence has placed at the head of our nation & sex, is one who can sympathise with us, not only in benevolent aspirations, but in the dear & sacred hopes that unite the children of our common Saviour."[6]

Beecher hoped to train fifty thousand women as teachers, many to be sent out to the frontier as agents of civilization. Education in the West was something of an obsession with the Beecher family. From their home in Cincinnati, Catharine's abolitionist sister Harriet Beecher Stowe and her professor husband, Calvin, advocated for improvement in educational opportunities in the nation's western states and territories. Their father, one of the nation's most prominent ministers, Lyman Beecher, had spent over a decade arguing in favor of the Protestant reformation of American lands previously belonging to Catholics and heathens. In 1835, Reverend Beecher declared that it was "plain that the religious and political destiny of our nation is to be decided in the West. There is the territory, and there soon will be the population, the wealth, and the political power." It was "equally clear, that the conflict which is to decide the destiny of the West, will be a conflict of institutions for the education of her sons, for purposes of superstition, or evangelical light; of despotism, or liberty." For many Protestant Americans, Manifest Destiny was also a religious war between righteous Protestants and Papist Catholics.[7]

Lyman Beecher had visited with Sarah when she was last in Washington in the 1830s, in order to gain support for his efforts to spread Protestantism in the West. Sarah, in her familiar role as James's assistant, asked him to "address a communication" to her "on topics on which he wished to consult" James.[8]

But Catharine presented her plan to the First Lady not on behalf of her father, and not for James to consider. This was a communication between two women, on a subject of "deep interest & anxious reflection" to both of them. And it was a matter that Beecher believed to be above party. Catharine Beecher was every bit the Whig, while Sarah was a Democrat. And yet she reached out to the First Lady not as a partisan, but as a woman with a shared interest in Christianizing and civilizing the frontier. Educating women as teachers would not only bring light to the "darkness" of the frontier, she told Sarah, but fight poverty by providing the thousands of poor women in America's cities a means of supporting themselves.

And it might do more. "I am not without hope," Catharine wrote, "that this enterprise, if it succeeds, will benefit, not only the poor & oppressed of our sex, but contribute to the usefulness & happiness of many, who amid elegant luxuries & ease, are yearning for some mode of spending their time according to the spirit & example of our lord and savior." Despite the bias against their "sex," Beecher was convinced that "if ladies will work as they may work in this effort, it will soon be conceded, that a woman of energy and developed talent, can do as much as a man." She included with her letter a copy of her most recent book, *The Duty of American Women to Their Country.* The header of each page posed a dare to readers, impossible to ignore: "AMERICAN WOMEN! WILL YOU SAVE YOUR COUNTRY?" Beecher's message, to both the First Lady and to readers, was clear: *"It is in the power of American women to save their country."* Sarah was never one to back down from a challenge.[9]

THE PRESIDENT AND FIRST LADY could, quite literally, see the writing on the wall. When Sarah and James entered the White House they found a map of North America hanging in the president's office, a remnant of either Jackson's or Van Buren's years in office. It was a grand map, printed on paper sections that had then been glued together like a puzzle on a linen backing. A ten-year-old map was bound to be out of date. It would likely have featured the Erie Canal, which connected the Great Lakes and surrounding farmland to New York City, but not the railroads that facilitated trade and communication in the Northeast and the Mid-Atlantic region, or the new cities of the Midwest, cities created by the new transportation network. Nor would it have revealed the massive growth of the metropolises of the eastern seaboard from European immigration and the internal flow of rural New Englanders from farms to cities. But the eastern half of the map was nonetheless a hive of activity, dotted with the familiar states, cities, towns, and ports of the long-settled United States.

The map's western half, however, was a relative void, an open expanse of blank paper seemingly waiting to be inscribed. The uncharted territory west of the Mississippi failed to capture the extent of Indian power in the region, or to demarcate the domains of non-sedentary peoples like the Comanches, who exacted tribute over vast expanses and inhibited settlement by Mexicans in land that according to European law belonged to Mexico. Meanwhile, joint control by the British and Americans of the land known as the Oregon Country since 1818 lent the northwestern corner of the map a displeasing ambiguity.[10]

There was a great deal for James and Sarah to contemplate about this map. Lands to the west of Texas offered great promise to slave-holders like themselves looking to grow rich from cotton production. The Mississippi cotton plantation James purchased in 1834 had thus far failed to turn a profit, but he was determined that it would. Whether or not he realized that the expansion of slave territory would dramatically increase the value of his slaves, he knew the value to planters of fertile land in slave territory.

James's interest in expansion was not entirely driven by self-interest. The Oregon Country was just as alluring to northerners as Texas had been to southerners. James had implicitly promised his supporters in the North that he would take the entirety of the Oregon Country from Great Britain, including British Columbia, even if it required war, and turn that territory into free states. For a true territorial expansionist, any blank territory on a map of North America presented a call for action.

That spring Sarah received two letters that offered dueling perspectives on the First Lady's role in the nation's Manifest Destiny. Alex Jones, a leading Democratic journalist and admirer of Sarah's, sent her an editorial he published at the end of March 1845 in the *New York Journal of Commerce*, titled "The Fruits of Peace and of War." Sarah, as a Christian woman, was expected to agree with Jones's sentiment. "Blessed are the Peace Makers: There is not a declaration in Holy Writ which is more emphatically true, even in a temporal sense. . . . Let the world keep at peace for thirty or forty years more." But John Rees, a pious New York shipmaster, assured Sarah two months later that "I know something of my bible," and the holy book left no doubt about America's Manifest Destiny. Rees told Sarah that he could clearly "discern the face of the times, for God writes them in legible characters to be read and known by all men, that is, the extension of our wide spreading Empire."[11]

As a woman and a Christian, Sarah's manifest role was as peace-maker. But if God, quite legibly, called for the expansion of the United

States, and she knew the value of the West—to the poor, to women, and to the nation's security—who was she to reject the possibility that war might bring on a greater, lasting peace?

This issue was far from abstract on the Texas border in the spring of 1845. Texians actively courted Sarah even before inauguration day. When John Price of Galveston hoped to start a Democratic "paper of the right stamp" in the Republic of Texas, he wrote to Sarah, promising that his paper "shall be a perfect skinning machine!" It would also contain "a separate Department of vary Exquisite things served up in Oriental Style for their Ladys particularly—in which they will find some & perhaps many things on:

> Texas bays and Texas flowers!
> And Texas in her own rest hours.
> Together with the reasons why
> Her star shined yellow amidst the skies.

He asked Sarah to tell "the Col" "not to forget Galveston!"[12]

Although Congress had invited Texas to join the Union before James was inaugurated, matters on the southern border degenerated during the spring and summer of 1845. Mexico never accepted Texas's independence or its territorial claims. Texians claimed a boundary at the Rio Grande, although the historical boundary of Mexican Tejas ran 150 miles to the north, at the Nueces River. When the Lone Star Republic accepted the U.S. offer of annexation, on the Fourth of July 1845, Mexicans called for war. James ordered the navy to assemble in the Gulf of Mexico, and directed the commander of the Pacific flotilla to seize San Francisco should war break out. In June 1845, he directed Major General Zachary Taylor, commander of troops in the Southwest, to march his four thousand soldiers to Corpus Christi, on the northern edge of the disputed territory, and to await further orders. When the two new Texas senators arrived in Washington in April 1846, Sarah had them to the White House for dinner and invited Sam Houston to tell "something of his battles in Texas."[13]

In the meantime, James had to deal with Oregon. Thousands of American settlers had made the arduous trek by covered wagon to farm its fertile soils, and they were anxious to see British claims to the region extinguished. But Britain's navy was the most powerful in the world, and its claims to the region equally formidable. Northwestern Democrats believed that all of Oregon, including British Columbia, rightfully belonged to the United States. Congressmen attacked Britain, and called for war if it did not acknowledge U.S. rights in the region. It was a delicate situation. The United States could hardly fight two wars at once, and yet only months after entering office, James faced the possibility of exactly that.[14]

At the end of September, John Catron wrote Sarah a long letter about the current political situation. Whig calls to step down from potential wars with both Britain and Mexico were, in his view, politically suicidal. It was a "singular truth," he noted, that the people "of the East" knew almost nothing about the people "of the West"—that they "suppose us a wild horde" and that "the mass is ignorant altogether of political matters, and follows leaders, merely. . . . How gross this error is, you & I equally well know." Westerners were thrilled by Polk's martial attitude, by "the energy and strength displayed . . . regardless of party trammels, as a decided exhibition of national will & national power." At this point, nothing less than a "gross blunder on the part of the administration" could revive the Whig Party.

While "the pervading idea of the West" was "not a wish to whip or bully Mexico," Catron was quite sure that should Mexico's army "cross the Rio Grande . . . it would hardly be possible to save . . . the provinces next [to] that river. The rush then to the border would be like pigeons to the roost. Called or un-called, our young men would go in thousands, armed . . . well enough to sweep the poor Mexican Indians like a prairie fire through dead grass." With an utterly insincere nod to the value of peace, Catron added, "Such an unmooring of our war loving and restless population is to be feared, and I am happy that the Prsdt. has taken the very best course to avoid it." His message was clear: for Polk to win the affections of the West, to gain Mexican territory without directly invading Mexico, and to prostrate the Whig Party once and for all, all he needed to do was order Taylor's forces to the Rio Grande, and then either wait for or incite an international incident.[15]

CATRON HAD WRITTEN JAMES in a similar vein over a month earlier. But it wasn't until Sarah received her letter that James bothered to
respond. They must have discussed the letter, most likely late at night
in their shared office. "We will not commit an act of aggression unless
Mexico should strike the first blow, and in that event we will go on the
offensive & make a short war of it," he wrote. And then matters moved
quickly. About two weeks after Sarah received Catron's letter, William Marcy, the secretary of war, directed Taylor to move "as close as
circumstances will permit" to the Rio Grande. Less than a week after
the cabinet agreed on "concentrating our naval forces at Vera Cruz"
in view of "the probability of a revolution" in Mexico, Sarah hosted a
dinner for thirty to forty members of Congress where she was the only
woman present.[16]

It was easy to see where matters were heading, particularly among
men who looked for honor in a war with Mexico. John Catron and
Lyman Beecher weren't the only men to turn to Sarah when they
wanted to influence the course of Manifest Destiny. An 1846 New
Year's present from the Polks to their neighbors in Columbia, Gideon
and Mary Martin Pillow, was acknowledged by a thank-you note written by Gideon rather than Mary. Admitting that wives were usually
accorded the job of writing thank-you notes, Pillow explained, "In a
contest for the honors," Mary "yielded to her husband's pleasure." He
had "long sought an excuse to address" Sarah, and now that he had
one, he wasn't going to let it pass. "I have seen so many handsome
things said about you" in the newspapers, he wrote, "that I would
expect you had become somewhat vain, did I not know that these were
the natural fruits of the head and heart that I always told you were
intended to adorn the White House."

Pillow was full of flattery. "I think the President had better look out,
else he may be supplanted in the affections of the American Free-men,
and may have opposition from a quarter he little expects it." Then he
got down to business. All "eyes are turned to the Foreign intelligence
as indicating the prospect of peace or war. We all prefer peace, but if
we cannot have an honorable peace instead the surrender of our rights,
let war come, and in such a context, the energies of the nation, almost
to a man, may be demanded in defense of the country." Pillow boasted
of no extraordinary intuition, but he was convinced that James was

"destined, under Providence, to . . . march . . . this nation to future greatness," he told Sarah.[17]

Pillow didn't have to tell Sarah that he was anxious for a military commission. She understood clearly. Nor did he have to wait long to get it. James had just enough time to resolve the Oregon situation before Mexican soldiers crossed the Rio Grande. In a masterstroke of diplomacy and domestic politics, Polk appeased northern expansionists by publicly claiming that Oregon belonged to the United States and asking Congress to terminate the joint occupation, while at the same time secretly inviting compromise from London. In late April 1846, Congress passed a joint resolution to end the joint occupation of Oregon with Britain, and invited the two countries to settle the matter amicably. Polk signed the bill, and with a clear message that he was willing to compromise and hand over the northern portion of the territory to Britain, had it sent across the Atlantic. Fully expecting the British to comply with a settlement that was very much in their interest, he turned his attention to Mexico.

General Taylor, who had no great respect for James Polk or the war he appeared to be instigating against Mexico, took his time reaching the Rio Grande. It was clear to him and to many of his officers that the residents of the disputed territory south of the Nueces considered themselves Mexican. They fled when the U.S. Army approached. But Polk had heard Catron. He began drafting a war message to present to Congress even before receiving news that Mexican soldiers had crossed the Rio Grande and attacked U.S. forces on April 25, 1846.[18]

The day after learning of the attack, James sent a war message to Congress. In the strongest possible language he excoriated Mexico, elided the truth, and demanded—not that Congress declare war, but that it recognize a war already in existence. He informed them that "now, after reiterated menaces, Mexico has passed the boundary of the United States, has invaded our territory and shed American blood upon the American soil." It wasn't true, of course. Objective observers saw clearly that it was the United States that had invaded Mexico. Nor was it true that "notwithstanding all our efforts to avoid it," war "exists by the act of Mexico herself." But no one could argue with the fact that Taylor's army was under attack and needed immediate reinforcements. "We are called upon by every consideration of duty and patriotism to vindicate with decision the honor, the rights, and the interest of our country," James insisted.[19]

As Catron predicted, westerners rejoiced. Volunteers poured into recruiting offices, particularly in western states: Illinois, Missouri, Kentucky, and Tennessee. There were more men than the army could handle. Sarah was shocked to read in "the Nashville papers" that her own brother John had left for Mexico in command of a Tennessee volunteer company. Once again, it appeared, John had failed to communicate a matter of crucial importance. She wrote immediately to her sister-in-law, Sarah Williams Childress, to confirm the story.[20]

Fortunately, her fears were unfounded. John and the majority of his company changed their minds about serving in the army when they learned that Polk insisted that volunteers serve a twelve-month enlistment. John sheepishly admitted that "most of the company as well as myself being unwilling to be absent from home for so long a time, without the emergency was greater, declined the service, and another company was taken in our stead." One imagines the embarrassment he felt explaining to his brother-in-law why he had decided to stay home, particularly after the publicity surrounding his promised sacrifice.[21]

Enthusiasm for the war in the eastern states was somewhat more muted, particularly in the Northeast, where both Whig and Democratic congressmen voted for the war despite privately acknowledging that the president had lied about Mexicans shedding American blood on American soil. There were plenty of men in the Northeast who were enthusiastic volunteers, but also voices protesting the war as designed to increase slave territory. Slaveholders, including Tennessee slaveholders, felt no misgivings about this point. In July 1846, James made Gideon Pillow a brigadier general. Less than a year later he was promoted to major general.[22]

And suddenly America was at war. Two weeks after the congressional vote, Joanna Rucker wrote her cousin that Washington was filled with "wars and rumors of wars!" On Friday, May 29, "a regiment of several hundred soldiers marched up to the president's house." Joanna admitted that "some of the soldiers were very ordinary looking men, but when my heart enlarged at the thought of beholding those that were willing to defend and die for their country, I forgot but that they were the finest looking in the world." It all happened so quickly, Joanna could "scarcely realize that we are actually in war." She was "certain I have no patriotism until I see the soldiers and hear the drums, and then I wish to be a man."[23]

Unlike her niece, Sarah never expressed a desire to be a man. She understood how to put the White House to work in the service of the nation. She increased the number of weekly receptions at the White House, and transformed them to reflect the war now under way. One of her greatest innovations was musical. She had enjoyed the Scottish march "Hail to the Chief" as a girl, so much so that she painstakingly recorded both the words and score in her Salem Academy copybook. At the outset of the war she directed the Marine Band to perform the march at large events in order to announce James's arrival. This not only imbued gatherings with a martial flavor, but also ensured that her unassuming-appearing husband would be noticed and acknowledged as commander in chief even in the largest crowds.[24]

Regardless of the newly martial music, Sarah's receptions during the course of the war continued to be celebrated for their "republican simplicity." An admirer noted, "There is no extra formality exhibited when a Secretary or some other high officer of government presents himself" in the White House. "The quiet, unheralded citizen receives a polite and cordial salutation, as well as the rich man or the Minister of State." A visitor to the White House in the first months of the war was particularly struck by "Mrs. Polk's patriotic sentiments. A gallant lieutenant, just back from the bloody but glorious conflict at Monter[r]ey was there also; and as she carried back his thoughts to the distant field of his fame, he caught the inspiration, and dwelt briefly upon some of the thrilling incidents of those scenes." It was an "animated conversation."[25]

Sarah understood the need to honor the military in a time of war. Visitors to wartime receptions at the Polk White House noted the frequent presence of uniformed army and naval officers. None of the "Mexican lions," as they were called, at the 1848 New Year's levee "attracted more attention than the handsome and dashing General Shields," an Illinois Democrat who won praise as a brigadier general of the volunteers, and delivered a speech during the dinner praising the war. "He can talk as well as fight," offered one admirer afterward. Shields put his patriotism and sacrifice on display at the levee. "He still carries his left arm in a sling and the ladies have provided him with ribbons enough to keep it tied up for half a century." Guests during the course of the war included not only officers and soldiers, but also William Prescott, a historian whose best-selling 1843 *History of the Conquest of Mexico* was popular reading among American troops.[26]

While the war started with a burst of enthusiasm, a series of thrilling victories by Zachary Taylor's army on the Rio Grande, as well as the easy conquest of California and New Mexico, were not enough to sustain the support of the people. Americans, including James, assumed the war would be a quick affair. But although the United States secured Texas, California, and New Mexico by the end of the summer of 1846, Mexico refused to surrender. James pulled the army from Taylor, whom he disliked and resented, and gave it to another Whig officer, Winfield Scott, who bombed the walled port city of Vera Cruz at a great loss of civilian life and property, and then, following the same route taken by Hernán Cortés, marched to Mexico City, capturing the capital in a series of bloody engagements in September 1847.[27]

Yet Mexico still refused to surrender. The army settled in for a long, wary occupation of Mexico's capital. With fighting at a standstill, the public began to turn against the war, and against the president. There had been too many casualties, soldiers were being shot by guerrillas on a regular basis, and disturbing reports of atrocities against civilians committed by men in American uniform circulated in U.S. newspapers.[28]

Bad news poured into the White House. Sarah heard from families of servicemen about the "many sorowful days—and sleepless nights" caused by the "Mexican mania." When an officer returned home to Cincinnati "a walking specter" and reported "seven-hundred sick in the hospital" in Perote, in the state of Vera Cruz, a frantic grandfather wrote to Sarah in hopes of intervention.[29] Sarah made a courtesy call on a Washington, D.C., mother of a young lieutenant killed in action, "to condole with the heart broken mother, on the untimely and savage death of her gallant and darling son." But according to a reporter, the First Lady was met not with thanks, but incredulity. "Tell me not of resignation," the woman addressed Sarah. "Tell me Madam, if you can, for no one seems able to answer me—for what was this wicked war brought upon our country? Why was my noble son sent to be murdered in that barbarous country?" The First Lady's response went unrecorded.[30]

Family members provided war news from Tennessee. When two

hundred volunteers spent the night in Murfreesboro on the way to Mexico, "they drank and caroused all night, and the next morning, Sunday as it was, the drum & fife called them to start . . . the streets were filled with Negroes & children, some of the school-boys ran off with the companies to Nashville wishing to go to Mexico." Half a dozen young men wished to join, but their parents were opposed. News had also made it to Murfreesboro that the American army had lost two thousand men attempting to take Mexico's capital. Sarah's niece hoped it was a false report.[31]

Sarah also heard from her sister-in-law about the war. James's brother William married wealthy thirty-one-year-old Mary Louise Corse on June 29, 1847, and immediately afterward joined the 3rd Regiment of United States Dragoons as a major. Inspired by Sarah's "systematic course of reading," Mary Louise dedicated herself to following her "example," but with a husband in Mexico, she was unable to marshal Sarah's focus. She found it "very difficult to concentrate my ideas, they will fly off to Mexico in spite of all my effort."[32]

In November 1847, Mary complained to Sarah about her "low spirits." She admitted to "gloomy forebodings by day, & ill dreams at night. . . . I awaken in agony & tears. Oh! this war, this horrid war, when will it cease, what does the President think about it? It must cause him a vast deal of anxiety." But not as much anxiety as it caused Mary once she realized she was pregnant. "My dear friend will you be kind as to enquire of the President for me . . . is there any chance of the Major's making a visit home early in the Spring?" Mary didn't attempt to hide her disdain for the war: "That 'bold Huzzah' will have a great deal to answer for one of these days."[33]

Other women turned to Sarah for help as well. The widow of a New York volunteer killed in the march to Mexico City wrote Sarah for help getting her husband's pension. She and her four-year-old had been patiently waiting for "the pension due my child." They had no money for food. "The vexations and delays of the officers of the government are killing me by inches," she pleaded. She hoped Sarah could intervene, and believed she would, because she knew from her reading that Sarah was a kind woman. "I somewhere saw in the journal of a foreign lady an account of her interview" with Sarah, she wrote. "She said you made so many kindly inquiries after her and her family at home that it brought the tears from her eyes and this may perhaps have in my misery suggested the idea of taking the liberty of addressing you."[34]

A YEAR INTO THE CONFLICT, with no end in sight, it was becoming clear that war with Mexico would neither unify the nation behind the Polks nor annihilate the Whig Party. Instead it was becoming a political liability. Whigs won control of the House of Representatives during the midterm elections, and called for an immediate end to the war. An anonymous Ohio letter writer signing themselves "the Devil" threatened James that "the spirits of those you have murdered will eternally ho[v]er round you in this world, and when I get you to my regions, they shall each punch you for 24 hours with the Mexican bayonets!"[35]

Each evening the couple met in their shared office and worked together, analyzing policies late into the night. Because Sarah was in charge of reading and editing the press that James read, she was able to limit his exposure to the many vindictive partisan attacks on his presidency. But when a Massachusetts newspaper condemned her as a hypocrite who, despite "her piety . . . lov[ed] most cordially all plunder, robbery, murder, and every other sport for the sake of slavery," no censor protected her feelings.[36]

Sarah dismissed the protests just as her husband had done. "Of course there were some opposed," she told a Nashville reporter, "there is always somebody opposed to everything." But until the end of her life she maintained that the acquisition of Texas, California, and New Mexico were "among the most important events in the history of this country." As the nation divided over war, Sarah's role as conciliator became ever greater. "Mrs. President" invited political opponents to dinner, deploying her political skills in the dining room and parlor. James noted in his diary that at the end of one such dinner Henry Clay promised Sarah he would "visit her drawing room soon" and that "he had heard a general approbation expressed of her administration, but that he believed there was some difference of opinion about her husband's administration." Playing along, Sarah "replied pleasantly that she was happy to hear from him that her administration was approved, and added, if a political opponent of my husband is to succeed him, I have always said I would prefer you, Mr. Clay, and in that event I shall be most happy to surrender the White House to you."[37]

Vice President Dallas believed that Sarah held too much power, but marveled at her social skills. He wrote home to his wife in Philadelphia after overhearing a conversation at a wedding between Sarah and a woman disgruntled with the administration, in order to explain exactly how the First Lady was able to win over opponents of her husband.

After a little conversation, Mrs. P. said suddenly though kindly, "why have you never been to see me? I have often wanted to invite you, but feared I should intrude, as you had never called." "Pray, Mrs. P., don't let us talk upon the subject." "Oh! but I am sincerely anxious to know." "Since you press me—remember I would cheerfully abstain—but the cause is simply the inexplicable and inexcusable treatment of my son-in-law Mr. Irwin."

"But that ought surely to be set down to politics, and not be permitted to interfere with personal intercourse." "Ah! Mrs. Polk, you have never been a mother, or you would know that a mother feels much more keenly than her children every wrong they suffer."

Dallas closed his dialogue by noting that "the ladies found they liked each other, and separated most graciously." As the vice president related it, the story was not necessarily flattering to Sarah, since it implied that she lacked empathy because she was childless. But the fact that she won the friendship of a former opponent of the administration proved her worth as a political actor, and her abilities as a conciliator were far more valuable to the Polk presidency than maternal empathy.[38]

As in previously stressful moments in James's career, such as the Tennessee gubernatorial elections, he demanded that Sarah do more. He twice asked her to return a call to Benjamin Butler, U.S. attorney for the Southern District of New York. Butler was one of the powerful men who opposed the war, and he appeared willing to desert the Democratic Party for a new Free Soil Party, composed of northerners who opposed the extension of slavery into territories gained from Mexico. "Under the circumstances I think you should make it a point to return the call," James told Sarah. This one could not be delegated to the nieces.[39]

Nor was James above using Sarah's domestic skills to appease other politicians. His close friend Robert Armstrong wanted a brigadier generalship. James closed his letter denying the request by telling Armstrong that his daughter "Little Rachel visits us very often and calls Mrs. Polk, aunt, as affectionately and familiarity, as if she had been raised in our family. She spent from last Saturday evening until Monday morning with us. . . . Mrs. Polk takes as much interest in her, as if she were her own daughter."[40]

The conquest of Mexico City in September 1847 should have resulted in a peace treaty, yet somehow the occupation drew on, month after month, without word of a settlement. As dissent against the war grew in intensity, Sarah started carrying a heavy ornamental mother-of-pearl fan, brought back from Mexico for her by General Pillow. She admitted that it was too unwieldy for use, but she carried it to state dinners anyhow. It was a symbol of U.S. victory, and she had long been accustomed to carrying heavy weights on James's behalf.[41]

James, unfortunately, was in a poor position to appreciate her efforts on behalf of the war. Never robust, the overworked president began declining during the second half of his term. By his own admission, his "constant confinement to my office and great labour for many days past" left him increasingly "enfeebled and prostrated." Sarah begged him to take a vacation, but his deep sense of duty made it impossible. Although in "the habit of taking exercise on horseback all my life," James stopped exercising in October 1846, not long after coming into conflict with General Taylor over his actions south of the Rio Grande. As James complained in his diary, he was "so incessantly engaged into the onerous and responsible duties of my office" that he didn't mount a horse for the next six months.[42]

The chairman of the House Committee on Foreign Affairs called on Sarah to warn her that James "was wearing himself out with constant and excessive application, that if he did not take some recreation, he would die soon after the close of his term." He suggested that she "insist upon his driving out morning and evening; that she must order her carriage and make him go with her." Sarah, who understood her husband's destructive work habits better than anyone, attempted to follow the advice. Day after day she ordered their carriage, "and the carriage waited and waited, until it was too late. It would have been obliged to wait all day, for somebody was always in the office, and Mr. Polk would not, or could not, come," she later recalled. It was hopeless. "I seldom succeeded in getting him to drive with me."[43]

Instead she focused on limiting his exposure to both bad news and people who might upset him. No longer did she simply intervene when men like Lyman Beecher wished to speak to her husband, or stop strangers at the foot of the grand staircase before they disturbed James with job requests. By the start of 1847, if a politician hoped to speak to James, he did well to be on good terms with Sarah.

John Van Buren was one recipient of the First Lady's wrath. Son of the former president, Van Buren was an antislavery Democrat who spent much of 1847, in James's words, "making violent political speeches against my administration" and drumming up support for a new Free Soil political party. As a Democratic leader, he made repeated calls on the president, who, "of course, treated him courteously in my own parlor."

But Sarah banned the younger Van Buren from White House social events. "On two or three occasions I had decided that he should be invited to dinner," James wrote in his diary, "and in each case Mrs. Polk had countermanded the order. . . . On one of these occasions I was amused when she told me she had burned John Van Buren's dinner ticket, which I had requested my Private Secretary to send to him."

Van Buren was a traitor to the Democratic Party, but his political views don't fully explain the vehemence of Sarah's reaction. Whigs made regular appearances at White House dinners. Equally unforgivable was Van Buren's lack of respect for the First Lady herself. He "so far neglected the courtesies of life as not to call and pay his respects to her," and thus, Sarah proclaimed, "he should not be honoured with an invitation to dinner." Eventually Van Buren caught on and made a formal call on Sarah. But he still wasn't invited to dinner.[44]

That virtually no one critiqued Mrs. James K. Polk's aggressive politicking is due to several factors. Opponents of the administration believed that Sarah, as a pious Christian, might be a moderating force in the seemingly bloodthirsty administration. When James was preparing his annual message in December 1847, the *New York Herald* offered a "hope that, with the aid of the chivalric spirit of Mrs. Polk, he will throw out a message that will reflect credit on himself and the country, and astonish the whole world."[45]

James's supporters, on the other hand, recognized that Sarah's "affable manners" went a long way toward "allaying the opposition that is ever apparent in times of national trouble." Sarah appeared to be so much more *reasonable* than James. This was why it was left to her to appease John C. Calhoun after James removed him as secretary of state. Franklin Pierce, one of Sarah's "most cordial and constant friends," said he would rather discuss politics with Sarah than with her husband. George Bancroft expected to hear from his "great and good friend" Sarah directly while he was abroad serving as minister to Great Britain, and repeatedly told James as much.[46]

And she had power. Politicians had long understood the need to cultivate Sarah to get to James. Before the Polks entered office, Thomas Hart Benton wrote directly to her on behalf of the minister of the Presbyterian church where Andrew Jackson worshipped, to determine which church she and James would worship in. Catron wrote to Sarah to promote his ideas about the war. Gideon Pillow wrote to her in order to gain a commission. And from faraway Havana, U.S. consul Robert B. Campbell sent her "a small box of sweetmeats" after his "lamented wife" died of yellow fever. Campbell hoped to return home to South Carolina, and the possibility that Sarah's intervention might result in a more desirable position clearly influenced his gift.[47]

Other men cultivated Sarah not because they wanted something from James, but because they understood the extent of her control over aspects of White House political life. When Thomas Ritchie, editor of the administration newspaper, the *Washington Union*, wanted to read the communication between the president and Captain Hiram Paulding, commander of the sloop of war *Vincennes*, he turned to Sarah, requesting that the First Lady let him read it, "if convenient," and promising to "make not a line of Extract from it, without your full consent." And her power was recognized beyond political circles. A police officer, fired without explanation, wrote Sarah asking if it was because he had asked the driver of her carriage to move from a spot where it blocked traffic. "It was suggested by a friend that I might have been so unfortunate to have incurred, on a certain occasion, at the Capitol grounds, the displeasure of the lady of our Chief Magistrate." A great deal had changed since James had first run for governor of Tennessee, including the willingness of men to recognize and acknowledge Sarah Childress Polk's political power.[48]

———

IN THE SUMMER OF 1847, Sarah and James temporarily parted ways—he for a two-week tour of New England, and she for a longer trip to Tennessee to visit family and oversee the construction of their new home.

James had campaigned on the promise of only serving one term in office, a decision he wrongly believed would unify his party. He began thinking about retirement almost as soon as he reached the White House. Only a year into his presidency, Joanna Rucker reported that the president "talks a great deal of anticipated enjoyment after his term expires." When James learned, in the fall of 1846, that Felix Grundy's Nashville mansion was up for sale, he imagined himself occupying it, and was willing to buy it, sight unseen, without knowing "what extent of back ground, or yard, there may be. Nor do I know anything of the back buildings." What he did know was that Grundy's Palladian-style brick home had been the finest in Nashville when it was built in 1820, and it had no doubt dazzled the young student when he visited. Provided Nashville resident Vernon Stevenson could vouch that the exceptionally high price ($10,000, not including a vacant lot behind the property that James also wanted) was reasonable, he wanted it. "I prefer it to any other," he repeated, "and desire to buy it."[49]

Sarah was less convinced. The house needed work. Among other issues, the roof leaked, and Felix Grundy's son-in-law, John Bass, intended to continue living in the home and pay the Polks rent. Sarah made clear to James that "the house would require thorough repairs and modernizing, before she would be willing to occupy it," and that "this will cost a considerable sum." James admitted that this was a matter in which Sarah was "so much interested," but when had she ever denied him anything? Her husband had earned the right to live in Judge Grundy's home and to rename it Polk Place as a way of reminding himself as well as Nashville that he had thoroughly surpassed even Grundy for honors and laurels.[50]

James closed the deal as quickly as possible, paying $13,000 for the house and vacant lot. He optimistically told friends that he was purchasing the property "long in advance" of when it was needed so that "I will have full time to cause the necessary repairs and improvements to be made." By "I" he meant Sarah. It was a tall order, as was responsibility for a home that was set to rival the new capitol building under construction just a block away. Sarah admitted to her sister-in-law that she dreaded "the vast responsibility" of keeping up the property.[51]

Bass, who was living in the house, recommended repairing the roof at once. James had no intention of doing any such thing. Indeed, he refused to make any repairs until Sarah could get down to Nashville and take charge of the proceedings. James had strong views about the necessary remodeling. The building's current Palladian style felt stuffy, and Greek Revival was in fashion. Polk engaged a builder to transform the façade by changing the shape of the windows, flattening the roof, and adding a great portico with fluted columns and Corinthian capitals.[52]

But it was Sarah who was in charge of refurbishing the house and bringing it up to, if not presidential standards, then at least the standards a former U.S. president deserved. Despite her clear reservations about the condition of the Grundy mansion, she accepted this duty with the same equanimity with which she had met all of James's requests. "Mrs Polk will visit her friends in Tennessee in June," James wrote Bass, "and will at that time—in consultation with yourself, Mr Stevenson, and Judge Catron, determine upon the improvements to be ordered." Responding to news about Sarah's coming "reconnaissance," Bass assured the president that he was happy "to act as her aide de camp on so important an occasion," but his use of military terminology suggests some discomfort at the perceived power arrangement. Felix Grundy's son-in-law, renting his wife's family home from the great legislator's former student, knew Sarah's visit could only result in discomfort for himself, and quite possibly in orders he might not want to receive from a woman.[53]

As Sarah headed south, James went north. It was their first separation since moving to Washington. Although James's tour of New England was "of the most gratifying character. . . . Nothing of a party or of an unpleasant character has occurred anywhere," as he told his wife, he missed her terribly. He wasn't the only one. At every stop on the tour "the friends of the President were earnest and sincere in regretting the absence of his honored lady," according to the journalist who accompanied James. In New York, a little girl residing in an asylum for the deaf told the president that she "regretted (and the regret was everywhere general) that he had not brought Mrs Polk with him."

James Buchanan wrote Sarah from Portland, Maine, that "there was nothing wanting to make our party everything it ought to have been but your presence." When Buchanan added that "we have got along as well as could have been expected in your absence," he was likely speaking for himself as well as for James. Back in Washington the secretary of state socialized with Sarah a great deal. When Sarah and her nieces wanted a male escort for charity events, dinners, or, on one notable occasion, a convent graduation ceremony, Buchanan was their preferred companion.[54]

James clearly enjoyed reporting his victories to Sarah, not only well-delivered speeches, but also good press, and a warm public embrace seemingly at odds with the outcry over his war. "I have seen many hundreds of thousands of people of all ages and sexes," he marveled. "The newspapers, though they give a general account of the tour, furnish, but an imperfect idea of it. The manner of my reception and the consideration paid me far exceeded any thing which I had anticipated."[55]

But once he was back in Washington his spirits sank. He fretted that Sarah might have met with an accident when he didn't hear from her, being unable to account for the failure of her letter to reach him. He ordered her to write to him, and was quick to respond to letters from others reporting her whereabouts, never directly thanking his correspondents but rather making clear that he was glad to hear that Mrs. Polk had arrived safely. He closely tracked her whereabouts, crowing at one point that news that she had reached Nashville on July 8 "verifies my predictions made some days ago." He could only admit "the truth," which "is I miss you very much, and am already becoming impatient for your return." Her description of events in Murfreesboro led him to respond, "I wish I could have spent the day with you."[56]

The following evening he wrote simply out of affection, to "let you know how much I miss you in the White House." He had given a dinner party in Sarah's absence, and Mariah's son, Henry, noted that "things was a heap straighter when Miss Sarah was here." James, reporting the anecdote to Sarah, plainly agreed.[57]

Sarah was fully occupied with the responsibilities of family and home. She enjoyed John Catron's escort to middle Tennessee, entertaining him along the way with political news, including a detailed report of a "Splendid Speech" Polk cabinet member John Y. Mason delivered in Chapel Hill, North Carolina. When they reached Columbia on Sunday evening, July 10, the "truth of affection" displayed by James's mother posed a dramatic contrast, in Catron's eyes, with "the Smiles of office seekers and fawning for place" Sarah lived with back in Washington. Sarah also visited her mother, whose welfare was an ongoing concern. After Joanna Rucker left the White House and returned to Murfreesboro, she wrote Sarah on a regular basis. She was concerned to see that her grandmother "lives alone and leads a lonely life. I often ask her if she has a message for you. But she sends none."[58]

Elizabeth Childress clearly needed attention, but Sarah's main business was their new home. John Catron had overseen construction in her absence, and sent her positive reports that may have helped distract from the increasingly "red hot shot" being "poured onto Mr. Polk" because of the divisive war. "Congress seems to be slashing away at the President," Catron wrote her. Fortunately, this war, unlike the Second Seminole War, was not going to break down the administration "as a few naked Indians in Florida" did to the "regime of Mr. Van Buren."[59]

Three months after Sarah returned to Washington, William's wife, Mary Louise, visited Nashville and reported "your house not as much advanced, as I had imagined."[60] Whatever frustration Sarah must have felt about the slow progress was placed in perspective by the news a week later that Nashville was "shattered by the explosion of a powder magazine." Matilda Catron sent the bad news. "There is not a house in Nashville or within three miles distant that is not injured by the explosion." Matilda rushed to Sarah's new house immediately after the explosion, and confirmed that the walls were solid. Unfortunately, "there is not a window nor door but have received too much injury to repair for present use." She left "two carefull negroes" in charge of the house, and promised to call there frequently on her evening walks.[61]

Neither the unsettled state of affairs in Mexico nor the explosion in Nashville prevented Sarah and James from celebrating their twenty-fourth wedding anniversary on New Year's Day 1848. James gave Sarah an enameled gold pendant watch, made in Europe, displaying a bucolic river scene on the dial. It's possible he intended the image to remind them of the promise of their lives after the White House. He engraved it "to Mrs. Jas. K. Polk from Jas. K. Polk Jan. 1, 1848."[62]

In February 1848, the long-hoped-for peace treaty between the United States and Mexico finally arrived in Washington. It was a peculiar and not entirely welcome one, as it had been signed by a disgraced American diplomat acting contrary to James's orders, and brought less territory to the United States than anyone in the cabinet desired. But with opposition to the war growing, and Whigs in control of the House of Representatives, the treaty left James in a quandary. Were he to reject it, Congress would likely refuse to vote him money to continue the war, and he might lose California. We have no way of knowing if James discussed the Treaty of Guadalupe Hidalgo with Sarah, but given that he stayed up late the night it arrived, they almost certainly discussed it at length. And given Sarah's record of advising James, it seems likely that she concurred with her husband that he had no choice but to accept it. On February 21, 1848, President Polk presented the Treaty of Guadalupe Hidalgo to Congress.[63]

The United States had conquered Mexico. The defeated republic handed over nearly half of its original territory in return for $15 million. The Polk presidency added more than eight hundred thousand square miles of territory to the United States as a result of negotiations over the Oregon Country and the U.S.-Mexican War.

When Catharine Beecher wrote Sarah in order to enlist her assistance in civilizing the frontier, this was certainly not the outcome she hoped for. America's greatest female reformer and most powerful female politician agreed in principle that America's women had the power to enact its Manifest Destiny, and that "if ladies will work as they may work in this effort, it will soon be conceded, that a woman of energy and developed talent, can do as much as a man." But they had very different visions of what that destiny would entail. Beecher's Whiggish vision of an American West domesticated and Christianized by female teachers was a great distance from Sarah's Democratic dream of Mexico conquered by young men with guns.[64]

As much as Sarah agreed with Beecher that it was "in the power of American women to save their country," she never did advocate in favor of Beecher's plan to settle women in the West. On the contrary, the First Lady lent her support to a very different outcome when she led a fund-raising drive in support of destitute Mormons driven from Illinois because of their doctrine of polygamy, and then later signed on to an appeal to women in other cities to help the Mormon refugees. In an era when religious persecution of Catholics and other religious minorities was widespread (Lyman Beecher himself warned of the threat posed by Catholic settlement in the West), Sarah's position was not the easiest to adopt. Mormons were even more reviled than Catholics. But these acts of charity aligned with James's personal and public support of religious tolerance. James personally donated ten dollars toward the relief of the Mormon refugees, and agreed to arm a regiment of Mormon soldiers to fight in the U.S.-Mexican War, and to ultimately settle the Great Salt Lake region. Thanks to the Polks, the women in the West would not be Protestant schoolteachers, they would be Mormon wives.[65]

Upon his return home, General William Worth, one of the heroes of the war, presented Sarah with a life-size, three-quarter-length portrait of Hernán Cortés. Worth claimed he had a colonial painting copied for the First Lady, but scholarship on the Cortés portrait makes clear that it was no 1840s copy. In other words, Worth presented Sarah Polk with a valuable and most likely looted colonial portrait. The First Lady was happy to offer a place in her home to the painting, "trusting it may prove an agreeable incident in the brilliant retrospect of the last four years." Journalists later noted how appropriate it was for General Worth, "one of the conquerors of a party of Mexico," to present a picture of Cortés, "the original conqueror of that great and beautiful country, to Mrs. Polk; for it was during Mr. Polk's administration that this vast and valuable territory was gained for the United States."[66]

Sarah proudly hung the portrait in a state parlor in the White House, where guests might easily contemplate the comparison between her husband and the man who conquered the Aztec Empire. For the rest of her life the painting occupied a place of honor in her home. It remains on display in the James K. Polk Ancestral Home, in Columbia, Tennessee, looted testimony to the role of the Polks in the course of America's Manifest Destiny.[67]

7

I shall be glad to be on <u>exterior</u> terms of personal intercourse with him. . . .
to go thro' the hypocritical ceremony of shaking hands with him, Polk, with
that fine manly Lady his wife, if possible, on all occasions to show that I
respect and admire her. I mean to be revenged on [the] Pres[ident].

—CHARLES INGERSOLL TO JAMES BUCHANAN, June 16, 1847

BEFORE THE WAR ENDED, James was already counting "the
weeks and days until his term expires." Given Whig control of the
House of Representatives, and sectional tensions produced by northern support of a proviso submitted by Pennsylvania Democrat David
Wilmot to ban slavery from any territory taken from Mexico, who
could blame the president for fantasizing about his future life in the
Grundy mansion in Nashville? Unfortunately, the Treaty of Guadalupe Hidalgo brought little improvement to either James's health or
Sarah's workload.[1]

The final year of the Polk presidency was fraught with political dissent. With Mexico secured, Congress needed to determine the status of
slavery in the new territories. But each discussion seemed to heighten
tensions between the South and the North. And James's refusal to
run for reelection left the Democratic Party in disarray. None of the
candidates hoping for the 1848 nomination stood a chance of beating
the Whig candidate, General Zachary Taylor. Taylor was not only the
savior of the Battle of Buena Vista, the most celebrated victory of
the entire war, he was also a political outsider. Moreover, he had issued
no statements on any important political issues, so voters could imag-

ine him any way they wished, and his ownership of a Louisiana cotton plantation and eighty-one slaves reassured southerners that he would never interfere with their right to bring their human property into new territories. Taylor was the perfect candidate for a nation fracturing over slavery.[2]

James always asserted that the question of slavery was peripheral to the war, but the status of slavery in the new territories was a matter of profound significance not only to the slaves themselves, but also to the balance of power between the North and South. The public knew that the Polks were slaveholders, of course, but James pretended to a disinterest in the expansion of slavery that was belied by his actions. Unbeknownst to the public, he began secretly purchasing slave children to labor on the plantation as soon as he got into office.

Or rather, Sarah and her brother purchased them. A president of the United States could not purchase slaves while in office without jeopardizing his reputation in the North. While James was running for office, his good friend Gideon Pillow circulated a letter insisting that James never bought slaves unless doing so would unite a family through the purchase of an enslaved husband's wife, an enslaved wife's husband, or the child of an enslaved parent. And indeed Sarah had at times insisted that James make such acquisitions for Childress family slaves.[3]

But when it came to the plantation, James's priorities could not have been more different; his goal was to make a profit, and his purchases were of a sort that would particularly horrify the public. James specified that he wanted young people for his plantation, between the ages of twelve and twenty-one, although he had no scruples about buying children as young as ten or eleven. Dafney, purchased at age ten, was married off at age twelve to Giles, who was himself only thirteen when he was bought by James. All of these young people at one point or another before arriving at the Polk Plantation had been ripped away from their families. Family reunification was hardly a priority for James and Sarah Polk when it came to cotton production.[4]

James employed John Childress to help him acquire human property for the plantation, with Sarah as mediator. When John made a purchase, it sometimes was Sarah who gave him the money. John then conveyed the money and specification to a third man. Sarah's brother wrote her in July 1846 to inform her that he had "drawn upon" James "for the amount of money he wanted me to invest in property for him." John's purchase at the president's request and with his money was "a boy about 14 yrs old of yellow complexion, for $450. A good sized plow boy and seems to be well disposed." When Sarah traveled to Tennessee earlier that spring, she repaid her brother for the purchase of several slaves, including "a girl in her fourteenth year, of good size, appearance & of sprighty active habits," whom John stated would "be much more valuable to you" than the "boy" John traded away. Sarah helped purchase two thirteen-year-old girls that year. One of them, Jane, later remembered that she was just "a girl half grown" when she arrived at the Polk Plantation.[5]

What John left unsaid was that the reason a "sprighty" thirteen-year-old girl like Jane was more valuable than a healthy boy was because the girl was, or would soon be, old enough to bear children. Not that he needed to tell the Polks this. When Jane arrived at the plantation she noted that eighteen-year-old Dafney, purchased only six years before, already had "a large family of children" with Giles. Jane followed in her footsteps, marrying a Polk Plantation slave and giving birth to at least four children over the next decade. As Thomas Jefferson himself noted less than thirty years earlier, "I consider a woman who brings a child every two years as more profitable than the best man of the farm," because "what she produces is an addition to the capital, while his labors disappear in mere consumption."[6]

The annexation of Texas dramatically increased the value of slave property; it meant new opportunities for planting cotton, a crop that depended on slave labor. As a result, enslaved people sold for 30 percent more in 1846 than they had before James entered office. In 1849 the Polks were no longer in debt; indeed, they were finally on the way to becoming rich. Having finally secured his finances, James could tune out the sectional discord and look forward to leaving office. But his denials of further political ambition failed to convince the Democrats who begged him to run for a second term. A highly secretive man who confided only in his wife, and frequently misled members of his own party, James Polk made many more enemies than friends during his presidency.[7]

As always, it was up to Sarah to repair these relationships. Some of her efforts were successful. Pennsylvania Democrat Charles Ingersoll was no friend of the president's: he referred to James as "stupid" and "selfish" in private correspondence with James Buchanan, and vowed to "be revenged" on him. Yet he was willing to "go thro' the hypocritical ceremony of shaking hands" with James in order to show his admiration and respect for "that fine manly Lady his wife."[8]

But the opportunities for anyone to shake hands with James were limited by his declining health. He rarely felt well for more than a day at a time. He suffered from recurrent gastrointestinal disorders, and was completely worn out by the end of the day. He spent most of the summer of 1848 in bed, too sick to attend to anything more than the most important work.[9]

It was left to the "fine manly Lady his wife" to host their receptions. Sarah canceled the two weekly soirees she had added for the duration of the war, yet because men were now used to talking to her rather than her husband, her cares hardly abated. In June the vice president reported that Sarah was present at a reception by herself, and "the President was invisible, having chills & fever. Mrs. Polk looked well. She has resolved on being one half in eclipse for the rest of this Summer, and will receive only one evening in the week." A month later he again stopped by the White House, intending to "present" two rising young men "to Mrs. Polk," but was disappointed to learn she was unavailable, having "discontinued receptions except on Tuesdays." The three men had to content themselves with a visit to James's study, which Dallas called a "pis aller," or last resort, since James was "under the weather in health and spirits."[10]

THE SUMMER OF 1848 was not an ideal time for James to fall sick. The Polk presidency left the nation immensely larger, and richer, than it had been when Sarah and James arrived in Washington, but also badly fractured over the issue of slavery. The Wilmot Proviso to ban slavery from any territory taken from Mexico passed the House of Representatives, where northerners outnumbered southerners, but could not get through the Senate, where southerners held the majority. The Democratic Party fractured over the proviso, and was unable to find a candidate that appealed to both northern and southern Democrats.

When Lewis Cass of Michigan emerged from the party's nominating convention in June, James committed to supporting him. But northern Democrats opposed to slavery joined with Liberty Party men to support the nomination of Martin Van Buren and a new Free Soil Party. James needed the party faithful to rally around Cass. Sarah's close friend Aaron Brown rose to the challenge, but Gideon Pillow declined, blaming an ankle wound received during the war.[11]

Nor was the election the only political issue requiring finesse. A divided Congress was faced with establishing territorial governments, and the status of slavery, in California, Oregon, and New Mexico. On July 27 they passed a bill organizing all three territories, but outlawing slavery in only one, Oregon, leaving the issue in California and New Mexico to the Supreme Court, which seemed likely to uphold the rights of southerners, who had already moved slaves into those territories. James signed the bill, but made his allegiance with southerners clear by affirming his view that slavery was legal south of the Missouri Compromise line of thirty-six degrees, thirty minutes, including southern California.[12]

Sarah sent James to bathe in the famous mineral waters of Bedford Springs in an attempt to repair his health, but was herself too busy hostessing to join him. He found that the waters of the springs soothed his chronic intestinal complaints. But the separation from Sarah was excruciating, and almost immediately after leaving he declared himself "impatient" to get back to Washington. He dutifully reported on all the "highly respectable and fashionable people" at Bedford Springs, and attended a ball, as Sarah played hostess at the White House. Her brother John chastised her for not writing more frequently; she had been "so chary of letters recently" that no one in the family had the slightest idea what she was up to. This was a bit much coming from the brother who had failed to invite her to his own wedding.[13]

Sarah continued to filter the news for James, so it's very likely she was aware of the July convention in Seneca Falls, New York, "to discuss the social, civil, and religious condition and rights of women." The demand of assembled women for political rights was mentioned in at least one of the Washington, D.C., papers Sarah was in the custom of reading. But the claims by some recent historians that Sarah "encouraged James to address the group" are unfounded. There is no evidence that Sarah or James took an interest in the events in upstate New York.[14]

The fine manly lady in the White House said very little publicly about women's rights. Like most Americans, she opposed the idea of women voting. She was a southern Democrat, after all. Women's rights were hardly more popular with southern Democrats than was abolitionism. But just because Sarah wasn't at Seneca Falls doesn't mean her views on women fully conformed to those of her section and party. During her years in public life she had met and corresponded with a variety of powerful women who hoped to uplift women by promoting their authority in the domestic sphere. Catharine Beecher imagined her a partner in expanding women's power. The editor of *Godey's Lady's Book,* Sarah Josepha Hale, sent poetry. Another leading exponent of the doctrine of separate spheres, Lydia Sigourney, sent Sarah a volume of her *Illustrated Poems* after Sarah invited her to the White House. The editor and dime novel author Ann Stephens sent her the *Cabinet of American Literature.*[15]

And as a First Lady who took pride in reading the books sent to her, Sarah was exposed to some of the most radical currents of the day, including the explosion of print culture in the 1840s devoted to sex and reproduction. In 1845, a well-known lecturer on birth control asked her to endorse a revised edition of his best-selling volume *Womanhood,* a "valuable female work of some repute" that included information about female sexual anatomy, pregnancy, birth, and miscarriage. It also offered advice about birth control (much of it wrong), and for close readers, how to induce abortion with the use of botanicals (tansy, rue, pennyroyal, motherwort) that had long histories as abortifacients.[16]

Sarah did not endorse the volume, but she clearly supported less radical reforms to women's economic status. When a justice from the Pennsylvania Supreme Court came to dinner near the close of the Polk presidency, he was thrilled to hear the First Lady express her support for his recent decision in favor of expanded property rights for women. Sarah asked him to send her a copy of the full opinion. The decision in question, McCullough's Appeal, 12 Pa. 197, was far from radical. It offered legal justification for ignoring previous laws that prevented widows from remarrying and keeping property left to them by their husbands.[17]

But Justice Ellis Lewis was so pleased by Sarah's embrace of his position that he sent her, in addition to the decision, a letter he had published in favor of the rights of women. Under the heading "The Liberty of the Press—The Writ of Habeas Corpus—and the Rights of Women: The trinity in the creed of freedom throughout the civilized world," Ellis bemoaned the situation of America's women. "By marriage, the civil existence of woman is almost extinguished. Her personal property becomes the absolute property of her husband. Her real estate becomes substantially his for life; her rights of action are also his if he choose to reduce them into possession." Nor was this all. "The exclusion of females from offices which they might fill with propriety, and from all profitable employments, the reduction of their wages to a pittance insufficient to sustain life, and the neglect of their education" were "evils as alarming in their influence upon the welfare of society" as they were unjust. He asked that Sarah consider the essay a " 'Valentine' to the Ladies in general, and to yourself in particular as standing at the head of them." Clearly he hoped that she agreed with the editors of a popular women's magazine that his letter made him "Woman's Champion."[18]

Judge Lewis considered Sarah a friend of women's rights. Given her experiences as First Lady, the many appeals made to her by poor and suffering women, and her correspondence with Catharine Beecher, she was probably sensitive to these issues. James certainly was. He had often seen "mothers dispose of their property among their children, and afterwards become dependent on them," with "unpleasant" results. When his sister Lydia was widowed he advised her to keep her portion of her estate under her "exclusive control." A year and a half later, he reiterated that were he in his sister's place, "I would retain my own property."[19]

How Sarah responded to Justice Lewis's tribute to women's rights is impossible to know. Like the vast majority of her correspondence, any thank-you note has been lost to posterity. What's clear is that neither James nor Sarah was willing to advocate in public for the companionate marriage that sustained them and the Polk presidency, let alone to go further and push for expanded rights for women. Sarah had deliberately cultivated a deferential persona in order to connect herself to Andrew Jackson and the traditional values of piety, simplicity, and patriarchy, which Democrats held dear. Furthermore, she had made that patriarchal image work for her, providing cover for outsized political power that was not nearly as deferential as it appeared. She didn't need to ask anyone for women's rights.

CHARLES INGERSOLL never was revenged on James, although he was one of many northern Democrats to reject his party's candidate in 1848 out of disgust over the seeming proslavery course of Manifest Destiny under the Polk administration. Although Lewis Cass never served in the Polk administration, Ingersoll, chairman of the House Committee on Foreign Affairs, admitted voting against him, because "no one knew better than he what a necessary thing it was to the country that this administration should not be continued." When Elizabeth Blair Lee, a committed Democrat, met Ingersoll after Zachary Taylor's 1848 victory was confirmed, she "laughed at him for turning Whig. After a good deal of fun & Merriment, I told him I heard he voted the Whig ticket openly. 'I swear I didn't,' he said laughing all the time. 'I am the perfectest Democrat in the city & am just buying a pair of new gloves to go see Mrs. Polk & condole.' "[20]

Not long thereafter Sarah took a final short trip without her husband. Her destination was New York City, where she planned to buy furniture for Polk Place. She took her two resident nieces with her, and left hostess duties in the hands of Knox's wife, Augusta, who met visitors in the parlor along with the president. James was supportive of Sarah's trip. "As you leave home so seldom I hope you will take full time for your visit." But he also expected daily letters, and fretted when they didn't arrive. He wasn't used to being alone. When a missing letter finally arrived, several days later than James expected, he responded with what he described as a "woman's letter"—chatty, with a postscript full of gossip. His relief was palpable.[21]

The final months of the Polk presidency were difficult ones for Sarah. Her mother's mental state continued to be a concern. Sarah's faithful correspondent Joanna, who was valiantly struggling to follow her aunt's habit of daily reading, continued to ask her grandmother if she had a message for Sarah, "but she never has any." And the house was weighing on her. Looking to the future, Sarah purchased her first cookbook, Mrs. A. L. Webster's *Improved Housewife*. It was finally time to learn how to make her own butter.[22]

But Polk Place was still under construction. This despite the daily visits of Vernon Stevenson, who even checked on the house on a Sunday, "for which sin I claim your prayers," he wrote Sarah. The blame lay with an epidemic of cholera, a highly contagious waterborne disease that was ravaging cities throughout the Southeast. "The cholera excitement . . . has taken off one or two workmen," Stevenson wrote Sarah, and "scared off some others." Her niece also warned them that "the cholera is very bad in Nashville" and that she and James should plan on staying in Murfreesboro "with us untill it has abated."[23]

Not that Murfreesboro was safe from the "alarm & excitement in regard to the cholera." Sarah's sister Susan was forcing her family to drink ginger-pepper-brandy tea for its "anti-cholera" properties, and both she and their brother John were worried about their mother, who was unwell from "this influenza that is prevailing."[24]

John's family was also doing poorly; his teenage daughter Mary wrote her aunt a guilt-inducing missive that was unlikely to make Sarah want to leave Washington. "After writing to you several times and receiving no answer, I concluded that you had forgotten me. . . . You know it is discouraging for one that dislikes to write to receive no response. . . . We have had some severe attacks of the cholera. . . . Ma and I have been very sick." The younger children, including seven-year-old Bettie, and a baby named Martha, were also sick. There was talk of Elizabeth moving in with one of her children, but seeing how "she could not bear the noise of children and there are at each of her children's houses large families," they all feared "such a life would not suit her."[25]

The very young and very old, as well as individuals who were sick and weak to begin with, were most likely to succumb to cholera. The Childresses were fortunate that they lost only one child, baby Martha, before the epidemic subsided. The rest of the family, including young Bettie, survived. Remarkably enough, Elizabeth Childress survived as well. By March 1849 she was well enough that she was "very busy, having her yard and garden put in order." Susan's daughter Sarah Rucker wrote Sarah "that these preparations were for you." When the Childresses learned that the Polks were considering taking a meandering tour through the cities of the South on the way home, family members again raised concerns about cholera. New Orleans was believed to be particularly susceptible to the disease. Elizabeth Childress, who for months had refused to send any message to Sarah or James, at last felt the need to do so. She was "much distressed at the thought of your going so near the cholera," she wrote via Joanna, but that "if any body escapes" she looked forward to taking care of them.[26]

WHILE THE CHILDRESSES STRUGGLED with cholera, and Sarah planned their route to Tennessee from Washington, the nation began the process of saying goodbye to the First Lady. But the success of her public persona as a pious, humble public servant left little room for celebrating, or even acknowledging, that Sarah Childress Polk was also a "fine manly Lady" and political actor.

Consider the profile of the outgoing First Lady published in *Sartain's Union Magazine*. Author Mary Andrews Denison likely had the best of intentions when she set out to write about the outgoing First Lady. Quite likely she planned on conducting research, or at least finding out the basic facts of Polk's early life. But she was a busy woman, a married twenty-four-year-old journalist who was on her way to wealth and fame as the author of eighty potboiler dime novels that would eventually sell more than a million copies. Her first dime novel, *Edna Etherill, the Boston Seamstress*, was published when she was only twenty-one.

"Mrs. Polk, though as far removed as possible from what would be called a politician, has yet taken pains to make herself well informed on public affairs," Denison declared. "One who knows her intimately says, there are not twenty days in a year, that she does not spend a certain time each day, in reading the leading public journals—not those filled with trashy, 'fashionable' literature, but the solid productions of sterner intellects. . . . Though perfectly acquainted with politics, yet with a rare judgment, and a comprehension of womanly delicacy, she seldom makes them a subject for conversation."[27]

It was inevitable that Denison would get some things wrong. Sarah was far from an open book. Certain elements of her family background, as we've seen, were opaque. Denison's assertion in the first sentence of the profile that Sarah was born in Buckingham, Virginia, may have originated from the pen of an earlier author. Her claim that Sarah "had the misfortune, in early life, to lose her mother" is harder to justify, given that Sarah's mother was still very much alive, and an ongoing source of anxiety for her three children. Just as perplexing was the statement that "in the tender years of childhood" she "was much of the time away from home. . . . Thrown, to some extent, upon her own resources, with no mother's guiding hand or approving smile, she early displayed an independence of mind, and a strength of will, joined to remarkable perseverance, which few acquire until the ripeness of middle age." Nor was it correct that Sarah avoided "fashionable literature." Sarah was not only an early subscriber to the preeminent fashionable magazine, *Godey's Lady's Book,* but she valued the magazine highly enough to send it, along with other "Ladys newspapers," to her nieces back in Tennessee when she was done reading them.[28]

Most likely Mrs. C. W. Denison embarked on the hard work of biography in the same spirit as the patriotic chroniclers of America's founding generation. Parson Mason Locke Weems, who wrote the very first biography of George Washington, including the completely fabricated story of young George chopping down the cherry tree, was said to write "without fear and without research." Sarah Childress Polk, Denison believed, was just as worthy of emulation. "As a wife, a benefactress, a friend, she is a model for every woman to imitate, whether of exalted or lowly estate." And as a novelist, Denison had a clear sense of what such a woman should be. Denison would become famous for imagining "purer, sweeter, and nobler" women than "are often found in real life." The Sarah Polk whom she profiled was just as pure and as sweet as any of the heroines in her novels. "There is a perfection in her character" that revealed itself in her "eminent piety, and the purity of her life and conversation," in the "sweetness of her countenance . . . the affectionate warmth of her reception," and the "ease in her deportment" even when "richly and most becomingly dressed." First Lady Sarah Polk was nothing less than "a sweet exemplification of lowliness." By this she meant that the First Lady was modest, delicate, and retiring, in short, "the furthest thing from a politician."[29]

Except when her husband's career required her to be political. For what better evidence of a woman's lowliness, in the best sense of the word, than her commitment to do everything in her power to advance her husband? Sarah was willing to make herself "familiar with much that would have burdened others" because she loved her husband. "Whatever was identified with the public career of her husband . . . interested her," Denison asserted, and offered as evidence of her lowliness a story that would be difficult to interpret as anything other than political. "While Mr. Polk resided in Tennessee, a story was put in circulation, calculated to injure his reputation as a public man. He was, at the time of which we speak, several hundred miles away from home." An editor "repaired to Mrs. Polk, and made known the circumstances to her. She instantly led him into her husband's private office, and selecting different journals and manuscripts, referred immediately to the page and paragraph containing proofs of her husband's nonparticipation in the plot imputed to him. These were soon published to the world." When James "accidentally met with a paper, containing a complete refutation of the falsehood," he exclaimed "in extreme, but delighted surprise, 'Why! This is indeed singular—who could have done it? No one but Sarah knew so intimately my private affairs.'" This is a nearly accurate rendering of Sarah's work on James's campaigns, with the important caveat that James would hardly have been surprised at Sarah's actions on his behalf because, more often than not, he was the one directing her.[30]

But with the exception of politics practiced on behalf of one's husband, First Lady Sarah Polk "was as retiring, as gentle, as though the public eye had never scanned her conduct, and the public tongue never sounded her praise." If the aim of Denison's portrait was not verisimilitude but instruction, then a tragic childhood was a fitting start for our heroine. And "lowliness" rather than political acumen was an appropriate summation of her time in the White House. Yet on both accounts Denison was wrong. One can blame Denison for her mistakes, but it was Sarah's own efforts that allowed the public to remember her as "a sweet exemplification of lowliness" rather than the "fine manly Lady" she actually was.[31]

THE FINAL WEEKS in the White House were bittersweet for the First Lady. James had a tremendous amount of last-minute legislation to deal with, including how to admit California as a state without alienating either the North or the South, and whether to establish a Department of the Interior. All of which left him completely "worn down" with "excessive fatigue" each night. And they were turning over the White House to a Whig general whom James had openly antagonized. As thousands of Americans left the cities of the eastern seaboard in search of gold in California, Sarah was consumed with the minutiae of their move and the drama of handing over the White House to new occupants. She likely never heard that her fame had taken on hemispheric proportions. Gold Rush travelers reported seeing her likeness hanging on the wall of the alcalde's office in Gorgona, Panama, in a room decorated with four lithographs, three biblical "Marys," and the fourth, "wonderful to behold . . . still another Mary—a black-haired, red cheeked, staring young woman in a flaming red dress and ermine tippets, a pink rose in her hand, and underneath, the inscription: MARY, WIFE OF JAMES K. POLK, PRESIDENT OF THE UNITED STATES!" The only realistic aspect of the image was the hair: Sarah's was still jet black at age forty-five. Time had indeed "dealt kindly" with Mrs. Polk.[32]

Washington etiquette helped with the transition of power. President-Elect Taylor called on James, and a few days later Sarah threw a White House dinner party, her last, for the incoming president. Leading figures in each party, the cabinet, and other luminaries were invited. Diplomatically seating herself between Taylor and his defeated Democratic opponent, Lewis Cass, she managed her forty guests in such a manner that "not the slightest allusion was made to any political subject." James was pleased and also somewhat surprised that "the whole company seemed to enjoy themselves."[33]

Three days later, James and Sarah said goodbye to the congregation at the First Presbyterian Church, shaking hands with their fellow parishioners. At 3 a.m. the morning after the inauguration they left Washington by steamboat. Their party included James's enslaved servants Elias and Henry, Henry's enslaved wife, Millie, the Polks' White House steward, Henry Bowman, assorted Tennessee friends, and Sarah's two nieces, Sarah Polk Rucker and Virginia Hays, who took advantage of their final evening in Washington to attend Taylor's inaugural ball without the escort of their uncle or aunt. James was optimistic. He felt "sure I shall be a happier man in my retirement than I have been during the four years."[34]

But Sarah kept her thoughts to herself. James's health was a concern, and she had failed to see the construction of Polk Place completed in time for their arrival. The future was unclear. What would she do in Nashville besides keep up her palatial new mansion? Everything at Polk Place was designed to impress. She purchased the fanciest cooking stove available, complete with a copper boiler of the very latest design. It was a fitting place to try out that new cookbook.[35]

IN DECEMBER 1848, the House of Representatives voted on the Wilmot Proviso for a third time, and for the third time passed it on a strictly sectional vote. James made it clear he would veto the bill if it passed the Senate. Northerners were outraged at his proslavery bias. But it was southerners who began talking openly about secession as a legitimate recourse against northern "interference" with their property rights.[36]

Yet the outgoing First Lady and her husband each felt satisfied with their accomplishments. Sarah was showered with praise. The March 1849 issue of *Peterson's Ladies National Magazine,* a cheaper competitor to *Godey's Lady's Book,* offered a six-stanza poem in tribute to "To Mrs. James K. Polk." It honored Sarah as "some bright dame of ancient Rome, Modest, yet all a queen should be," and suggested that it was easy to forget she was "the highest in the land" because she was "all that was lovely, meek and good." The author, Ann Stephens, had long admired Sarah. Now she admitted that she "half forgot thy state, in love of thy bright womanhood."[37]

Newspapers universally praised Sarah's "excellent example and devoted character," asserting that "she has pursued a course and exerted an influence that will make her memory dear to the hearts of Christian people everywhere." No one seemed to doubt that, as one published letter put it, "in full view of the nation" Sarah illustrated the "power of true piety in a manner worthy of all praise and of imitation. . . . She leaves the capital universally esteemed. Mrs. James K. Polk is a true Christian, and in the highest sense, *a lady.*"[38]

A lady, indeed; and in the highest sense. Letter writers from around the country, "in common with thousands of others," assured her of their "regard & esteem." They hoped that her retirement would be sweetened by knowing "how highly the Christian public appreciate the example you have been enabled to set, and its happy influence, not only at the Seat of Government, but throughout the land. It is a great thing for a people to see the Lord's day, and the Lord's house habitually honored . . . and the wife of a Chief Magistrate taking occasion to show, both in public and private, that she is not 'ashamed of Jesus,' but rather glories in His name." By "sustaining the dignity & honor of her high position," an admirer from Boston wrote to James, "yr most excellent lady . . . has filld the measure of her countrys house, in her appropriate sphere, by filling the full measure of the character of an American Woman."[39]

James had always garnered less affection than his wife, and the close of his presidency was no exception. Perhaps this made him vulnerable to the appeal of a final valedictory tour. Sarah had missed the New England tour the summer before. She hadn't seen the crowds that greeted him, or the affectionate addresses of speakers in a region that had been unrelentingly hostile to his administration. A southern tour could be a companion piece, one that would allow Sarah to witness and participate in his public acclaim. So he willingly acceded to a circuitous route home with stops at over a dozen southern cities, providing him maximum exposure to the public, a trip that, conveniently, would be paid for by his hosts along the way.

Sarah may also have relished a final moment in the spotlight. And given that their home was still under construction, they were in no great hurry to return to Nashville. They met crowds of well-wishers in Fredericksburg, Richmond, Petersburg, Wilmington, Charleston, Savannah, Macon, Montgomery, Mobile, and smaller towns along the way. There were bands playing patriotic music (but never on Sunday), including "Hail to the Chief," banners and fireworks, speeches about Manifest Destiny, and lovely receptions in hotels and ballrooms. "Universal approbation" for Sarah's "womanly and sensible course" as First Lady contributed to the "tributes of respect" at every stop. The couple were fêted in every town along the route, just as Andrew Jackson had been twelve years earlier.[40]

But the schedule was grueling. Sarah was so tired in Macon that she skipped the grand ball held in their honor. The following day they were caught in a rainstorm, attended a banquet with four hundred guests, and were up until two in the morning at yet another grand ball.

When they reached Montgomery, James was visibly unwell, with a disturbing cough. The public wanted their president. Assembled throngs at every stop demanded that James speak, and he "felt it was right to do so." But it was becoming abundantly clear to Sarah that this trip had been a mistake. She tried to cut his addresses short because she couldn't shake the "feeling" that his "life was at stake."[41]

That feeling became more pronounced when a passenger on their steamship down the Alabama River died of cholera. Reports circulated that cholera was rampant in New Orleans as well. When they reached the Crescent City the local arrangements committee assured them that the cholera reports were overblown and that the town was perfectly safe. James agreed to attend a dinner in their honor, but Sarah took him home early. She wanted to leave the city immediately, but James's physician told her that while it would be fine for her to flee the city, James could not do so "without seeming to undervalue the honors the city has been arranging for him." Ignoring the recommendations of both doctor and local arrangements committee, she asked for immediate transportation to Nashville. The committee in charge of James's reception insisted there was none available until the day originally planned for their departure. The people of New Orleans demanded their allotted time with the president.[42]

But Sarah didn't care. Ignoring protocol, she thanked the committee and organized alternative transport on a steamer upriver to Memphis. After a passenger on that boat died of cholera near Baton Rouge, she refused to allow James to disembark in Natchez, "much to the disappointment of the people of that city." By the time they reached Memphis, three more passengers had died, and James was very weak. When Millie was diagnosed with cholera the following day, the entire Polk party was thrown into disarray. Fortunately, her case was a mild one.[43]

A month after leaving Washington they finally arrived in Nashville. Although a doctor summoned to examine the president reported him free of cholera, he was far from well. After bearing witness to James's "feebleness," the *Nashville Union* reported that "the most intense anxiety for his health has pervaded the city." An old friend who met with the Polks soon after they returned to Nashville noted that "Mrs. Polk looked as natural as life, with scarce a perceptible change in the four years of absence. But Mr. Polk had changed until I scarcely knew him.

From a pure black, his hair had become perfectly white. It did not change to a silver gray, but to a milk white. . . . He looked care-worn and tired." The change in circumstance struck the friend as poignant. "When he left for Washington, his escorts were thousands," he noted. "Now that his power and patronage is gone, his faithful wife alone remains by his side, and doubtless he is glad they are gone."[44]

AFTER A BRIEF VISIT to their unfinished home, James and Sarah spent ten recuperative days with family in Columbia, followed by a visit of similar length to Sarah's family in Murfreesboro. They welcomed sisters and brothers, nieces and nephews. They allowed their mothers to fuss over them. And they met with well-wishers, including a memorable visit from the teachers and students of the Columbia Female Institute, who paid a call on the couple at James's mother's house not long after they arrived. Aaron Brown's daughter, a student at the school, offered a "beautiful complementary address to Mrs. Polk," and afterward Sarah met and shook hands with each of the two hundred visitors.[45] Near the end of April they finally returned to Nashville. Polk Place, still under construction, was a scene "of great disorder and confusion." Their steward, Henry Bowman, had gone directly to Nashville after their arrival in Tennessee, and made the most of the three weeks before James and Sarah joined him, getting carpets put down, furniture unpacked, and two or three rooms made habitable so that the Polks could move in. But "numerous boxes of furniture, books, groceries, and other articles forwarded from New York, New Orleans, and Columbia, Tennessee, were piled up in the halls and rooms." Elias, Henry, Millie, and some of their other enslaved people settled into wood-framed quarters behind the main building. James and Sarah were overjoyed to be in their new home at last. To the degree possible given the ongoing renovation, "the parlors were thrown open" as they received "old and new friends."[46]

Late spring was beautiful, and they passed an exceedingly pleasant month together in their new home, visiting with friends, organizing furniture, hanging paintings, and overseeing enslaved workers installing trees and shrubs in the unfinished landscape of the generous grounds. Sarah and James discussed finally visiting Europe. Neither had ever left the country, but travel writing in *Godey's Lady's Book,* as well as letters from friends George and Elizabeth Bancroft in England, where George was serving as minister to the Court of St. James's, piqued Sarah's interest. They started planning a trip for the following year.[47]

And they discussed James's historical legacy. With a Whig in the White House, he fretted about the future of his accomplishments. It was easy for him "to foresee, that they will, upon some subjects widely depart from" the policies he had successfully pursued, "and that to that extent, the administration must be unsuccessful, if not disastrous to those who conduct it, and to the party in power." It seemed clear to James that an accurate recording of the previous four years was essential to the preservation of his legacy, and that such a recording was unlikely to happen without his intervention. He could not let the Whigs write the history of the Polk presidency.

In early May 1849, James wrote his former secretary of war, William Marcy, about "the great importance, of having presented to the country, a truthful and reliable history of the remarkable events which were crowded into my Presidential term, and especially of the war. . . . Bancroft could do it well," he admitted. "I had thought of writing to him, and calling his attention to the subject." But Marcy's "knowledge of facts, and the considerations, upon which we acted, especially after Mr. B. retired from the Cabinet, and more particularly as relates to the war, would be more extensive and minute than his could be." Would Marcy himself undertake the work? On Sarah's behalf, James invited William and Cornelia Marcy to Polk Place for an extended visit. They could discuss it further then.[48]

Visitors reported seeing James in his garden that May, behind the great iron fence that enclosed the property, with obvious energy and "erect bearing" that "gave promise of long life." But just a month after they settled into their new home, cholera returned to Nashville. James determined that they would be safer in the country, and insisted that they leave town. Sunday, June 3, the day before their intended departure, Sarah came downstairs to find James lying on a sofa. He told her he would be unable to attend church with her. She responded, "Well, I will go by myself. You cannot always be with me." But he asked her to stay. "Sarah, I do not want you to go. I am too unwell." He never got up again. Sarah sat by his bedside, so consumed with his illness that she didn't notice that their enslaved cook, Matilda, also developed cholera and soon died. A friend sent his own cook to Polk Place and hired a different cook for himself. James's mother arrived, along with other Polk relatives. Sarah failed to notice anything but that her husband was dying.[49]

Healthy adults had a good chance of surviving cholera in 1849. But James's constitution was never strong. Repeated bouts of malaria, as well as chronic diarrhea, had plagued him his entire adult life, and the incessant work and stress of his presidency left him gravely compromised in a struggle with deadly bacteria. His final decline was swift. During a moment of lucidity he attempted to talk to Sarah about their finances. He assured her that "he had so settled the property that it could not be taken from her; that the plantation in Mississippi would support her." Dolley Madison's poverty late in life had affected him deeply. He promised her that Dolley's experience would never be her own, that "his wife should be placed beyond the need of public or private beneficence." Sarah asked him not to speak about it, but he insisted.[50]

When the end was near he made an unexpected and upsetting request. He asked Sarah to call a minister of the Methodist Church to his bedside so that he could be baptized. Jane Polk called her own Presbyterian pastor to try to convince her son to reconsider. Surely he would join the Presbyterian Church, the church that had sustained the women in his life, the church where he had worshipped most Sundays his entire life. He refused, and revealed that back when he was governor he had determined that "when he did embrace Christianity" it would be as a Methodist. Neither Mother Jane nor Sarah had known.

That James had kept such a secret from Sarah must have cut her deeply. He was an intensely secretive man, but Sarah believed she was privy to his secrets. In the presence of Mother Jane, and Sarah, and at least one Presbyterian minister, he was baptized a Methodist. And in the presence of Mother Jane, and Sarah, and at least one friend, he died, less than two weeks after falling ill. The funeral sermon was preached in the Methodist church, as he requested.[51]

James K. Polk, the youngest man to become president, now had the distinction of being the youngest to die. The news stunned Washington. Elizabeth Blair Lee met with friends who were "not very tender of Mr. Polk." She, for one, felt "sorry" for Sarah, whom she knew to be devoted to James. But as for James, she expected "few will mourn deeply."[52]

The depth of Sarah's bereavement defies easy description. Partners in both work and love, she and James had shared a harmonious life together for twenty-five years, more than half her life. Because they spent so much time together, because James had no close male friends, because they had so long lived at a distance from relatives, and because they were childless, they were more dependent upon each other for emotional solace than most couples at their stage of life. James admitted that Sarah knew his "private affairs" better than anyone else. Sarah felt the same way about James. He was just fifty-three years old. They should have had at least another decade together. She was a widow at age forty-five, and saw no path forward, no purpose for continuing. All she could see was that her "life was then a blank."[53]

ALTHOUGH THE EX-PRESIDENT'S official cause of death was listed as "complicated," rather than "cholera," city authorities insisted on his rapid burial in the Nashville City Cemetery outside of town, along with the rest of Nashville's cholera victims. Matilda, the Polk's cook, had been interred in the cemetery's "negro ground" four days earlier. Sarah arranged for a funeral at the Methodist church that Polk had joined on his deathbed, listened as the minister praised his accomplishments and great "moral" character, and then laid him to rest not, as he wished, at home, but in a fine walnut coffin in Felix Grundy's family plot, thanks to Grundy's son-in-law, who hastily found space for the ex-president.

The grieving widow spent the following eleven months trying to bring his body back home, where it belonged. She put William Strickland, the prominent Philadelphia architect who designed the Tennessee capitol building, in charge of constructing a sufficiently monumental edifice to serve as James's final resting place. Strickland created an imposing marble monument shaped like a temple, surrounding James's four-foot-tall tomb. An epithet in his honor covered three sides of the tomb. The fourth side was left blank, reserved for Sarah. By the time

James's remains were finally transferred to Polk Place, on May 22, 1850, the monument was complete.[54]

IT APPEARED to Elizabeth Childress that her daughter was all too ready to take her place by James's side. Sarah had nursed her mother after Joel Childress's sudden death in 1819, willingly leaving Salem Academy and her education behind. Now it was her mother's turn. Hoping to bring Sarah back from her grief, she made a radical suggestion. What if Sarah raised her little grandniece, Sarah Polk Jetton, whom everyone called Sallie? Sarah had been close to Sallie's mother, Mary Childress Jetton, who had been left an orphan when Sarah's elder brother Anderson and his wife both died. Mary looked to her aunt Sarah for advice on both large and small matters, and Sarah sent her gifts.[55]

But Mary died in childbirth, leaving Elizabeth with the care of a motherless newborn great-granddaughter. Sarah had been in Washington at the time of Sallie's birth and Mary's death, but heard about her regularly from family members. In the summer of 1848, Sarah Rucker wrote her aunt, "I saw little Sally Jetton a short time since, you have no idea how much she has grown, she is very pretty and the greatest fidget I ever saw." It was Mary's dying wish that the First Lady might have a hand in the upbringing of her little namesake. Elizabeth hoped that "the sunny presence of childhood might enliven the then desolate home."[56]

Sarah agreed to allow Sallie into her home. Sallie was three when she was delivered to Polk Place, just a few months after James's death, and one imagines quite terrified by the scene that greeted her. The great marble pillars in front of the house were draped with black, and her aunt Sarah was still "inconsolable in her grief." Newspapers, unanimous in their sympathy because "even her late husband's political enemies speak of her as being a most worthy and estimable woman," reported that Sarah had "almost entirely secluded herself from society."[57]

Not that America had forgotten about her. Evidence that her star still shone brightly is suggested by the offerings at Mathew Brady's Daguerreian Gallery in New York City. Only 10 of the 107 portraits of "distinguished persons" on exhibit at Brady's in the summer of

1851 were women. Sarah shared the honor with Dolley Madison, Abigail Adams, and the famous Swedish soprano Jenny Lind. But Sarah seemed to forget about everything outside her grief.[58]

Not even the double wedding of two of her nieces, Joanna and Sarah Polk Rucker, pulled her out of her depression. Joanna was twenty-seven and Sarah twenty-one when they married in a joint ceremony, officiated by the esteemed Methodist minister John B. McFerrin in Murfreesboro on November 6, 1850. Both women had shared the First Lady's life in the White House. Sarah Rucker was with the Polks at the end of their White House sojourn, and had accompanied them back to Tennessee. Joanna had devoted two years to lifting the First Lady's burdens at the start of James's term, primarily by returning social calls. She had kept in close contact with her aunt since, and had not only become Sarah's most faithful correspondent, but also the niece who worked the hardest to impress and please her aunt.[59]

Nevertheless, Sarah did not attend the wedding. And she proved utterly unprepared for the care of a small child. It was John Catron's contention that because Sarah had "always been absorbed in political and social affairs," she was "not the one . . . to have the charge of a little child." Sarah was lucid enough to know she needed help, and turned, as usual, to Childress nieces for help. Sixteen-year-old Mary Childress and fifteen-year-old Susan Rucker, neither of whom had been old enough to visit the White House, settled instead for a long visit with their widowed aunt and three-year-old Sallie. Sarah hired a nurse to take care of Sallie, and purchased a subscription to *Mrs. Whittelsey's Magazine for Mothers,* published by Henry M. Whittelsey, New York. As Elizabeth Childress had hoped, Sallie brought "new light and life into the echoing halls and stately parlors" of Polk Place. Sarah may have wanted to disappear from view, but Sallie Jetton would not allow it.[60]

Nor would her finances. In his will James acknowledged his dependence on Sarah, not only her devotion during "all the vicissitudes" of his political life, but also her "prudence, care and economy" in financial matters. He made her executor of his will—a somewhat unusual role for a woman of Sarah's class and station, and evidence of James's respect for her abilities—and gave her full discretion to dispose of his assets, excepting Polk Place, in which she was granted a life interest.[61]

The bulk of those assets were tied up in the 920-acre Mississippi plantation that he had assured Sarah would support her in her later life. Yet James added a curious note about people they owned, most of whom struggled to pick cotton under some of the most brutal conditions known to enslaved people in North America. Were he to outlive Sarah, he wrote in his will, "it is my intension to emancipate all my slaves, and I have full confidence, that if at her death she shall deem it proper, she shall emancipate them."[62]

It's easy to see in these words an admonishment to Sarah to consider their slaves as people rather than property, and as entitled at some point in the future to their freedom. But there is good reason to believe James added this sentiment to his will for purposes of public consumption rather than a sincere intention to free his human property. He was becoming increasingly concerned with his historical legacy in the final months of his life. As sectional tensions worsened, it was easy to see that public sentiment was turning against slavery, and that the very survival of the "peculiar institution" was in danger. That George Washington had freed his own slaves upon his death had always been understood to be to the first president's credit.

But given that James had assured Sarah on his deathbed that she would be saved from poverty by the profits of the plantation, it's hard to imagine that he had any intent to do away with that income source. If he intended to free his enslaved people, he certainly would have discussed it with Sarah. And had he ever suggested to Sarah that their slaves deserved to be free, she almost certainly would have ensured that this became the case. It's difficult to imagine that a wife as devoted as Sarah would ignore her husband's dying wish.

But the clearest evidence that James had no late-in-life change of heart regarding the humanity of his enslaved people was that the day after he wrote this will, he surreptitiously purchased an additional half dozen "very young slaves" for their plantation, in the same manner in which he had, with Sarah's help, been secretly buying slaves throughout his presidency. James offered a vision of Sarah as emancipator while ensuring that she would become something very different upon his death: a cotton planter.[63]

8

PROFIT AND LOSS

The negrose seem to be much troubled as bout there master. But since they have learned theh be Long to you the are something beter reconciled.

—JOHN MAIRS TO SARAH CHILDRESS POLK, August 19, 1849[1]

I F IT'S TRUE that James K. Polk's presidency was only possible with the help of Sarah, so too was it true that Sarah could only do what she did because of the unacknowledged labor of enslaved servants. Because her slaves took care of her household, did her laundry, cooked her meals, cleaned her home, and tended the garden, she was able to focus on politics. Slave labor paid for the carriage, the fine French garments, and all the other material objects that defined Sarah's identity as a fine lady and social equal to the wealthy women who commanded Washington society. The enslaved people on their plantation grew and harvested the cotton that paid for James's political campaigns, and allowed him the freedom to neglect his legal practice when he was out of office. And they also enabled Sarah to advance his interests. These men and women were truly dependent on Sarah and James, but they were also the vehicle by which Sarah, who was herself dependent on James, was able to flower into a political actor.[1]

Sarah Polk had owned slaves her entire life. Her wealth was slave-based, her appeal as a marriage prospect based in part in her dowry's nine inherited slaves, her work on her husband's behalf facilitated by her slaves' labor, her prospects as a widow secured by her plantation slaves. Like most white women who owned slaves, Sarah was invested in a paternalistic understanding of her relationship to her slave property. It was an important part of a southern plantation mistress's identity that, as a moral Christian, she provided the love and care for "her" enslaved people that transformed them from property to family. The claim that white women were sentimentally attached to their slaves was universally asserted by slave owners to help justify slavery, despite ample evidence that women could be as brutal as their husbands to their human property.[2]

There is a great deal of evidence that Sarah initially considered herself the very best sort of slavemistress. The responsibility that she felt for the slaves she employed in her home did not extend to freeing them, or to paying them, or to any measures that might improve their lives if they would disrupt hers. But Sarah was no doubt convinced that she was a "good" slavemistress, and that she protected her slaves from the worst excesses of enslaved life, both excessive corporal punishment and the breakup of families through sale.

It had always been James's contention that Sarah was overly indulgent of "her people," meaning the Childress family slaves, and more particularly those people left to her in her father's will. When Sarah was first married and the enslaved people she received from her father were removed for sale, she had sheltered teenaged Mariah over the objections of her mother and brothers. Mariah ran away "to" Sarah, and Sarah rewarded her fidelity by insisting that James buy Mariah from the Childress creditors.

But the limits of Sarah's solicitude were made obvious when Mariah was shipped off to the first Polk plantation in Tennessee. James was desperate for laborers, and perhaps Mariah had already met the slave from a neighboring plantation whom she would later marry, Henry Carter. But Sarah understood that Mariah would have preferred to remain a lady's maid in her employment than a cotton picker. Despite this predictable betrayal by the woman who claimed to protect her, Mariah maintained the pretense of affection for Sarah, and in return Sarah convinced James to purchase Henry Carter so the couple could live together. Sarah later insisted that James employ Mariah and Henry Carter's son, also named Henry, as a house servant in Tennessee and eventually in the White House.[3]

Mariah was smart. She took advantage of the opportunity to train herself as a weaver, and proudly informed Sarah in 1841 that her new skills had increased her value by thirty dollars. Mariah didn't hesitate to ask for information from the First Lady, particularly when it pertained to her son, Henry. In 1847 the Polk Plantation overseer added a postscript to a letter to James: "Marier request me to give heir respects to you and her Mistes and if you pleas in the next Leter your rite me to let hir nough hough hir sone Henry is iff well and houg he is doing."[4]

Sarah asked James to intercede on behalf of other Childress family slaves, and his experiences with Harbert, whom Sarah inherited when he was just three years old, taught James the value of regarding her wishes. Harbert was perpetually "unruly," so much so that James made the decision to banish the young man to Gideon Pillow's Mississippi cotton plantation, but only after Pillow promised Sarah that he would return Harbert to her at some point. That point came sooner than Pillow, or James, wished. After Harbert's mother protested to Sarah, she demanded that James not only get Harbert back, but also purchase his wife, Mary, and son, Lewis, both of whom were owned by Pillow.[5]

James set aside his presidential duties to negotiate with Pillow. "As we own his mother Mrs. Polk has . . . a desire that I should get him back," he wrote. Pillow was resistant. Harbert was "as valuable a boy as I can get," Mary was the plantation's "valuable" cook, and their seven-year-old son, Lewis, was "a very likely & smart & stout boy" and "large for his age . . . one of the drivers for my gin the past season, though he was small for that business." James ultimately paid $1,436 for all three of them, $100 more than he believed they were worth.[6]

Sarah's self-image as benevolent stood in stark contrast to her efforts on behalf of slavery. As wife of the Speaker of the House, she helped her husband pass the "gag rule" tabling without discussion any petitions against slavery. As First Lady she promoted a war that expanded slave territory. And she believed slavery to be part of God's plan. James liked to repeat a story from early in their White House tenure, what he described as Sarah's "acumen" on the topic. Gazing out the window at slaves working the grounds on a hot July afternoon, Sarah interrupted her husband from his writing with the assertion that "the writers of the Declaration of Independence were mistaken when they affirmed that all men are created equal." When James suggested this was just "one of your foolish fancies," Sarah elaborated. "There are those men toiling in the heat of the sun, while you are writing, and I am sitting here fanning myself . . . surrounded with every comfort. Those men did not choose such a lot in life, neither did we ask for ours; we were created for these places."[7]

James's death left Sarah owner of the fifty-six people on her 920-acre plantation, and however much she might believe her life to be over, what had actually changed was the power she now held over other lives. Abolitionists understood that there was no such thing as a "good" slaveholder, and that it was impossible for any man or woman who held the power of life or death over another individual to remain unsullied by the experience. Frederick Douglass described the "fatal poison of irresponsible power" as inevitably turning slave-owning women "of the kindest heart and finest feeling" into "demons." While James was alive it was possible for Sarah to imagine herself the protector of "her people." But the events of the 1850s would make clear the impossibility of imagining oneself a benevolent slaveholder when your people were growing cotton for export in Mississippi.[8]

JAMES WAS DETERMINED to "make more money or loose more" when he purchased the Yalobusha planation in 1834. Because they were absentee owners, the Polks were not privy to either the day-to-day workings of the planation or the sufferings of its workers, but they were highly aware of its balance sheet. Polk's overseers, like all slave drivers, understood that their job was to extract profit from human bodies and that they would be fired if they failed to do so to the owner's satisfaction. They were not fired for working slaves too hard or for whipping them unnecessarily.

Not surprisingly, the result was that the Polk Plantation's most successful overseers were also the most brutal. Plantations on the cotton frontier have been described by historians as "slave labor camps," where planters expanded their operations by purchasing enslaved people from traders as quickly as they could, and then torturing them into picking cotton "faster and more efficiently than free people." The Polk Plantation was worse than most. Infant mortality was higher than on comparable plantations, and the mortality rate among young women was much higher than average. At least seven of the twenty-one women on the Polk Plantation died young, six of them within a few years of arriving in Yalobusha County. There was also a remarkably high rate of flight by male slaves. Premature deaths, desperate acts of running away, and the sales of errant slaves together weakened the sense of community on the Polk Plantation that sustained slaves throughout the South. Only nine of the twenty-one slaves that James sent to Mississippi in 1835 were still there twenty-five years later. Only two survived to old age.[9]

The fact that Polk's slaves ran away more often than did slaves on other plantations was in large part due to the bleak conditions on the plantation. But Sarah's reputation for sheltering slaves from abuse also played a role. She did nothing to remove the overseers her slaves complained about, but she pressed for special treatment for the bondspeople she inherited, including Matilda, Harbert, and another inveterate runaway by the name of Jim. James's sisters in Tennessee also harbored runaway slaves from the Mississippi plantation, and took their sides against overseers. By 1841, Polk's slaves in Mississippi regarded Tennessee through the lens of nostalgia. It was, they claimed, "a place of parridise." It seemed within reach, so they fled, some of them regularly.[10]

One of the Polks' more brutal overseers, Isaac Dismukes, blamed James for the bad behavior of his slaves. Noting that slaves "runaway from all" the Polk overseers, he suggested that if James were more manly the problem would resolve itself. "You wil have to bea the man that wil have to stop that amongst your negroes." The solution Dismukes suggested was torture, whippings so intense and prolonged that the slaves would be forced to submit to plantation discipline. James conceded to Dismukes's disciplinary strategy, despite complaints from his sisters and their husbands about the overseer's brutality.[11]

But torture wasn't enough. The Yalobusha plantation continued operating at a substantial capital loss until the 1844 election. As we've seen, Manifest Destiny was a winning issue for the Polks in more than one way. Texas annexation won James the White House, and its impact on the value of slaves made him rich. James made nearly $9,000 (more than a quarter of a million dollars today) in capital gains from the value of his slaves over the course of his presidency.[12]

Not only did the slaves themselves considerably enrich the Polks during James's presidency, but so too did the plantation. It averaged a profit of $2,700 a year for the four years he was in office (about $81,000 today). The Polks' total expenses during four years in the White House were $54,000, a little more than half of his salary during those four years. So although he entered the White House $16,000 in debt, mostly due to election expenses, he was soon solvent, thanks to his planation. He used the entirety of his plantation profits to purchase nineteen additional slaves in order to expand his operation.[13]

Although Sarah helped James purchase slaves for the plantation, had visited the plantation on several occasions in the early 1840s, and had intervened on behalf of Childress family slaves in Mississippi, there is no evidence that she was involved in the management of the property before James's sudden death. Sarah, who had worried about the responsibilities of ownership of Polk Place, was unprepared for the reality of plantation management. Just before James died, cotton prices stumbled, and then fell dramatically, the result of political upheaval in Europe. Within weeks of becoming widowed, she had to face the deteriorating situation at the plantation. Rather than do so directly, she enlisted a mutual friend to write to the Polk's Plantation's overseer, John Mairs, who had been in place since the early days of James's presidency. He had run the plantation with little supervision, but now, in the midst of 1849's growing season, he found himself taking orders from Sarah, whom he had never met.[14]

We have no record of what Sarah said to Mairs in that first letter, because it, like the vast majority of her letters, has been lost to posterity. Mairs responded in August 1849. He addressed his letter to "Sarah Polk wife of the Late Ex-president James K. Polk." Noting that James's death was "very unexpected and most distressing to me," he added that the slaves "seem to be much troubled as bout there master," no doubt because they feared the breakup of the plantation and the destruction of their community through sale. "But since they have learned theh be Long to you," he wrote, "the are something beter reconciled."[15]

One can only imagine the relief among the slaves at Polk's Yalobusha plantation when they learned that the plantation and their families would remain intact. The fact that a woman who believed herself benevolent was now their mistress may have been cause for optimism, spread by the people who knew Sarah best: Mariah and her husband, Henry, and Harbert and his wife, Mary. Mariah and Harbert could testify that Sarah had served as a moderating force in the Polk home and had prevented James from breaking up their families.

From that time on Mairs wrote Sarah regularly, usually once a month. He addressed her as "Mrs. Sarah Polk," the only person among dozens of correspondents over seven decades who did so. Mairs was not an educated man, and had he realized that she referred to herself as "Mrs. James K. Polk," no doubt he would have done likewise. But she never corrected him.

If Mairs thought it strange to work for a woman, he showed no sign of it. Daniel Graham and Sarah's brother John acted as her advisors in business matters, with John in charge of most deliveries to the plantation, but from the outset Mairs made his monthly reports to Sarah, and at least pretended to take direction from her. He appealed to her, rather than her brother or Graham, to make the important decisions at the plantation. In his second letter he asked for instructions about the marketing and sale of her cotton. "You have not givin me enny dy Recttions About your coten. . . . Please give me some Dy Recttions about the coten or eny thing els you want don. We have packed 22 Bals of coten I will sen you the wats and numbers."[16]

She turned to one of Jane Walker's sons-in-law, William Pickett, to market her cotton from his firm's base in New Orleans, and less than a year after James's death, in the early spring of 1850, made a visit to the plantation. Mairs reported that "the Negros was muched pleased to hear that you was coming doune to sey them." When he asked for a raise, Sarah gave it to him. His $550 salary was generous, but during the first years of Sarah's ownership of the plantation Mairs appeared to deserve it. In 1852, Pickett attributed the "unusually high price" her cotton fetched to the "beautiful manner" in which the overseer "prepared" her cotton "for the market." In reality, it was the slaves under Mairs's control who prepared Sarah's cotton so beautifully, but white men and women who owned slaves generally spoke about the work of their slaves as if it were their own. As an absentee owner, Sarah was insulated from thinking about the hard labor of cotton production.[17]

This does not mean Sarah had no responsibilities. She still had to decide when to sell her cotton, an all-important decision upon which hundreds if not thousands of dollars could be made or lost. Pickett made suggestions: "The market may keep up for some time, and even get better—but I am decidedly in favor of selling at present," he advised on November 9, 1849. But whether to do so was ultimately Sarah's call. Pickett was solicitous of Sarah. He invited her to "call on" him in New Orleans. But she was a wary owner, on the lookout for fraud. Pickett reported on the condition of all her cotton, and sent regular copies of the "stock" report for the New Orleans markets, including cotton.[18] But when Sarah believed the price on the cotton exchange unfair, she complained. When she noticed an unidentified expense in her "account sales," she asked for clarification.[19]

She was also responsible for provisioning the plantation. Every spring, her agent bought supplies in New Orleans, on Sarah's orders, and had them sent upriver when the Yazoo was high. She purchased three dozen pairs of brogans, heavy and stout low-cut work shoes, hard and clumsy, for men and women. Children went barefoot. And adult slaves received "Campeachy hats," like the ones worn by Mexican peasants in the fields of Campeche, in order to protect them from the brutal southern sun. Practicality at a cheap price, rather than the comfort of the slaves, was Sarah's goal in both cases. Most plantations had to purchase cheap slave cloth from the North, but Sarah was fortunate at the outset of her plantation management that Mariah, whom she had once harbored, could weave an impressive seven yards of cloth a day, enough to make summer clothes for the plantation's slaves, and fabric for winter garments as well. "Negro Cloth" was notoriously poor in quality and rough in texture. Mariah almost certainly made better. Sarah purchased blankets (said to be of decent quality), as well as other supplies for the plantation—rope, twine, bagging, iron, and steel. Mairs occasionally complained that she had not bought enough steel or iron, but in general her provisioning seems to have met with his satisfaction.[20]

When William Pickett left his firm in 1857, he continued to court her business, as did a number of other middlemen anxious to "solicit the consignment of your crop of cotton." Pickett, who had moved to Memphis, encouraged Sarah to begin shipping cotton from that city instead of New Orleans. In July 1857, he predicted that the Mississippi and Tennessee Railroad would within a year "perhaps penitrate as far

as Granada [its destined point] and maybe within a very short distance
from your plantation." Two months later he was more adamant, assuring her that "a majority of the planters in that county [Yalobusha]
will now ship their crops to Memphis." He promised her she would
"receive more for" her crop in Memphis than New Orleans. But Sarah
chose stability over risk, even at the cost of family ties, and stuck with
her firm in New Orleans.[21]

One scholar who analyzed the Polk Plantation in detail suggested
that Sarah's "close oversight of the plantation is worthy of commen-
dation." And the remarkable financial success of the plantation in her
hands suggests that she was a canny businesswoman, perhaps more
so than she could have imagined. During the ten years that she was
sole owner, the plantation itself increased in value by $4,000. But her
success may well have been due more to luck and forces outside her
control than to skill. The end of revolution in Europe in 1849 led to a
worldwide cotton boom, while both northerners and southerners felt
cautiously optimistic about the decline in sectional tensions following
the Compromise of 1850. Sarah's cotton was selling for 12.5 cents a
pound in 1856, and as of 1857 slave prices had doubled from the day
James entered office.[22]

Unlike most cotton planters, Sarah was conservative in her investments, and unwilling to maximize her profits when there was a potential for loss. James determined to grow cotton in Mississippi because
he hoped to become rich. But Sarah stuck with shipping from New
Orleans when her agent promised her higher profits in untested Memphis. She never expanded her holdings in order to grow more cotton.
And in contrast to James's policy of purchasing healthy young people
from dealers in order to expand the portion of his plantation under cul-
tivation, Sarah bought exactly one additional person, Alfonso. And she
purchased him because he was husband to her enslaved laborer Maria
Davis. She convinced her nephew Marshall to sell Alfonso in order to
keep the marriage together.[23]

She was also unwilling to go into debt. Most planters made regular
use of credit, often going into debt to their cotton agents. Sarah's agent
in New Orleans noted that she was "anxious to avoid" the "credit
system," and he managed her affairs with respect for her seemingly
unusual desires in this matter, reminding her, however, that he was

"always ready to supply your wants" if she did decide to proceed on credit.[24]

There were setbacks, including some serious ones. In 1853, boll weevils and rain decimated the crop, and the following year a fire at the Yalobusha River warehouse destroyed two-thirds of the crop. Although Sarah held insurance on the cotton, it did not cover accidents taking place in the warehouse, so she lost a great deal of money. But this loss was offset by the considerable increase in the value of the men and women she owned.

On April 25, 1855, Perkins had "further disasters to your cotton" to report, a remarkable series of unfortunate events that led him to conclude, "A fatality seems to attend your Crop of Cotton this year."

> The 55 bales <u>not burned</u> at Troy were shipped on a Keel boat as soon as there was sufficient water in the river, which Keel boat was sunk in the Yallobusha before reaching a reshipping point. Your cotton was recovered in a damaged condition and again shipped on board the steamer <u>"Texana"</u>—and this boat took fire in the Yazoo river & was consumed with most of her cargo.

The cotton that survived one fire, and then survived a watery grave, only to be burned in a second fire, remarkably resulted in less loss than had the Troy cotton, due to insurance. "This cotton was insured at $50 a bale, a high valuation and more than it would probably bring in the market." Perkins promised to look into it and in the meantime asked her to "instruct" him "what you will have done with the proceeds of the cotton." He provided a final settlement in a letter dated January 18, 1856.[25]

But even in those two terrible years, Sarah's profits were still 10 percent a year. Overall the plantation provided her with an 11 percent average profit.[26]

OF COURSE, that 11 percent profit came at a sharp cost. When Sarah inherited the plantation, it was home to fifty-five enslaved people, and more than half the children died before reaching the age of fifteen. During Sarah's first ten years of ownership, thirty-six babies were born into slavery on the plantation. Thirty slaves, including seventeen babies, died, and plantation births outnumbered plantation deaths by 12 percent. This was an improvement from the period before Sarah took over management, but it was substantially less than the 23.5 percent average population increase among slaves elsewhere in the South in the 1850s. Dafney and Giles, the slave couple who were married, in Dafney's words, when "we were neither of us hardly grown," lost six of their ten children before they reached adulthood. There was so much death in their family that in later years Dafney was unable to recall exactly when she lost each of her children.[27]

Not only was infant mortality higher on Sarah's plantation than on most, but the mortality rate among young adults was dramatically higher than the norm. Most of the Polk Plantation was flat and wet, clearly "unhealthy ground." For purposes of surveillance, overseers crowded the slaves into cramped quarters, facilitating the spread of infectious disease. In 1852 six Polk slaves died of pneumonia, bacterial infection, and whooping cough. That fall and winter so many enslaved people were ill that they left one-sixth of the cotton crop to rot in the fields. In 1853 five enslaved people suffered from dysentery, and in 1854 the plantation was hit with typhoid fever, both of which resulted in excruciating suffering. Most of the men and women who labored on the Polk Plantation had been purchased from the upper and middle South, so to their peril they lacked resistance to malaria, a debilitating and frequently deadly disease endemic to the Deep South. And clearly John Mairs pushed some of the laborers until they died, despite his assertion to Sarah when many of the men and women were "unwell with bad colds" that "I am not pushing, think it better to lose a little tim than a negro." Young black men and women, children, and newborn babies on the Polk Plantation suffered and died painful, unnecessary deaths all the time.[28]

But these tragedies were, by definition, abstract to an absentee owner. Overseers were paid to terrorize slaves for profit, but they were equally responsible for providing plausible deniability to their employer, to protect the owner from the reality of the indignities and tortures and death endemic to plantations. So although it is fair to say that compared to many other slave owners Sarah was a "good mistress" to the slaves with whom she developed personal relationships,

Sallie, age seventeen, on James's tomb. *George N. Bernard, Photographer, 1864. Library of Congress Prints and Photographs Division.*

A Union soldier in the side yard of Polk Place gazes reverentially at James K. Polk's tomb, 1862–1865. *Photograph by T. M. Schleirer from the Collection of Herb Peck. Courtesy of the Tennessee Historical Museum.*

Newly sworn-in president Andrew Johnson issued this blanket pass to Sarah to sell her cotton without constraint or tax, June 3, 1865. *Andrew Johnson Papers, Library of Congress.*

Polk Place as seen from the North Portico of the Tennessee Capitol Building. Polk Place was clearly visible from the State House, and was within easy shot of Union cannons, as this photo, taken during Union occupation, makes clear. *Courtesy of the James K. Polk Memorial Association, Columbia, Tennessee.*

Elias Polk, in the only known image of any of the Polk family enslaved people. *Courtesy of the James K. Polk Memorial Association, Columbia, Tennessee.*

Captain Marshall Tate Polk, flanked by two fellow Confederate officers. *Courtesy of Dr. Bill Shultz.*

Two images of the interior of Polk Place, ca. 1880. *Courtesy of the James K. Polk Memorial Association, Columbia, Tennessee.*

Sarah Childress Polk, age seventy-five, 1878. *Courtesy of the James K. Polk Memorial Association, Columbia, Tennessee.*

Sarah Childress Polk and her family, 1889. Sarah is seen here with Sallie, George, and Saidie Polk, and their unnamed dog. *The Miriam and Ira D. Wallach Division of Art, Prints and Photographs: Print Collection, The New York Public Library.*

Frances Willard. Willard, the president of the Woman's Christian Temperance Union, helped build support for the temperance cause by celebrating Sarah's model of womanhood. *Library of Congress Prints and Photographs Division.*

Mrs. Elizabeth Childress Brown. *Courtesy of the Tennessee State Library Association.*

Sallie and Sarah, ca. 1870. *Courtesy of the James K. Polk Memorial Association, Columbia, Tennessee.*

those acts count for little when weighed against her liability as a slave owner. She treated Mariah, and some of the other Childress slaves, as individuals, and occasionally did benevolent acts in their favor. Quite likely, she felt sorrow when she heard about Mariah's death, at age thirty-seven, of unexplained spasms stemming from a chronic gynecological condition. She and Sarah had a long history, after all, one that stretched back to Sarah's life in Murfreesboro, before her marriage. But the ability of slave owners to maintain distance from the suffering of the people they owned, suffering that was ultimately their responsibility regardless of the mediation of an overseer, reveals the basic and inescapable corruption of slavery. The only truly benevolent slave owner was the woman or man who freed all their slaves.[29]

Sarah had other tragedies to contend with in the early 1850s. Both of her recently married nieces, Joanna and Sarah, died in childbirth within three years of being married, just three months apart. Joanna had lived with her aunt for two years and adored her. She directly modeled her behavior on her aunt Sarah's, turning to her for direction about what to read and how to spend her time, years after the two were separated. The same minister who officiated at the joint wedding of the two Rucker daughters returned to Murfreesboro in December 1853 to preach their joint funeral sermon. Although Sarah did not attend the wedding, she most likely made the trip to Murfreesboro for their funerals.[30]

And despite Sarah's lifelong aversion to breaking up slave families, she was ultimately responsible for the separation of three. The first two came after Mother Jane's death in 1852, and Sarah's culpability might not have been clear to her. Jane Polk held a life interest in three of the people on Sarah's plantation. After her death, all three became Jane's grandson Marshall's property. Sarah proposed to exchange slaves with Marshall in order to preserve the marriages of two of the slaves, but for reasons that remain unclear, all three were moved to Marshall's plantation in Bolivar against their will, and with much distress to the Polk Plantation community.[31]

But her decision in 1856 to sell Harbert after years of "protecting" him was entirely her own. She could blame no one else. Mairs couldn't handle him any better than had previous overseers. Mairs was adamant that thirty-six-year-old Harbert was a "bad boy," and after his fifth attempt at escape, Sarah sold him away from his wife, Mary, and their teenage son, Lewis.[32]

If Sarah ever had any taste for plantation management, she lost it with Harbert's sale. She stopped writing monthly letters to John Mairs, and he responded in kind. His own lack of enthusiasm was no doubt colored by the fact that Sarah owed him $339.06 in back wages in 1857. The crop the following year was disappointing, just 129 bales, or 20 bales below average. Mairs had difficulty mustering his usual enthusiasm for the enterprise. "I am in hops we will be more fortunate this year," he wrote Sarah in January 1858.[33]

But Mairs wasn't trusting his salary to fortune. Using every weapon at his disposal, he pushed the slaves so hard that something snapped. On November 1, 1858, Mairs threatened to whip one of the enslaved men, and the rest fought back. Led by Giles and Manuel, the slaves armed themselves with "axes, hatchets, clubs, scythes, stones, &c. . . . and swore they would die to a man before one of their party should be whipped." It took seventy-five white men, one of whom was seriously injured, to subdue an uprising that the newspapers proclaimed a great "negro rebellion." Giles and Manuel were indicted for "conspiracy to make rebellion," an offense punishable by execution, and taken to jail.[34]

But thanks to Sarah's intervention, Giles and Manuel were not put to death. The attorney she hired on their behalf requested and received a change of venue to Tallahatchie County, and then successfully challenged the indictment on the grounds of habeas corpus. After an initial mistrial, Giles and Manuel returned to prison. Sarah petitioned the presiding judge for bail, again on the grounds of habeas corpus, and after paying $3,000, brought both men back home on the last day of January 1860.[35]

Three thousand dollars was a tremendous amount of money, but it's worth asking why a Mississippi judge allowed the ringleaders of a widely publicized slave rebellion to post bail at any price. After all, they were returning to the same plantation, and the same slave community, where they had reportedly armed their fellow laborers with weapons and faced down their overseer. One has to conclude that Sarah received special treatment from the court. The drawn-out nature of the legal proceedings also suggests that the state of Mississippi felt some misgivings about putting to death two slaves once owned by President

Polk. Sectional tensions had never been higher, and the publicity surrounding such an execution would not have reflected well on either the
South or its labor system.[36]

Nor is it clear why Sarah agreed to pay such an outrageous sum in
bail, particularly given that Mississippi law reimbursed slave owners
for half the value of their executed human property. The average price
of an enslaved person in 1860 was $800. If Sarah thought of the two
men strictly as property, if she wished to punish them, or if her abiding interest was in the submission of her plantation's slave community,
she would never have brought them back home. Giles and Manuel's
fate remained uncertain as the case made its way through the appeals
process in the beginning of the 1860s. But Sarah's bond was never
discharged.[37]

Cotton plantations had very little to recommend themselves to their
owners beyond profitability. But that was generally enough. Despite
the high death rate at the Polk Plantation, a slave uprising, and repeated
unforeseen disasters with the crop, Sarah's plantation did exactly what
James intended: it provided his widow with a steady income. It was
still doing so two weeks after Giles and Manuel returned to Polk Plantation, when Sarah sold away "the undivided one-half" of her plantation and fifty-six slaves. The purchaser was James M. Avent, who had
several years earlier married twenty-three-year-old Mary Childress,
the niece who lived with Sarah at Polk Place shortly after James's
death. Avent, almost twenty years older than Mary, had capital to spare
and dreams of getting rich on cotton after a career as an attorney in
Murfreesboro.[38]

It's unclear what motivated Sarah to take the highly unusual step of
selling an "undivided" half interest in her plantation and its people to a
step-nephew. There's no evidence that she was in need of money. The
1860 census listed the value of her personal property at $105,000, and
Polk Place itself at $110,000. She was clearly tired of plantation man-
agement, and according to testimony from the Polk Plantation slaves,
their home came "under" Avent's "management" starting in 1860. It's
possible that the rise of the antislavery Republican Party raised Sarah's
concern about the future of the peculiar institution, although it would
be several months before the party would name Abraham Lincoln
their 1860 presidential candidate. She may well have been motivated to

assist a niece who had provided her with comfort after James's death. What is clear is that although James suggested in his will that Sarah might at some point free their slaves, she did no such thing. Saving Giles and Manuel's lives was a benevolent act, but her benevolence had clear limits. Instead of liberating "her people," she turned them, and the capital gains they represented, into cash. She sold out her benevolent pretentions for $30,000.[39]

But half ownership was still ownership. In the view of both the residents of the plantation and the federal government, it remained very much Sarah Polk's property. The 1860 census listed her as owner of sixty slaves in Mississippi. She continued to profit from her plantation's cotton throughout the Civil War. And of the twelve former slaves living on or near the Polk Plantation who provided testimony years later, not one identified Avent as the owner of either themselves or the plantation where they labored. Lewis, whose father, Harbert, was sold away from him when he was seventeen, gave clear testimony in 1887 that "I formally belonged to Mrs. J. K. Polk and lived on the Polk Plantation." Caroline, the daughter of the plantation midwife, agreed. "We were all owned by President James K. Polk and his widow after his death."[40]

Despite the nearly universal assertion by scholars that Sarah sold the plantation in 1860, it wasn't until 1870 that she and the Avents sold "the tract of land known as the 'Polk Plantation'" to a third party for $10,000, a fraction of its prewar value. The loss hurt Avent far more than Sarah, given that he had paid her $30,000 for half ownership of the land and its occupants ten years earlier. From a business perspective, Sarah had done quite well for herself.[41]

DESPITE SARAH'S BUSINESS SUCCESS, the decade after James's death was a struggle. Apart from weekly appearances in pew 137 at the Nashville First Presbyterian Church she rarely left Polk Place. Beyond that initial trip to visit John Mairs and her plantation in 1850, she appears to have left town only to visit family in Columbia and Murfreesboro. She cut back on shopping; her decreased expenditures reflecting her circumscribed public life rather than diminished finances. She still had to care for Sallie, of course, and continued to buy shoes from the likes of Nashville's Daniel and Ben Winter ladies' fashionable shoemakers, and hats from New Orleans' Olympe millinery and fancy dry goods store. But the sum total of these purchases was just a fraction of those in the past. Rather than buy new dresses for herself, she chose instead to remake her Washington frocks.[42]

By 1853 she had begun entertaining again, although her limited purchases of claret ($1.50 a bottle) and champagne ($1 a bottle) from the liquor and wine retailer George Grieg were also a fraction of her past expenditures. In 1854 the Tennessee legislature began what would be a yearly tradition of making a "New Year's call" on Sarah at Polk Place. The First Lady, dressed in mourning, was said to have received them "with that courtesy, grace, and hospitality for which this excellent lady is so distinguished." Nieces were visiting again, none more frequently than John Childress's teenage daughter Bettie, who enjoyed helping her aunt with the receptions.[43]

When Congress granted Sarah franking privileges, allowing her to mail letters without paying for postage, it was an honor never before shown to a First Lady. But Sarah wrote few letters in the 1850s. Instead she read. She had always been a reader, but after James's death she plunged into British history. In 1850 she ordered eleven volumes on the *Lives of the Queens of England,* carefully inscribing "Mrs. James K. Polk" in each of them. She plowed through Thomas Macaulay's *History of England* and William Shakespeare's complete works. Turning her head toward the continent, she read French scholar Arsène Houssaye's *Men and Women of the Eighteenth Century,* and a collection of biblical lectures by a divinity professor at King's College London. She received Martin Tupper's *Proverbial Philosophy* from her "sincerely attached friend" Ann Wright in 1849. In taste and content these volumes marked a return to her reading habits at Salem Academy: books about powerful women, books about serious philosophical matters. Sarah was reading for her own pleasure now, and the topics that pleased her were telling. She was thinking about her own legacy, about female power, and about religion. There is no need to explain the Shakespeare: in the mid-nineteenth century everyone loved him.[44]

About the only American volume she acquired in the first years after James's death was Sheppard M. Ashe's *Monterey Conquered: A Fragment from La Gran Quivera; or, Rome Unmasked.* Ashe's tribute

to the heroism of Tennessee volunteers in Mexico was a thoroughgo-
ing celebration of Manifest Destiny in classical garb. Following "the
star of Empire Westward," Ashe attempted to "sing his country—her
political and religious destiny—her arms and institutions—her unaffected manners, and moral worth." Admitting that his seven-canto
epic poem was a "freak of Fancy," Ashe was likely aware that *Monterey
Conquered* was no *Iliad* or *Odyssey*. But Sarah's attraction to the piece
is easy to understand. Ashe, a minor functionary in Tennessee politics
and a committed Democrat, had been an acquaintance of James's, and
his poem closely reflected Sarah's convictions about the justness of the
war and James's heroic place in it.[45]

> Thou son of Washington! my harp in vain
> Would sing thy praise; for the wild surging main
> Doth chant, and winds, where'er our banners play,
> Acknowledge thee. Thy glory shall remain
> Eternal as the hills of Monterey;
> And a whole nation, bursting party's chain,
> Invite their only living Washington to reign.[46]

James was "Augustus, worthy of some noble song," leading his

> countrymen, thus armed with right
> To scourge yon vain, intolerable foe
> And make them feel and own Columbia's might,
> By sparing when their capital lies low;
> Then offer peace, that all the world may know
> Americans take no delight in blood,
> And unprovoked had never struck the blow.

Opponents of the war, by contrast, were "the base of a degener-
ate age."[47]

Sarah thought about her own place in history, happily submitting
to an interview with Mrs. E. F. Ellet, author of the volume *Women of
the Revolution,* when she visited Nashville "to collect reminiscences
of the Pioneer Women of Nashville." Sarah took the "liberty" of rec-
ommending a female friend to Ellet, "as one that might be interested
in her object." Expressing her own finely developed views of the eti-

quette of social calls, she offered the following advice to her friend: "If you are not disposed to receive this literary Tourist, you need not be at home."[48]

As the bushes and trees about Polk Place burst into flower in the spring of 1852, Sarah discovered her interest in the outside world also revived. "Although my spirits have undergone such a trial in the death of my lamented husband, time has calmed me" she wrote to her brother-in-law William, who had recently been elected to Congress. Given the sectional divisions in the Democratic Party, there was a real possibility that another dark horse presidential candidate would win the party's nomination in June. "I find that I cannot now withdraw my mind from the political affairs of my country," she admitted to William. While she did not "claim to have patriotism," she told him, a life spent "with one so pure" as James was "calculated to make lasting impressions. His devotion to the interest of the country, was *self*-sacrificing." She made a request of the congressman: "I . . . would like for you occasionally to give me some of the items of news, & speculations as to the probabilities of coming events, believing I have some character for discretion. I hope that you will not be afraid to put on paper your views that are not intended for the public. Will our friend Donelson get the Census printing? Who is your candidate for the Presidency?"[49]

And in fact, the Democratic Party still needed her. When Democrats gathered in Nashville prior to the election of 1856, the assembled military companies paid a call on Sarah. The *Nashville Union* reported that "having been so much identified with public life, and partaken so fully of the sentiments of her illustrious husband, for long years the pride and support of the Democratic party, it is but natural that she should continue to feel a lively interest in the success of the Democracy and the consequent ascendancy of its principles."

But while Sarah found the convention tribute "gratifying" and admitted to being a "cordial well-wisher for the triumph of our party on this and all other occasions," she refused to publicly comment on the election because to do so would be unladylike. The *Nashville Union* approved entirely. "She maintains inviolate that ladylike reserve and abstinence from all overt political action, so becoming to one of her age and position in the esteem of the American people irrespective of party."[50]

Of course, Sarah's "ladylike reserve" from "overt political action" was, as always, a façade. Late in life she claimed that she had never recommended friends for office, on the grounds that it was "undignified to make such solicitations," and were she successful, "it would be heralded over the country that she was now meddling with politics." She was clearly worried that public acknowledgment that she was politically active would "render her liable to the loss of whatever influence she might possess." Yet she continued to exercise her influence by calling in political favors. Earlier that year she had drawn on the political capital she still held in Washington, writing to Secretary of War Jefferson Davis to request a brevet for an officer friend. Davis promised to present the officer's name to President Franklin Pierce for the honor.[51]

James Buchanan's election in 1856 fully captured Sarah's attention. Although she had at one time mocked his sexuality, he had been her close friend and frequent companion in the 1840s. And, of course, he had been James's secretary of state. His elevation to president brought back a host of pleasant memories.[52]

It also returned her to power as a source of political information. When James had asserted that no one knew his affairs as closely as did his wife, he received no contradiction. Her work as communications director of his political campaigns provide her with an intimate knowledge of his papers. Her secretarial assistance during his presidency only deepened that archival knowledge. Buchanan, like other political insiders in the 1840s, was well aware that Sarah had full command of presidential paperwork.

During the third year of his presidency, Buchanan found himself at odds with Britain over the northwestern boundary of the United States, which was supposedly settled in 1846, to the Polk presidency's great credit. He turned to Sarah Polk for assistance. Apologizing that his public duty required him to bother her ("& I know, in your opinion, will justify it"), he turned immediately to business. "You will doubtless recollect the Oregon negotiation," he wrote. Although Minister to Britain Louis McLane was clear about the boundary between British-controlled Vancouver Island and the U.S.-controlled San Juan Islands, the British government now claimed additional territory. McLane, who died in 1857, wrote a number of letters to the president that might now buttress the American position. Would Sarah be willing to locate an account of the conversation between McLane and British foreign secretary Lord Aberdeen about the matter dated "on or about the 18 May, 1846"? Buchanan would be gratified to hear from her "as soon as it may be quite convenient."[53]

What Buchanan most likely did not know was that after James's death, Sarah kept his office exactly as he left it, and spent "day after day among the papers and relics, recalling to memory the times of which they speak. Nothing is more delightful to her than this indulgence," a visitor wrote. She was so comfortable in his office that "she now has a clear idea and perfect familiarity with the position occupied by any paper she desires to lay her hand upon."[54]

Sarah knew exactly where to find the McLane correspondence. Although she responded almost immediately, she apologized that "absence from my house prevented an earlier reply." The combination of erudition and political acumen beneath a veneer of deference was vintage Sarah, an indication that despite her self-imposed exile from Washington, she was still mentally engaged in the world of politics. "At your request I have examined the correspondence of my Husband + Mr. McLane, on the subject of the Oregon Negotiation," she wrote Buchanan, "and find the letter you suggest, dated May 18, 1846, which I have enclosed." While "there are many letters marked <u>private</u> + <u>confidential</u> from Mr. McLane, I have not read the correspondence carefully," she demurred. "Perhaps I have not selected such as may contain the information you desire." She included a second letter, one he had not requested, "dated April 30, 1846, giving the interview with Lord Aberdeen on the subject." She added, "I will take pleasure to communicate any information that may be in my possession."[55]

James Buchanan knew Sarah well, had known her for decades, and their correspondence on the Oregon boundary reminded him of how much he missed her. He pleaded with her to visit with him and his niece Harriet Lane, who was serving as First Lady for the first bachelor president. "I recollect with particular pleasure our agreeable and friendly social intercourse 'in the auld lang syne,'" he wrote.

> I have ever cherished for you the most respectful and friendly regard. Why can we not meet again? Why will you not visit Washington during the present autumn or the next Session of Congress? Miss Lane &

myself would give you a most cordial welcome to the White House, where you could pass a few months. In common with your numerous friends, we should be delighted with such a visit. I am now in my 69th year & am heartily tired of my position as President. I shall leave it in the beginning of March, 1861, should a kind Providence prolong my days until that period, with much greater satisfaction than when entering on the duties of the office. Pray do come. I should not ask this great favor, were I not thoroughly convinced that there would not be the least shadow of impropriety in your compliance with this my earnest request.[56]

Any awkwardness in Buchanan's tone, and the reference to "impropriety," no doubt stemmed from entirely baseless rumors in the penny press that he was "about to marry the widow of the late President Polk." Sarah, of course, knew this was ridiculous. But Buchanan would nonetheless have been embarrassed. His solicitation to Sarah was sincere, and it would, as he told her, have been "a great favor" for her to join him for a few months of what had devolved into a spectacularly controversial presidency. Her presence might remind Sarah's "numerous friends" of better days, before abolitionists and proslavery settlers had turned "popular sovereignty" in the Kansas Territory into a bloodbath, and Congressman Preston Brooks of South Carolina had beaten Massachusetts senator Charles Sumner into unconsciousness on the floor of the Senate. Sarah belonged in Washington, but Buchanan was no longer sure he did.[57]

Sarah thanked the president for the invitation to visit Washington, "+ the offer of the hospitalities of the 'White House.'" She enjoyed the "reminiscences of my life in Washington. . . . And the appearance that I am remembered by friends, will brighten some of the quiet hours of my retirement." But she remained unmoved. Polk Place was her place now. She sent her regards to Miss Lane, and asked the president "to return me the letters" at his "pleasure." She signed her letter, as always, "Mrs. James K. Polk."[58]

9

NEUTRAL GROUND

If I have asked for anything which it would be inconsistent or improper to grant, of course I will not expect to receive it. —SARAH CHILDRESS POLK

JUNE 15, 1861, marked the twelve-year anniversary of James K. Polk's death. Sarah woke and dressed in the somber costume of deep mourning, dull black fabric without ornamentation—not because of the anniversary, but because she always dressed this way. Convention suggested two years of mourning for widows, with deep mourning reserved for the first year. By the second anniversary a widow was entitled to color, to jewels, to sartorial rebirth.[1]

But Sarah offered no concessions to the passage of time since her husband was stolen from her. She was perennially bereaved and her home bore the same weight of tragedy. Sallie was now fourteen. Yet despite her teenage energy, and the presence of a twenty-three-year-old Irish servant and at least five enslaved people, including Elias, who had lived with Sarah for the entirety of her married life, James's ghost was the governing spirit of Polk Place. The public rooms Sarah kept exactly as he had liked them; private rooms were crammed full of his things. She passed a portion of each day by his tomb in the yard, imagining what he might think or say, how he would advise her. His loss still felt strange, but not the mourning. Had she not foreseen this crypt nestled in a welcoming garden back in her days at Salem Academy?

She had the proof right there, in the form of a fine piece of needlework showing "a tomb gleaming white through the foliage of surrounding trees." She could easily see the tomb through her bedroom window, a "daily reminder of the blissful reunion awaiting her in the near future."[2]

Of course, she missed James even more on the important anniversaries: birthdays, their wedding, and above all June 15. But this year something was different. In the midst of her sorrow she felt a distinct sense of relief that her husband had been spared the madness that engulfed the country. Within the week Sarah would see the Confederate flag flying over the recently completed Tennessee capitol building. At least he was spared that.

The coming years would prove Sarah's greatest challenge, but that challenge was eased by the knowledge that "the wisdom of providence" spared her husband from its "dreadful scenes." Whichever side he chose, she knew "he would have been misunderstood, and possibly maligned, and would surely have drunk a bitter cup of sorrow." She missed him, but she also saw "that it was better as it was." Better that she weather the crisis alone. Of course, she knew she was never truly alone—his spirit was with her just as surely as his body occupied that crypt in the garden. She faced the future convinced she could navigate a path that would have made him proud.[3]

When Tennessee voters went to the polls in November 1860 to vote for the sixteenth president of the United States, they faced a choice between three candidates, none of whom was Abraham Lincoln. Southern voters could choose between the official Democratic candidate, Stephen A. Douglas; the "Southern Democratic" Party's candidate, secessionist John C. Breckinridge; and James's old Whig nemesis, Senator John Bell, who was Tennessee's most esteemed living politician and was running as the nominee of the newly formed Constitutional Union Party. Tennessee, Kentucky, and Virginia gave their votes to Bell by a thin margin. The rest of the South cast its lot with Breckinridge and secession. None of their votes prevented Abraham Lincoln's victory with 59 percent of the Electoral College, and only 40 percent of the popular vote. Lincoln's outsized Electoral College victory reflected the fact that 71 percent of white Americans lived in the North. Southerners had long warned that unless they captured

more territories, northern growth would render them politically pow-
erless. In 1860 those fears were realized.

Lincoln's election and the subsequent secession of South Carolina
in December forced southerners to consider the future in an entirely
new light. Sarah, like the majority of her neighbors in Tennessee and
the states of the upper South, initially sided with the Union. James's
younger brother William was a staunch Unionist who vocally supported Stephen A. Douglas in 1860, no doubt in part because John Bell
and James had been lifelong rivals. Tennessee voters rejected a call
for a secession convention in February 1861 after leading Unionists,
including Bell, delivered rousing speeches in favor of the Union's salvation just a block from Polk Place.[4]

But by the time Lincoln took office and six more southern states
had joined South Carolina, Unionism in Tennessee was waning. Lincoln had assured Bell in a private meeting that the United States would
not use force against the wayward states, and he repeatedly asserted in
public that he would not interfere with their slave property. John Bell
and other Unionists initially argued that slavery would be safer within
the Union than outside it. But when the Union army refused to surrender the garrison at Fort Sumter, Bell reconsidered his allegiance. In
April he called for Tennessee to align with the Confederacy.

William was left holding the flag of Unionism. In May he chaired a
Union gubernatorial convention that had to adjourn precipitously when
secessionists threatened the Unionists with bodily harm. Although his
Democratic allegiances left a great deal to be desired in the eyes of old
Whig Unionists in the state, he was suddenly the most prominent man
left standing, and thus the default gubernatorial candidate. William's
work ethic never approached that of his oldest brother, and he did not
have a Sarah behind the scenes doing political work on his behalf. But
he ran the best campaign he could, delivering sixty speeches over the
summer's brief gubernatorial campaign.[5]

It was an uphill battle. Tennessee voters remained deeply divided.
A majority of voters in the mountainous east continued to oppose
secession, while Nashville voters were split. As elsewhere in the South,
density of slave ownership corresponded closely with support for
secession, and while residents of eastern Tennessee owned few slaves,
the remarkably fertile lands to the south and west of Nashville were

home to a large slave population and enthusiastic secessionists. In a June 8, 1861, referendum, Tennessee voters chose secession by a two-to-one margin, despite nearly 70 percent of East Tennessee voters preferring to stay in the Union. On June 17, the new Confederate flag, the "Stars and Bars," was raised above the capitol building.

Tennessee was the last state to secede, but its soldiers wasted no time. By the following day the army there was twenty-five regiments strong, with three more on their way to Virginia to fight the Yankees. Only three of Tennessee's congressional representatives remained in Washington. Senator Andrew Johnson and the other two holdouts all hailed from the Unionist east. Not surprisingly, secessionist incumbent Isham G. Harris handily won the gubernatorial race against William Polk in August 1861. William put his Unionism into action, and signed on as an aide to U.S. general Thomas Crittenden.[6]

Choosing sides would have been painful for James, but it was distinctly less so for many others in Sarah's circle. The biggest slaveholders in middle Tennessee were, as a group, the earliest supporters of secession. Many of them were also, unsurprisingly, among Sarah's family and friends. Leonidas Polk was first cousin to James's father, from the wealthier branch of the Polk family. He owned a vast plantation just outside Columbia on the "Rattle and Snap" tract, named after the dice game in which his father reportedly won the property. By 1840 he was the largest slaveholder in Maury County, surpassing even his neighbor Gideon Pillow. Leonidas and James were friendly but not friends, particularly after Leonidas threw his support behind Henry Clay in 1844. President Jefferson Davis commissioned Leonidas a major general the very same day that Tennessee joined the Confederacy.[7]

Gideon Pillow went to work building a Provisional Army of Tennessee even before the state seceded. As soon as Tennessee joined the Confederacy, Pillow was named a brigadier general under Leonidas. But the two commanders proved a toxic combination. Less than three months after Tennessee formally joined the Confederacy, Leonidas ordered Pillow to invade neighboring Kentucky, which had declared neutrality. The invasion forced the Kentucky legislature to call for support from the Union and drove a majority of Kentucky residents to favor the Union cause. It was one of the great blunders of the war. In December, Pillow and Leonidas argued, and Pillow resigned from the army. Regretting his rash decision, he appealed to his old friend President Jefferson Davis to reinstate him. It was a decision Davis would soon regret.[8]

In February 1862, Pillow badly mismanaged the Battle of Fort Donelson, on the Cumberland River. Under the command of the relatively unknown Ulysses S. Grant, the Union army captured the fort, and Pillow surrendered his army's twelve thousand men—but not himself. He fled across the Cumberland in a small boat. Grant's capture of Fort Donelson, along with more prisoners than in all previous American wars combined, made him a national hero. It also opened up the Cumberland River, and thus Nashville, to Union forces.[9]

Pillow informed an enormous assembled crowd in the Nashville Public Square that Confederate forces would make "no stand" to defend the city. Attempting to calm the crowd, he promised, "The Federals will be with you only for a time, and I pledge you my honor that this war will not end until they are driven across the Ohio River." Then he left for his estate in Columbia. The mayor of Nashville surrendered to Major General Don Carlos Buell on February 23, 1862, giving Nashville the distinction of not only being the last state capital to join the Confederacy, but also the first to leave.[10]

The city of thirty-seven thousand people, including fifteen thousand slaves, was of clear strategic value to both sides. It was a regional center for the distribution of goods, and a key transportation hub. Ohio was accessible by river, while five railways connected Nashville to Louisville and Atlanta. It was also one of the South's few industrial centers, home to seventy-three manufacturing establishments before the war. By the time the Union army arrived, many of them had been converted to the war effort, turning out cannons, muskets, gun carriages, ball and shot, swords, percussion caps, and gray uniform cloth.[11]

There was, initially at least, little question where Sarah's sympathies lay. Although she repeatedly asserted, and likely believed, that her husband had given his life for the Union, she was a plantation owner, a southerner by birth and inclination, and a Democrat who had long maintained the need to protect the rights of states from the encroachment of the federal government. That the former First Lady was president of a "Society of Nashville Ladies, organized for the purpose of making clothing for the Confederate Army," was reported as far away as Boston in May 1861, well before Tennessee joined the Confederacy, and before William ran for governor. The same week as Sarah's Confederate clothing efforts circulated in the press, the *Baltimore Sun* reported that she was elected president of a "Soldiers' Friend Society," to "take care of families of men in service."[12]

Given Sarah's seclusion since James's death, and the fact that even as First Lady she preferred to join societies rather than lead them, her embrace of the challenges of two leadership positions is difficult to fathom. But it's not hard to understand why Nashville's women turned to their most famous sister in this moment of need, or why Sarah rose to the challenge. Placing the First Lady at the top of the masthead would validate women's war work as both important and safely within women's sphere of influence. Since her years in the White House, Sarah had epitomized the glory of female dependence and deference, the First Lady who was a lady first. She was still in the minds of Americans a "sweet exemplification of lowliness." There was no better way to prove the propriety of activism by southern women than through Mrs. James K. Polk's involvement.

Although Sarah had shown little enthusiasm for sewing since her days at Salem Academy, she, like countless other southern women, turned her attention to provisioning the Confederate army. It's easy to imagine women gathered at Polk Place sewing uniforms, and Sarah with gray cloth draped over her black gown. But after General Grant's army captured Fort Donelson, Sarah, like other Nashville residents, faced an immediate and profound decision. Should she stay at home, or flee to the safety of Confederate lines? The Mississippi plantation she now jointly owned with James Avent was open to her. Her brother John was adamant that she move there. Any "unprotected woman" who remained "in a city invaded by a victorious army" would incur "frightful" risks. No need to spell out what those risks were: southerners spread mostly untrue stories of vicious Union soldiers and freed slaves who took vengeance on their owners. In other words, were Sarah to stay in Nashville, she faced the possibility of rape or murder at the hands of Union soldiers and emboldened slaves. As one middle Tennessee newspaper put it, a Union invasion would mean facing "two powerful and blood-thirsty foes, the one without and the other within," and "a fate to our wives and children equal to the sacking of a city by barbarians."[13]

Were Sarah lucky enough to avoid assault, it seemed highly likely that Union officers would confiscate her home, which, valued at $110,000, was one of the finest in Nashville. Leaving Polk Place would ensure its confiscation, but at least she could escape to the plantation with her valuables. Once the Union army arrived, there was no guarantee that any of the things she loved, James's things, would remain under her protection. Across the South, women of Sarah's race and class faced the choice between remaining and protecting their property or leaving and protecting their virtue.[14]

Of course, she couldn't very well flee with James's crypt. His final wishes were clear on the matter—his crypt would never leave Polk Place. And so Sarah decided she wouldn't either. She told her family that "she was at home, and intended to stay at home, and that if her house should be blown up or burned up, she would pitch a tent on the lawn beside Mr. Polk's tomb, and stay there." She understood that her position was tenuous, but many elite Confederate women assumed they had the right to male protection, even by the Union army, on account of their sex and class. Nor were they necessarily mistaken: the Union army agreed with them sufficiently to write the protection of female noncombatants into its laws of war. Perhaps no other southern woman had as much claim to protection by the U.S. government as Mrs. James K. Polk. Sarah's lifetime of political negotiations provided her with the faith that she could leverage her position as First Lady. It was time to draw on some of the benefits of deference she had stockpiled for years. She raised an American flag outside the front door, and waited.[15]

There was no saying what might happen. "If they come and we can't defend ourselves we are prepared to welcome them to a pile of ruins," one elite Nashville woman wrote to a friend. The Confederate army would surely "fire every place that could afford them quarters or in any way benefit from them." Some retreating troops tried just that. Nashville became "a supreme pandemonium" as Confederates set fire to their vessels, tore up train tracks, and literally burned bridges to keep them out of Union hands.[16]

As Union forces came into view, Nashville's residents descended into an "uncontrollable panic. People were rushing madly about with their most valuable possessions in their arms; every valuable vehicle was put into use to carry the fleeing crowd from the city," wrote a

Confederate officer. The "ceaseless clamor of excited voices" was almost "deafening," and "hysterical women, half laughing, half crying, dragged their children behind them, too much excited to know what they were doing, but impelled by the nervous dread that if they did not move the Yankees would catch them."[17]

A great crush fled the city. And then all became quiet as Nashville shut down. "Not a house in the city open. Not one," wrote one resident five days after the arrival of the army. Miraculously enough, the coming of the Yankees brought none of the threatened terrors. There was no mass uprising of slaves against their masters, and the soldiers were a far cry from the imagined barbarian hordes.[18]

And General Buell's overtures were friendly. One of his first proclamations was designed to protect civilian property. Soldiers were "forbidden to enter the residence or grounds of any citizen, on any plea, without authority." Sarah was a diplomat by trade; surely she could navigate this crisis. Judge John Lea, a longtime friend, was charged with meeting the Union army on the outskirts of town. Before doing so he visited Polk Place and asked Sarah, "What shall I say to General Buell for you?" Putting on her best smile, she replied, "Tell him I am at home."[19]

A FEW DAYS LATER, after the commander of the federal army set up his headquarters at the nearby St. Cloud Hotel, he sent a note to Polk Place asking permission to "pay his respects to the widow of an ex-President of the United States." Sarah wrote back, inviting Buell and his guests at 11 a.m. the following morning. She correctly predicted that this would not be a small reception, and corralled friends and neighbors into helping her with her entertainment. Buell arrived with "nearly every commanding general in and around the city, eighteen or twenty in number." Over the course of their hourlong meeting, Sarah proved a gracious host, even offering a tour of the house, focused, of course, on James's great legacy and "curiosities that he received as president."[20]

Rather than providing verbal proof of her allegiance to the Union, she allowed her actions to demonstrate that as a First Lady, she stood above the current crisis. Whether she directly said so or not in that first meeting with General Buell, the officers who visited her left with the distinct understanding that she considered Polk Place neutral ground, set apart by the presence of James's tomb and many objects from his presidency.

The meeting was a success. The officers who left Polk Place were charmed, even delighted. Sarah received Brigadier General William Haines Lytle "with great grace and cordiality. . . . She is still very handsome & elegantly mannered—I am very glad I called," he wrote his wife. "Mrs. Polk is a very social old lady and a very good looking woman too," N. G. Markham, a soldier in the 18th Michigan, wrote to his wife about his own visit to Polk Place. "She has got a very nice residence and seemed to enjoy herself very well." A formal visit to Mrs. Polk became a required event for each succeeding federal commander in the Nashville area, almost all Union officers, and a number of enlisted men as well. That Sarah's wartime hospitality was widely appreciated is suggested by the testimonial she received years later from Union general Galusha Pennypacker of Philadelphia as "a soldier's reciprocity to a high-toned Southern woman who had been good to him and his men."[21]

Yet this version of the encounter was not remotely the way Sarah's meeting with Buell was reported in the national press. And it was widely reported; Mrs. James K. Polk's meeting with the Union officers was understood to be a matter of national interest, and covered accordingly. For a month northern papers reprinted the account of an "eye witness" to the meeting with Buell under the title "Mrs. Polk the Traitor." The eyewitness claimed that when Sarah and a "niece, daughter of the ex-reverend General Leonidas," met Buell and the other officers, she "seemed determined that no doubt should be entertained as to her sentiments." "General," the First Lady was said to have stated. "I trust this war will speedily terminate by the acknowledgement of Southern independence." In response to her effrontery she received a lecture about her husband's great sacrifice to the Union, one that left her silent and, the writer implies, ashamed.[22]

The absurdity of this story should be evident. There was no one more polite than Sarah Polk, or less likely to bring up an unpleasant issue unnecessarily. Attacking the aims of her powerful guests would not only have been counterproductive to her goal of appeasing her

visitors, but also a sin against decorum. Nor was she likely to have
expressed such a clear political view; her career had been devoted to
obscuring the direct expression of her political beliefs behind the veil
of deference.

And then there is the supposed presence of General Leonidas Polk's
daughter in her house. The young ladies from that branch of the family were among the few nieces who never spent time with the First
Lady, because the two branches of the Polk family did not socialize.
Clearly Leonidas's daughter was inaccurately placed on the scene to
remind northern readers of the Polk family's Confederate ties.

The *New York Evening Post* reported a different meeting, but one
little more flattering to Sarah. According to the *Post*, an unnamed general who had met with Sarah made it clear that "no doubt remained
of the lady's faith in the southern cause. She took occasion to say that
although the people of the United States once made her husband president, the abolitionists did not do it."[23]

Sarah Polk's allegiances were of more than ordinary interest for
several reasons. As the widow of James K. Polk, she was a living representative of America's expansionist past, and her betrayal of the Union
would signify the truth of Republican claims that the U.S.-Mexican
War was fought for the expansion of slavery. For those Republicans
who asserted that the government had long been under the sway of
a "Slave Power" intent on consolidating slavery at the expense of
free labor, Sarah's embrace of secession appeared not only likely but
inevitable.

And at the same time, Sarah represented southern womanhood.
Few aspects of secession initially shocked northern sentiments more
than the vehemence with which the South's white women embraced
their cause. They insulted Union soldiers with abandon, and aided the
Confederacy in countless, seemingly unfeminine ways. They smug-
gled goods under their skirts; they hid munitions. Could any of them
be trusted? With reports circulating of the active dissent of southern
women, it was easy to project the same sentiments on Sarah.[24]

But Sarah's allegiance was also called into question within the
South. Female patriotism was a serious matter for the new Confederate
nation, and policed accordingly. Sarah explicitly conformed to many
of the obligations expected of patriotic women: she made provisions

and she tended to the sick. But by flying an American flag, Sarah made it clear that she rejected the central tenet of Confederate nationalism, which was that the Confederacy was in fact a nation.[25]

Her willingness to meet with Union officers, in particular, led many southerners to question Sarah's loyalty to their cause. Criticism of the fact that she treated federal officers "with a courtesy that ought not to be extended to the invaders" was so widespread that a Georgia paper felt driven to justify her "cool politeness" to Union officers. The paper explained that her attitude stemmed from past association, and that many of the officers in question "are old acquaintances and some received their appointments from her husband." Extracts from "Northern papers" proved, according to this supporter from Georgia, that she "never sought to conceal her sympathy for the Southern cause." She rightly recognized these visits as "courteous acknowledgements of her dignified position and personal worth, and it would be unwomanly in her to repel them with insult or taunt." While northerners were quick to attribute treachery to a southern woman, southern supporters justified her behavior by pointing to norms of female decorum. Sarah was a paragon of deferential womanhood; her behavior offered a reproach to more assertive women. The Georgia reporter wasn't sure whether "the ladies of the South are called upon, by any true instinct of patriotism, to treat *mere courtesies* from the enemy with scorn or contempt."[26]

This is not to say that Buell or any other Union officer knew Sarah to be true to the Union. They did not. "She claims, I am informed, that she is a Union woman," Brigadier General John White Geary wrote his wife with some skepticism in 1863. Although Geary had been the recipient of a lucrative patronage appointment from President Polk in 1849, he seemed a bit amazed that Sarah "insists upon the retention of the *franking* privilege which was granted her some years ago by Congress." When Geary later found himself in Nashville with "more time than I could well dispose of," he decided to stop by Polk Place. Sarah met him, as she met all officers, "with great warmth and cordiality." She gave him a picture of Polk Place, featuring James's tomb, to take home with him, and "made many expressions of extreme unconditional loyalty, of which I took notice as she had been represented as somewhat rebellious in the early part of the war."[27]

What neither Geary nor any other officer knew was that Sarah was concealing precious Confederate property. Hidden in Polk Place were boxes of silver, jewelry, and diamonds, as well as fine paintings and portraits owned by neighbors who brought them to her before fleeing the city. When officers of the Tennessee Historical Society in the capitol building discovered their building "open and abandoned to any and all that saw proper to go into it, and especially to straggling soldiers who came with the advance guard of the U.S. Army," they also turned to Sarah for help. The recording secretary, forty-one-year-old Anson Nelson, knew Sarah through his work as city tax collector. He hastily gathered up valuables and took them to Polk Place, asking her to take care of them for the society. "She very generously consented to put them in a safe place and keep them until they should be called for by proper persons, to be returned to the Capitol." Not one of the valuables given to Sarah for safekeeping was lost, but countless items left behind at the historical society were destroyed over the course of the war.[28]

The Union army's reception elsewhere in Nashville hadn't been nearly as pleasant as in the drawing room of Polk Place. The population was hostile; the "ladies of Nashville" were "as full of treason as they are in occasional cases of loveliness," according to the *New York Times*. Passing two young ladies in the street, a soldier heard one say to the other that she wished she "had the eyeballs of the Yankees to play marbles with." Indeed, Sarah's hospitality, whatever her true feelings, was notable in that it existed at all. Another elite Nashville woman wrote a friend on the eve of the Union invasion that she hoped to be able to "entertain" a large number of Yankees, and poison them. "I would with pleasure give each a cup of coffee and I think it would be the last any of them would ever drink." In Murfreesboro one of James Avent's female relatives said simply, "I hope I will die before I am found receiving a Yankee."[29]

Polk Place was an "island of grace" in a hostile city, in large part because Sarah had the tact to avoid political discussion when entertaining Unionists. She flew the American flag, and was careful to say, when asked, that given his great sacrifice to the nation, her dearest husband would never have supported secession. But when one of the generals leaving Polk Place asked Elias, who was standing at the steps, uncovered head bowed in respect, what he thought of "the situation," Elias promptly responded, "I'm for the rights of the South in the territories." This "unexpected answer raised the hearty laughter of the whole party," and the observation by one officer that "you'd better not ask another darkey his political opinions in his section of the country."[30]

Northerners could be forgiven for finding Sarah's "neutrality" less than amusing. A *New York Times* correspondent who accompanied General Grant was not charmed by her when he visited Polk Place soon after Buell. He reported that Grant and his staff were received "courteously, but with a polished coldness that indicated sufficiently in which direction her sympathies ran—she was simply polite and ladylike; in no case patriotic." She expressed neither sympathy for the South nor "anything that might be construed into a wish for the success of the Government." She hoped, she said, "that the tomb of her husband would protect her household from insult and her property from pillage; further than this she expected nothing from the United States and desired nothing." The reporter was appalled. "As the widow is of more than ordinary intelligence, and owes the ample fortune which smooths the declivity of her old age to the Government, it is somewhat strange that she should be at once so blindly ignorant of the true character of the present war, and so ungrateful." Five days later the same story appeared in the *Richmond Times-Dispatch*, offering just as much reassurance to Confederates as it did concern to northerners.[31]

This did not quell General William Tecumseh Sherman's suspicions. When he visited Sarah he made it a point to question her about James's inaugural address, "which not only contained expression of attachment and loyalty to the Union, but also affirmed that it should be preserved forever indissoluble." Sarah responded, "Those are good sentiments, sir." Sherman was unconvinced by her mild expression of loyalty to the Union. But what mattered was that both General Sherman and First Lady Sarah Polk kept up a façade of her neutrality. It's no critique of Sarah's ample tact and charm to surmise that the main goal of the repeated visits of Union officers to Polk Place was something other than refreshments. She was a threat that they needed to neutralize. And Union officers were aware that they desired her allegiance, even if only in pretense, in order to maintain Union sentiment in the state.[32]

Abraham Lincoln entered the war assuming that secessionist sentiment throughout the South was limited, and that the great mass of loyal civilians would embrace a stable Union presence. Were this the case, of course, the quick securing of Tennessee in early 1862 should have resulted in widespread civilian celebration. When Andrew Johnson became military governor of Tennessee in March 1862, he had high hopes that Lincoln was right, and was convinced that a conciliatory approach was the best means of reuniting Nashville citizens with their country. Forgetting Elias's endorsement of the expansion of slave territory, Union officers asked Sarah if Elias might be included in the delegation welcoming Johnson, as a link to James, and a happier history. Sarah agreed, and so Elias Polk helped escort Johnson into Nashville.[33]

Whether or not Elias kept his opinions to himself, Johnson quickly learned that secessionism ran deep in Nashville. From the beginning, his governorship was less than auspicious in Tennessee's biggest city. As the leading political representative of the interests of eastern Tennessee, and an avid Unionist, he was an unpopular figure in Nashville before he became governor, and Union generals worried about "fierce hatred to Governor Johnson, to him personally more than officially." Nashville's secessionists considered his rule dictatorial. Although Nashville was home to some vocal and powerful Unionists, the mass of white residents appeared openly hostile to the Union.[34]

Losing Sarah Polk's allegiance was not a risk the Union army was prepared to take. They recognized that their hold on Tennessee was far more fragile than it appeared. The fact that the Union held the city throughout the war obscures the strength of Confederate sentiment, sentiment that never fully disappeared because the Confederate Army of Tennessee was so very tenacious. In November 1862, Nathan Bedford Forrest moved against Nashville's defenses, and Confederates in the city were convinced salvation was at hand. The Union army beat them back definitively, Unionists believed.[35]

But southern sympathizers never lost hope, even after John Bell Hood's forces lost Atlanta to Sherman's Union forces in the summer of 1864. Hood, hoping to draw Sherman out of Georgia, marched north to Tennessee and dug in outside the Nashville city limits. Two weeks before Christmas 1864, Hood's army was within sight of the city limits. The faith of Nashville's Confederates, they thought, might

finally be rewarded. But in two days of fighting, the Union army over-
ran the Confederate trenches and forced Hood's damaged army to
retreat to Mississippi.[36]

Nor was Sarah's allegiance of local importance only. Visiting President Polk's grave was a highlight for thousands of troops who landed in
Nashville and encamped outside of town. The 10th Indiana Volunteer
Infantry marched directly to Polk Place after landing in Nashville, and
were thrilled when "Mrs. Polk came out on the veranda and greeted us
kindly, the boys responding with cheers." The loss of First Lady Polk
to the Confederacy would have been a serious public relations failure
for the Union, one that would leave the army in the uncomfortable
situation of punishing a First Lady who until the war was still widely
beloved both north and south of the Mason-Dixon Line. The Union
army needed Sarah in its camp just as surely as she needed it in hers.[37]

IT WASN'T EASY remaining in Nashville through the course of the
war. The city almost immediately experienced shortages of coffee,
liquor, and staple products. When the Union army arrived, thousands
of slaves fled to Union lines. As Nashville became the center of the
Union's western war effort, a permanent garrison of ten thousand U.S.
Army troops seized buildings for barracks and hospitals. They also
commandeered slaves for military work, many of whom had previously been employed cleaning the streets. Filthy streets produced out-
breaks of communicable disease. With roads, bridges, and railroads
damaged, the economy stagnated, a situation exacerbated by the fact
that the occupation army barred almost all civilian travel, trade, and
industry.[38]

There was a real threat of widespread famine. First Confederate
and then Union troops set upon the farmers close to Nashville. The
fertile farmland of middle Tennessee was called upon to furnish the
Union army with food and draft animals for the remainder of the war,
leaving little to spare for urban residents. War refugees sought shelter
in the city, which struggled to feed and house them. By the summer of
1863 even wealthy Nashvillians like Sarah had to contend with vastly
inflated prices and shortages of basic staple products. In 1862 a work-
ingman might earn two dollars a day, but by September of that month

a cord of wood cost fourteen dollars. By January 1864 there wasn't a cord of wood for sale in Nashville for less than thirty dollars. Crime increased, as did conflicts between civilians and the military. Despite Buell's order to respect local property, few yards or homes, besides Sarah's, remained safe from depredations.[39]

Given the larger goal of reintegrating the citizens of Nashville back into the nation, military commanders struggled with how to best ensure compliance among an openly hostile civilian population. It seemed obvious that one of the best methods was to ask Confederates to sign an oath of allegiance to the Union. Initially they limited this demand to politicians and other leading figures: the more prominent the individual, the more pressure to prove him- or herself loyal. "It is a happy thing these days to be obscure, & a man's safety *now*, depends on his insignificance," wrote one nervous Nashville woman.[40]

As Johnson grew to understand the depth of Confederate support, he expanded the loyalty oath requirement to any civilian with known pro-southern sentiments. In December 1862, Union military commander General William Rosecrans ordered all Nashville citizens who had facilitated rebellion by speech or action to take an oath to the Union, and insure it with a bond, within a two-week period. The punishment for noncompliance was imprisonment. In March 1863, he expanded the order to all whites not known to be Unionists.

Not everyone complied. Former Tennessee senator Alfred O. P. Nicholson of Columbia, a close friend of both the Polks and the Johnsons, refused to take the oath, boldly claiming that "he had been a sympathizer with the South, and was still a sympathizer with the Rebellion, and that he had made up his mind to take the consequences before he would take the oath." When a flabbergasted Johnson attempted to corroborate the story with the post commander in Columbia, the commander blamed Alfred's wife, Caroline. "Nicholson did not speak of you," the post commander told Johnson, "but seemed under the influence of his wife who is like many other women here intense bitter & unbearable." Caroline threatened that Alfred would "rot in jail" before she would consent to his taking the oath.[41]

Regardless of whether Johnson believed Caroline Nicholson to be responsible for his friend refusing to take the oath, he repeatedly responded favorably to the "pleas of rebel ladies." He allowed Elizabeth Harding, wife of an imprisoned Confederate, and owner of Nashville's fanciest plantation, Belle Meade, to travel to visit her husband. He also ordered the Union army to protect Belle Meade's breeding stock and racehorses, which were the finest in Nashville.[47]

But Governor Johnson didn't hesitate to exile women whom he believed suspect, sometimes sending them to Canada or to the North, but most often to places south of Union lines. James's cousin Mary Polk Yeatman, wife of a Confederate officer, was allowed to stay in Nashville after taking the loyalty oath. By the end of May, almost ten thousand men and women had sworn the oath, while others fled south.[43]

While Johnson hoped to persuade Nashvillians of the Union cause, General Rosecrans supported more drastic measures, particularly the use of military police. He established a secret police force under the command of Colonel William Truesdail, to root out disloyalty. Truesdail's determination was such that Governor Johnson admitted to President Lincoln that the secret police were "causing much ill feeling and doing us great harm." One of Truesdail's chief targets was the Nashville's Ladies' Aid Society, which the Union army suspected of smuggling contraband quinine and other necessities to Confederate troops. He clashed so often with this organization that his warning to his operatives, "Don't trust women," became an unofficial slogan. One reason that Truesdail was so hated by Nashville dwellers is that he threw women in jail, although not nearly as many as he wished to.[44]

According to the *Boston Post*, none other than Sarah Childress Polk headed the Nashville Ladies' Aid Society. Yet not only was Sarah never under threat of a jail term, but she never swore an oath to the Union. Regulations specified that only individuals who had proven their loyalty via oath would be provided coal for the winter. Provost marshals across occupied Tennessee "coerced patriotism" by requiring loyalty oaths in exchange for desperately needed supplies that the army controlled.[45]

And yet Sarah asked for and received coal, precisely when "it is most convenient for me to put it away." Governor Johnson made the stakes with regard to the treatment of Mrs. Polk clear in a letter to commanding officer William Utley in October 1863. "As to whom Mrs Polk is, her high character &c I need not write to you, but trust you will give her letter, and the matters of which it treats such consideration as it deserves, coming from such a respectable source, and relating to a matter of . . . importance to the Government, and National troops."[46]

In February 1864, a reporter from the *Cincinnati Times* who was visiting Nashville had the good fortune to encounter Sarah in her front yard as he made the requisite tourist's visit to Polk Place. He was astounded to find that the "elderly female in 'weeds' " seemed happy to grant him an interview. After she insisted that since the time of James's death she hadn't attended "a party or gathering of any kind" except funerals, or the occasional dinner while "on business" with James's other executors, the conversation turned to "Mrs. Polk's secessionism," of which "much has been said." He allowed Sarah to defend herself against accusations of "being a bitter Secessionist," particularly in relation to the Nashville Ladies' Aid Society.[47]

"I never was a Secessionist, and I don't think I ever will be one," Sarah stated. "I always said there was no excuse for the course taken by misguided Southern friends. I said that Mr. Lincoln was constitutionally elected, and that that election should be acquiesced in by every true patriot. I go, sir, for my Government, my whole Government." She admitted that her name was "placed before the public . . . in a connection that may have engendered in some minds doubts of my loyalty, but was placed against my wishes and remonstrances. But inasmuch as it was done for a humane and charitable purpose I said nothing about it." Yes, she loved the South, but she invited the nation to understand that this was because she was a woman:

> I do not deny . . . that my womanly sympathies are with the South, and that I often catch myself exulting over the successes of the Confederate arms, but this is only when my reason is taken prisoner and my judgment temporarily suspended at the bidding of my sympathies, prejudices and affections. I was born in the South . . . my surroundings have all been Southern. . . . Is it, then, reasonable to suppose that . . . I can throw off, as I would a garment, all the affections, all the prejudices (if you please) of a long life? And yet, dear sir, notwithstanding all this, I long, and pray, and yearn for a restoration of my distracted country to its former peaceful and happy condition.[48]

The journalist offered little commentary, instead deferring to the preferences of "this retiring and truly modest woman." His failure to question her narrative was no accident. He, like the Union generals who gave her a free pass to assert her own neutrality, were in effect repaying her for her deference to men. The journalist reported with approval that Mrs. James K. Polk was a woman for whom "it could truly be said that 'It is a name and an attainment to shun as much as possible the public gaze.'" Her allegiance to the South and leadership of the Nashville Ladies' Aid Society shed doubt on her assertions of patriotism, but her claim to being a private woman kept the "public gaze" from investigating that narrative too closely.[49]

OF COURSE, the reality was quite a bit more complicated. Sarah was not neutral, and virtually all her efforts during the war supported the South. Her initial energies, in the spring of 1862, were focused on saving the life of her nephew, Confederate artillery captain Marshall Polk. Marshall lost a leg at the Battle of Shiloh in early April and was taken prisoner. Although he was "kindly" treated in northern hospitals, his heart rate remained dangerously elevated after surgery. His situation was dire.[50]

The Polks never adopted Marshall, but Sarah's devotion to him was intense. It was widely acknowledged that he was her "darling." She made it her mission to bring him home. "I have never seen her so much concerned about anything since her Husband's death," wrote a close family friend. Sarah turned to commanding general Henry Halleck to secure his release, and her appeal was granted. For weeks Sarah tended to Marshall, whose situation remained critical. Ten days after his arrival, Polk family friend Malvina Grundy Bass visited Polk Place, and "very much fear[ed] that Capt Polk will die." But Marshall recovered, and his aunt returned him to the Confederate army on crutches.[51]

Sarah then turned her attention to the care of other wounded soldiers. She became "assiduous in her attentions to the sick in the hospitals, devoting a large portion of her time in visiting the sick, and furnishing them with everything that would in the least contribute to their comfort." Although Sarah was far from alone among elite southern women in her hospital work, it won her praise in the North and the South. A New York correspondent condemned the "shesessionists" of Nashville for their "ultra Southern sentiments" and "energetic animosity," but made an exception for "the venerable Mrs. James K.

Polk," who was renowned for her "charity and attention" to the sick in local hospitals.[52]

Sarah tended to both Union and Confederate wounded, but expended her political capital in support of the Confederacy. Her most public intervention took place in September 1864, when she petitioned President Lincoln on behalf of four Confederate soldiers, or, as she put it, "4 fatherless, destitute, simple hearted, uneducated Southern youths," requesting that they "be reprieved in order that they may prove themselves innocent of the charges for which they were under death sentence." In addition to the petition, which was signed by other prominent Tennessee women, Sarah included a personal letter appealing to the president. Lincoln reprieved the men.[53]

This was not the only time she drew on her political capital to secure the comfort or release of Confederate soldiers. Sarah had built personal relationships with dozens of politicians over the years. Many of them had received patronage from James during his political career, and some of those relationships deepened after James's death. In 1863 she sent ten dollars and a note to the commander of the prison at Rock Island to be handed to an unknown soldier, with the order that the money be turned over to "this boy immediately and you will much oblige me."[54]

She also secured the release of her nephew John Childress Jr. from prison. John was only sixteen years old when the war started, with an enthusiasm for battle that was matched only by his bad luck. He was captured almost immediately after joining the Confederacy, and jailed at Camp Chase in Ohio. Sarah wrote immediately to Ohio governor David Tod to plead for his release "on a parole of honor or by a bond that he will not take up arms again," basing her claim on the grounds of John Jr.'s youth, "not 17 years of age," and the fact that he was in service at Fort Donelson "only a <u>few days</u> before the battle," as well as on Tod's own "position and high character." An indirect reference to "many recollections of the past" only hinted at the debt Tod owed the Polk family. David Tod, like James, had the misfortune in the 1840s to run as a Democrat in a Whig state. When he lost the governor's race in 1846, James took pity on him and appointed him minister to Brazil. "You have the power to confer on me a favor, that will be ever remembered with gratitude," she wrote Tod. Tod granted that favor.[55]

NONE OF SARAH'S political relationships would prove to be as valuable as the one she had formed with Andrew Johnson. When Johnson served his first term as governor of Tennessee in the mid-1850s, he and his family were frequent guests at Polk Place. Their relationship was cordial enough that Sarah lent him books to read. She appealed to Johnson repeatedly for the release of friends from prison, for special dispensation from federal law, and for a variety of other favors.[56]

Many of those favors were on behalf of her brother John's family. In 1860, fifty-four-year-old John Childress, his wife, and their seven children, including eighteen-year-old Bettie (who as a child survived cholera), were living on their very valuable farm outside Murfrees-boro. He was a regular visitor to his mother's home nearby, and with the neighboring Avents, co-owners of the Polk Plantation with Sarah. But Murfreesboro was far from peaceful. After the Union army captured the town in 1862, both John Childress and James Avent were arrested and jailed, along with ten of the town's other leading men. "There is no knowing who will be next," wrote Avent's relative Kate Carney. "For it seems though [sic] most polite are the first arrested & I verily believe, if a person did not open his mouth, they would have them taken up on suspicion of his having looked contrary to his established rules."[57]

The men were released in late May, after swearing an oath to the Union, but less than two weeks later James Avent was arrested a second time. Mary Childress Avent and her two young sons fled to Polk Place and the protection of her aunt. Sarah picked up her pen and wrote to Governor Johnson. Appealing to his sense of chivalry, she requested Avent's parole so that "he may go home to his distressed family." The appeal was successful, and Johnson released him soon after. This was the first of many requests that Sarah made to Johnson over the course of the war, requests that grew ever larger, and almost all of which he granted. She made another request on behalf of the Avents, in order to prevent one of their slaves from being impressed by the Union army, but the majority were on behalf of John Childress, and ultimately her own fortunes.[58]

The Avents remained in Murfreesboro as Confederate troops began to mass nearby in hopes of regaining the town. But John and his family packed up their belongings and escaped to northern Georgia later that summer. Whether they were escaping from the Union or the Confederate army was unclear, a fact that would cause a great deal of trouble for both John and Sarah in the future. But in one respect, at least, it was a highly fortuitous move. In Georgia, twenty-year-old Bettie Childress met a "gallant" Confederate major general by the name of John C. Brown, and married him not long thereafter.[59]

On January 2, 1863, the Union army secured permanent control of Murfreesboro at the Battle of Stones River, one of the deadliest engagements of the entire war. This was no gift to Sarah, who suddenly found herself responsible for John's property, at the same time that she lost his help in looking after their mother. Compounding matters was eighty-one-year-old Elizabeth's rapidly degenerating health. Sarah successfully appealed to Union soldiers to protect her mother's property, and as Elizabeth declined, repeatedly received Union escort to visit Murfreesboro both before and after her death, on May 25, 1863.[60]

Sarah was devastated by her mother's death, and felt the want of companionship deeply. She had female friends in Nashville, several of whom, including Malvina Grundy Bass, reached out to her during her mother's last illness. Sarah was grateful, but Malvina herself died almost immediately after Sarah's mother, and her Nashville companions were no substitute for family. Sarah was possessed by the desire to see Sister Jane. Jane would be a comfort; she knew what it was like to lose a mother. Sarah sent news to Jane through their niece Naomi Hays that "her mother is dead," and "that she is very anxious to see her." If Jane didn't "come up there soon," Sarah vowed she would "try to come" to Columbia.[61]

But Columbia was also under siege, and without mail service. A recent "Yankee raid" had subjected the inhabitants to "various" unspecified "bad things," including, though not limited to, the theft of horses, mules, and the entire contents of smokehouses. Leonidas Polk lost seventy-one horses, leaving his daughters "grieving over the loss of their riding-horses." Jane Walker was more fortunate. Union soldiers forced their way into her house, looking, they claimed, for hidden Confederate soldiers, "but the Colonel apologized upon hearing she was a sister of James K. Polk" and took nothing.[62]

In the end Sarah did not get to see Jane: the situation in Murfreesboro didn't allow it. The Union army "appropriated" John's furniture
after he fled, and squatters moved into his home. Sarah set aside her
grief over the loss of her mother and focused her energies on securing
John's property. Her efforts were heroic. According to family history,
after John Jr. was released from prison he rode up to the family home
"to look things over" disguised in a Union uniform, and then turned
the squatter occupying his family home over to military authorities. In
fact it wasn't John Jr. who returned the property to family hands, but
Sarah.[63]

Although Governor Johnson recognized that any complaint on the
part of Mrs. James K. Polk had political implications and was a matter
of "equal importance" to the "Government, and National troops," as
to "the parties concerned," Sarah had a much harder time convincing
the lower-level supervisors who had the power to release John's property. She sent letter after letter adamantly insisting that her brother was
loyal to the Union. "I must be allowed to repeat that my brother did not
'abandon' his home," she wrote. "He left when the Confederate Army
was concentrating at Murfreesboro. Two months before" the Union
took control of the town. John was no Confederate. "He has nothing
to do with the army in any form whatever and expects to return as soon
as he can remove his family." Her multiple letters to supervising agents
and the provost marshal requesting that John's property be returned to
him, or at the very least "the Piano & the mirror," were all declined.
Not dissuaded by repeated rejection, she sought permission in March
1864 to ship a trunk of "ladies wearing apparal" to her brother through
Union lines in Chattanooga. When her request was rebuffed on the
grounds that it was illegal, she apologized to Colonel Parkhurst, the
provost marshal general, that "the usages of war prohibited a comply-
ance" at the time of her request. With her head held high, she offered
a wish that "when communications are open I can have the privilege
of sending it."[64]

In early April, Sarah turned to the governor for help. A week before
the intended sale of the Childress property the governor requested
that the sale be postponed long enough to give Sarah time to present a
memorial to the secretary of the treasury. That appeal was successful.
Secretary of the Treasury Salmon P. Chase had the "great pleasure to

be able to relieve" Sarah's concern by ordering the authorities to surrender John's furniture to him. Chase was apologetic. "It is not my
wish that the agents of this Department shall take or retain possession
of any furniture or like property unless it has been really abandoned,
and even then, only for the purpose not of depriving the loyal owner
of it, but to preserve it for the rightful proprietor," he assured her.
Unsurprisingly, given this outcome, she breezily asked Parkhurst for a
pass for her brother to visit her in Nashville.[65]

SARAH'S SUCCESSFUL APPEALS on behalf of her brother and Confederate soldiers, the consideration she received from the army regarding her mother's property and death, and the implicit understanding
occasioned by the continuing visits of Union officers to Polk Place,
emboldened her to pursue her own affairs.

Sarah's finances, like those of other white southerners, were devastated during the war. Her investments consisted of slaves, cotton,
and state bonds. Her 50 percent stake in the Yalobusha plantation was
her sole source of income during the war. The Union army placed an
embargo on cotton sales, and backed it up with naval reinforcements to
prevent illegal smuggling of cotton out of New Orleans. The president
himself was the only one who could issue a permit for a southerner to
bring cotton north for sale.[66]

Sarah's firm in New Orleans was left holding an entire season's
worth of cotton that was impossible to sell. But unlike most southerners, she was in the position to work around the ban on cotton. In
November 1864 she turned to her old friend Andrew Johnson, now
vice president–elect, for a "special permit, to bring into the Federal
Lines a small lot of cotton." Having successfully appealed to Lincoln
only three months earlier for a reprieve of the death sentence handed
down on four young Confederates, she turned now to Johnson "to
solicit most earnestly, your interest in my behalf, with the President
of the U.S." She entertained "a confident belief, that if the request is
placed before him showing my necessity, he will be kind enough to
grant me this privilege. I most respectfully ask it as the Widow of an
Ex-President of the U. States."[67]

Were her status not enough to persuade President Lincoln, whom she rightly predicted would see the letter, she drew on her status as a dependent on the basis of both age and sex. "I am now <u>60 years</u> of age, retired from the active scenes of life, and can not provide for myself." It was a powerful appeal, and for the second time that fall Lincoln granted Sarah Polk her wish. She was allowed to import sixteen bales of cotton into Union lines.[68]

Less than two weeks later she wrote to the general who oversaw the first delivery for "another favor; to give me permit to bring into Memphis a few bales more of Cotton." Again, she was explicit in her appeal on the grounds of dependence. Expenses, she claimed, would consume "almost the whole amount that I can get for the 16 bales" she had already received permission to ship. She would like to ship an additional hundred bales from Mississippi to Memphis, and then north. "I ask this favor solely for the purpose to get means to live on. And to prevent the saddest of all evils in old age: dependent poverty. I am now 60 years of age, and cannot provide for myself." She felt sure that he would "sympathise with me in the desire to save something to live on in the decline of life." Sarah was canny enough to recognize that a second appeal to Lincoln was unnecessary, and that the earlier permit might be interpreted in a flexible manner. And again she judged correctly, for a second time receiving permission to ship what was now a substantial quantity of cotton through Union lines. When requesting permission to ship more of her cotton, she testified that it "was produced by my laborers, who was and are supported by me, & receives a portion of their product."[69]

This was not an entirely accurate representation of the situation on the Yalobusha plantation. While the Emancipation Proclamation abolished slavery in Mississippi on January 1, 1863, the enslaved people on the Polk Plantation didn't learn of their freedom until 1865. Although the Polks' enslaved people were entitled to farm small plots of land on their days off, there is no evidence that Sarah or anyone else was paying the laborers on the Polk-Avent plantation in 1864. Nor, of course, were they paid before emancipation.[70]

But by this point, Sarah had become an expert at learning how to craft an appeal that would win her special treatment. She was indefatigable in pursuit of her own interest, repeatedly requesting (but never demanding) that her voice be heard and her privilege acknowledged.

Her excuse for never taking no for an answer was one she had cultivated over decades in politics: her deference to men. "If I have asked
for anything which it would be inconsistent or improper to grant, of
course I will not expect to receive it," she wrote to Union officers.
Her decorum enabled her to push past the customs and laws that were
designed to hold her back. Sarah made it clear that it was up to the men
in charge to determine what she was entitled to, but she did so in the
knowledge that her approach made it difficult for them to deny her the
means for her support. It's fair to say that her deferential pose never
paid better dividends than during the Civil War.[71]

But Sarah wasn't done with cotton in 1864. In March 1865 she wrote
Vice President Johnson asking forgiveness for "my perseverance, and
I do fear annoyance," as well as "your interest + influence in my behalf
in relation to the favor I have been soliciting from the President. You
have some knowledge of my pecuniary circumstances. The necessity
to provide means to live on, is my object. The sale of some cotton is my
resource, and all I have to meet my daily expenses + deferred demands
against them." Asking for "a permit + safe conduct, into federal lines"
to sell a hundred bales of cotton, she hoped, "will not conflict with the
public good . . . and will be a favor, gratefully acknowledged by me,
the proceeds of which will relieve me of much embarrassment."[72]

A month later President Abraham Lincoln was assassinated by
John Wilkes Booth. Nashville theater attendees had recently enjoyed
watching Booth and his more talented brother perform *Othello* at the
Nashville Theatre. Sarah was not among them; she never went to the
theater. Newly sworn-in president Andrew Johnson sent her, by military telegraph, a blanket pass lifting "all restrictions on cotton, including the twenty five percent tax." She need not ask again. She could ship
as much cotton as she pleased.[73]

In July 1865 the new president granted her one last favor. Reminding Johnson of his acquaintance with her niece Bettie (most likely from
meetings at Polk Place), Sarah requested a pardon for Bettie's husband, Confederate general John C. Brown. Johnson issued the pardon.
It was a decision he would come to regret.[74]

AND WHAT ABOUT THOSE LABORERS? How did the human beings
owned by Sarah Polk fare during the Civil War? When the Union

army arrived at Polk Plantation on August 19, 1863, the season's cotton crop had been "laid by," and field hands were occupied with the sort of mundane tasks that could wait for the end of the harvest. That Wednesday, many of them were cleaning out a turnip patch. Overseer George W. Peel had just enough advance warning of the army's arrival to order twenty-seven-year-old Charlie, who was owned by James Avent, to "take the mules and horses off and hide them in a certain canebreak." When he returned to the turnip patch, Charlie discovered that "the Yankees had done come through" and commandeered ten valuable mules as well as two saddles and bridles. Nor was that all they left with: "All the boys was gone off the place" as well.[75]

The Polk Place overseer claimed the army "took" ten Polk slaves. Jane, the onetime "sprighty" thirteen-year-old Sarah had helped purchase for the plantation in 1846, claimed her husband, Manuel, was "carried off" by the Union army. But the men may have seen it differently. The Emancipation Proclamation of January 1, 1863, not only declared "all persons held as slaves" in the rebel states "henceforth free," but it also provided for receiving those former slaves into the armed service of the United States. The opportunity to take up arms against the Confederacy was a matter of great celebration among black Americans. By the time the Union army reached the Polk Plantation, thousands of former slaves had joined the United States Colored Troops. Close to 10 percent of Mississippi's black male population, almost eighteen thousand men, served in the Union army.[76]

Some enslaved men resisted enlistment because they worried about the safety of loved ones left at home. Women and children were subject to retribution by angry owners, and the very real possibility of mistreatment, including rape, from raiding soldiers. But many, if not all, of the black men on the Polk Plantation had a taste of armed rebellion when they took part in the insurrection against overseer John Mairs in November 1858, including Giles and Manuel, who were still awaiting trial. It's far more likely that they willingly embraced the Union offer of freedom and a uniform than that they were taken by force, even when it meant, in Manuel's case, leaving his wife, Jane, and three living children behind. Or in the case of Giles, leaving his wife, Dafney, with five living children, including an infant less than a month old.[77]

One of the ten Polk men returned to the plantation within days. The rest marched a hundred miles north to La Grange, Tennessee, where on August 24, 1863, they enlisted together for a three-year term in the U.S. Colored Infantry. In one week they had gone from slaves to soldiers. "We were all together," remembered Harbert's son, Lewis, who at age twenty-four was a generation younger than some of his companions. Seventeen years earlier, Gideon Pillow had described Lewis as "a very likely & smart & stout boy" when haggling with James over his value. He was still likely and smart, but no longer a boy.[78]

After another young man from the Polk Plantation deserted four days after enlisting, Lewis and the remaining seven Polk men chose to cast their lot with the Union army. Not only had they all, in the words of Lewis Polk, "formally belonged to Mrs. J. K. Polk and lived on the Polk Plantation," but they had at this point known one another most or all of their lives. Thirty-nine-year-old Alfonso was Manuel's brother. Five of the men were within five years of age of one another. Alfonso's son John was ten years old and a frequent playmate of the elder living children of Giles and Dafney. Manuel and Giles were the same age. Giles and Lewis left behind wives with "suckling" babies born just weeks apart, and the two men promised each other that if one of them should die, the other would care for the family they left behind.[79]

They remained together as much as possible during five months of post and garrison duty at La Grange and Moscow, Tennessee. In January 1864 their regiment marched to Memphis, where they gained the designation of Company E of the 61st United States Colored Troops, and forty-five-year-old Addison Polk died of smallpox. The 61st remained on garrison duty in Memphis until July, when they first saw action in Tupelo, Mississippi. Under the command of Union general Andrew Smith, the 61st USCT helped defeat Confederate forces under cavalry general Nathan Bedford Forrest. This was no ordinary victory for the USCT. Forrest was among the most reviled of all Confederates for commanding the troops that massacred more than a hundred black Union soldiers after their surrender at Fort Pillow, Tennessee, just three months earlier. Victory at Tupelo was fittingly sweet.[80]

Over the course of an eventful summer, the Polk men battled the Confederacy on at least four separate occasions, and were again victorious over Forrest's Confederate troops in Memphis in late August. They remained in Memphis for the remainder of the year, and spent the spring of 1865 marching first to Louisiana, then to Florida, and finally to Alabama.

It was on the march in Alabama that Giles Polk died of congestive heart failure on May 15, leaving widowed Dafney and his five children behind on the Polk Plantation. Alfonso outlived him by less than a month, dying of fever in Mobile. The loss of three of their number was not unusual: black soldiers were far less likely to return home alive than white soldiers, and in comparison to white soldiers, who were twice as likely to die of disease than war wounds, black soldiers were ten times more likely to die of disease than in battle.[81]

The five surviving Polk men remained in Alabama until mustered out on December 30, 1865. They all returned to the Polk Plantation. Manuel was reunited with his wife, Jane, and their three children. Lewis, keeping his promise to Giles, determined to care for Dafney and her children. Following a pattern typical among freedpeople in the Mississippi Delta, most of the former Polk Plantation residents left the plantation immediately after the war, but didn't venture far. In 1866, a core group of the Polk freedpeople "put in a crop" at "the place next to ours." But the following year they returned to Polk Plantation as sharecroppers.[82]

It might be difficult to understand why the men and women formerly owned by the Polks would voluntarily return to the unhealthy ground where so many of their friends and family died. But freedom was a complex matter for newly emancipated people, and more likely evaluated in terms of family, safety, and paid labor than physical distance. To maintain your family free from violent interference by white people while being paid for your labor meant that you were free. In the coercive landscape of the postwar South, many freedpeople discovered their best chances for freedom were in the neighborhood they knew best. And despite everything that happened at the Polk Plantation— despite sickness, violence, and death—for Dafney, Manuel, Jane, Lewis, and others, their shared history, family ties, and community meant that Yalobusha was home.[83]

Manuel and Jane had two more children after the end of the war, while still living and working at the Polk Plantation. When Manuel began drawing his veteran's pension, he did so from the Polk Plantation. More than twenty years after the war's end, a core group remained in the immediate neighborhood, able to confirm shared memories about their experiences in slavery and the coming of freedom. One of the benefits of freedom was the opportunity to choose a new surname, and a few of them did, one from Polk to Avent. But most remained Polks, on land they continued to refer to as the "Polk Place."[84]

MATTERS AT THE NASHVILLE POLK PLACE were somewhat different. As a loyal state, Tennessee was exempted from the Emancipation Proclamation. Governor Johnson called for the immediate emancipation of Tennessee slaves in August 1863, but slavery didn't end legally in the state until February 1865. Slaves in Tennessee were forced to free themselves, and the majority did so by physically removing themselves from their former owners.[85]

It's possible to interpret the murder-suicide of enslaved twenty-seven-year-old Susan Polk in November 1861 in this manner. According to the coroner, Susan killed her three young children before taking her own life while "in a fit of insanity," but we have no way of knowing what was going through the young woman's head. Sarah left behind no commentary about the event, nor about the death of another Polk Place slave, twenty-six-year-old Nancy, from a burn two years later, beyond excusing her inability to return social calls on account of being "a little scarce of servants." But, of course, Sarah Polk had never enjoyed returning social calls.[86]

Nancy, Susan, and Susan's three young children may well have been the only enslaved Polks to leave Polk Place during the war. There is no evidence that anyone at Polk Place fled to Union lines or volunteered to fight in a black regiment, as did the men of the Yalobusha plantation. Seven men with the last name Polk show up in registers of black men employed by the Union army in Nashville, so it's possible that one or two of the unnamed enslaved men who were listed in the 1860 census as living at Polk Place were impressed by the Union, but none of the "contraband" Polks have familiar first names. And when the Union army attempted to impress Jerry, one of her enslaved people, Sarah secured his exemption by appealing, once again, to her good friend Andrew Johnson. If it was the case that none of her other enslaved people were requisitioned by the army, it was likely because Sarah was once again receiving special treatment.[87]

The black residents of Polk Place may well have asserted their assumed freedom by working less, or not at all, as did the slaves of her neighbors. Her friend Malvina Bass noted in June 1862 that the "darkie men are more obedient and are better than usual" because "intelligent Contrabands don't want to lose good homes," but that "the women are becoming insolent and lazy." Sarah's niece Naomi Hays reported that as soon as federal soldiers arrived in Columbia, "many darkies ran off," although her own family's enslaved people remained at their posts, albeit with a decided lack of enthusiasm. "I have concluded to be a dining room servant after the war," Naomi thoughtlessly joked, "being the surest way of getting fed, and not any hard work."[88]

Six African American freedmen were still living with Sarah four years after the end of the war, at least one because he claimed loyalty to the First Lady. That was sixty-year-old Elias Polk, the slave given to James and Sarah as a wedding present, and the man who greeted Governor Johnson. The 1870 census listed Elias as owning $5,000 worth of personal property, a remarkable amount for a freedman, and working as a porter in the state senate. In the decades following the Civil War he became one of Nashville's leading black politicians, while continuing to live, as he had since age eighteen, in a home with Sarah Polk. Elias never stopped deferring to the Polks, and it's largely because of that allegiance that his name isn't better known today.[89]

Elias ended up on the wrong side of history. Despite his enslavement, he appears to have fully internalized the Jacksonian democratic perspective, claiming to have been "'a democrat from conviction' since 1834, having imbibed his partisanship from listening to the private conversations of Calhoun and Polk."[90] That perspective extended to what many considered the subjugation of his own race. Not that he considered himself subjugated. According to newspaper reports, he claimed that President Polk once offered him his freedom. They were traveling through Wilkes-Barre, Pennsylvania, when "several white men approached him and asked him if he didn't know he was free. They told him that he was in a State where a man could not hold slaves, and all he had to do was leave and his master couldn't do a thing."[91]

Elias supposedly rejected the offer. "Do you think I would go back on the President dat way? No, sir. You don't know me I'd sooner die than run off." President Polk rewarded his loyal slave for his fidelity. "The President happened to be near and heard this. He was greatly pleased, and the next day surprised his faithful valet by speaking of it and told him whenever he wanted his freedom he could have it. When his master died Elias remained with the family." Whether or not James offered Elias Polk his freedom, Elias's response to General Buell and the other Union officers when they first visited Sarah in 1862 was likely no feint—he did support the rights of southerners to bring slaves into the territories. And he wasn't afraid to say so. During the Civil War he welcomed one visiting general to Polk Place by remarking that the general "looked like a good conservative gentleman, . . . like his good old Master who was dead and gone."[92]

After the war Elias's politics remained Democratic, and, in the view of the vast majority of freedmen, radically offensive. The Democratic Party openly embraced white supremacy. But Elias was a founding member of a "Colored Democratic Club" and spoke out against northern Republican "carpetbaggers" sent by the Johnson administration to help rebuild the state's political infrastructure. In 1869, he spoke at a meeting of black leaders in Nashville on the subject of migration. He insisted that freedmen could live peacefully in Tennessee if they would "just leave the white man's politics alone." While being considered as a Democratic candidate for the legislature, he put that philosophy into action, working with southern white Democrats to wrest control of the legislature from Republicans, actions that led to violent attacks by political opponents, and "wounds which were almost fatal in their results, received because of his firm adherence to his party."[93]

But Elias never wavered, "in spite of the great odium in which it brought him with the people of his own race." He remained an outspoken Democrat. He was listed as one of the "prominent colored men" who supported Horace Greeley in 1872. In 1875 he was quoted in newspapers from Massachusetts to San Francisco for his support for Andrew Johnson's Senate race. When Johnson was nominated, "Elias Polk, an aged colored man, the trusted body-servant of President Polk, came in, saying that he had not felt so happy since 1844, 'when master beat Clay.'" In 1880 he "delivered a brief speech warmly indorsing" the platform at the Tennessee Democratic Convention.[94]

Although Elias remained Sarah's fierce advocate and supporter until the end of his life, he eventually chose to leave Polk Place for the excitement of Washington and "being back again among the great men of the nation and in the midst of scenes where he had spent so many happy days." By the time he left, his $5,000 was gone. But like Sarah, Elias understood patronage and knew how to get by in a system that marginalized him. In 1881 he was working as a laborer for the Forty-Seventh congressional House of Representatives, at a salary of $720 a year. The rise of Grover Cleveland, "a typical Democrat of the old-school," pleased him greatly in part because Cleveland reminded him of James. Elias, who claimed to have "shaken hands with every other President since 1826," had the opportunity to shake Cleveland's hand in 1886, and died soon thereafter.[95]

Southern Democratic papers enthusiastically eulogized Elias, "the colored carriage driver of President Polk," and enjoyed quoting him about the "many a narrow escape from the fury of the ignorant nig-gahs have I had for voting and speaking my sentiments so freely." As "one of those old-time colored people who feel that they are members of their employers' family," Elias, in continuing to live with Sarah long after the end of slavery, reassured southern whites that black Repub-licanism was a carpetbagger plot. Elias Polk offered support to their dearest wishes—that their servants only hated them because they were manipulated by abolitionists. His death, and Sarah's sorrow over los-ing "the body servant of her husband," were reported nationwide. "I sincerely regret his sudden demise," Sarah was quoted as saying. "He was always a trusted and faithful servant." As for Elias, Sarah was never far from his thoughts. In his final interview, he discussed her contributions to Washington life, and bragged that she still "did all her own correspondence, without aid of glasses."[96]

One obituary that Elias would have particularly appreciated ran in the *St. Louis Globe-Democrat*. When "Mr. Polk and his bride had removed to their home Mr. Polk's father sent Elias to him. Elias had grown up with his young master, and was never a slave." It wasn't true, of course. Elias was property, given as a wedding present from Sam Polk to his oldest son. But by publicly insisting that James K. Polk's political views were also his own, Elias was not only able to shape the conditions of his freedom after emancipation, but to retro-spectively erase slavery from his past. It was a particularly skillful use of deference.[97]

WHEN ELIAS'S POLITICAL STAR began to rise at the close of the war, the members of the Tennessee legislature resumed their annual visit to Polk Place. The representatives offered a resolution in their hostess's honor. "You were in the line of the advancing and receding hosts, in the very gulf-stream of the war, but the mad passions engendered by the conflict were ever calmed in the presence of your abode." Sarah was delighted by this tribute, since it was exactly what she herself believed.[98]

She was happy to embrace the fiction of her neutrality even as she joined other elite white women across the South in the hard work of reconstructing order out of chaos and helping southern men find honor in defeat. Ladies' Memorial Associations, formed in the immediate aftermath of war across the South, took charge of memorializing the Confederate dead with proper burials and monuments in their honor. When Nashville women hoped to sanitize "unwomanly" political activism in the name of the Confederacy at the start of the war, they put Sarah at the head of the Ladies' Aid Society. At the close of the war they embraced yet another activist agenda that required the imprimatur of America's leading model of pious and deferential womanhood, Mrs. James K. Polk. Sarah was at the head of a committee to purchase land for a Confederate cemetery near Nashville.[99]

Like the First Lady, the southern women directing these memorial associations were adamant that they were ladies first. It was no coincidence that these women referred to themselves as "ladies." In the wake of Confederate defeat, white southern women adopted an explicitly deferential position in relation to their husbands and brothers. The Civil War overturned both racial and gender hierarchies: black people were no longer enslaved, and white women, left at home without the aid or protection of white men, had proven self-sufficient and capable of jobs previously considered outside their sphere. The humiliation of Confederate defeat left southern white men badly in need of reassurance that they still held authority, as men, over women, if no longer over slaves. White women were happy to provide this reassurance. To say that they were ladies implied that there were gentlemen protecting them.[100]

"Southern ladies naturally shrink from contact with the outside world," one memorial association announced, explaining, "Southern women frankly acknowledge their dependence on southern men." They embraced Sarah in part because her deferential womanhood was their explicit ideal. But the hard work of Confederate memorialization would undermine their professed dependence in ways the "ladies" of the South failed to foresee.[101]

SARAH PURCHASED a volume of Milton in 1865, and, one imagines, plunged into *Paradise Lost*.[102] It was an appropriate choice for a white southerner at the close of America's deadliest war. She could easily have imagined herself as Eve, thrust out of Eden. In coming years a host of historians would point to the war with Mexico that she and James oversaw as the origin for the Civil War. Her onetime visitor Ulysses S. Grant would call that war the nation's "sin" for which the Civil War was "punishment." Among the many things lost during the Civil War was the legacy of that earlier war.[103]

James was clearly concerned about his legacy after he left office, but his overtures to William Marcy came to nothing, and he hadn't lived long enough to find a biographer. At the close of the Civil War, Sarah thought she might have found the right person: Henry Randall, author of the popular *Life of Jefferson*. Sarah wrote President Johnson with yet another request: Would he give "his approbation" to Randall composing a " 'Life + Times' of my husband ex President Polk"? With the support of the sitting president, including an interview or two, writing a biography of the controversial and short-lived expansionist would be a far more attractive prospect for a biographer of ambition. Sarah assured Randall that Johnson would "be disposed to extend" this "favor" to her. "My personal relations with President Johnson have been of an agreeable character. During his term as Govr. Of the State, Senator in Congress & Military Governor, I received from him marked attention," she wrote, with considerable understatement.[104]

But Randall wasn't at all sure he wanted to get involved with the Polks. He made his reservations clear in a private letter to President Johnson. He would embark on a biography of James K. Polk only if he first received reassurance from the president on two points. First, he needed to know "whether Mrs. Polk, or her friends, entertained feelings which would lead her, or them, to expect the work in question to be tinged by any prejudices against those who have been instrumental in putting down the Rebellion." Second, Randall asked Johnson to intervene with Sarah, if necessary, so that Randall could "fill my canvas properly" and "take the true standpoint in respect to some of those important & mooted questions in President Polk's career." In other words, could Johnson vouch that Sarah was not, in fact, a Confederate? And could Johnson ensure the publication of a critical biography, one that revealed the ugly side of the U.S.-Mexican War? Johnson failed to reply, and Randall declined Sarah's offer. No one appeared anxious to write the biography of James K. Polk.[105]

Sarah had every right to set aside her concern about the unwritten biography and focus instead on her success during the Civil War. She had kept Polk Place safe. Soldiers never ransacked its grounds, and James's tomb was untouched. In the immediate aftermath of the war she still had faithful Elias by her side, proudly carrying on James's Democratic legacy. It was much easier for her to focus on the praise offered her by the Tennessee legislature for her neutrality than to take Republican condemnations of the Polk presidency seriously. For the moment she could ignore what Republicans wrote. Sarah didn't read those sorts of books anyway. But she would soon find it impossible to ignore them.

10

A Lady at my advanced age has but little influence at the present time.

—SARAH CHILDRESS POLK TO WILLIAM H. POLK, March 31, 1877

SARAH SURVIVED for forty-two years as a widow while only once leaving Tennessee. After her mother's death she claimed that nothing, other than church attendance, "could tempt her from Polk Place," and actively promoted the impression that she was a hermit in "the beloved home chosen and prepared for her by her husband." She dressed in mourning until the end of her life. In 1870 a critic of the First Lady claimed that her "morbid exclusiveness rendered her unsociable, and her Christian virtues, too much inclined to austerity closed her house to every form of gayety."[1]

Nothing could have been further from the truth. Her correspondence makes it clear that she was no hermit, and that when she left home it was in well-tailored black outfits accessorized with the brooch featuring James's profile, the one he had commissioned for her when they lived in the White House. Polk Place, moreover, was a lively and complicated space. The First Lady had grown used to visitors during the Civil War and continued to cultivate them through the 1870s. Visitors to Nashville were told that that "the old lady . . . liked to receive strangers," and even uninvited visitors were sure to receive a warm welcome from the First Lady, who was known to open her own door on Sunday, when her servants had the day off.[2]

One out-of-town journalist ushered into Polk Place met Sarah as she was leaving the house. She happily shook his hand, then apologized. "I have an appointment at this hour it is quite imperative I should meet, or I would be pleased to entertain you," she offered. "I pray you will excuse me, and make yourself as much at home in my house and on my grounds as if I were here." Her servants, who were used to visitors, would show him the house. "People call every day to see me," she said, laughing, "to see how a woman lives that lived in the White House once, and I value the attention very highly." That "prominent men of all classes and callings" visited her was widely acknowledged as one of the "public marks of respect . . . shown to Mrs. Polk as it has been no other lady's fortune to receive."[3]

Visitors received a set tour of the relic-filled interior of Polk Place, culminating with a visit to James's tomb. A coffin-shaped knocker on the front door set the tone. Visitors contemplated the "half-faded landscapes," valuable historical pictures, and other relics of "ancient elegance" in the downstairs rooms, including James's inaugural addresses as governor and president, both of which were printed on white satin and hung exactly as James wished. Next came a visit to James's second-floor study, with its fine view of the capitol building. "Here are his books, his paper, his pen and all the little articles that betoken an apartment in daily use; as if he had just stepped out and would soon return," a visitor marveled. Sarah kept it "just as he left it. . . . It is kept in order by her own hands."[4]

Polk Place played an important role in Nashville's social world. The Tennessee legislature's annual New Year's visit was a well-known feature of the yearly calendar. Sarah welcomed the entire legislature into her reception room, introduced them to friends and family with "a general shaking of hands and complimentary remarks," and then ushered them into "a spacious dining room, where was spread before them a variety of wines and edibles sufficient to satisfy the appetite of any epicure." Following White House tradition, Sarah extended her New Year's Day hospitality to the general public in the late 1860s. Interested visitors could learn the exact hours from local newspapers.[5]

In the years after the war the staff at Polk Place became experts at such receptions. Sarah received the religious, political, scientific, literary, and industrial societies passing through Nashville with the "gracious courtesy which had long before won for her such a high place in the nation's regard, a place that probably no other woman had held so continuously." Over the course of the 1870s, Polk Place hosted the Grand Chapter of Royal Arch Masons, the Odd Fellows, the Sons of Temperance, the American Association for the Advancement of Science, the National Education Association, the National Association of Fire Engineers, and the General Assembly of the Presbyterian Church, who came to "evince their sincere respect for her whose life has been so pure and blameless, and whose Christian Character is so shining an example." President Rutherford B. Hayes and his wife, Lucy, visited Polk Place in 1877, afterward extending an invitation to Sarah to attend a second reception for the presidential party at a private home. Sarah politely declined.[6]

In 1881, Sarah stopped opening her house to the public on New Year's Day, and informed both houses of the legislature that "owing to her advanced age" she could no longer receive them collectively.[7] Yet she still received large groups at Polk Place. Increasingly the hard work of entertaining was entrusted to Sallie, who continued living in Polk Place with her husband, George Fall, after they were married during the Civil War. When the National Grange of the Order of Patrons of Husbandry called on Mrs. Polk in November 1884, Sallie and George helped with the reception, along with at least fourteen of Sallie's friends. It was "the lady whose high and noble character had endeared her to the people of the whole country" they came to see, however. Sarah received each member politely.[8]

As the decades passed, Sarah's mania for keeping everything in Polk Place as it was when James died seemed increasingly poignant, or odd, depending on one's perspective. And there were many people who could provide a perspective, because, as Sarah put it at an elaborate and very well attended surprise eightieth birthday party in 1883, "notwithstanding the natural feebleness" of her "advanced years," she was still determined to "entertain all who called" on her.[9]

Sarah continued to entertain callers because her entertainments had a purpose. Her entertainments had always had a purpose. During her decades in Washington she entertained to advance the political agenda she shared with her husband. During the Civil War she entertained officers, soldiers, and journalists in order to maintain the illusion of her neutrality while aiding the Confederacy. In the 1870s and 1880s, she faced new challenges, only some of which, she learned, could be resolved by entertaining "all who called."

THE END OF THE WAR brought a return to normalcy to Polk Place. Her brother John was back in Murfreesboro, although with her mother gone, Sarah felt little desire to visit. Columbia was more of a draw, and Sarah made the forty-five-mile trek, by her own account, once every three or four years. But after Sister Jane's funeral in October 1876, Columbia also lost a great deal of its allure. There were still numerous Polk nieces and nephews in town, but Sarah turned seventy-three the year of America's centennial. She had already outlived most of her contemporaries, and was beginning to slow down. When John died eight years later, Sarah was eighty-one, and no longer physically able to travel to Murfreesboro for the funeral.[10]

Fortunately, there were plenty of friends and family who were happy to visit her. These days they were just as likely to be nephews as nieces. She developed warm relationships with two of William Polk's sons, and a niece who had been too young to visit the Polk White House. By the early 1870s, John's daughter Bettie and his son John Jr. were both living in Nashville along with their families.[11]

Unfortunately, many of these visitors, family included, wanted something from her. Friends and relations continued to believe she had political connections and the power to bestow a job. They failed to recognize that, as Sarah put it, "a Lady at my advanced age has but little influence at the present time." Sarah had spent enough time as First Lady responding to requests for jobs to have gained a clear understanding of the power of a well-placed letter of recommendation, or direct request for patronage from the right person. She had made use of that knowledge to lobby for friends and relatives in the decades since, usually with success.[12]

But in 1873 the U.S. economy collapsed, and the world plunged into the first global depression. Suddenly Sarah was inundated by demands for assistance. Typical of the requests she faced was that of an old and "very poor" friend in Columbia who turned to her for help finding her doctor husband a job. By March 1877 the requests for assistance had grown "so numerous" that Sarah was forced to admit, "I could not know how to select from them, even if I thought that I could be successful."[13]

Her nephew William turned to her for advice in 1875 as to whether he should move from Warrenton, North Carolina, to Nashville "to get a business situation." She apologized that she was "so little connected with business matters" that she had no information, but she advised against it. "Hard Times has thrown hundreds out of employment," plus "Board + expenses so great in the city" that he would do better to follow his mother's advice "that a course of reading at present, would be best for you." Unbowed, the young man asked Sarah to help find him a position in Washington, D.C. She took longer responding to this letter, apologizing for "not replying" and offering as an excuse that she was "now advanced in life, and often times out of health." She couldn't help him. "I know but few persons at present day in Washington—my generation has passed away—and others taken their place." Once he applied for a position she would recommend him "+ will do so with much pleasure," but she warned him that "your mother can do more for you through the Rep[resentative] or Senator in the Congress, than I can do." A few months later she provided him with a letter for an unspecified position in Washington, but declined to write on his behalf a second time when he looked to gain a spot at the post office.[14]

But when Sarah learned that William was planning on attending America's very first World's Fair, the 1876 Centennial Exhibition in Philadelphia, she responded with great enthusiasm. The celebration, marking the hundredth anniversary of the signing of the Declaration of Independence, promised to be a spectacle of unequaled magnificence. Thirty-seven countries were participating, and millions of visitors were expected. Among the many novelties that Sarah would have enjoyed was a Woman's Pavilion, "originated and paid for by the women of America, and devoted to the exclusive exhibition of woman's art, skill, and industry."[15]

The First Lady received many pressing invitations to attend. A Union general to whom Sarah had been kind during the Civil War had conveyed to her the invitation of "some of the citizens of Philadelphia" to attend the exhibition. The president of the Pennsylvania Railroad offered to place a palace car at her disposal during her stay. She also received an official invitation from the organizers, one of the "distinguished few favored" with such an honor.[16]

She was clearly tempted, no doubt in part because her own reputation was at that very moment under attack. Sarah, like many other wealthy southerners who professed loyalty to the Union during the Civil War, filed a claim for $2,040 with the federal government for property taken from her by the Union army. In her case the property in question was "ten head of very serviceable mules" along with two saddles and two bridles, taken from her Yalobusha plantation. Two former enslaved people who worked at the Polk Plantation testified on her behalf. The efforts of a seemingly wealthy First Lady whose loyalty had never been proven to gain reimbursement from the federal government for plantation property struck many northerners as deeply wrong. Although Congress passed a famine relief bill to assist starving southerners immediately after the war, and adamantly refused to exact vengeance against southern women, it was difficult to forget about female support for the Confederacy.[17]

In 1874 the Claims Commission refused to meet Sarah's claim. Not only did "the depositions of two colored servants . . . appear to have been written by the claimant's attorney," but the commission shed doubt on Sarah's word, concluding that her own testimony was insufficient evidence to "prove loyalty." The commission determined to investigate the claim themselves. That the federal government questioned her loyalty made national news.[18]

When a friendly senator moved to take up the matter of Sarah's claim on the government a second time, in July 1876, a New England Republican announced that he had "received some evidence touching the loyalty of Mrs. Polk" and demanded that the "truth of the evidence" receive full investigation by the appropriate committee before coming to a vote. It took another month before the act for the "Relief of Mrs. James K. Polk" was finally enacted by the House and Senate, and Sarah received $1,500 in recompense for property taken from her cotton plantation. That fall the New York press reported that she would in fact attend the Centennial Exhibition. She clearly wanted to, but in the end she politely declined the invitations extended to her.[19]

Sarah's success in receiving recompense for her plantation property inspired other southerners who hoped to justify their actions during secession. The *Richmond Enquirer* noted that what was said of Sarah, that while loyal to the Union she "deeply sympathized with her friends and neighbors," could be said of "hundreds who even fought throughout that struggle. They loved the Union, but could not desert their friends."[20]

IN 1877, Sarah's social life was vastly improved by the return of her beloved nephew Marshall Tate Polk, whom she had nursed back to health during the Civil War. After the war was over, he started a newspaper in Bolivar, Tennessee. Marshall "held a high social position in Nashville, and the state," and, much to Sarah's joy, was appointed state treasurer in 1877.[21]

But Sarah's pleasure in Marshall's political elevation, and his company, were of limited duration. Six years after his appointment, investigators discovered that he had embezzled $400,000 from the state treasury. He fled to Texas, but was captured days after his escape. In July 1884, he was convicted of fraud and sentenced to thirteen years' imprisonment. He died from "a disease of the heart" less than a year into his confinement. Marshall's "disgraceful defalcation and subsequent imprisonment" drove the Boston Herald to conclude that Sarah's fate, despite her fortune and "rare circle of devoted friends," was little better than that of "Mrs Harrison, Mrs Taylor, Mrs Lincoln, and Mrs Garfield," all of whom "became widows while at the White House." Sympathy for the First Lady, whose "last days . . . have been much embittered by the disgrace," was widespread.[22]

Fortunately, Sarah still had Sallie. In the darkest period of Sarah's life, Sallie's "child life, her studies, her entrance into society" had given "needed interest to Mrs. Polk's life." Now Sallie had a daughter of her own, Sarah Polk Fall, who was born in Polk Place in 1871. The family called her Saidee to distinguish her from the other two Sarah Polks in the household. As Sarah grew increasingly feeble, Saidee's growth "into womanhood" became the focus of her attention, and the reason for entertaining. Sallie wanted the best for her daughter, and Sarah agreed. If Sarah in her grief after James's death had held Sallie at arm's length, now, late in her life, she was happy to dote on the baby born in Polk Place. With Sallie's help, she was finally able to appreciate the quiet pleasures of motherhood.[23]

Well into the 1880s Sarah hosted social events designed to promote the social advancement of Sallie and Saidee, some of which received coverage in the local newspapers. In 1875 she hosted the Nashville Reading Club, composed of the "elite of the city." Doctors, professors, and married and single women followed an elaborate program that concluded with Saidee doing a recitation.[24]

Sarah's social efforts on behalf of Saidee reached their apogee in 1885 when she hosted a debutante ball in the young woman's honor. The scene of "exceptional splendor and brilliance" was lauded as the "apex of local society events." Sitting beneath an oil portrait of James, Sarah was "the first lady of the land in all which that word conveys," according to a guest at the party. She wore a black silk dress covered in jet beads, and along with it the ever-present cameo of James. It was a "brilliant entertainment" reported as far away as Baltimore. The following New Year's Day, the sixty-second anniversary of her marriage, she helped host a New Year's reception at Polk Place.[25]

In the years following, Polk Place continued to host impressive entertainments, but Sallie and Saidee played hostess. Sarah made only brief appearances at these events, and sometimes did not appear at all, although she continued to promote the social aspirations of the other two Sarah Polks of Polk Place. In 1886, she wrote a letter of introduction for Sallie and Saidee to First Lady Frances Folsom "Cleaveland" at the "Executive Mansion" in Washington, D.C. In shaky handwriting she asked the new First Lady and the president to extend their hospitality to her grandniece and great-grandniece during their visit to the White House "in this the evening time of my life." The recommendation had the intended effect, and the Clevelands entertained the two women during their Washington visit.[26]

The following year, five months after Elias's fatal final trip to Washington to meet the president, Sarah repaid the Clevelands for their courtesy when she hosted a presidential visit. Several thousand people gathered outside Polk Place to catch a glimpse of the honored duo on their Sunday afternoon visit. Sarah set her Sabbatarianism aside for the occasion as she invited the governor and other "gentlemen of prominence" to join in the reception. The eighty-four-year-old First Lady stood as she welcomed the twenty-two-year-old First Lady and the president. The Clevelands recognized the gesture as an homage to Dolley Madison, who always stood when former president John Quincy

Adams entered a room. The honored guests admired her reception parlor, where "every picture is hanging just as President Polk arranged them in 1849." The president and Sarah exchanged compliments, and the two First Ladies compared their experiences in Washington. Sarah invited the company to enjoy refreshments, including seventy-five-year-old sherry. After each guest had been offered a glass, the party moved out to the garden to pay their respects at James's tomb.[27]

Sarah freely admitted that she "was always a poor correspondent." In her "advanced age" she found herself less able to reply to letters, even from family members.[28] But during the last years of her life she gave away a great number of mementos, including James's letters, to friends and relatives who asked for them. She sent a presidential portrait to a niece in St. Louis in 1888. The grateful recipient, who addressed the envelope of her thank-you letter to "Mrs. Ex President Polk," invited Sarah to join the "Lady's Humane Society" she had recently organized with fifty members "from the cream of St. Louis society." Adding Sarah's name to their masthead would be an honor, she wrote, as "your name . . . stands higher than any woman's in our land."[29] Sarah wrote back, in a barely legible scrawl, thanking her niece for the "beautiful and kind letter," but apologizing that she could not comply with the request because she was suffering "under a nervous debility from old age."[30]

She wasn't too debilitated to turn out on July 4, 1888, to open Cincinnati's Centennial Exposition by "electric signal" from Nashville.[31] Given that one of the primary goals of the exposition was to showcase Cincinnati's ingenuity, there was something fitting about the First Lady's spectral appearance by means of telegraph and "time gong," a nationalized time signal from Nashville that triggered the ringing of gongs. Sarah would have remembered that one of the first uses of the newly invented telegraph was to announce James's nomination as Democratic candidate in 1844.[32]

She was thrilled to have been asked to signal the start of the exposition, and played up the event. She chose to sit herself at a mosaic marble table inlayed with an eagle that had been given to James upon his retirement by the American consul to Tunis. It was one of her most prized reminders of their White House years. She invited prominent Nashville men and women as well as journalists, friends, and family to gather around her—a scene that printmakers determined merited illustration. At the appointed time, she "clicked the instrument, and in a moment there came an announcement from the Queen City that the electric current had done its work." As one newspaperman waxed, "Could the vast assemblage at Cincinnati have seen the lady, now fast completing her eighty-fifth year, herself inspired by the enthusiasm of the moment, keenly alive to the occasion, bright, vivacious and heartily enjoying it, but still preserving the stately dignity which has always characterized her, their enthusiasm might well have been increased." Sarah turned to her companions and exclaimed, "Can we not all say, 'Praise God, from whom all blessings flow?' It all comes from Him."[33]

This was not Sarah's first public experiment with new technology. In 1877 two professors conducted a demonstration with "sound telegraphy" by setting up a telephone in Polk Place and connecting it via copper wire with a second across the street. The participants were unsure how to pronounce the name of the device. "Is it '*Tele*phone' or 'Telep*ho* ne' or '*Teleph* o-ne,'" one visitor asked, only to be told to "take your choice."[34] Sarah admitted that she "had lived a long career, had witnessed many changes, but never so many as had occurred within the past twenty-five years." It seemed to her "that the people of this age were living at the rate of railroad speed and electric flashes and that nothing was too difficult to be accomplished." But she "was pleased to know that in the busy whirl of the world she was still kindly kept in remembrance and the many courtesies and tokens of esteem with which she was presented was a source of very great pleasure in this the evening of her life."[35] Then Sarah took the opportunity to provide some "interesting reminiscences" about James's presidential term.[36]

THOUGHTS OF JAMES rarely left her mind. The rise of the Republican Party was not good for the memory of the U.S.-Mexican War. President Grant's contention that the war with Mexico was "one of the most unjust ever waged by a stronger against a weaker nation" and that the Civil War was "our punishment" for that "transgression" became the consensus view in the decades after the Civil War. While Grant had been a member of James's own Democratic Party in the 1840s and 1850s, as a Union general and Republican president he accepted the antiwar Whig Party as his present party's forebears. James didn't live long enough to realize that the U.S.-Mexican War was a pyrrhic victory for the party, because ultimately the views of Whigs, who maintained that the war was unjust, immoral, and part of a land grab on the part of slaveholders, held sway. The 1847 resolution by the Massachusetts House of Representatives that "an offensive and unnecessary war is one of the highest crimes which man can commit against society; but when is superadded a war for the extension of slavery, its criminality stands out in the boldest possible relief" had become the reigning view among the reigning political party of the postbellum period.[37]

James's reputation suffered along with that of his signature achievement: if the war was a crime, he was the criminal. Sarah yearned to vindicate his actions and to uphold his legacy. It was her duty, one she accepted not with resignation but with gratitude. She alone had the power to remind Americans of the "great accomplishments" of the Polk presidency. It would be the defining work of her waning years.[38]

Sarah made it clear that she welcomed what others might consider an "intrusion" on her privacy as "pleasing to her" because it was offered "to the memory of her husband." Mrs. Polk was "fond of recalling incidents of Mr. Polk's administration, and is proud of his career," the *Baltimore Sun* reported. "In fact, she thought Mr. Polk's administration was second to none, and she would not even except the results obtained by Mr. Jefferson." When a reporter asked her if the constant inquiries of strangers weren't intrusive, Sarah demurred. "I feel an exquisite pleasure in giving items of valuable information, especially to young men, concerning Mr. Polk's public and private life, for of course I deem it a life eminently worthy of emulation."[39]

Sarah rarely missed an opportunity to reflect on the Polk presidency in public. In March 1875 she presented the Tennessee Historical Society with a pen, made from an eagle quill, that James used to sign his first message to Congress, the joint resolution to admit Texas as a state, and the Treaty of Guadalupe Hidalgo. In 1879 she expressed regret to a reporter that opposition to the war had been "very harassing to Mr. Polk." But, she continued, brightening, "it was a very great thing. What would the United States be now without the Californias—the direct result of the war?" Five years later she asserted that "the acquisition of Texas and the results following the Mexican war—that is, the adding of California and New Mexico in the territory of the United States"—were "among the most important events in the history of the country, and that fact is becoming more and more apparent. The country was advanced by those acquisitions, and has ever since reaped benefit from them."[40]

It was wishful thinking on Sarah's part that the country was becoming increasingly appreciative of the U.S.-Mexican War. If anything, hostility toward the war had intensified since the 1860s. As it became more difficult for people to remember a time when the Southwest belonged to Mexico, the sacrifices American soldiers made to gain that territory also faded from memory. Veterans of the war experienced this in a particularly profound way. After Congress awarded veterans of the War of 1812 pensions of eight dollars a month in 1874, the newly founded National Association of Veterans of the Mexican War lobbied Congress to receive their own pensions. Although by the end of the 1870s Mexican War veteran groups were meeting on a regular basis in thirteen states, from California to Louisiana to Massachusetts, and by 1893 over five thousand veterans had applied to receive one of the National Association's official badges, the lobbying organization was notably less successful than the Grand Army of the Republic on which it was modeled.

For thirteen years Mexican War veterans were thwarted by northern Republicans who pointed to the presence of former Confederates among the surviving veterans and denounced the pension bill as "a southern war claim." After finally obtaining pensions in 1887, Mexican War veterans were more often charged in pension abuse exposés than were soldiers from other wars. Efforts by veterans to erect a national monument, to preserve battlefields in Texas, and to establish a home for invalid veterans were also blocked by Congress.[41]

But many journalists, particularly in the South, were receptive to Sarah's message. "The millionaire owes his wealth to this source," wrote the *Raleigh Register* about the Mexican cession, "and there is no doubt that the steps taken and points gained by James K. Polk deserved the highest estimate that could be put upon it by a grateful country."[42]

Sarah often introduced her reminiscences with the suggestion that her time in the White House was "a delightful memory" that she never tired of sharing with others. Although "the responsibility was great, we had a comparatively happy life" in Washington, she recalled. "I hardly recall anything which marred the pleasure of our social life there."[43]

But those reminiscences always vindicated her husband. When visitors remembered that Polk's nomination was unexpected, Sarah agreed that it was a surprise to the country "when so young and comparatively unknown a man as Mr. Polk was nominated to compete against one so famous as Mr. Clay." But she "demurely observed" that "the surprise was still greater, especially to Mr. Clay's party and to Mr. Clay himself, when Mr. Polk was elected."[44]

Sarah recognized the risk in too closely investing James's legacy in the U.S.-Mexican War, however just and wise she believed that war to be. So she reminded the public of his other virtues and accomplishments whenever possible. During an era rocked by political scandals, from the graft of urban machine politicians ("Boss" William Marcy Tweed's Tammany Hall embezzled $200 million from the New York coffers) to the Crédit Mobilier and Whiskey Ring scandals of the Grant presidency, Sarah took pains to remind Americans of the high moral standards of her own husband's presidency. "It is my happiest thought that no criticism of Mr. Polk's integrity during a long public career, in various exalted positions was ever made to my knowledge," she told a reporter from the *Indianapolis Sentinel* in 1881. "His judgment may have been impugned, but not his honor."[45]

And for the first time in her life she put her political partisanship on hold, cultivating Republicans as assiduously as she once did Democrats. Given the dominance of the Republican Party nationally, this made good political sense, but contemporaries interpreted her diplomacy as stemming not from political calculation but from her "lady like reserve." Although "it was natural that she should ever feel a lively interest in the success of the Democracy and a wish for the ascendency of its principles," wrote one author, "yet holding inviolate . . . her sense of what was due her position, she could not distinguish between parties in receiving public marks of respect."[46]

George Bancroft, who forty years earlier as secretary of the navy had made a patronage appointment on Sarah's request, also found himself absorbed with the legacy of the Polk administration. Bancroft was one of America's leading historians, and like Sarah he was troubled by the partisan attacks against the administration he had served in. Hoping to "do something for the memory of our friend James K. Polk," he asked a Nashville acquaintance in 1887 to "ask Mrs. Polk if she would let me take some of Polk Papers back to Wash. to be copied and returned immediately. I propose to draw his character and especially the results of his administration; and a full and just statement of them is of great interest for the whole nation." Sarah agreed, and Bancroft set off to visit his "old friend" at Polk Place.[47]

They spent several days together in Nashville, beginning with a public reception thrown by Sarah in Bancroft's honor that was praised as "one of the most brilliant of social events" as far away as Milwaukee. Sarah was pleased by the party and "the reminiscences that the occasion recalled," telling a reporter, "it reminded me of the receptions at the white house when Mr. Bancroft and I received together."[48]

While the former secretary of the navy and the First Lady combed through James's papers, picking out materials for his proposed history of the Polk administration, Bancroft marveled at Sarah's command of the material. He also learned that she had decided opinions about both events and people of the era. When the two of them came across a letter referring to cabinet member John Y. Mason, Bancroft announced that he took "no stock in Mason." As he recounted the scene to a friend, "the madam Mrs. Polk replied 'Why he was a great friend of Mr. P's.' I preferred not to respond." Bancroft was clearly chagrined, admitting, "I do not know that such a remark about him ever escaped me before."[49]

After Bancroft returned home, Sarah gathered a chest full of materials she hoped he would use and mailed them to the former secretary. Bancroft had an assistant make copies of the papers, and returned the originals to the First Lady. They stayed in close touch in the following years (at Sarah's eighty-sixth birthday the eighty-nine-year-old Bancroft referred to himself as her "truest" and "oldest" friend), but her hopes of seeing a proper biography of her husband by America's foremost historian faded along with his health.[50]

Bancroft wasn't the only scholar looking to Polk Place for evidence about the Polk administration. In the first months of 1888 she received a barrage of letters from *Appletons' Cyclopaedia of American Biography*. As the editors prepared the fifth volume of their mammoth encyclopedia, they repeatedly turned to Mrs. Polk for assistance. Would she be kind enough to fill out a form, and include any facts "that may prove of interest in writing a brief sketch" about herself "to be added to that of her distinguished husband"?[51]

She failed to respond, perhaps because none of the questions on the form remotely related to the power she exercised from 1844 through the Civil War. How was she expected to respond to question five, about "official positions" held; question six, about "inventions or other achievements that ought to be mentioned in a sketch of your life"; or question seven, asking for the "exact titles of books you have written (or edited) . . . or, if an artist, names of notable pictures you have painted"?[52]

Not that Sarah had ever been particularly forthcoming about her life. Another frustrated biographer complained in 1870 that "Mrs. Polk, though ever willing to converse, and always enriching the conversation from her ready store of information and observation, is remarkably reticent in regard to her own life. Her most familiar friends fail to persuade an account of incidents relating purely to herself." When asked about her family history in 1890, she claimed not to know the date or place of her own parents' marriage, or her maternal grandmother's maiden name. "In those early times concerning which you are asking," she explained, "there was not so much appreciation of the relation of current events to history as there is now, and it was seldom that note was made of those events."[53]

Somehow *Appletons'* managed to collect enough material without Sarah's help to compose a portrait of the First Lady that was inaccurate in only a few details. It was not true that she "abolished the custom of giving refreshments to the guests" at her many receptions; indeed she continued to serve wine and sherry at Polk Place receptions after James's death. But the distinction the Polks drew between hard liquor and wine made less sense in the prohibitionist culture of the 1890s than it did in an earlier era. *Appletons'* portrait of Sarah largely understood her popularity as stemming from her morality. While the portrait discussed her appearance in detail and noted her "courteous manner, sound judgment, and many attainments," her church membership and moral reforms as First Lady took precedence, while her political skills vanished from view. Having no children, Mrs. Polk dedicated herself not to James's political career, but rather to a depoliticized domestic ideal. She "devoted herself entirely to her duties as mistress of the White House."[54]

Sarah saved her response, not surprisingly, for the more important matter of her husband's representation in the volume. The editors had a tremendous number of questions. They wrote her once asking her to identify the material from which James's tomb was constructed. They sent her two requests that she help identify the date and place of a portrait of James they intended to use, wondering if it was "taken from life . . . when about sixty or sixty-five years of age." (Given that James famously died at age fifty-three, this could hardly have reassured her.) They wrote her on a separate occasion wondering if she might use her "influence" with George Bancroft to urge him to write the article on James for their volume, and again after Bancroft declined. They then asked her to proofread the entry about James.[55]

Sarah responded to this barrage of letters in a shaky hand, writing directly to the chief editor of the *Cyclopaedia*. She was sorry about Bancroft's "inability to furnish the sketch you desired," confirmed that the photograph of James in their possession was not taken during his presidency, but "after his return home. At the time his health was declining rapidly. I think in April 1849, and he died June 15, 1849, aged 54." That she was unable to remember James's age at death suggests her own decline in her eighty-fifth year of life. She invited the editors to call on her "if the notes I have are not satisfactory." She would do all to assist them "that my health will permit."[56]

James's portrait fully repaid Sarah's efforts. While it expressed understandable skepticism about James's claim at the start of the U.S.-Mexican War that "American blood" had been spread on "American soil," and admitted that "it may still be too soon to judge" his "public career . . . with entire impartiality," he emerges from the generous portrait exactly as Sarah remembered him: "ever solid, firm, and consistent . . . generous and benevolent." The portrait rejected the abolitionist assertions of his day, saying that he was "not a slavery propagandist, and consequently had no pro-slavery policy," and going so far as to argue that he went out of his way to keep slavery out of Oregon. His "private life was ever upright and blameless," so much so that "the esteem in which he was held as a man and a citizen was quite as high as his official reputation." Finally, "whatever the motives of the executive as to Texas and Oregon, the results of the administration of James K. Polk were brilliant in the extreme."[57]

Sarah may have felt no need to answer inquiries about herself from *Appletons'* or any other sources because she already had plans for her memoir. The vice president of the Tennessee Historical Society, Anson Nelson, visited her with his wife, Fanny, once a week, a habit they had established during the "early days" of the Civil War, after Sarah agreed to hide the Historical Society's valuables from the Union army. Sarah "was exceedingly kind to me and mine" during the war, Anson later remembered. When the couple proposed to help her write an autobiography, she happily concurred. She began collecting materials for the posthumous memoir by the mid-1880s, and conducted informal interviews during the Nelsons' weekly visits. They understood that any biography of Sarah would also be a history of her husband's accomplishments, but they also believed that Sarah Childress Polk was a figure of significance in her own right.[58]

SARAH WAS ALSO coming to a new understanding of her own political importance. No relationship formed in the final decade of her life was more important to her than her friendship with Frances Willard, the outspoken leader of the Woman's Christian Temperance Union. The WCTU was a radical organization with profoundly conservative goals, formed in Ohio in 1874 by female activists committed to "protecting the home" against social threats, above all the dangers of alcohol. WCTU members engaged in nonviolent protest at saloons, and used moral suasion to gain pledges of total abstinence from alcohol.

As president of the nationwide organization starting in 1879, Frances Willard adopted a "do everything" policy in order to effect a variety of interlocking moral reforms, and claimed sweeping powers for the organization and its members in the name of protecting children. The WCTU created a "Department for the Suppression of Impure Literature" and petitioned the government to pass censorship and obscenity laws. Members worked vigorously to end the use and sale of alcohol at the local, state, and national level.[59]

In Willard's hands the WCTU quickly grew into the largest women's organization of the nineteenth century, with a distinctly different vision of the meaning of women's rights than that promoted by Elizabeth Cady Stanton and her allies. WCTU members were religious Christians. They understood "home protection" as a women's rights issue, and grounded their "domestic feminism" in Christianity and female authority over the domestic realm, not liberal individualism. Most believed that political action was "unladylike" and would not have joined a women's suffrage campaign. Indeed, WCTU representatives explicitly distanced themselves from Stanton and "that wedge driven into the best interests of society technically known as 'woman's rights'"[60]

Only the Wyoming, Utah, and Washington territories extended full voting rights to women in the early 1880s. But Willard convinced the WCTU membership that only by securing the franchise would women implement the reforms necessary for "home protection." Under her leadership the WCTU grew from twenty-seven thousand to almost two hundred thousand members in just a decade as she lobbied Washington for voting rights for America's "crusading women."[61]

Willard first visited Sarah in 1881, and was so taken by her "Christian example" that she omitted no opportunity to continue their conversation in the following years. Upon her return home from Nashville after that first visit she called a meeting of representative women from ten southern and eight northern states to a health resort in Dansville, New York, popular with reformers. The purpose of their assembly was to "honor Mrs. James K. Polk" with a portrait that could hang in the White House next to James's official portrait. Sarah's "noble character is a heritage of which the womanhood of the nation is justly proud," concluded the assembly, and Sarah deserved a place in the White House.[62]

Willard clearly admired Sarah, but she also recognized that Sarah's stature in the South could prove useful to building support for the temperance movement among southern white women. The South in 1881 was "virgin territory for women's organizations." While northern women had been associating together for reform causes for half a century, southern women stayed home. Although the temperance movement was congenial to southern women, and many southern men, southerners were deeply suspicious of "activist" women.[63]

But Sarah Polk challenged no prejudices, and Willard's appreciation of a "representative southern lady" went a long way toward reassuring southerners that the reformer was both a "womanly woman" and sympathetic to the South. Willard promoted Sarah as a symbol of national reconciliation. The national drive to place a portrait of her in the White House was evidence, Willard pointed out, of "a new expression to the kind and fraternal feelings cherished in so many hearts both north and south." National reconciliation could serve as a springboard for national reform.[64]

By October the "faithful portrait" was finished, "replete with the fires of intellect, and bearing the calm gaze of a resolute will a face whose lines combine the true woman graces with that force of character, that power, which is seen in the portrait of the good and strong of her sex in all ages." Willard's national assembly of women asserted that Sarah "is still remembered in the annals of the White House, for her easy grace and dignified simplicity. It is only the truth to say that she won there a fame beyond that acquired by any other lady of the White House." As for the portrait, "what worthier tribute, indeed, than thus to say that she is deemed worthy to occupy a place by the side of her husband's portrait, as a fit testimony to coming ages of the women of the nineteenth century."[65]

Frances Willard understood that national veneration for Sarah Polk's practices of womanhood could both justify female activism and serve as a force of national reconciliation. Sarah seems to have come to a similar conclusion herself, and was ready to act on it. In August 1886, she penned a letter to a representative of the Grand Army of the Republic in her own hand, reminding the nation of her public stature and the sacrifice she had made for the Union. "Before I die," the former First Lady wrote,

> I would that mine eyes could see the grand reunion of my beloved country in the city where my dear husband lies—see the veterans of the North encamping in amity where they once did in anger, and those who wore the gray shaking hands with their fellow countrymen in the fellowship of a common destiny. I cannot but think the meeting of the grand army of the republic in Nashville in 1887 would be the grand turning point in the complete reconciliation of the land my husband presided over, and whose unity is dear to my own heart.[66]

While Sarah referenced James, the appeal was, for once, firmly about herself—*she* wanted to see the GAR in Tennessee, *she* thought it would be a turning point in reconciliation, and it was dear to *her* heart. It was a grand appeal, to the entire nation, and also the open acknowledgment of her political significance as an individual.[67]

Willard held the national meeting of the WCTU in Nashville that same year. After meeting privately with Sarah, she brought a hundred or so members of the convention to Polk Place to meet the First Lady. Many other members of the union visited Polk Place, in groups, over the course of the national meeting. A delegate from New York brought her baby to meet the First Lady. Sarah, clearly inspired, told her visitors, "If I were younger, I would certainly attend your meetings."[68]

If Willard was entranced by Sarah's "noble character," so too was Sarah taken by the world-famous reformer's exercise of power. Sarah's unqualified admiration was "excited by the undreamed of powers developed in women by the novel circumstances of modern times." The course of women's political activism was astounding to her. The entrance of women into partisan politics that she had witnessed and participated in had flowered in manners she could never have imagined. Christian women like herself were organized, harnessing their combined power to change laws that harmed their families and society.[69]

This delighted her. When another newly formed women's organization, the Daughters of the American Revolution, invited Sarah Polk to join their board of directors as an honorary vice president in 1890, she happily accepted. The DAR, composed of women who claimed relation to Revolutionary War patriots, promoted a historically grounded patriotism as a means to uplift society and address the inequality and social unrest of the late nineteenth century. They believed that the knowledge of what "forefathers and mothers . . . sacrificed for home and country" might allow Americans "to comprehend the price of the legacy left, and to realize that if we hold this magnificent inheritance," the nation's "institutions must be kept pure, her laws just, her government upright." Mrs. James K. Polk entirely endorsed the patriotic mission of the group, which was so close to her own. She was "extremely grateful," she wrote, "to be associated with such an order."[70]

It may have appeared to Sarah in the 1870s that she had "little influence." As she was inundated by requests to help out-of-work friends and relatives find employment, the contrast with her previous power must have seemed stark. But a decade later it was becoming clear, both to her and to the nation, that Mrs. James K. Polk's influence extended beyond patronage, and that her "noble character" had influenced a new generation of Christian women to organize for what they understood to be the betterment of society.

THE NATION ASSUMED that Sarah was rich, but her finances never recovered from the losses of the Civil War. Rumors that she owned $40,000 in state bonds appear to have been inflated, and although James's tomb and the surrounding gardens were always well tended, by the early 1880s Polk Place itself began to show its age. Repairs were put off; paint was peeling. Sarah repeatedly renovated her old dresses rather than buying new ones, adding panels of lace and otherwise "making over" fine French garments. Renovating older garments was a common strategy in the nineteenth century, and often a marker of ingenuity rather than poverty. Quite often the labor required to remake an item of clothing was more than starting from scratch.[71] Sarah only remade her mourning clothes. Her beautiful White House dresses she preserved "to be transmitted as heirlooms to her grand-niece."[72]

Her pecuniary situation markedly improved after the assassination of President Garfield in 1881. When Congress moved to grant his widow, Lucretia, a $5,000-a-year pension, Tennessee senator Howell E. Jackson suggested that the annual "invalid pension" be extended to all other widowed First Ladies. Sarah welcomed the considerable sum and, in scrawled handwriting, thanked Senator Jackson for rendering her "in the evening of my life, so comfortable + happy."[73]

Sarah still attended services at the First Presbyterian Church, and continued to do all her own correspondence, without glasses. And she remained as interested in politics as ever.[74] Her "mental vigor" unbowed, she was happy to speak to a reporter from the *New York Telegram* about the similarities between the presidential elections of 1844 and 1884, pointing out that "the question then, as now, was largely about the tariff." She also noted that both elections hung on the New York vote. "You see," she told the reporter, "my increasing age has toned down my ardor in such matters although I always take an interest, a deep interest, in state and national affairs."[75]

One marker of how far attitudes toward political women had evolved between 1844 and 1884 was that the reporter took Sarah's political perspective seriously, noting that during James's "administration Mrs. Polk was his Prime Minister in everything in counsel, and was such a helpmeet as was fitted to stand by the side of the first man in the nation." In her "custom" of "interesting herself in all matters pertaining to national affairs," she united herself with her husband. She "extended her hand in a hearty greeting that told of the warm cordiality that won her friends in the White House and wherever she is known." Another difference was the stunning fact, left unmentioned by Sarah, that a woman was running for president. Belva Ann Lockwood, an attorney, author, and activist, was the official candidate of the National Equal Rights Party. For the first time in American history, a woman's name appeared on official ballots.[76]

In 1886, Sarah hosted the Democratic gubernatorial candidate, telling him that "the brilliant canvas you are making reminds me of the days of '44." Two years later, a reporter noted that "although her vision was not quite so clear nor as strong as it was a short time ago, she still reads the papers with as much zest and genuine interest as she did when her husband was President of the United States."[77]

In August 1889, Sarah stood for an hour exchanging "pleasant words" with seventy-five teachers (representing every U.S. state as well as Canada) who repaired to Polk Place for an afternoon reception in the middle of their national convention on the future of education. Sarah marveled at the "great change in public sentiment regarding the respectability of labor." Forty years earlier a married woman of "culture and high character" was "barred" from "social equality" with women of Sarah's class, simply because she taught school. But in the 1880s, Sarah noted, it was now "considered proper for young ladies, when they leave school, to teach or to do something else for themselves." She pronounced it "beautiful to see how women are supporting themselves, and how those who go forward independently in various callings are respected and admired for their energy and industry." It was as if Catharine Beecher's dream of a nation of independent female schoolteachers had finally come true. Two months later, Sarah celebrated her eighty-sixth birthday, remarking to a visitor that her life had known "but one great sorrow, the death of her husband."[78]

In 1890, after discussing the question of admitting female members, the Tennessee Historical Society invited the eighty-seven-year-old First Lady to join as an honorary member, the first woman so honored. Their attempt before the Civil War to convince her to donate to the young organization had met with limited success, although she did promise the society a portrait of her husband. But the invitation was not cynical. The Historical Society was fully aware of the extent of their coming bequest from the First Lady, given that the society's vice president, Anson Nelson, witnessed Sarah's will in 1885. Sarah left her library to the state of Tennessee, several valuable portraits to the Historical Society, and a small bequest in the memory of her brother John. A second bequest to the last surviving Rucker niece, Susan, was removed in an amended version of the will written in 1888, after Susan also predeceased her aunt. The rest of her much-diminished estate she left to Sallie Fall. As for her final resting place, that was a foregone conclusion: "I wish my remains to repose beside those of my husband wherever that place may be."[79]

GEORGE BANCROFT died in January 1891, his biography of James unwritten. Sarah was sorry, of course. But she was now reconciled to death. She spoke frequently about Divine Will and started quoting passages from her favorite psalms with regularity. Two months later she herself fell sick, but recovered within a few weeks. Her final major undertaking was Saidee's wedding, which, like Sallie's, would take place in the parlor of the only home either of them had ever known. But at age eighty-seven, Sarah was no longer capable of extended exertion. Saidee insisted that if Sarah was unable to attend the wedding in the parlor, the wedding would occur upstairs by her bedside. In May 1891, Saidee was married, in the parlor, with Sarah present.[80]

On a sultry Wednesday afternoon in August, after a ride in her carriage, Sarah collapsed on her way upstairs. She refused dinner, and didn't leave her bed again. Over the course of two days she gradually faded away. Sallie didn't leave her side. On Friday evening, August 14, surrounded by her loved ones, Sarah announced, "I am ready. I am willing to go. Praise God from whom all blessings flow!" Sallie Fall, overcome with emotion, asked her aunt a final question, one she had likely carried with her since childhood: "Darling, do you love me?" Sarah responded, "I do. I do. We have lived together a long time, peacefully and happily." She placed her hands on her niece's head and offered her a blessing, then lay "quite still, breathing naturally. A slight sound came from her lips, and the name 'Sallie' was feebly whispered, but nothing further could be understood." It was her last utterance.[81]

The state legislature lowered the flag at the capitol building to half-mast. "The bells throughout the city are mournfully tolling and sympathy and regret are heard from the masses of people," reported the *Philadelphia Inquirer.* They had all "respected her as one of the noblest of her sex." Tributes poured in from around the country and as far away as London, some addressed to Sallie, and some to her brother John's son, John Childress Jr., who was now her closest male blood relation. The family refused a military escort for the funeral, preferring a private burial in the yard, alongside James. Her name and dates of birth and death were inscribed on the tomb, along with a brief summary of her accomplishments, as she herself wished them to be stated. She was "a noble woman, a devoted wife, a true friend, a sincere Christian."[82] The *New York Herald* noted, "Her cultured and refined womanly qualities did much to make her husband's administration popular."[83]

With the exception of her bequests to the Historical Society and to John Childress's heirs, Sarah left the entirety of her estate, including Polk Place, "to my niece, Mrs. George W. Fall, whom I reared from infancy, and who is to me as a daughter." Unfortunately, Polk Place was not hers to give. With Sarah's death, the fact that the president had left "one of the queerest wills that was ever left to be probated by an intelligent man" became a matter of general discussion.[84] James's will, written forty-two years before Sarah's death, left Polk Place in the hands of the state legislature, to be "used and enjoyed by such one of my blood relations, having the name of Polk as may be designated by the state" for the extent of that individual's life, at which point the legislature would locate another Polk to occupy the home. If at some point there was "no such blood relation bearing the name of Polk," then the state could choose another of James's blood relations to "enjoy" the property. It would be the responsibility of the occupant of Polk Place "at all points in the future to preserve and repair the tomb which may be placed or erected over the mortal remains of my beloved wife and myself, and shall not permit the same to be removed, nor shall any buildings or other improvements be placed or erected over the spot where the said tomb may be."[85]

James intended his tomb, and home, to become a shrine occupied by worthy blood relations and administered by the legislature, in perpetuity. The will "must have been made in his last illness when his mind was failing," North Carolina Republican politician Daniel R. Goodloe wrote William Polk's widow from Washington when he heard the news, "for in his prime he never would have made such a one."[86]

According to James's will, Sarah agreed to both the distribution of Polk Place and "joint interment of their bodies" on the premises. And despite the generalized disbelief that greeted the will upon Sarah's death, the ultimate disposal of Polk Place was not exactly held in secret during her life. When the prominent Chicago businessman and philanthropist Harlow Higinbotham visited Nashville in 1886 to meet with "the leading bankers + merchants," he naturally made time to visit "the President Polk mansion," where he was pleasantly entertained by Sally, Saidee, and Sarah, whom Higinbotham described as "quite frail." Higinbotham was shocked by the poor condition of the house. "The mansion is very old and quite out of repair," he wrote in his diary. He was well aware that Sarah only had the use of the property for her life. Because "her life hangs by a silken thread" and "there is no arrangement to reimburse the family for money spent in repairing, it is neglected."[87]

Sarah may well have acceded to James's wishes in 1849 regarding the disposal of their home. But a great deal had changed in the ensuing forty-two years. Sarah knew who should inherit the estate. And James's wishes were impossible to fulfill, for a variety of reasons. By 1891, it was unclear which Polk was either the closest relative or the most deserving.

At one time Marshall would have been the obvious choice, but newspapers around the country reminded their readers that "a few years ago he became a defaulter to a large amount and fled the country, finally dying in Mexico. His dishonesty cut him and his family off, and just how the matter will be settled is now a mystery." The *New York Tribune* succinctly concluded, "There are no other deserving members of the family bearing the Polk name: and now that Mrs. Polk is dead the courts will have to decide the matter. It is not believed that the document will stand a legal test." It is worth noting that when contemplating "deserving" members of the family, no one considered the children of any of the former enslaved people, in Nashville, or in Mississippi, who kept the name of Polk after becoming freedmen.[88]

There was one clearly deserving member of the family not bearing the name of Polk, of course. And that person was Sallie Fall. Sallie's given name was Sarah Polk Jetton. Had Sarah adopted her, her middle name would have become her surname. But Sarah Polk Jetton never became Sarah Jetton Polk, because Sarah did not adopt her. Nor was Sallie a "blood relation" of James's. So despite caring for Sarah until her death, despite being raised by Sarah in Polk Place, and remaining in Polk Place after marrying, and then raising her own daughter, Saidee, in that same home, and despite Sarah's clear wishes that Sallie inherit the estate, Sallie had no chance of doing so under the terms of James's will. She may have been "as a daughter" to Sarah, but Sarah did not make her a daughter.

Of course, had James adopted Marshall in 1843, when he entered their home as a ward, or had Sarah adopted Marshall after James's death, in 1851, when Tennessee passed a General Adoption Act "to authenticate and make public record of private agreements of adoption," there would have been no need for James to look wistfully toward a future when the Tennessee legislature would determine which among his accomplished nephews, or perhaps nieces, was the most deserving Polk of the generation. Inheritance would have been a simple matter, particularly given that James died long before Marshall's downfall and disgrace. Nineteenth-century adoption law codified the propriety of widows adopting children in order to "keep the testator's property in the channels by him intended." But neither James nor Sarah chose to adopt. Death spared her from learning the true cost of their choice in this matter.[89]

William Polk's thirty-year-old son, Tasker, was the first to contest the will. If he did not quite rise to James's standards of worthiness, he had at least avoided jail and disgrace. William's widow, his third wife, Lucy, had been writing Sarah on a regular basis for decades, never failing to extol her son's virtues. And Sarah had acknowledged Tasker's preeminence, to a point. Three years before her death, Sarah sent Lucy a watch to be presented to Tasker. Sarah explained that James had wanted the Polk family heirloom to go to a family member.[90]

But James had nine siblings, and by 1891 there were dozens of heirs. Fifty-five of them, including two who had visited Sarah and corresponded with her for years, combined forces and contested the will in chancery court. Sallie Fall, using the little power left to her, refused to leave Polk Place. She tended Sarah's and James's graves, but otherwise let the house and grounds fall into disrepair. She had the stable condemned and torn down, then requested a reduction in rent. The Polk cousins were convinced she was "watching her chance to get the house cheap" once the case was settled. When Sallie claimed that her husband's insolvency left her unable to pay rent, the Polk cousins unsuccessfully tried to evict her.[91]

After several years of litigation, the courts found the will invalid, on the grounds that it set up a perpetuity and established a "home of nobility," neither of which was legal in Tennessee. James's heirs agreed that they "would not sell any part before removing the remains and tomb" of the former president and First Lady. But after the heirs claimed to be unable to come up with "money for the removal," the legislature borrowed $1,500 for the purpose, and in 1893 James's tomb, which was now James and Sarah's tomb, was moved to the grounds of the Tennessee statehouse. Although the heirs had hoped to "remove the bodies <u>without ceremony</u>," the "sacred dust" of the president and his wife were reinterred in an elaborate service that left many attendees in tears.[92]

In June 1897 the property was divided into lots and sold to the highest bidder. Polk Place itself was sold for a little over $20,000, and the heirs divided the remaining profits, which were only a fraction of what they had initially hoped for. In April 1900, Polk Place was torn down and an apartment building, named after the Polk family, was erected in its place. But not even the apartment building achieved anything close to perpetuity. By 1950 the "Polk Apartments" had given way to a parking lot. A hotel now occupies the former location of Polk Place. The only evidence that Sarah and James Polk once lived at that address is a small marker, difficult to find even by those who are looking for it.[93]

If the heirs felt any deep regret about disregarding the wishes of the dead, they didn't put it down on paper. Sallie and George Fall moved into a house down the street, where she attempted to re-create the interior spaces of Polk Place in much smaller rooms. Paintings, furniture, and the rest of Sarah's precious things were crowded together. Sallie named her new home "Polk Memorial Hall" and opened it to the public. It was an easy walk to the statehouse. She continued caring for Sarah's tomb with a fidelity that came naturally.[94]

Epilogue

SALLIE POLK FALL was more than just the daughter whom Sarah should have adopted; she was also a Childress by blood, granddaughter of Sarah's older brother, Anderson. If Sarah and James were in fact partners and equals in a companionate marriage, shouldn't the surviving Childresses have had a stake in Polk Place as well as the surviving Polks?

Not according to Tennessee law, which recognized Sarah's interest in her husband's estate, but not the interests of her sister and brothers, or any of their issue. In 1891 the only states that treated property acquired during a marriage as "community property" were states carved from former Spanish territory, most notably California, where the more equitable property conventions of the Visigothic Code still held sway. The rest of America followed the patriarchal conventions of British common law. Had Tennessee law allowed for inheritance by a "worthy" Childress, things might have turned out differently.[1]

Sallie wasn't the only Childress descendant with a better claim to "worthiness," according to the standards of the time, than the Polk progeny who sold off Polk Place. At the time of Sarah's death, two of John's children had emerged as particularly notable: John Childress

Jr., and Bettie Childress Brown. Both had benefited from Sarah's intervention during the Civil War and lived in close proximity to their aunt
in Nashville at the time of her death. Both were wealthy, political, and
shared their aunt's "appreciation of the relation of current events to
history." Like Frances Willard, they found inspiration in Sarah's deferential politics and persona, her lifelong insistence that she was a lady
first. But the Childresses carried her legacy in a strikingly different
direction than did Willard.[2]

After Sarah twice appealed to President Johnson to secure the
pardon of Bettie's husband, General John Calvin Brown, the couple
moved in 1865 to the small market town of Pulaski, where Brown had
established a legal practice prior to the Civil War. John Calvin was
known in Pulaski; it was a place where it would be easy for him to
make a difference. He was thirty-seven. Bettie was twenty-three. Bettie plunged into domestic life: the first of her four children, a daughter,
was born in 1865. Like her aunt Sarah, she joined the local ladies' auxiliary of the Confederate Home and Camp. John Calvin plunged into
politics.[3]

The Browns had once been one of Tennessee's leading Whig families. John Calvin's older brother, Neill, helped found the state's Whig
Party in the 1830s, and in 1847 ran for governor on a platform oppos-
ing the Polks' war with Mexico. It was a winning strategy. Neill defeated the incumbent candidate, Sarah and James's close friend Aaron
Brown. The residents of the Polk White House shared their dismay
with Tennessee's Democracy, which returned to its familiar position
as the minority party.

When President Zachary Taylor appointed Neill minister to Russia,
John Calvin took up the Whig mantle at home. In 1860 he was a vocal
Unionist, and an elector for John Bell's Constitutional Union Party.
But when Tennessee joined the Confederacy he enlisted as a private.
He moved up the ranks quickly, proved calm in battle, spent six months
in a Union prison at Fort Warren, Massachusetts, was repeatedly
wounded, and by the time he surrendered his troops in April 1865 had
been made a major general. He was also, needless to say, a Democrat.[4]

The Childresses always had good timing. John Calvin and Bettie
Childress Brown arrived in Pulaski at a remarkable moment. In the
month before Christmas 1865, or in the summer of 1866 (in later years

no one could quite remember which), a small group of young men decided to form a club, they claimed, for the purposes of their own amusement. They gathered in the law office of Judge Jones, near the center of the small town. They were six or seven in number, aimless, bored, frustrated, even angry. Many had, like Bettie Childress's family, experienced the humiliation of seeing their homes and property occupied by squatters, or family members jailed on suspicion of Confederate sympathies. Some had, like John Calvin, spent time in Union prisons during the war. There were all former Confederate officers, young, well educated, and starting adult life in a manner very different than they had once imagined. Like the Childresses and John Calvin Brown, they all claimed Scottish heritage. They determined to keep their membership a secret, to only appear in public in disguise, and, they claimed, to play tricks on the unsuspecting residents of Pulaski.

But first their club needed a name. One of them suggested the *kuklos*, the Greek word for "citizen." Nothing divided the well educated, like themselves, from the poorly educated in the first decades of the nineteenth century as clearly as did a knowledge of Greek. James K. Polk knew the language, had excelled at it at the University of North Carolina. Henry Clay, to his lifelong embarrassment, did not.[5]

Kuklos resonated on another register as well. The most prominent college fraternity of the period was Kuklos Adelphon, or "Old Kappa Alpha." It started at the University of North Carolina in 1812, just a few years before James Polk and Sallie's grandfather, Anderson Childress, arrived on campus. By midcentury it had spread across the South, to the campuses of more recently established colleges, and in towns where alumni gathered. It's unlikely that John Calvin Brown's alma mater, Jackson College of Columbia, Tennessee, had a chapter before the war. Given that the Union army leveled the school, we can say definitely that there was no postwar chapter. But the alma maters of other Pulaski college graduates almost certainly did. The young men settled on an initiation ceremony based on that of Kuklos Adelphon, and anointed their secret club the Ku Klux Klan, adding the final syllable because it sounded right. They thought the alliteration lent the term an extra degree of mystery. Their regalia, with white masks, high coned hats designed to make them appear especially tall, and long flowing white robes, was designed to evoke ghosts.[6]

The founders always claimed their intentions were benign, and that they appeared in public strictly for the purposes of their own amusement and in order to recruit new members, which they did with surprising ease. But young white southern men had a long tradition of finding amusement in violence toward black people. And given the social dislocations of the end of slavery and the enfranchisement of black men, white men had never felt a greater need to assert their physical authority than immediately after the war.

Within a year of the founding of the Pulaski Klan, men dressed in the Ku Klux uniform, flying the Ku Klux flag, began terrorizing and killing freedmen, revisiting the violence of slavery on men and women who were no longer slaves. When the Tennessee General Assembly conducted an investigation into Klan violence in middle and western Tennessee in 1868, they were inundated with testimony from hundreds of black men and women in Pulaski, in Murfreesboro, in Columbia, in every county, who had been whipped, raped, beaten, shot at, and threatened with death by men in white robes. W. A. Kelly, a former Union soldier and farmer near Columbia in Maury County, was luckier than some of the other freedmen he knew. After he voted in a local election, fourteen masked and armed men came to his house at ten or eleven at night, broke down his door, and fired at him as he escaped out the window. They "presented a pistol" at his "wife's head" and "swore they would kill" him, and kill his wife as well, if she didn't give them his money. After looting their house, stealing his money, and tearing up his army discharge papers and "certificate of registration," they "turned the stock" out into his fields and left just before daybreak.[7]

By the time the Tennessee legislature collected this testimony, black men and women across the South had fallen victim to Klan raids. The primary goal of this reign of terror was to "redeem" the region from the control of the Republican Party. When W. A. Kelly was asked if he thought "any Union man" who advocated "the cause of the Republican Party" would be "allowed to live" in Maury County "without being molested," Kelly replied definitively, "I do not. I believe he would be killed." Dafney, Lewis, Jane, and the other Polk freedpeople in Yalobusha, Mississippi, faced similar terrors as Klan members proudly shot, lynched, and burned those they deemed "bad negroes."[8]

Lynch law proved a remarkably effective political tactic. With the

Klan playing armed enforcer, the Democratic Party began a revival. Pulaski, birthplace of the Klan, not coincidentally led the way. Between the spring and fall elections of 1868, middle Tennessee's Republican majority evaporated. John Calvin Brown helped write a new state constitution allowing former rebels to vote and instituting a poll tax to prevent voting by former slaves. By 1870, Tennessee was fully redeemed, its black citizens disenfranchised, and a Democrat, from Pulaski, no less, elected governor of the state.[9]

That the new governor was reported to be one of "the first members of the Ku Klux Klan," and later a Grand Dragon of the Realm of Tennessee, should come as no surprise. Nor is it surprising that the new governor was John Calvin Brown. John Childress Jr.'s son later claimed that his father was one of the founders of the KKK. Given that John Jr. was nowhere near Pulaski at the time, it seems impossible that Bettie Childress's brother witnessed the birth of the Klan. But Bettie's husband most certainly did.[10]

If the election was a disaster for the Republican Party, it was far more so for black Tennesseans. But it was a family victory for the white Childresses. Bettie, who was "noted as one of the most elegant and cultivated ladies in the state," was now Tennessee's First Lady, just like the aunt who had secured her husband's pardon. And her brother, John Jr., had helped them get there: although just twenty-five years old, he managed the campaign that elected his Democratic brother-in-law to the governor's mansion. His career was launched. John Jr. became chairman of the Democratic Party of the state of Tennessee, a position he held for twenty-five years. Nor was his influence limited to Tennessee. His plans for Confederate commemoration spanned the entire South. John Jr. was reportedly the first person to suggest the construction of a monument to Jefferson Davis in the former capital of the Confederacy, Richmond. He headed up the movement, reaching out to like-minded sons of the Confederacy as far away as Atlanta for the purpose. He then employed an agent to travel throughout the South collecting funds for the monument.[11]

Visitors to Polk Place noted the remarkable physical resemblance between the state's new First Lady and pictures of her famous aunt at the same age. Bettie Childress delighted in the comparison, which validated her place in the Childress and Polk family legacy. Bettie's experience assisting Sarah "in receiving the General Assembly and other distinguished visitors from all parts of the world" at Polk Place over the years paid handsome dividends. Sarah's niece was arguably a greater success as Tennessee's First Lady than Sarah had been thirty-five years earlier. Governor Brown was reelected to a second term, something James had failed to accomplish. During her two terms as the state's First Lady, Bettie "filled her high position with graceful dignity. Her entertainments were frequent and elaborate, and she gave much assistance to her distinguished husband."[12]

Bettie and the governor visited Sarah frequently while in office, often in the company of their brother, John Jr., and his new wife. The capitol building, after all, could not have been any closer to Polk Place. Sarah enjoyed the attention, as well as her access to power. In 1871 she asked the governor to appoint a "special friend" of hers as superintendent of the penitentiary, "if consistent" with his "sense of Public duty." She recognized that "this is a departure from any usual custom," but she would consider it a "kindness" to her.[13]

Bettie loved to gaze on the portraits of her aunt in Polk Place, particularly one painted when Sarah was First Lady. "Everyone" agreed that this portrait in particular resembled Bettie more than Sarah. She asked her aunt to leave it to her, and Sarah agreed to do so in front of Bettie's friends and a reporter. Bettie tried but failed to follow Sarah's path from Nashville to Washington. In 1874, General Brown ran for the Senate as a Democrat. He was beaten by former president Andrew Johnson, the man who had pardoned Brown at Sarah's request. Johnson no doubt experienced the victory as a small vindication after watching his beloved Tennessee redeemed by the Democrats four years earlier.[14]

General Brown left politics; he went to work for the railroads, which was where the real money lay in the late nineteenth century. Although he no longer had an office in the capitol building, he and Bettie bought a mansion on Spruce Street, a few blocks from Polk Place. Family socializing continued to be easy, perhaps more so, now that Sarah and Bettie had so many common experiences to share.[15]

No doubt Bettie and Sarah discussed Sarah's vice presidency in the Daughters of the American Revolution, because she joined soon after her aunt. But in the wake of Sarah's death, Bettie lost her interest in the national association. The DAR, like the Woman's Christian Temperance Union, sought reconciliation in the name of national female unity at a moment when reconciliation gained national prominence. The vision of a reunited America, a vision Sarah had promoted in the late 1880s, became a kind of national religion in the last decade of the nineteenth century after the North allowed southern Democrats political home rule and vigilante violence in the name of white supremacy. Reconciliationist pageantry, complete with shared reunions of "Blue" and "Gray" veterans, suggested to many, particularly in the North, that it was time to consign sectional division to the past. If old soldiers could put aside their differences, then perhaps the nation could at last become whole again.[16]

But Bettie's allegiance lay not with country but with section. Not to the American Revolution but to the role of the Confederacy, in what she liked to call "the War between the States." Like her, many white southerners believed their "Lost Cause" was noble, that the North only won because of its superior numbers, and that the racial and social order of an imaginary "Old South," where slaves were happy and women on a pedestal, was vastly preferable to late-nineteenth-century northern society.[17]

Elias Polk's veneration of the Polk family thrilled them, because his sycophancy offered proof that the racial order of the Old South had been just. For these white southerners, most of whom had been too young to fight, the Confederate cause was something to celebrate, to venerate, and to cling to. When John Childress Jr. set to work raising money for Richmond's proposed Jefferson Davis statue in 1893, he and other members of Nashville's Young Men's Democratic Club raised $1,800 in the first year of their work, in the midst of a national economic depression, in a region that had not yet recovered from the financial devastation of the Civil War.[18]

John's wife helped out from her position on the "committee of ladies." The thousands of women across the South who were active in memorial associations in the 1860s and 1870s had taken the lead in commemorating the valor of southern men. Their increasingly political activities included establishing a Confederate Memorial Day, and public homes for destitute widows and orphans of Confederate soldiers. Many of them became enthusiastic advocates of terrorizing freedpeople. According to firsthand accounts, committees of ladies joyfully sewed Ku Klux Klan uniforms. The daughter of one of Alabama's original Klansmen argued that women were the driving force behind the Klan: "Southern men and women supported the Civil War, southern women and men supported the Klan."[19]

In 1893, many of the women working for Confederate commemoration under the umbrella of the "Ladies Auxiliary of the Confederate Home and Camp" purchased Sarah's posthumous memoir. The "charmingly written" and "elegant book" was available from bookstores across the South for just $1.75, and was advertised in the *Confederate Veteran,* a new magazine started under the auspices of John Childress Jr. to promote the work of commemoration. As narrated by Anson and Fanny Nelson, Sarah Childress Polk's life story revealed the power of Christian womanhood to shape American politics and inspire others. Her life was nothing less than a testimony to the power a strong Christian woman could wield in society.[20]

But her story was also one of fidelity and devotion: to James, to his tomb, to his memory, to home, and to nation. With "the waters of oblivion . . . silently engulfing" the "glory" and "grief" of "the epic of the Confederacy," it became clear, at least to one group of elite Tennessee women, that the time had arrived to lead rather than to follow. Emboldened by their pro-Confederate activities, white southern women embraced unreconstructed Confederate nostalgia as a means of expanding their sphere of influence. They, not their husbands and brothers, would vindicate the South.[21]

On September 10, 1893, Bettie Childress Brown joined with her friends and neighbors to organize a new hereditary society, devoted to honoring "the memory of those who served and those who fell in the service of the Confederate States; to protect, preserve, and mark places made historic by Confederate valor; to collect and preserve the material for a truthful history of the War between the States." They committed to placing Confederate monuments across the South, to remind the coming generations of the heroism of Confederate soldiers, and the justness of the cause for which they fought. They also pledged "to record the part taken by Southern women in patient endurance of hardship and patriotic devotion during the struggle." Like other women's organizations of the period, they expanded upon the traditional understanding of women's role as moral guardian to claim political authority equal to that of men. It was a radically broad agenda for an intensely reactionary group of women. None of them seemed to notice that in the gender order of the Old South, the one they yearned for, their female activism would have been unthinkable.[22]

Their first convention, the following year, was held in Nashville. Bettie, "a pioneer in the work," labored tirelessly to promote the new group. When the National Association of the Daughters of the Confederacy changed its name to the United Daughters of the Confederacy in 1895, Bettie Childress Brown was elected the association's first president. President Brown immediately published a letter in the leading southern newspapers "setting forth the need for this association, calling on the Southern people to rally to it, and pleading for the organization of chapters." Although membership was limited to relatives of Confederate veterans and women who served the Confederacy, the UDC grew rapidly. During its first year of existence, 20 chapters were organized. Within three years there were 138 chapters. By 1912, forty-five thousand Daughters belonged to 800 chapters. This was but a fraction of the membership of the WCTU or the Daughters of the American Revolution. But the United Daughters of the Confederacy were motivated, they were organized, and they were determined to redeem their Old South.[23]

Women like Bettie Childress would ultimately prove more resistant to appeals for reconciliation then would the South's white men. For the United Daughters of the Confederacy, activism in the name of conservative tradition was driven by resentment, because they believed that the glory of the Old South, where white women were venerated and protected, and had not needed to prove their equality, had been stolen from them. But it was also driven by love, and a conviction that the best way to prove your love for those who died was to continue fighting for the thing they died for. The UDC took as their motto "Love makes memory eternal." It was a sentiment that Sarah surely would have agreed with, one that captured all that she stood for in the second half of her life, even as it erased from memory her accomplishments in Washington. Although Sarah Childress Polk rose to political power by crossing boundaries, skillfully manipulating both men and women, and analyzing politics with a focus nearly as intense as that of the husband who worked himself to death, in public memory Mrs. James K.

Polk was celebrated as something quite different, a First Lady who was a lady first, whose politics had been driven by love and by a widow's responsibility to protect and cherish the memory of her lost husband. It wasn't untrue, but nor was it the whole story.[24]

Sarah never did leave Bettie the portrait she coveted. Although Bettie was convinced it resembled her "as much as it once did" Sarah, perhaps Sarah saw things differently. In the end the portrait did not go to the niece who chose section over country, but to Sallie Fall, the niece who should have been a daughter, and whose devotion matched her own.[25]

The Childress Family

JOEL CHILDRESS (1777–1819) m. Elizabeth Whitsitt (1781–1863)

  Anderson Childress (1799–1827) m. Mary Sansom (died 1821)

    MARY CHILDRESS (1821–1847; died in childbirth) m. Robert B. Jetton (1818–1887)

      Sarah Polk "Sallie" Jetton (1847–1924) m. George B. Fall

        Sarah Polk "Saidee" Fall (1871–1936)

  Susan Childress (1801–1878) m. Dr. William R. Rucker

    ELIZABETH RUCKER (1820–1843)

    JOANNA LUCINDA RUCKER (1822–1853; died in childbirth)

    WILLIAM HENRY RUCKER (1825–1827)

    SARAH POLK RUCKER (1828–1853; died in childbirth)

    SUSAN CAMILLA RUCKER (1835–1888)

    WILLIAM READE RUCKER (1838–1883)

    JOEL CHILDRESS RUCKER (1841–1874)

  Sarah Childress (1803–1891) m. James Knox Polk (1795–1849)

  Benjamin Childress: Died in infancy

  John W. Childress (1807–1884) m. Sarah Josey Williams (1815–1850)[*]

    MARY CHILDRESS (1834–1894) m. James Monroe Avent (1816–1895)

    JAMES CHILDRESS (b. about 1836)

    ELIJAH CHILDRESS (b. about 1839)

    ELIZABETH (BETTIE) CHILDRESS (1842–1919) m. John Calvin Brown

    JOHN W. CHILDRESS JR. (1845–1908) m. Mary Lyon

---

[*] John W. Childress had nine additional children with his second wife, Mary E. Phillips (1829–1900).

JOSEPH PHILIP CHILDRESS (b. about 1847)
MARTHA CHILDRESS (1848–1849)
Elizabeth Childress: Died in infancy

Some of Sarah Childress's Enslaved People

Matilda
   HARBERT (b. 1820, sold 1856) m. Mary
     Lewis (b. 1839)
Mariah (1814–1851) m. Henry Carter (1812–1852)
   HENRY (b. 1831) m. Millie

The Polk Family

SAMUEL POLK (1772–1827) m. Jane Knox (1776–1852)

James Knox Polk (1795–1849) m. Sarah Childress (1803–1891)

Jane Maria Polk (1798–1876) m. James Walker (1792–1864)

   SAMUEL POLK WALKER (1814–1870)

   JAMES HAYES WALKER (1816–1902)

   JOSEPH KNOX WALKER (1818–1863) m. Augusta Tabb (1824–1860)

      Maria Polk Walker (1843–1872)

      Henry Tabb Walker (1844–1928)

      Sarah (Sallie) Walker (1846–1903)

      Joseph Knox Walker Jr. (1847–1857)

      Samuel Polk Walker (1848–1932)

      Augusta Tabb Walker (1850–1860)

   JANE CLARISSA WALKER (1820–1899)

   MARY ELIZA WALKER (1823–1900) m. William Pickett (1820–1884)

   SARAH NAOMI (SALLY) WALKER (1825–1916)

   ANNIE MARIA WALKER (1827–1854)

   LUCIUS MARSHALL WALKER (1829–1863)

   ANDREW JACKSON WALKER (1834–1910)

   OPHELIA LAZINSKA WALKER (1837–1839)

   LEONIDAS POLK WALKER (1839–1840)

Lydia Eliza Polk (1800–1864) m. Silas M. Caldwell (1794–1846)

   SAMUEL POLK CALDWELL (1818–1885)

   JAMES MONTGOMERY CALDWELL (1828–1868)

Franklin Ezekiel Polk (1802–1831)

Marshall Tate Polk (1805–1831) m. Laura T. Wilson

   EUNICE POLK (1828–1842)

   MARSHALL TATE POLK JR. (1831–1884)

John Lee Polk (1807–1831)

Naomi Leetch Polk (1809–1836) m. Adlai O. Harris (1800–1862)

    AMELIA HARRIS (b. 1831)

    MARIA HARRIS (b. 1829)

    LAURA HARRIS (b. 1831)

    MALVINA HARRIS (b. 1837?)

Ophelia Clarissa Polk (1812–1851) m. Dr. John B. Hays (1796–1868)

    JANE VIRGINIA HAYS (1830–1857)

    MARIA NAOMI HAYS (1838–1864) m. William E. Moore

William Hawkins Polk (1815–1862) m. Belinda Dickinson (1815–1844)

second marriage—Mary Louise Corse (1816–1851)

    JAMES KNOX POLK (1849–1912)

third marriage—Lucy Eugenia Williams (1826–1906)

    WILLIAM HAWKINS POLK JR. (1855–1886)

    TASKER POLK (1861–1928)

Samuel Washington Polk (1817–1839)

Some of James K. Polk's Enslaved People

Elias Polk (1806–1886) m. Mary

Manuel (b. 1824) m. Jane (b. 1834, bought 1846)

Charles (b. 1825) m. Rosetta (b. 1833, bought 1849)

Giles (b. 1818, bought 1831) m. Dafney (b. 1828, bought 1839)

Maria Davis (b. 1831, bought 1847) m. Alfonso (b. 1827, bought 1853)

Henrietta

Acknowledgments

It took me a long time to realize that admitting ignorance is the first step in enlightenment, and that few things are more valuable to a writer than constructive criticism. If my books have gotten better over time, it's thanks to these core realizations, as well as the luck of having some brilliant friends who are as generous as they are gifted.

All of which is to say that this book exists thanks to the assistance of many people. My first debt is to Charles Sellers, who was not only unabashedly enthusiastic about this project when I first broached it with him, and has continued being a source of encouragement and historical analysis in the years since, but also gave me the kind of present that every historian dreams of. Before I drafted a single chapter, Charlie presented me with three large boxes of primary research for the unwritten third volume of his James K. Polk trilogy. These boxes contain hundreds of pages of notes taken at archives around the country, decades ago, all organized chronologically and by topic. I have tried to do justice to them in this volume. Thanks also to Caroline Merchant, who welcomed me into her home and gave me a suitcase to bring Charlie's notes home in. The two of them will recognize the debt that this project owes to them, and may even see a reflection of their enviable collaboration in James and Sarah Polk's happier moments.

When I set out to build an archive of all of Sarah Polk's correspondence, I had no idea of the extent to which I would come to depend on the skill and generosity of archivists. I owe special debts to three Tennessee scholars who repeatedly took time out of their busy jobs to assist me with my research: Tom Price, director of the Maury County Archives and formerly curator of the James K. Polk Home in Columbia, Tennessee; Tom Kanon, supervisor of manuscripts at the Tennessee State Library Association; and Michael David Cohen, editor of the *Correspondence of James K. Polk*. All three helped me track down sources, happily scanned material, and answered a truly embarrassing number of questions (they know how many!) over several years with remarkable good humor.

During a memorable visit to Columbia, Tom Price provided a mind-expanding historical tour of the Polk Family Home and its special collections, bought me lunch, and then, after a full day of nonstop Polk discussion, invited me on a tour of the plantation district outside Columbia proper. All of this had a dramatic influence on my understanding of the Polk family and the role of slavery in middle Tennessee. The extent of Tom Kanon's assistance is suggested by the fact that at one point he read a very long master's thesis in the TSLA archives on my behalf, in order to answer a very short question.

Michael David Cohen provided me with a remarkably thorough (and deservedly critical) line edit of an early draft of this book, for which I am very much in his debt. He shared his research with me and, not insignificantly, the only known example of James Polk laughing. And he did me the tremendous favor of introducing me to Lisa Childs of Arkansas, whose remarkable research uncovered the Civil War and Reconstruction fates of many of the enslaved people on the Polk Plantation. Many thanks to Lisa for so generously sharing this material. I'm not sure what marvelous thing I did in a previous life to deserve the help of these historical experts, but I am grateful. It's no exaggeration to say that this book would not have been completed without their help.

I was extremely lucky to make the acquaintance of Kay McKnight at the Salem College Archives early in this project. Kay not only conducted research on my behalf in Salem, but also introduced me to Bobby Bennett, who generously allowed me access to his private collection of Polk materials, including a previously unknown letter from Joel Childress to his fifteen-year-old daughter, Sarah. My thanks to both of them. I also received valuable assistance from Dawn Eurich at the Burton Historical Collection, John Holtzapple at the Polk Family Home, Tal Nadan at the New York Public Library, Jennie Cole at the Filson Historical Society, John Lodi and Gena Henderson at the Rutherford County Archives, William Thompson at the Mississippi Department of Archives and History, Yalobusha plantation owner Don Sides, filmmaker Brian Rose, and Dr. Bill Schultz. Aaron Scott Crawford was not only generous with his research, but a marvelous help puzzling out (what now appear to be) rather basic aspects of the Democratic political scene in 1830s and 1840s Washington and Nashville.

I owe the National Endowment for the Humanities thanks for a Public Scholar Fellowship in 2016–17, which provided me with the time to complete my manuscript. And I don't often enough thank fate for landing me at Penn State University. "Happy Valley" has proven an ideal place to live and to work. University administrators, particularly dean of liberal arts Susan Welch, and history department head Michael Kulikowski, have proven remarkably supportive of my research agenda. Without course releases and research funds this book (and my previous books) would have taken much longer to complete. Penn State also provided me with a series of marvelous research assistants: Xiangyun Xu, Kathryn Falvo, Emily Seitz, and Mallory Huard. Robert K. Colby and Evan Rothera also conducted research on my behalf.

It's a pleasure to have the opportunity to publish a second book with Andrew Miller at Alfred A. Knopf. Andrew has proven himself a model editor, a gentle critic who clearly loves history and is willing to line-edit repeated drafts. His suggestions for strengthening what I wrongly thought was a great first draft vastly improved the final project. Knopf editorial assistant Zakiya Harris also provided a careful reading and suggestions that did a great deal to strengthen my narration and argument. Thanks also to my book agents, Sydelle Kramer and Susan Rabiner, for their representation and sage advice.

I am in debt to too many of my historian colleagues. I would like to thank audiences at my presentations on Sarah Childress Polk over the years, particularly at the McNeil Center for Early American Studies at the University of Pennsylvania, the University of Wisconsin, the Center for Presidential History at Southern Methodist University, and at annual meetings of the Organization of American Historians and, my intellectual home, the Society for Historians of the Early American Republic. Thanks also to Jennifer Boittin, Tom Chaffin, Catherine Clinton, Richard Doyle, Dan Feller, Lori Ginzberg, Melissa Gismondi, Cassandra Good, Nancy Isenberg, Ari Kelman, Catherine E. Kelly, Patrick Kelly, Susan Lee Johnson, Charlene Boyer Lewis, Seth Rockman, Anne C. Rose, Adam Rothman, Joshua Rothman, and Michael Vorenberg for their helpful suggestions during the course of my research and writing. My colleague Anthony E. Kaye didn't get to read this book, but his thoughts on slavery and community, shared over the years, went a long way toward shaping my approach to these topics. His correspondence during the final months of his life about material in this book is a testimony both to his generosity and his historical acumen. I'm sorry I can't thank him in person.

William Blair, Andrew Burstein, Cathleen Cahill, Patricia Cline Cohen, Emily Conroy-Krutz, Rebecca Edwards, Martha Few, Caitlin Fitz, Mary Kelley, Alexis McCrossen, Charles Sellers, Alan Taylor, Elizabeth Varon, and Andrew Zimmerman each read and commented on early drafts of this project. To say that their assistance was crucial to making this book better is a radical understatement. My kind readers challenged me to dig deeper, rethink central assumptions, and recognize what I didn't know. I didn't always follow their advice as well as I should have, which not only reflects poorly on me, but explains any remaining errors of fact or interpretation. I would also like to thank my two educated "lay readers," Robin Briscoe and Jane Lee Macintosh Greenberg, who helped me see my own work from a nonhistorian's perspective. For longer than I think either of us can believe, Penny Grove has helped me keep my life in order with ridiculous good cheer. And, as always, I acknowledge Alexis McCrossen, who continues to be the best friend anyone could ask for. Thanks to her, and to my other wonderful friends who have kept me sane during a difficult stretch of my life.

The Greenbergs know how much I love them: Mike, Ken, Jessica, Barb, Aunt Sheila, and the nephews. As for my kind, brilliant, wonderful children, Jackson and Violet, there are no words to express my gratitude for your presence in my life.

I dedicate this book to two women whose examples have shaped my understanding of both my own world and that of Sarah Polk. The first is my mother, Jane Lee Macintosh Greenberg. The second is Mrs. Paul A. Greene, who always insisted that "a lady rises above it." I'm very sorry that Mrs. Greene passed away before she could see the influence of those words in print.

Notes

ABBREVIATIONS USED IN THE NOTES

CS	Charles Sellers Collection
JKP	James K. Polk
JC	John Childress Sr.
LOC	Library of Congress
NCSA	Lucy Williams Polk Papers, North Carolina State Archives
NDA	*Nashville Daily American*
NYH	*New York Herald*
SCP	Sarah Childress Polk
TSLA	Tennessee State Library and Archives
UT	University of Tennessee Polk Correspondence

PREFACE: MRS. POLK'S 1848

1. The term "First Lady" did not come into use until the 1850s, but I employ it in this project because it so nicely encapsulates the special status of the president's wife.
2. Elizabeth Thacker-Estrada, "True Women: The Roles and Lives of Antebellum Presidential Wives Sarah Polk, Margaret Taylor, Abigail Fillmore, and Jane Pierce," in *The Presidential Companion: Readings on the First Ladies*, ed. Robert Watson and A. Eksterowicz (Columbia: University of South Carolina Press, 2003), 86; Valerie Palmer-Mehta, "Sarah Polk: Ideas of Her Own," in *A Companion to First Ladies*, ed. Katherine A. S. Sibley (Malden, MA: Wiley-Blackwell, 2016), 158–75.
3. Elizabeth Benton Frémont, *Recollections of Elizabeth Benton Frémont* (New York: Frederick H. Hitchcock, 1912), 15.
4. Laura Holloway, *The Ladies of the White House* (New York: U.S. Pub. Co., 1870), 462; "A Visit to Mrs. Polk," *Alexandria (VA) Gazette*, October 29, 1859.
5. "Bolting Among the Ladies," *Oneida Whig*, August 1, 1848; Judith Wellman, "The Seneca Falls Convention: Setting the National Stage for Women's Suffrage," *History Now,* Gilder Lehrman Institute of American History, http://oa.gilderlehrman.org/history-by-era/first-age-reform/essays/seneca-falls-convention-setting-national-stage-for-women%E2%80%99s-su, accessed October 15, 2015; Lisa Tetrault, *The Myth of Seneca Falls: Memory and the Women's Suffrage Movement, 1848–1898* (Chapel Hill: University of North Carolina Press, 2003).

6. John Smolenski, "From Men of Property to Just Men: Deference, Masculinity, and the Evolution of Political Discourse in Early America," *Early American Studies* 3, no. 2 (2005): 253–85, quote on 258.

7. William Dusinberre, *Slavemaster President: The Double Career of James Polk* (New York: Oxford University Press, 2003), 184–85.

8. "From *Sartain's Union Magazine* Mrs. James K. Polk," *Pittsfield (MA) Sun*, February 28, 1850. Lori D. Ginzberg has noted that female political activism in the decades before the Civil War was obscured by both an ideology of separate spheres and the efforts of women to conform to the ideal of nonpolitical womanhood. Lori D. Ginzberg, *Women and the Work of Benevolence: Morality, Politics, and Class in the Nineteenth-Century United States* (New Haven, CT: Yale University Press, 1990).

9. Anson Nelson and Fanny Nelson, *Memorials of Sarah Childress Polk: Wife of the Eleventh President of the United States* (New York: Anson D. F. Randolph and Co., 1892), 33. Gregory P. Downs makes the argument that a politics of dependence, what he calls "American patronalism," emerged during the Civil War, and has been missed by scholars. The politics of deference Sarah Polk practiced predates Downs's patronalism but is otherwise a similar practice of political power from a position of dependence. Gregory P. Downs, *Declarations of Dependence: The Long Reconstruction of Popular Politics in the South, 1861–1908* (Chapel Hill: University of North Carolina Press, 2011), 1–3.

10. Frances E. Willard and Mary A. Livermore, eds., "Polk, Mrs. Sarah Childress," in *American Women—Fifteen Hundred Biographies with Over 1,400 Portraits: A Comprehensive Encyclopedia of the Lives and Achievements of American Women During the Nineteenth Century* (New York: Mast, Crowell & Kirkpatrick, 1897), vol. 2, 577–78.

11. "Memorials of Sarah Childress Polk," *The Nation* 55 (October 27, 1892): 325.

12. National Woman Suffrage Association, *Report of the International Council of Women, Assembled by the National Woman Suffrage Association, Washington, D.C., U.S. of America, March 25 to April 1, 1888* (Washington, DC: Rufus H. Darby, 1888), vol. 1, 32; Nancy Isenberg, *Sex and Citizenship in Antebellum America* (Chapel Hill: University of North Carolina Press, 1998), 5–6; Lori D. Ginzberg, *Untidy Origins: A Story of Woman's Rights in Antebellum New York* (Chapel Hill: University of North Carolina Press, 2005); Julie Hirschfeld Davis and Jada F. Smith, "Get to Know the Historical Figures on the $5, $10 and $20 Bills," *New York Times*, April 21, 2016.

13. Barbara Bennett Peterson, *Sarah Childress Polk: First Lady of Tennessee and Washington* (Huntington, NY: Nova History Publications, 2002), 31; John Reed Bumgarner, *Sarah Childress Polk: A Biography of the Remarkable First Lady* (Jefferson, NC: McFarland, 1997). Bumgarner makes ample use of Martha McBride Morrell's *"Young Hickory": The Life and Times of President James K. Polk* (New York: G. P. Dutton, 1941) and Jimmie Lou Sparkman Claxton's *Eighty-Eight Years with Sarah Polk* (New York: Vantage, 1972). Carl Sferrazza Anthony's *America's First Families: An Inside View of 200 Years of Private Life in the White House* (New York: Touchstone, 2000) draws liberally from Mary Ormsbee Whitton's romanticized and footnote-free *First First Ladies, 1789–1865: A Study of the Wives of the Early Presidents* (New York: Hastings House, 1948), while misquotations in Betty Boyd Caroli's popular *First Ladies: From Martha Washington to Michelle Obama* (New York: Oxford University Press, 2009) have led many later authors to problematic conclusions. Caroli cites Charles Sellers's award-winning *James K. Polk*, vol. 1, *Jacksonian, 1795–1843* (Princeton, NJ: Princeton University Press, 1957), for her claim that "when Sarah and James married, his relatives supposedly thought that she displayed 'a great deal of spice and more independence of judgment than was fitting in one woman'" (Caroli, 34). But

what Sellers wrote was quite different: "Some may have felt that she displayed more independence of judgment than was fitting in a woman; and one of the townsmen proved himself a perceptive judge of character when he noted that 'her eyes looked as if she had a great deal of spice'" (Sellers, 93). Caroli's statement suggests that James's family thought Sarah too independent, when there was no suggestion in the original account that anyone in his family was less than enraptured by his new bride. The Caroli interpretation has been quoted repeatedly. See, for instance, Margaret Ripley Wolfe, "The Feminine Dimension in the Volunteer State," *Tennessee Historical Quarterly* 55, no. 2 (Summer 1996): 120.

14. See, for instance, Bumgarner's narration of Sarah refusing to marry James Buchanan, drawn from Claxton. There is no evidence that Sarah "stated that she had too much respect for her beloved husband ever to change her name," or that "romance" ever entered her "thoughts." Bumgarner, *Sarah Childress Polk*, 127–28. Claxton's book was published seventeen years before the state supreme court in New York ordered Vantage to pay $3.5 million in damages to twenty-two hundred authors it had defrauded. "Jurors' Vanity Press Review: Publisher Defrauded Authors," *New York Times*, April 7, 1990; Jim Milliot, "Vantage Press Closes," *Publishers Weekly*, December 19, 2012.

15. All of this rich source material has been carefully preserved by the Massachusetts Historical Society: www.masshist.org/adams/louisa_catherine_adams.

16. SCP to William H. Polk, April 25, 1875, Polk Papers, PC 75, 4, Correspondence 1875–1877, NCSA.

17. When documenting events, rather than Sarah's views of events, I have attempted wherever possible to corroborate material in *Memorials* with other sources. Nelson and Nelson, *Memorials of Sarah Childress Polk*.

18. Holloway, *The Ladies of the White House*, 461.

19. Scholars who promote well-written narrative history, as well as those who practice it, have shaped my approach here. Ivan Jabolonka makes a compelling argument in favor of literary, accessible, jargon-free history: "not lowering the requirements for the social sciences, but on the contrary raising them, by making investigations more transparent, procedures more honest, research more audacious, and words better adjusted. . . . By switching from discourse to text, we can proceed so writing produces a net gain for epistemology." Ivan Jabolonka, *History Is a Contemporary Literature: Manifesto for the Social Sciences* (Ithaca, NY: Cornell University Press, 2018), xii. Annette Gordon-Reed's narrative of the Hemingses of Monticello demonstrates how fruitful conjecture can be in writing the history of enslaved people. Annette Gordon-Reed, *The Hemingses of Monticello: An American Family* (New York: Norton, 2008); Lorena Walsh's approach to writing the group history of a multigenerational slave community has also been influential. Lorena S. Walsh, *From Calabar to Carter's Grove: The History of a Virginia Slave Community* (Charlottesville: University Press of Virginia, 1997).

20. Robert P. Watson, "The First Lady Reconsidered: Presidential Partner and Political Institution," *Presidential Studies Quarterly* 27, no. 4, Rules of the Game: How to Play the Presidency (Fall 1997): 805–18, quotes on 810, 811.

21. Rachel Sheldon has recently argued in her book *Washington Brotherhood* that due to a variety of local circumstances, extra-official spaces became, if anything, even more crucial to the functioning of Washington political life in the antebellum decades then they had earlier. Sheldon reveals that important political alliances and decisions were inevitably made outside the halls of Congress—in social clubs, boardinghouses, and private homes. Sarah Polk's facility in this realm was of crucial importance to but-

tressing her husband's position—she set the conditions for the president to form alliances and influence others. Rachel Sheldon, *Washington Brotherhood: Politics, Social Life, and the Coming of the Civil War* (Chapel Hill: University of North Carolina Press, 2013).

CHAPTER I. BLACKBOARD, MAPS, AND GLOBES

1. Donald Detwiler, *Rutherford County, Tennessee Deaths and Estate Settlements*, vol. 1, *1804–1849* (Murfreesboro, TN: Rutherford County Historical Society, 2008), 31; Susan G. Daniel, *Rutherford County Tennessee Pioneers* (Murfreesboro, TN: Rutherford County Historical Society, 2003), 52; William S. Speer, *Sketches of Prominent Tennesseans: Biographies and Records of Many of the Families Who Have Attained Prominence in Tennessee* (Nashville: Albert B. Tavel, 1888), 26.

2. Alan Taylor, *American Revolutions: A Continental History* (New York: Norton, 2016), 251–80.

3. "Charter of Carolina, 1663," in *The Colonial Records of North Carolina*, ed. William L. Saunders (Raleigh, NC: P. M. Hale Printer, 1886), vol. 1, 20–33.

4. Speer, *Sketches of Prominent Tennesseans*, 26; Richard Carlton Fulcher, *1770–1790 Census of the Cumberland Settlements* (Baltimore: Genealogical Publishing Co., 1987), 181; William Heth Whitsitt, "Annals of a Scotch-Irish Family: The Whitsitts of Nashville," *American Historical Magazine and Tennessee Historical Society Quarterly* 9 (1904): 239, 241.

5. Quoted in Tom Kanon, "The Kidnapping of Martha Crawley and Settler-Indian Relations Prior to the War of 1812," *Tennessee Historical Quarterly* 64, no. 1 (Spring 2005): 14; James Seagrove to William Knox, May 24, 1792, *American State Papers: Indian Affairs*, ed. Charles J. Kappler (Washington, DC: Government Printing Office, 1904), vol. 1, 296; Kristopher Ray, *Middle Tennessee, 1775–1825: Progress and Popular Democracy on the Southwestern Frontier* (Knoxville: University of Tennessee Press, 2007), 26–27; Mark Renfred Cheathem, *Andrew Jackson, Southerner* (Baton Rouge: Louisiana State University Press, 2013), 26.

6. Ray, *Middle Tennessee*, 28–33, quote on 28.

7. Donald B. Dodd and Wynelle S. Dodd, *Historical Statistics of the South, 1790–1970* (Tuscaloosa: University of Alabama Press, 1973), 50.

8. "Treaty with the Cherokee a.k.a Treaty of Hopewell, 1785," Nov. 28, 1785. | 7 Stat., 18. *American State Papers: Indian Affairs*, vol. 2, 8–11; Daniel, *Rutherford County Tennessee Pioneers*, 52.

9. Important facts about the early history of the Whitsitts and Childresses are frustratingly obscure. One of James K. Polk's biographers claimed Sarah's parents were married in Campbell County, Virginia, and when questioned about this late in life, Sarah herself thought he might have been correct, although she admitted that she didn't know where her parents were married, or when. But this appears highly unlikely. Legal documentation suggests that Elizabeth Whitsitt's father, John Whitsitt, was originally from North Carolina, not Virginia, and also offers evidence that Elizabeth was born in North Carolina, and was living in Tennessee by age nine at the latest. Judge Andrew Jackson oversaw John Whitsitt's sale of a "Negro boy named Jack about seven or eight years old" in Sumner County in 1795. An early narrative states that Elizabeth and Joel were married in Sumner County, and multiple land deeds place Joel Childress in Sumner County at the turn of the century. Whitsitt, "Annals of a Scotch-Irish Family," 239–41; Speer, *Sketches of Prominent Tennesseans*, 26. See also Daniel, *Rutherford County Tennessee Pioneers*, 52; Sumner County, Register of Deeds,

Roll #108, TSLA, vol. 1, August 1793–December 1797, p. 107; Thomas Waller to Joel Childress, Deed, Sumner County, Register of Deeds, Roll #108, TSLA, vol. 3, April 1800–October 1805, p. 210.

10. Anson Nelson and Fanny Nelson, *Memorials of Sarah Childress Polk: Wife of the Eleventh President of the United States* (New York: Anson D. F. Randolph and Co., 1892), 1–2; Thomas Waller to Joel Childress, Deed, Sumner County, Register of Deeds, Roll #108, TSLA, vol. 3, April 1800–October 1805, p. 210; Joel Childress to John Jetton Deed, Rutherford County, Register of Deeds, Roll #109, Tennessee State Library and Archives, vols. A–G, 1804–1808, vol. A, p. 36; Joel Childress to John Lawrence Deed, Rutherford County, Register of Deeds, Roll #109, Tennessee State Library and Archives, vols. A–G, 1804–1808, vol. A, pp. 35–36. On debates over Sarah's place of birth, see John Williams Childress, "The Childress Family of Tennessee" (typescript, 1960), Rutherford County Historical Society publication no. 16 (Winter 1981); Land Office, and Museum, Early Tennessee/North Carolina Land Records, 1783–1927, Record Group 50, August 10, 1811, TSLA, p. 942; Daniel, *Rutherford County Tennessee Pioneers*, 52.

11. Sydney E. Ahlstrom, *A Religious History of the American People* (Garden City, NY: Doubleday, 1975), vol. 1, 341–45, 387–88, 523–40; Christine Heyrman, *Southern Cross: The Beginnings of the Bible Belt* (Chapel Hill: University of North Carolina Press, 1997), 6–9, 267–68; Elizabeth Whitsitt Childress portrait courtesy of the Rutherford County Archives.

12. Heyrman, *Southern Cross*, 6–9.

13. Susan Childress Rucker portrait courtesy of the Rutherford County Archives.

14. Elizabeth Whitsitt Childress portrait courtesy of the Rutherford County Archives.

15. Genesis 1:28. Rebecca Edwards has argued that by the 1820s, female fertility was helping to drive territorial expansion, and that "Americans believed, in fact, that moving to 'fair and fertile territories' caused women to have more children." Rebecca Edwards, "Childbearing and U.S. Empire: The Case of the 1850 Oregon Donation Land Act," unpublished paper presented at the 17th Berkshire Conference on the History of Women, Genders, and Sexualities, June 2, 2017, p. 2.

16. Mary Beth Norton, *Liberty's Daughters: The Revolutionary Experience of American Women, 1750–1800* (Boston: Little, Brown, 1980), 74–75; Wilma A. Dunaway, *Women, Work, and Family in the Antebellum Mountain South* (New York: Cambridge University Press, 2008), 144–46.

17. Janet Farrell Brodie, *Contraception and Abortion in 19th-Century America* (Ithaca, NY: Cornell University Press, 1994), 2–86.

18. The most thorough study of conception in the Revolutionary era suggests that these views were far more unusual on the frontier than in urban centers in this period. Susan E. Klepp, *Revolutionary Conceptions: Women, Fertility, and Family Limitation in America, 1760–1820* (Chapel Hill: University of North Carolina Press, 2009).

19. Carol Berkin, *Revolutionary Mothers: Women in the Struggle for American Independence* (New York: Knopf, 2005), 4–11; Rosemarie Zagarri, *Revolutionary Backlash: Women and Politics in the Early American Republic* (Philadelphia: University of Pennsylvania Press, 2007), 19–22.

20. Abigail Adams to John Adams, March 31, 1776, *Adams Family Correspondence*, ed. L. H. Butterfield, Wendell D. Garrett, and Marjorie Sprague (Cambridge, MA: Harvard University Press, 1963), vol. 1, 370.

21. Benjamin Rush, *Essays Literary, Moral, and Philosophical* (Philadelphia: Thomas and William Bradford, 1798), 76–77.

22. Nelson and Nelson, *Memorials of Sarah Childress Polk*, 2.

23. "State vs. Joel Childress," Minutes of the Superior Court of North Carolina Including Mero District (Works Progress Administration transcript, 1938, TSLA), 2, 199–200; "State vs. Childress," in Andrew Jackson, *Legal Papers of Andrew Jackson*, ed. James W. Ely Jr. and Theodore Brown Jr. (Knoxville: University of Tennessee Press, 1987), 212–13.

24. Holger Hoock, *Scars of Independence: America's Violent Birth* (New York: Crown, 2017); Dickson D. Bruce Jr., *Violence and Culture in the Antebellum South* (Austin: University of Texas Press, 2011); Bruce C. Baird, "The Social Origins of Dueling in Virginia," in *Lethal Imagination: Violence and Brutality in American History*, ed. Michael Bellesiles (New York: NYU Press, 1999), 87–112.

25. Inventory of Joel Childress estate, April 12, 1820, Polk Papers, LOC; "Robbery," *Daily National Intelligencer*, July 15, 1818; "It will be recollected," *Mississippi State Gazette*, September 12, 1818.

26. Ahlstrom, *A Religious History of the American People*, vol. 1, 538–40.

27. Tennessee Division of Archives, Land Office, and Museum, Early Tennessee/North Carolina Land Records, 1783–1927, Record Group 50, December 11, 1810, TSLA, p. 466; 1810 Census, Census Place: Nashville, Rutherford, Tennessee, Roll #63, p. 10 (NARA microfilm publication M252, 71 rolls), Bureau of the Census, Record Group 29, National Archives, Washington, DC.

28. Dunaway, *Women, Work, and Family in the Antebellum Mountain South*, 144–46. On the role of cotton production in driving territorial settlement, see Adam Rothman, *Slave Country: American Expansion and the Origins of the Deep South* (Cambridge, MA: Harvard University Press, 2005), 45–54, 177–78.

29. A. W. Putnam, *History of Middle Tennessee; Or, Life and Times of Gen. James Robertson* (Nashville: Printed for the author, 1859), 585. On cotton, see Thomas Perkins Abernethy, *Frontier to Plantation in Tennessee: A Study in Frontier Democracy* (Tuscaloosa: University of Alabama Press, 1967), 150–52; Sven Beckert, *Empire of Cotton: A Global History* (New York: Knopf, 2014), 102–3.

30. Tennessee Division of Archives, Land Office, and Museum, Early Tennessee/North Carolina Land Records, 1783–1927, Record Group 50, December 11, 1810, TSLA, p. 466; 1810 Census, Census Place: Nashville, Rutherford, Tennessee, Roll #63 (NARA microfilm publication M252, 71 rolls), Bureau of the Census, Record Group 29, National Archives, Washington, DC; "Black Fox Camp Spring," Tennessee Historical Marker 3A 162; Goodspeed Publishing Company, *History of Tennessee from the Earliest Time to the Present* (Nashville, 1886), 97.

31. Dodd and Dodd, *Historical Statistics of the South;* Nelson and Nelson, *Memorials of Sarah Childress Polk*, 2; Lisa C. Tolbert, *Constructing Townscapes: Space and Society in Antebellum Tennessee* (Chapel Hill: University of North Carolina Press, 1999), 42–43.

32. Advertisements, *Nashville Whig*, December 28, 1813; *Nashville Whig*, January 3, 1815; Tennessee Division of Archives, Land Office, and Museum, Early Tennessee/North Carolina Land Records, 1783–1927, Record Group 50, December 13, 1812, TSLA, p. 323. See also Bradley and Benge to Joel Childress, Rutherford County, Register of Deeds, Roll #110, vols. H–L, 1811–1819, TSLA, vol. H, 227–28; John Steele Gordon, *An Empire of Wealth: The Epic History of American Economic Power* (New York: Harper Collins, 2004), 125.

33. The variety, quality, and number of household furnishings owned by the Childresses would have placed them "at the top" of society anywhere in the United States. Barbara G. Carson, *Ambitious Appetites: Dining, Behavior, and Patterns of Consumption in Federal Washington* (Washington, DC: AIA Press, 1990), 45.

34. Inventory of Joel Childress estate, April 12, 1820, Polk Papers, LOC; Susan Childress portrait courtesy of Rutherford County Archives. Mirrors were an especially valued feature in elite domestic interiors for their value in reflecting light. Carson, *Ambitious Appetites,* 45; Walter R. Borneman, *Polk: The Man Who Transformed the Presidency and America* (New York: Random House, 2009), 12.

35. Rebecca L. Smith, "History of Dilton," Rutherford County Historical Society publication no. 9 (Summer 1977): 67; *Nashville Whig,* October 25, 1814. Charles Sellers, *James K. Polk,* vol. 1, *Jacksonian, 1795–1843* (Princeton, NJ: Princeton University Press, 1957), 42–43.

36. *Nashville Whig,* September 27, 1814.

37. "She was out to see old Mrs. Smart who lives near Charlotte, the old lady is 87 years of age, knew you when you were a little boy & still insists upon calling you little Jimmy Polk." Marshall T. Polk, West Point, to JKP, May 1, 1849, LOC, Polk Papers; Robert W. Ikard, "Surgical Operations on James K. Polk by Ephraim McDowell, or the Search for Polk's Gallstone," *Tennessee Historical Quarterly* 43, no. 2 (1984): 121–31. Ikard argues that the surgery most likely left Polk impotent.

38. Nelson and Nelson, *Memorials of Sarah Childress Polk,* 3–4.

39. Ibid., 3.

40. While it's easy to imagine that "ornamental accomplishments" like proficiency at needlework, drawing, and the piano were the antithesis of serious learning, Catherine E. Kelly makes the convincing argument that at the finest women's schools the two were closely linked, and that reading was embedded in "a variety of polite practices." The primary difference between Abercrombie's School and Salem Academy was that there appears to have been very little reading or formal study at the former, not that "ornamental accomplishment" was missing from the latter. Catherine E. Kelly, "Reading and the Problem of Accomplishment," in *Reading Women: Literacy, Authorship, and Culture in the Atlantic World, 1500–1800,* ed. Heidi Brayman Hackel and Catherine E. Kelly (Philadelphia: University of Pennsylvania Press, 2008), 124–43, quote on 124.

41. "Female Education," *Godey's Lady's Book* 9 (September 1834): 143.

42. On the importance of refinement in the early American republic, and the place of academies like Abercrombie's within the evolving culture, see Catherine E. Kelly, *Republic of Taste: Art, Politics, and Everyday Life in Early America* (Philadelphia: University of Pennsylvania Press, 2016), 14–54.

43. Caroline O'Reilly Nicholson, "Reminiscences of an Octogenarian," Caroline O'Reilly Nicholson Papers, #547-z, Southern Historical Collection, Wilson Library, University of North Carolina at Chapel Hill, 39; Nelson and Nelson, *Memorials of Sarah Childress Polk,* 8–10.

44. Nelson and Nelson, *Memorials of Sarah Childress Polk,* 8–10.

45. Richard R. Beeman, *The Evolution of the Southern Backcountry: A Case Study of Lunenburg County, Virginia, 1746–1832* (Philadelphia: University of Pennsylvania Press, 1984), 78–79, 180–81; Nancy Isenberg, *White Trash: The 400-Year Untold History of Class in America* (New York: Viking, 2016), 105–32.

46. Isenberg, *White Trash,* 105–32.

47. "Rules of the Boarding School at Salem," 1805, Salem College Archives; Mary Kelley, *Learning to Stand and Speak: Women, Education, and Public Life in America's Republic* (Chapel Hill: University of North Carolina Press, 2006), 32, 263.

48. Claudia Jack, "Sarah Childress Polk," typescript manuscript, Salem College Archives; "Rules of the Boarding School at Salem," 1805, Salem College Archives.

49. "Rules of the Boarding School at Salem," 1805, Salem College Archives; Salem

Academy Class Schedule 1811, Salem College Archives; Maria Crockett to Robert Crockett, January 13, 1818, Crockett Family Letters, Salem College Archives.

50. Maria Crockett to Robert Crockett, February 24, 1818, Crockett Family Letters, Salem College Archives.

51. Maria Crockett to Robert Crockett, March 8, 1818, Crockett Family Letters, Salem College Archives.

52. Contents of Salem Academy Library in 1817, Salem College Archives.

53. Maria Campbell to Mary Humes, September 21, 1819, Campbell Family Papers, Box 4, Correspondence, David M. Rubenstein Rare Book and Manuscript Library, Duke University.

54. Ibid.; "From *Sartain's Union Magazine* Mrs. James K. Polk," *Pittsfield (MA) Sun*, February 28, 1850.

55. "Nashville Female Academy," *Nashville Whig*, January 10, 1821. Sally Dickinson, later the wife of James's leading middle Tennessee Whig rival, John Bell, was said to have attended Salem Academy at the same time as Sarah, although there is no documentation in the Salem Archives that this was the case. Goodspeed Publishing Company, *History of Tennessee* (Nashville, 1887), 735; Nelson and Nelson, *Memorials of Sarah Childress Polk*, 3–4.

56. Joel Childress to Sarah Childress, April 22, 1818, Private Collection of Bobby Bennett.

57. Ibid.; Bertram Wyatt-Brown, *Southern Honor: Ethics and Behavior in the Old South* (New York: Oxford University Press, 1982), 117–48; Stephen M. Frank, *Life with Father: Parenthood and Masculinity in the Nineteenth-Century North* (Baltimore: Johns Hopkins University Press, 1998), 160–71; Lori Glover, *Southern Sons: Becoming Men in the New Republic* (Baltimore: Johns Hopkins University Press, 2007), 9–17. Glover also notes that fathers were anxious to avoid conflict with sons, and "often wanted to be friends as much as parents," 32.

58. Joel Childress to Sarah Childress, April 22, 1818, Private Collection of Bobby Bennett. Stephen M. Frank notes that "the language of parental friendship was employed earliest and most often vis-à-vis daughters" in New England, but studies of the southern frontier suggest it was far rarer in this region of the country. Frank, *Life with Father*, 171; Joan Cashin, *A Family Venture: Men and Women on the Southern Frontier* (Baltimore: Johns Hopkins University Press, 1994), 25–26. Cassandra Good argues that in the decades after the American Revolution "friendships between elite men and women . . . were both common and highly valued." Cassandra Good, *Founding Friendships: Friendships Between Men and Women in the Early American Republic* (New York: Oxford University Press, 2015), 1.

59. "Died," *Essex Register* (Salem, MA), September 29, 1819; Will of Joel Childress, August 10, 1819, Rutherford County Archives, Record Book 4, 191–99; Division of estate of Joel Childress, November 26, 1822, Rutherford County Archives, Record Book 5, 242–45; Inventory of Joel Childress estate, April 12, 1820, Polk Papers, LOC, Microfilm.

60. Nelson and Nelson, *Memorials of Sarah Childress Polk*, 12.

61. Ahlstrom, *A Religious History of the American People*, vol. 1, 537–39.

62. Sellers, *James K. Polk*, vol. 1, *Jacksonian*, 74–75, 79.

63. J. Roderick Heller III, *Democracy's Lawyer: Felix Grundy of the Old Southwest* (Baton Rouge: Louisiana State University Press, 2010), 119.

64. Nelson and Nelson, *Memorials of Sarah Childress Polk*, 15–16.

65. Sellers, *James K. Polk*, vol. 1, *Jacksonian*, 76–78.

66. Ibid., 74.

67. Nelson and Nelson, *Memorials of Sarah Childress Polk*, 16–20.

68. Nicholson, "Reminiscences of an Octogenarian," 16; Nelson and Nelson, *Memorials of Sarah Childress Polk*, 16–20.

69. Nicholson, "Reminiscences of an Octogenarian," 3, 8.

70. M. C. Bass to Generals Harding and Barrow, June 24, 1862, Harding-Jackson Papers, 1809–1938, Tennessee Historical Society (Nashville).

71. Bill, January 1, 1824, Polk Papers, LOC; Amy Greenberg, *A Wicked War: Polk, Clay, Lincoln, and the 1846 U.S. Invasion of Mexico* (New York: Vintage, 2012), 29; Nelson and Nelson, *Memorials of Sarah Childress Polk*, 18–19; Nicholson, "Reminiscences of an Octogenarian," 5.

72. Tolbert, *Constructing Townscapes*, 14, 42–43; Eastin Morris, *The Tennessee Gazetteer; or, Topographical Dictionary* (Nashville: W. Hasell Hunt, 1834), 35, 107.

73. The slaves in Sarah's portion of the estate were Charles, Milly and Harbert, Joseph, Letty, Big Jim, Sarah, Crease, and Mariah. The total value of all nine slaves was $2,915. Division of estate of Joel Childress, November 26, 1822, Rutherford County Archives, Record Book 5, 243.

74. Marie Jenkins Schwartz, *Ties That Bound: Founding First Ladies and Slaves* (Chicago: University of Chicago Press, 2017), 97.

75. Caroline Nicholson recalled that Elias at the time was "just large enough to stride a barrel," but census records make clear that he was either seventeen or eighteen. 1870 Census, Census Place: Nashville Ward 5, Davidson, Tennessee, Roll M593_1523, p. 303A, Image 303131, Family History Library Film 553022; Nicholson, "Reminiscences of an Octogenarian," 16; Dusinberre, *Slavemaster President*, 7, 8, 202–3.

76. Harriet Ann Jacobs, *Incidents in the Life of a Slave Girl* (Boston: Published for the author, 1861), 55; Tolbert, *Constructing Townscapes*, 191–196, 220–221; Morris, *The Tennessee Gazetteer*, 35.

77. Tolbert, *Constructing Townscapes*, 205–6, Morris, *The Tennessee Gazetteer*, 35.

78. Sellers, *James K. Polk*, vol. 1, *Jacksonian*, 94.

79. Ibid.

80. Nelson and Nelson, *Memorials of Sarah Childress Polk*, 16.

CHAPTER 2. A SALON IN WASHINGTON

1. Anson Nelson and Fanny Nelson, *Memorials of Sarah Childress Polk: Wife of the Eleventh President of the United States* (New York: Anson D. F. Randolph and Co., 1892), 253. Sarah hung a portrait of Thomas Jefferson in the parlor of her home. Ibid., 144.

2. William Dusinberre, *Slavemaster President: The Double Career of James Polk* (New York: Oxford University Press, 2003), 203n7; Anderson Childress to SCP, December 21, 1825, Polk Papers, TSLA.

3. Anderson Childress to SCP, December 21, 1825, Polk Papers, TSLA.

4. JC to SCP, January 3, 1826, Polk Papers, TSLA.

5. Mary Jetton to SCP, September 25, 1845, Polk Papers, TSLA; Crystal Nicole Feimster, *Southern Horrors: Women and the Politics of Rape and Lynching* (Cambridge, MA: Harvard University Press, 2009), 8–9; Dusinberre, *Slavemaster President*, 84–85.

6. I am indebted to Annette Gordon-Reed for providing a framework for interpreting relationships in slave-owning households. Annette Gordon-Reed, *The Hemingses of Monticello: An American Family* (New York: Norton, 2008), 31–32. See also Thavolia Glymph, *Out of the House of Bondage: The Transformation of the Plantation Household* (New York: Cambridge University Press, 2008), 22–24; Elizabeth Fox-Genovese, *Within the Plantation Household: Black and White Women of the Old South* (Chapel Hill: University of North Carolina Press, 1988), 132–35.

7. Robert Campbell to JKP, November 3, 1846, Polk Papers, LOC.

8. Charles Sellers, *James K. Polk*, vol. 1, *Jacksonian* (Princeton, NJ: Princeton University Press, 1957), 111.

9. Caroline O'Reilly Nicholson, "Reminiscences of an Octogenarian," Caroline O'Reilly Nicholson Papers, #547-z, Southern Historical Collection, Wilson Library, University of North Carolina at Chapel Hill, 30–32.

10. W. D. Moseley to JKP, December 1, 1830, James K. Polk, *Correspondence of James K. Polk*, vol. 1, *1817–1832*, ed. Herbert Weaver and Paul H. Bergeron (Nashville: Vanderbilt University Press, 1969), 348.

11. Anne C. Rose, *Victorian America and the Civil War* (New York: Cambridge University Press, 1992), 175.

12. *Congressional Directory* 19, no. 1, 41. Wendy Gamber suggests some of the difficulties of boardinghouse life for families, including a lack of privacy and questions about women's "work" when housekeeping was "denied" them. Wendy Gamber, *The Boardinghouse in Nineteenth-Century America* (Baltimore: Johns Hopkins University Press, 2007).

13. Mary Boykin Chesnut, *A Diary from Dixie*, ed. Ben Ames Williams (Cambridge: Harvard University Press, 1980), 178; Rose, *Victorian America*, 175–77.

14. Nicholson, "Reminiscences of an Octogenarian," 31; Nelson and Nelson, *Memorials of Sarah Childress Polk*, 16–20.

15. JKP to Andrew Jackson, December 5, 1828, Polk, *Correspondence*, vol. 1, 213–14; Nelson and Nelson, *Memorials of Sarah Childress Polk*, 2, 33–34; Walter Johnson, *River of Dark Dreams: Slavery and Empire in the Cotton Kingdom* (Cambridge, MA: Harvard University Press, 2013), 107–20.

16. Sellers, *Polk*, vol. 1, *Jacksonian*, 96–99; Daniel Walker Howe, *What Hath God Wrought: The Transformation of America, 1815–1848* (New York: Oxford University Press, 2007), 212–13.

17. *Nashville Republican Banner*, July 10, 1839; Sellers, *Polk*, vol. 1, *Jacksonian*, 96–99.

18. Pennsylvania Constitutional Convention, *Convention of the Commonwealth of Pennsylvania to Propose Amendments to the Constitution* (Harrisburg: Packer, Barrett and Parke, 1837), vol. 2, 98. On Sarah's political views, see her 1884 *Nashville Banner* interview, in Nelson and Nelson, *Memorials of Sarah Childress Polk*, 198–200. For the political views of James K. Polk, Hugh White, and Sam Houston, see Sellers, *James K. Polk*, vol. 1, *Jacksonian*.

19. Nelson and Nelson, *Memorials of Sarah Childress Polk*, 28–30, 33.

20. Sellers, *James K. Polk*, vol. 1, *Jacksonian*, 111.

21. John C. Wormeley to JKP, December 27, 1826, Polk, *Correspondence*, vol. 1, 65. James also found it necessary to explain to his uncle that Sarah "spends the winter with me in Washington," but was in "good health." JKP to William Polk, December 14, 1826, Polk, *Correspondence*, vol. 1, 60.

22. Quoted in Barbara G. Carson, *Ambitious Appetites: Dining, Behavior, and Patterns of Consumption in Federal Washington* (Washington, DC: AIA Press, 1990), 2.

23. "Mrs. James K. Polk, the First Lady in the Land Thirty Five Years Ago—A Visit, and Pleasant Reminiscences of the White House," *Indianapolis Sentinel*, February 21, 1881; James Sterling Young, *The Washington Community, 1800–1828* (New York: Columbia University Press, 1966), 41–48; Nelson and Nelson, *Memorials of Sarah Childress Polk*, 30.

24. Jan Lewis, "Politics and Ambivalence of the Private Sphere: Women in Early Washington, D.C.," in *A Republic for the Ages: The United States Capitol and the Political Culture of the Early Republic*, ed. Donald R. Kennon (Charlottesville: University Press of Virginia, 1999), 122–51; E. Cooley, *A Description of the Etiquette at Washing-*

ton City (Philadelphia: L. B. Clarke, 1829), 50–56; Cassandra Good, *Founding Friendships: Friendships Between Men and Women in the Early American Republic* (New York: Oxford University Press, 2015), 164–87.

25. Andrew Burstein and Nancy Isenberg, *Madison and Jefferson* (New York: Random House, 2010), 273, 285–86; Catherine Allgor, *Parlor Politics: In Which the Ladies of Washington Help Build a City and a Government* (Charlottesville: University Press of Virginia, 2000).

26. Allgor, *Parlor Politics*, 239–42.

27. Ibid., 73.

28. Ibid., 73, 82.

29. Margery M. Heffron, *Louisa Catherine: The Other Mrs. Adams*, ed. David M. Michelmore (New Haven, CT: Yale University Press, 2014), 302–4.

30. Ibid., 301–2.

31. Susan Radomsky, "The Social Life of Politics: Washington's Official Society and the Emergence of a National Political Elite, 1800–1876" (Ph.D. diss., University of Chicago, 2005), 114; Allgor, *Parlor Politics*, 147–52.

32. Heffron, *Louisa Catherine*, 313–51, quote on 351.

33. Ibid., 4–5.

34. Ibid., 347.

35. Ibid., 326.

36. Melissa Jean Gismondi, "Rachel Jackson and the Search for Zion, 1760s–1830s" (Ph.D. diss., University of Virginia, 2017), 216–19.

37. Cooley, *Etiquette at Washington City*, 59–60; Rachel Sheldon, *Washington Brotherhood: Politics, Social Life, and the Coming of the Civil War* (Chapel Hill: University of North Carolina Press, 2013).

38. Levi Woodbury to Mrs. Woodbury, n.d., Levi Woodbury Papers, First Series (LC), CS.

39. JKP to William R. Rucker, Columbia, TN, September 4, 1828, Polk, *Correspondence*, vol. 1, 195; Gulian Verplanck to William C. Bryant, January 1, 1829, Bryant-Godwin Papers, Manuscripts and Archives, New York Public Library.

40. Charles Day, *Etiquette* (New York: Wilson and Co., 1843), 12; Radomsky, "The Social Life of Politics"; Carson, *Ambitious Appetites*, 117.

41. "Mrs. President Polk," *NYH*, June 3, 1879; Irving H. Bartlett, *John C. Calhoun: A Biography* (New York: Norton, 1993), 121–22.

42. Jean Baker, *Mary Todd Lincoln* (New York: Norton, 1987), 138–41.

43. Nelson and Nelson, *Memorials of Sarah Childress Polk*, 255.

44. Margaret Bayard Smith, *First Forty Years in Washington* (New York: Charles Scribner's Sons, 1906), 154; Lewis, "Politics and Ambivalence of the Private Sphere," 129–32; Frederika J. Teute, "Roman Matron on the Banks of Tiber Creek: Margaret Bayard Smith and the Politicization of Spheres in the Nation's Capital," in *A Republic for the Ages: The United States Capitol and the Political Culture of the Early Republic*, ed. Donald R. Kennon (Charlottesville: University Press of Virginia, 1999), 89–121.

45. Mary Louise Polk to SCP, November 5, 1847, Polk Papers, TSLA; Sarah Myton Maury, *An Englishwoman in America* (London: Thomas Richardson, 1848), 203–4; Nelson and Nelson, *Memorials of Sarah Childress Polk*, 50.

46. On the Eaton affair, see Kristin E. Wood, "'One Woman So Dangerous to Public Morals': Gender and Politics in the Eaton Affair," *Journal of the Early Republic* 17 (Summer 1997): 237–75; Allgor, *Parlor Politics*, 190–238; Andrew Burstein, *The Passions of Andrew Jackson* (New York: Knopf, 2003), 173–80; Peggy Eaton, *The Autobiography of Peggy Eaton* (New York: Charles Scribner's Sons, 1932).

47. Eaton, *Autobiography*, 64; Rudoph Bunner to G. C. Verplanck, January 9, 1830, Gulian C. Verplanck Papers, New-York Historical Society; Sellers, *Polk*, vol. 1, *Jacksonian*, 143; "Miss Augusta W. Cole," Daughters of the American Revolution, *Lineage Book*, vol. 36: 1901 (Harrisburg, PA: Telegraph Printing Co., 1912), 257.

48. Receipts, January 31, 1835, Polk Papers, LOC. Her subscription started with volume 2, January 31, 1831, and continued for three years, until the December 1834 issue. She paid $12 for this. A. Godey to SCP, January 24, 1835, Polk Correspondence, UT.

49. Nicholson, "Reminiscences of an Octogenarian," 39.

50. "Woman—At Home," *Godey's Lady's Book* 2 (February 1831): 97; "The Wife; or, Domestic Heroism," *Godey's Lady's Book* 3 (December 1831): 308.

51. "Love," *Godey's Lady's Book* 2 (May 1831): 237; "Happiness in the Marriage State," *Godey's Lady's Book* 2 (May 1831): 289; "She weeps over the trinkets he gave her," *Godey's Lady's Book* 2 (April 1831): 220.

52. "The Wife; or, Domestic Heroism," *Godey's Lady's Book* 3 (December 1831): 308; "Distinguished Females," *Godey's Lady's Book* 2 (February 1831): 63; "Female Education," *Godey's Lady's Book* 9 (September 1834): 144; "The Sentiments of an American Woman," Philadelphia, June 10, 1780, reprinted in *The Pennsylvania Magazine of History and Biography* 18, no. 3 (1894): 361–64; see also Linda Kerber, *Women of the Republic: Intellect and Ideology in Revolutionary America* (Chapel Hill: University of North Carolina Press, 1980), 206; Salem Academy Library Contents, 1817, Salem College Archives.

53. Nelson and Nelson, *Memorials of Sarah Childress Polk*, 206.

54. Ibid., 50.

55. Ibid., 53.

56. Ibid., 54; Sellers, *James K. Polk*, vol. 1, *Jacksonian*, 329–30; receipt, January 18, 1838, Polk Papers, LOC. Comparative pricing based on Federal Reserve Bank of Minneapolis, "Consumer Price Index (Estimate) 1800–," https://www.minneapolisfed.org/community/teaching-aids/cpi-calculator-information/consumer-price-index-1800, accessed June 11, 2017.

57. Dena Goodman, *The Republic of Letters: A Cultural History of the French Enlightenment* (Ithaca, NY: Cornell University Press, 1994), 91, 124; David Hume, "Of Essay Writing" (1742), in *The Age of Authors: An Anthology of Eighteenth-Century Print Culture*, ed. Paul Keen (Ontario, Canada: Broadview Press, 2014), 161; Steven Kale, *French Salons: High Society and Political Sociability from the Old Regime to the Revolution of 1848* (Baltimore: Johns Hopkins University Press, 2004), 2.

58. On the persistence of the salon in the nineteenth century, see Kale, *French Salons*, quote on 37.

59. John Catron to SCP, January 7, 1840, Polk Papers, LOC, Microfilm, Reel 19, Series 2; S. H. Laughlin to JKP, August 21, 1835, James K. Polk, *Correspondence of James K. Polk*, vol. 3, *1835–1836*, ed. Herbert Weaver and Kermit L. Hall (Nashville: Vanderbilt University Press, 1975), 271.

60. "Mrs. President Polk," *NYH*, June 3, 1879.

61. Dusinberre, *Slavemaster President*, xiii–xiv, 13, 203.

62. JKP to SCP, September 26, 1834, James K. Polk, *Correspondence of James K. Polk*, vol. 2, *1833–1834*, ed. Herbert Weaver and Paul H. Bergeron (Nashville: Vanderbilt University Press, 1972), 509; Dusinberre, *Slavemaster President*, 14–15.

63. Deposition of Caroline Drain, January 12, 1898, Deposition of Dafney Polk, November 3, 1888, January 11, 1898, Case of Dafney Polk, Case Files of Approved Pension Applications of Widows and Other Veterans of the Army and Navy Who Served Mainly in the Civil War and the War with Spain, National Archives, Record Group 15.

64. On petitioning, see Susan Zaeske, *Signatures of Citizenship: Petitioning, Antislavery, and Women's Political Identity* (Chapel Hill: University of North Carolina Press, 2003).

65. Sellers, *James K. Polk*, vol. 1, *Jacksonian*, 114–15; receipts, January 31, 1835, Polk Papers, LOC.

66. SCP to Mary Childress, January 22, 1832, Polk Papers, TSLA.

67. Joanna Rucker to SCP, Murfreesboro, TN, June 13, 1834, Polk Papers, LOC.

68. Jane M. Walker to SCP, February 15, 1837, Polk Papers, LOC, Microfilm, Reel 13, Series 2.

CHAPTER 3. COMMUNICATIONS DIRECTOR

1. "The Rutherford Dinner," *Nashville Union*, September 3, 1838; *Nashville Republican Banner*, September, 3, 1838; Charles Sellers, *James K. Polk*, vol. 1, *Jacksonian, 1795–1843* (Princeton, NJ: Princeton University Press, 1966), 355.

2. *Nashville Republican Banner*, September 8, 1838.

3. The opposition newspaper was sure James was prepared to announce before the Murfreesboro dinner. "The Campaign Opened," *Nashville Republican Banner*, September 5, 1838.

4. Melissa Jean Gismondi, "Rachel Jackson and the Search for Zion, 1760s–1830s" (Ph.D. diss., University of Virginia, 2017).

5. JKP to Robert B. Reynolds, April 3, 1839, James K. Polk, *Correspondence of James K. Polk*, vol. 5, *1839–1841*, ed. Wayne Cutler (Nashville: Vanderbilt University Press, 1979), 110–11.

6. John Bell to Henry Clay, May 21, 1839, Henry Clay, *Papers of Henry Clay*, vol. 9, *The Whig Leader, January 1, 1837–December 31, 1843*, ed. Robert Seager II and Melba Porter Hay (Lexington: University Press of Kentucky, 1988), 316; William Allen to JKP, April 6, 1839, Polk, *Correspondence*, vol. 5, 111; Sellers, *James K. Polk*, vol. 1, *Jacksonian*, 341, 362.

7. *Nashville Union*, September 5, 1838; John Bell to Henry Clay, May 21, 1839, *Papers of Henry Clay*, vol. 9, 316.

8. Thanks to Michael David Cohen for help with interpreting this request.

9. JKP to SCP, April 8, 1839, Polk, *Correspondence*, vol. 5, 112.

10. JKP to SCP, June 2, 1839, Polk, *Correspondence*, vol. 5, 139.

11. JKP to SCP, April 14, 1839, Polk, *Correspondence*, vol. 5, 113.

12. On the pastoralization of housework, see Jeanne Boydston, *Home and Work: Housework, Wages, and the Ideology of Labor in the Early Republic* (New York: Oxford University Press, 1990).

13. JKP to SCP, April 20, 1839, Polk, *Correspondence*, vol. 5, 115; JKP to SCP, April 22, 1839, Polk, *Correspondence*, vol. 5, 116; JKP to SCP, April 29, 1839, Polk, *Correspondence*, vol. 5, 117.

14. See, for instance, JKP to SCP, April 17, 1839, Polk, *Correspondence*, vol. 5, 114.

15. JKP to SCP, April 20, 1839, Polk, *Correspondence*, vol. 5, 115; JKP to SCP, May 13, 1839, Polk, *Correspondence*, vol. 5, 126.

16. J. G. M. Ramsey to JKP, June 28, 1839, Polk, *Correspondence*, vol. 5, 155.

17. Lori Glover, *Southern Sons: Becoming Men in the New Republic* (Baltimore: Johns Hopkins University Press, 2007), 13; Dallett Hemphill, *Siblings: Brothers and Sisters in American History* (New York: Oxford University Press, 2011), 89; JC to JKP, May 18, 1839, Polk, *Correspondence*, vol. 5, 127.

18. JC to SCP, January 20, 1834, Polk Papers, LOC, Reel 8, Series 2; JC to SCP, June 18, 1839, Polk Papers, LOC, Microfilm, Reel 18.

19. James Walker to JKP, July 12, 1839, Polk, *Correspondence*, vol. 5, 165.

20. JKP to William Rice, August 26,1839, Polk, *Correspondence*, vol. 5, 210.

21. JKP to SCP, May 2, 1839, Polk, *Correspondence*, vol. 5, 120–21.

22. JKP to SCP, May 2, 1839, Polk, *Correspondence*, vol. 5, 121; David Henkin, *The Postal Age: The Emergence of Modern Communications in Nineteenth-Century America* (Chicago: University of Chicago Press, 2006), 32, 72–73.

23. Lisa C. Tolbert, *Constructing Townscapes: Space and Society in Antebellum Tennessee* (Chapel Hill: University of North Carolina Press, 1999), 144.

24. Sellers, *James K. Polk*, vol. 1, *Jacksonian*, 371. See also M. R. Rucker to SCP, May 13, 1839, and J. W. Childress to SCP, May 27, 1839, both in the Polk Papers, LOC. On the masculine nature of urban public space, see Patricia Cline Cohen, *The Murder of Helen Jewett: The Life and Death of a Prostitute in Nineteenth-Century New York* (New York: Knopf, 1998). It's not clear if Sarah made the visit to the office of *The Democrat.*

25. JKP to SCP, May 18, 1839, Polk, *Correspondence*, vol. 5, 128–29; Sellers, *James K. Polk*, vol. 1, *Jacksonian*, 370, 372–73.

26. JKP to SCP, May 2, 1839, Polk, *Correspondence*, vol. 5, 121; JKP to SCP, May 18, 1839, Polk, *Correspondence*, vol. 5, 128–29; JKP to SCP, May 18, 1839, Polk, *Correspondence*, vol. 5, 128–129.

27. JKP to SCP, July 1, 1839, Polk, *Correspondence*, vol. 5, 159; JKP to SCP, July 7, 1839, Polk, *Correspondence*, vol. 5, 162.

28. Samuel H. Laughlin to JKP, August 10, 1839, Polk, *Correspondence*, vol. 5, 183; *Papers of Henry Clay*, vol. 9, 317; Robert B. Reynolds and Lewis P. Roberts to JKP, August 5, 1839, Polk, *Correspondence*, vol. 5, 176; Alexander O. Anderson to JKP, August 6, 1839, Polk, *Correspondence*, vol. 5, 178; J. L. Martin to SCP, August 23, 1839, Polk Papers, LOC, Microfilm, Reel 18, Series 2.

29. Aaron Brown to JKP, December 7, 1839, Polk, *Correspondence*, vol. 5, 332. When Aaron and his wife subsequently named their new daughter Sarah Polk Brown, she sent the infant a bracelet. Mary Brown to SCP, February 4, 1849, Polk Papers, TSLA.

30. Samuel H. Laughlin to JKP, August 10, 1839, Polk, *Correspondence*, vol. 5, 183; JKP to SCP, May 2, 1839, Polk, *Correspondence*, vol. 5, 121: JKP to SCP, May 12, 1839, Polk, *Correspondence*, vol. 5, 185.

31. SCP to JKP, June 25, 1839, Polk, *Correspondence*, vol. 5, 154.

32. Nelson, *Memorials of Sarah Childress Polk*, 60–63; Eastin Morris, *The Tennessee Gazetteer or Topical Dictionary* (Nashville: W. Hasell Hunt, 1834), 165.

33. Robert Barnwell Rhett to JKP, August 21, 1839, Polk, *Correspondence*, vol. 5, 202; Anson Nelson and Fanny Nelson, *Memorials of Sarah Childress Polk: Wife of the Eleventh President of the United States* (New York: Anson D. F. Randolph and Co., 1892), 63.

34. John Catron to JKP, September 1, 1839, Polk, *Correspondence*, vol. 5, 221; Caroline O'Reilly Nicholson, "Reminiscences of an Octogenarian," Caroline O'Reilly Nicholson Papers, #547-z, Southern Historical Collection, Wilson Library, University of North Carolina at Chapel Hill, 29; Daniel Craighead to JKP, September 3, 1839, Polk, *Correspondence*, vol. 5, 227; Nelson and Nelson, *Memorials of Sarah Childress Polk*, 16–20.

35. Daniel Craighead to JKP, September 3, 1829, Polk, *Correspondence*, vol. 5, 227.

36. In 1842 she wrote him, "I have received a letter for you from Irwin at Savannah containing $50 in Alabama money the balance he says on your note. I suppose half is Knox's though I have not said any thing to him on the subject. If I must give him his portion you must so write me." SCP to JKP, June 24, 1842, James K. Polk, *Correspondence of James K. Polk*, vol. 6, *1842–1843*, ed. Wayne Cutler and Carese M.

Parker (Nashville: Vanderbilt University Press, 1983), 74; JKP to William H. Polk, October 26, 1839, NCSA.

37. Sellers, *James K. Polk*, vol. 1, *Jacksonian*, 380–81.

38. Adam Rothman, *Slave Country: American Expansion and the Origins of the Deep South* (Cambridge, MA: Harvard University Press, 2005), 177–78; Sellers, *James K. Polk*, vol. 1, *Jacksonian*, 380–81.

39. John Catron to JKP, September 1, 1839, Polk, *Correspondence*, vol. 5, 221.

40. Nelson and Nelson, *Memorials of Sarah Childress Polk*, 63–64.

41. Sellers, *James K. Polk*, vol. 1, *Jacksonian*, 381.

42. Nelson and Nelson, *Memorials of Sarah Childress Polk*, 64.

43. Ibid., 66.

44. Ibid.

45. John Catron to SCP, January 7, 1840, Polk Papers, LOC, Microfilm, Reel 19, Series 2.

46. A. O. P. Nicholson to JKP, July 27, 1840, Polk, *Correspondence*, vol. 5, 519; Robert Armstrong to JKP, March 28, 1841, Polk, *Correspondence*, vol. 5, 664; J. George Harris to JKP, June 18, 1841, Polk, *Correspondence*, vol. 5, 699; SCP to JKP, June 18, 1841, Polk, *Correspondence*, vol. 5, 700.

47. JKP to Alexander O. Anderson, August 16, 1840, Polk, *Correspondence*, vol. 5, 541–43.

48. Andrew Jackson to JKP, December 19, 1840, Polk *Correspondence*, vol. 5, 603. See also Andrew Jackson to JKP, March 6, 1840, Polk *Correspondence*, vol. 5, 648; SCP to JKP, July 11, 1840, Polk, *Correspondence*, vol. 5, 511; SCP to JKP, December 31, 1840, Polk *Correspondence*, vol. 5, 609; Elizabeth R. Varon, *We Mean to Be Counted: White Women and Politics in Antebellum Virginia* (Chapel Hill: University of North Carolina Press, 1998).

49. SCP to JKP, August 11, 1840, Polk, *Correspondence*, vol. 5, 511; Sellers, *James K. Polk*, vol. 1, *Jacksonian*, 421–22.

50. SCP to JKP, December 31, 1840, Polk, *Correspondence*, vol. 5, 609; Sellers, *James K. Polk*, vol. 1, *Jacksonian*, 434–36.

51. SCP to JKP, April 8, 1841, Polk, *Correspondence*, vol. 5, 673; SCP to JKP, April 10, 1841, Polk, *Correspondence*, vol. 5, 675; SCP to JKP, April 14, 1841, Polk, *Correspondence*, vol. 5, 677.

52. SCP to JKP, June 25, 1841, Polk, *Correspondence*, vol. 5, 703.

53. SCP to JKP, December 31, 1840, Polk, *Correspondence*, vol. 5, 609; SCP to JKP, April 8, 1841, Polk, *Correspondence*, vol. 5, 673; SCP to JKP, May 2, 1841, Polk, *Correspondence*, vol. 5, 683; SCP to JKP, December 31, 1840, Polk, *Correspondence*, vol. 5, 609; SCP to JKP, June 18, 1841, Polk, *Correspondence*, vol. 5, 700; JKP to SCP, April 11, 1841, Polk, *Correspondence*, vol. 5, 676; JKP to SCP, April 16, 1841, Polk, *Correspondence*, vol. 5, 678.

54. Joseph Howard Parks, *John Bell of Tennessee* (Baton Rouge: Louisiana State University Press, 1950), 7; SCP to JKP, June 18, 1841, Polk, *Correspondence*, vol. 5, 700.

55. "Rules of the Boarding School at Salem," 1805, Salem College Archives; "Female Education," *Godey's Lady's Book* 3 (July 1831): 30.

56. J. L. Martin to SCP, August 23, 1839, Polk Papers, LOC, Microfilm, Reel 18, Series 2.

57. William R. Rucker to SCP, May 13, 1839, Polk Papers, LOC, Microfilm, Reel 18, Series 2.

58. JC to SCP, May 27, 1839, Polk Papers, LOC, Microfilm, Reel 18, Series 2. It would be nice to know if Sarah had the article placed in *The Democrat*. Unfortunately, there are no surviving issues from the month following John's suggestion.

59. JKP to SCP, April 16, 1841, Polk, *Correspondence*, vol. 5, 678; JKP to SCP, May 9, 1841, Polk, *Correspondence*, vol. 5, 686; SCP to JKP, March 28, 1841, Polk, *Correspon-*

dence, vol. 5, 665; SCP to JKP, April 19, 1841, Polk, *Correspondence,* vol. 5, 675; SCP to JKP, April 25, 1841, Polk, *Correspondence,* vol. 5, 681.

60. SCP to JKP, April 8, 1841, Polk, *Correspondence,* vol. 5, 673; SCP to JKP, April 14, 1841, Polk, *Correspondence,* vol. 5, 677.

61. JKP to SCP, May 9, 1841, Polk, *Correspondence,* vol. 5, 686; SCP to JKP, April 25, 1841, Polk, *Correspondence,* vol. 5, 681; Ephraim P. McNeal to SCP, June 22, 1841, Polk Papers, LOC, Microfilm, Reel 22, Series 2; SCP to JKP, June 25, 1841, Polk, *Correspondence,* vol. 5, 703; JKP to SCP, July 1, 1841, Polk, *Correspondence,* vol. 5, 705; JKP to SCP, July 6, 1841, Polk, *Correspondence,* vol. 5, 709; JKP to SCP, July 1, 1841, Polk, *Correspondence,* vol. 5, 705.

62. SCP to JKP, July 5, 1841, Polk, *Correspondence,* vol. 5, 706–7.

63. SCP to JKP, July 25, 1841, Polk, *Correspondence,* vol. 5, 716.

64. SCP to JKP, June 18, 1841, Polk, *Correspondence,* vol. 5, 700; SCP to JKP, July 5, 1841, Polk, *Correspondence,* vol. 5, 706.

65. SCP to JKP, July 29, 1841, Polk, *Correspondence,* vol. 5, 716.

66. JKP to Robert Armstrong, August 2, 1841, Polk, *Correspondence,* vol. 5, 717; William H. Polk to SCP, August 6, 1841, Polk Papers, LOC, Microfilm, Reel 22, Series 2; Hopkins L. Turney to JKP, August 12, 1841, Polk, *Correspondence,* vol. 5, 722.

67. Samuel H. Laughlin to JKP, September 1, 1841, Polk, *Correspondence,* vol. 5, 748; Samuel H. Laughlin to JKP, September 12, 1841, Polk, *Correspondence,* vol. 5, 757.

68. Sellers, *James K. Polk,* vol. 1, *Jacksonian,* 458–59.

69. SCP to JKP, July 1, 1842, Polk, *Correspondence,* vol. 6, 78.

70. John Catron to SCP, August 17, 1842, Polk Papers, LOC, Microfilm, Reel 23, Series 2.

71. JKP to SCP, October 9, 1842, photocopy held by the James K. Polk Project, University of Tennessee, Knoxville.

72. Nelson and Nelson, *Memorials of Sarah Childress Polk,* 68.

73. Ibid.

74. A. O. P. Nicholson to JKP, January 13, 1841, Polk, *Correspondence,* vol. 6, 616; JC to SCP, March 6, 1843, Polk Papers, LOC, Microfilm, Reel 24, Series 2.

75. SCP to JKP, March 3, 1843, Polk, *Correspondence,* vol. 6, 238.

76. SCP to JKP, May 29, 1843, Polk, *Correspondence,* vol. 6, 259.

77. JKP to SCP, April 4, 1843, Polk, *Correspondence,* vol. 6, 263.

78. JKP to SCP, April 7, 1843, Polk, *Correspondence,* vol. 6, 266; JKP to SCP, April 14, 1843, Polk, *Correspondence,* vol. 6, 272.

79. SCP to JKP, April 17, 1843, Polk, *Correspondence,* vol. 6, 273–74.

80. Ibid.

81. SCP to JKP, April 11, 1843, Polk, *Correspondence,* vol. 6, 271; JKP to SCP, June 9, 1843, Polk, *Correspondence,* vol. 6, 315; JKP to SCP, June 18, 1843, Polk, *Correspondence,* vol. 6, 318.

82. SCP to JKP, April 11, 1843, Polk, *Correspondence,* vol. 6, 271; SCP to JKP, May 3, 1843, Polk, *Correspondence,* vol. 6, 276.

83. JKP to SCP, May 8, 1843, Polk, *Correspondence,* vol. 6, 280.

84. SCP to JKP, May 23, 1843, Polk, *Correspondence,* vol. 6, 313.

85. JKP to Martin Van Buren, August 18, 1843, Polk, *Correspondence,* vol. 6, 332; JKP to Robert Armstrong, August 7, 1843, Polk, *Correspondence,* vol. 6, 331.

86. William Dusinberre, *Slavemaster President: The Double Career of James Polk* (New York: Oxford University Press, 2003), 87.

87. M. C. Bass to Generals Harding and Barrow, June 24, 1862, Harding-Jackson Papers, 1809–1938, Tennessee Historical Society (Nashville); Walter Durham, *Nashville: The Occupied City, 1862–1863* (Knoxville: University of Tennessee Press, 2008), 176.

88. Laura T. Polk to JKP, December 29, 1835, James K. Polk, *Correspondence of James K.*

Polk, vol. 3, *1835–1836*, ed. Herbert Weaver and Kermit L. Hall (Nashville: Vanderbilt University Press, 1975), 401–2; Sellers, *James K. Polk*, vol. 1, *Jacksonian*, 458–59.

89. Sellers, *James K. Polk*, vol. 1, *Jacksonian*, 459.

90. Ibid.

91. Marshall Tate Polk Jr. to JKP, September 29, 1843, Polk Papers, LOC, Microfilm, Reel 24, Series 2; Sellers, *James K. Polk*, vol. 1, *Jacksonian*, 459, 358–59.

92. Sarah Mytton Maury, *An Englishwoman in America* (London: Thomas Richardson and Son, 1848), 210; Stephen B. Presser, "The Historical Background of the American Law of Adoption," *Journal of Family Law* 11 (1971–72): 458–61; Gismondi, "Rachel Jackson and the Search for Zion, 1760s–1830s," 122–55.

93. M. C. Bass to Generals Harding and Barrow, June 24, 1862, Harding-Jackson Papers, 1809–1938, Tennessee Historical Society (Nashville).

94. "Mrs. James K. Polk, the First Lady in the Land Thirty Five Years Ago—A Visit, and Pleasant Reminiscences of the White House," *Indianapolis Sentinel*, February 21, 1881; "Mrs. President Polk," *NYH*, June 3, 1879.

95. Aaron V. Brown to JKP, December 9, 1843, Polk, *Correspondence*, vol. 6, 371.

96. Aaron V. Brown to JKP, January 22, 1844, James K. Polk, *Correspondence of James K. Polk*, vol. 7, *January–August 1844*, ed. Wayne Cutler and James P. Cooper Jr. (Nashville: Vanderbilt University Press, 1989), 44.

97. Aaron V. Brown to SCP, January 14, 1844, Polk Papers, LOC, Microfilm, Reel 25, Series 2.

CHAPTER 4. FEMALE POLITICIANS

1. On women and settlement in Florida, see Laurel Clark Shire, *The Threshold of Manifest Destiny: Gender and National Expansion in Florida* (Philadelphia: University of Pennsylvania Press, 2016).

2. Alfred Balch to Martin Van Buren, Tallahassee, April 3, 1840; Clarence Edwin Carter, *The Territorial Papers of the United States*, vol. 26, *The Territory of Florida, 1839–1845* (Washington, DC: Government Printing Office, 1962), 128.

3. Joel H. Silbey, *Martin Van Buren and the Emergence of American Popular Politics* (Lanham, MD: Rowman and Littlefield, 2005), 145–76; John Hallam, *The Diary of an Old Lawyer; or, Scenes Behind the Curtain* (Nashville: Southwestern Publishing House, 1895), 107–8; Timothy S. Huebner, *The Southern Judicial Tradition: State Judges and Sectional Distinctiveness* (Athens: University of Georgia Press, 1999), 65.

4. Alfred Balch to Martin Van Buren, November 22, 1842, Martin Van Buren Papers, Series 1, Reel 39, September 1841–November 1842, LOC Microfilm.

5. *Omaha Daily Herald*, October 28, 1879; Ben Perley Poore, *Perley's Reminiscences of Sixty Years in the National Metropolis* (Philadelphia: Hubbard Brothers, 1886), 130–31.

6. Elizabeth R. Varon, *We Mean to Be Counted: White Women and Politics in Antebellum Virginia* (Chapel Hill: University of North Carolina Press, 1998). Varon argues that women were "marginal to the discourse and rituals of partisan politics before 1840" (p. 74). "The Ladies Coming to the Rescue," *Hartford Daily Courant*, September 1840; Alfred Balch to Martin Van Buren, November 22, 1842, Martin Van Buren Papers, Series 1, Reel 39, September 1841–November 1842.

7. Alfred Balch to Martin Van Buren, November 22, 1842, Martin Van Buren Papers, Series 1.

8. Quoted in Charles Sellers, *James K. Polk*, vol. 2, *Continentalist, 1843–1846* (Princeton, NJ: Princeton University Press, 1966), 71–72.

9. Sellers, *James K. Polk*, vol. 2, *Continentalist*, 71; James K. Polk, "Letters of James K. Polk to Cave Johnson, 1833–1848," *Tennessee Historical Magazine* 1 (September 1915):

240–41. Although, as Tom Chaffin notes, Polk never actually used the term "Manifest Destiny," its enthusiasts flocked to his support. Tom Chaffin, *Met His Every Goal? James K. Polk and the Legends of Manifest Destiny* (Knoxville: University of Tennessee Press, 2014), 22–23.

10. "Texas—The Prospect," *The Liberator*, May 24, 1844; Amy Greenberg, *A Wicked War: Polk, Clay, Lincoln, and the 1846 U.S. Invasion of Mexico* (New York: Vintage, 2012), 38.

11. Quoted in Charles Sellers, *James K. Polk*, vol. 2, *Continentalist, 1843–1846*, 91; Greenberg, *A Wicked War*, 39.

12. George H. Hickman, *The Life and Public Services of the Hon. James Knox Polk: With a Compendium of His Speeches on Various Public Measures, Also a Sketch of the Life of the Hon. George Mifflin Dallas* (Baltimore: N. Hickman, 1844), 26; Poore, *Perley's Reminiscences of Sixty Years in the National Metropolis*, 321; Greenberg, *A Wicked War*, 39–41.

13. "The Responses to the Nomination of Mr. Polk," *Easton Gazette* (Maryland), June 8, 1844, vol. XXVII; "The Loco Foco Candidates," *Daily Atlas*, June 4, 1844; Caroline O'Reilly Nicholson, "Reminiscences of an Octogenarian," Caroline O'Reilly Nicholson Papers, #547-z, Southern Historical Collection, Wilson Library, University of North Carolina at Chapel Hill, 35.

14. "The Democratic Nomination at Last," *NYH*, May 31, 1844; Wendy Moonan, "Antiques: A Gothic Tale of a Bedstead Fit for a President," *New York Times*, November 3, 2000.

15. "Mrs. James K. Polk, the First Lady in the Land Thirty Five Years Ago—A Visit, and Pleasant Reminiscences of the White House," *Indianapolis Sentinel*, February 21, 1881.

16. John C. Catron to JKP, Nashville, July 17, 1844, James K. Polk, *Correspondence of James K. Polk*, vol. 7, *January–August 1844*, ed. Wayne Cutler and James P. Cooper Jr. (Nashville: Vanderbilt University Press, 1989), 355–57.

17. "Sarah Childress Polk," in *First Ladies: A Biographical Dictionary*, 3rd ed., ed. Dorothy Schneider and Carl J. Schneider (New York: Infobase Publishing, 2010), 70–78, quote on 74; "Colonel Polk at Home," *NYH*, November 16, 1844.

18. "The Lady of the President Elect," *Boston Evening Transcript*, published as *Daily Evening Transcript*, December 2, 1844. See also "Mrs. President Polk," *Portsmouth Journal of Literature and Politics*, December 14, 1844.

19. "Colonel Polk at Home," *NYH*, November 16, 1844.

20. "The Private Character of Mr. Polk," *Journal of Commerce*, reprinted in *NYH*, November 16, 1844.

21. Ibid.

22. "The Democratic Nominations," *Barre (MA) Gazette*, June 14, 1844; Anson Nelson and Fanny Nelson, *Memorials of Sarah Childress Polk: Wife of the Eleventh President of the United States* (New York: Anson D. F. Randolph and Co., 1892), 96, 43–44.

23. David S. and Jeanne T. Heidler, *Henry Clay: The Essential American* (New York: Random House, 2010), 172.

24. "The Democratic Nominations," *Barre (MA) Gazette*, June 14, 1844; Nelson and Nelson, *Memorials of Sarah Childress Polk*, 96, 43–44.

25. Nelson and Nelson, *Memorials of Sarah Childress Polk*, 79–80.

26. Ann Thomas to SCP, Liberty (now Bedford, VA), n.d; Varon, *We Mean to Be Counted*, 85–93.

27. "Gallant Harry, the song of the Clay club of Germantown," in John S. Littell, *The Clay Minstrel, or National Songster*, 2nd ed. (New York: Greeley and McElrath, 1844), 158; Varon, *We Mean to Be Counted*, 83–87; Ronald J. Zboray and Mary Saracino

Zboray, *Voices Without Votes: Women and Politics in Antebellum New England* (Lebanon, NH: University Press of New England, 2010); Nathan Sargent, *Public Men and Events, from the Commencement of Mr. Monroe's Administration, in 1817, to the Close of Mr. Fillmore's Administration in 1853* (Philadelphia. J. P. Lippincott and Co., 1875), vol. 2, 246.

28. Jayne Crumpler DeFiore, "COME, and Bring the Ladies: Tennessee Women and the Politics of Opportunity During the Presidential Campaigns of 1840 and 1844," *Tennessee Historical Quarterly* 15 (Winter 1992): 201, 203; "Progress of the Campaign," *Nashville Republican Banner*, July 17, 1844.

29. "Progress of the Campaign," *Nashville Republican Banner*, July 17, 1844.

30. *Nashville Republican Banner*, September 4, 1844; John Shofner quoted in Lisa C. Tolbert, *Constructing Townscapes: Space and Society in Antebellum Tennessee* (Chapel Hill: University of North Carolina Press, 1999), 78–79.

31. Ann Thomas to SCP, Liberty (now Bedford, VA), n.d.

32. "Presentation of the Texas Banner," *Nashville Republican Banner*, August 5, 1844.

33. Daniel Craighead to JKP, October 21, 1844, Polk Papers, LOC. Jayne Crumpler DeFiore notes that Democratic women were invited to a rally in Nashville on August 15, 1844. But this was unusual. "COME, and Bring the Ladies," 203.

34. DeFiore, "COME, and Bring the Ladies," 203. According to Elizabeth Varon, the Democratic Party in Virginia was somewhat more welcoming of female partisanship. *We Mean to Be Counted*, 87.

35. W. D. Moseley to SCP, December 1, 1830, James K. Polk, *Correspondence of James K. Polk*, vol. 1, *1817–1832*, ed. Herbert Weaver and Paul H. Bergeron (Nashville: Vanderbilt University Press, 1969), 348.

36. Elizabeth Bosworth to SCP, June 12, 1844, Polk Papers, LOC, Microfilm, Reel 26, Series 2; John W. P. McGimsey to JKP, September 27, 1844, and November 1, 1844, Polk Papers, LOC; Jane Frindlay to SCP, Cincinnati, March 25, 1845, Polk Papers, TSLA.

37. Ann Thomas to SCP, Liberty (VA), n.d., TSLA.

38. Sally Denton, *Passion and Principle: John and Jessie Frémont, the Couple Whose Power, Politics, and Love Shaped Nineteenth-Century America* (New York: Bloomsbury, 2007), 249; Tom Chaffin, *Pathfinder: John Charles Frémont and the Course of American Empire* (New York: Hill and Wang, 2002), 443.

39. Susan Radomsky, "The Social Life of Politics: Washington's Official Society and the Emergence of a National Political Elite, 1800–1876" (Ph.D. diss., University of Chicago, 2005), 30–37; Nicholson, "Reminiscences of an Octogenarian," 30–32, 84–85.

40. Daniel Walker Howe, *What Hath God Wrought: The Transformation of America, 1815–1848* (New York: Oxford, 2007), 688.

41. Nelson and Nelson, *Memorials of Sarah Childress Polk*, 78.

42. Lori D. Ginzberg, *Women and the Work of Benevolence: Morality, Politics, and Class in the Nineteenth-Century United States* (New Haven, CT: Yale University Press, 1990), 67–96, quote on 77.

43. Dallas to Mrs. Dallas, February 18, 1845, Dallas Papers, CS; Gilpin to Van Buren, February 24, 1845, Van Buren Papers, both quoted in Sellers, *James K. Polk*, vol. 2, *Continentalist*, 193; James K. Polk, *Correspondence of James K. Polk*, vol. 12, *January–July 1847*, ed. Tom Chaffin and Michael David Cohen (Knoxville: University of Tennessee Press, 2013), 287n3; Zboray and Zboray, *Voices Without Votes*, 146–47.

44. "A Memory of a Trip," *NDA*, March 2, 1889.

45. John Robert Irelan, *The Republic; or, The History of the United States of America* (Chicago: Fairbanks and Palmer, 1888), vol. 11, 675; Nelson and Nelson, *Memorials of Sarah Childress Polk*, 81.

46. "Seven Washington Belles no. 4—Sarah Childress Polk," *Idaho Statesman* (Boise), May 14, 1911; Leonard Jones to SCP, Shelby County, KY, December 26, 1844, Polk Papers, LOC, Microfilm, Reel 32; undated letter from "A Christian Friend" to SCP, Polk Papers, LOC, Series 9.

47. Undated letter from "A Christian Friend" to SCP, Polk Papers, LOC, Series 9.

48. E. S. Davis to SCP, March 7, 1845, James K. Polk Papers, Microfilm, Reel 34, Series 2.

49. Ibid.; Leonard Jones to SCP, Shelby County, KY, December 26, 1844, Polk Papers, LOC, Microfilm, Reel 32; Ginzberg, *Women and the Work of Benevolence*, 36–66.

50. Ginzberg, *Women and the Work of Benevolence*, 17, 75–77. Dix quote on 76.

51. Ann Thomas to SCP, Liberty (VA), n.d. See also A. D. Mitchell to SCP, Oakland, Bedford County, VA, May 1, 1845; Varon, *We Mean to Be Counted*, 89.

52. Nelson and Nelson, *Memorials of Sarah Childress Polk*, 49.

53. Joanna Rucker to SCP, December 1, 1847, Polk Papers, TSLA; Nelson and Nelson, *Memorials of Sarah Childress Polk*, 49.

CHAPTER 5. MRS. PRESIDENTESS

1. James D. Richardson, ed., *The Compilation of the Messages and Papers of the Presidents* (Washington, DC, 1901), 373–82; Charles Sellers, *James K. Polk*, vol. 2, *Continentalist, 1843–1846* (Princeton, NJ: Princeton University Press, 1966), 209.

2. Excerpts Concerning President and Mrs. James K. Polk (Diary of Elizabeth Dixon), December 6, 1845–January 1, 1846, TSLA. Original source: Elizabeth Dixon, "Excerpts from the Diary of Elizabeth Dixon of Connecticut, 1845–1847," Connecticut Historical Society, Hartford.

3. Henry Gilpin to Martin Van Buren, February 14, 1845, Martin Van Buren Papers. The average age of First Ladies before Julia Tyler was 51.7 years. Data drawn from Katherine A. S. Sibley, ed., *A Companion to First Ladies* (Malden, MA: Wiley-Blackwell, 2016). Sarah's height and weight are based on an analysis of textiles in the collection of the Polk Family Home, Columbia, TN.

4. Excerpts Concerning President and Mrs. James K. Polk (Diary of Elizabeth Dixon), December 6, 1845–January 1, 1846, TSLA; Sarah Mytton Maury, *An Englishwoman in America* (London: Thomas Richardson, 1848), 202. Maury said her "dark eye and complexion give her a touch of the Spanish Dama"; John W. Forney, *Anecdotes of Public Men* (New York: Harper and Bros., 1873), 312; Mary Cathryn Cain, "The Art and Politics of Looking White: Beauty Practice Among White Women in Antebellum America," *Winterthur Portfolio* 42, no.1 (Spring 2008): 27–50.

5. Sibley, *A Companion to First Ladies*, 75–158.

6. Robert Seager II, *And Tyler Too: A Biography of John and Julia Gardener Tyler* (New York: McGraw-Hill, 1963), 243–45, quote on 243; Sellers, *James K. Polk*, vol. 2, *Continentalist*, 62.

7. Seager, *And Tyler Too*, 248–49.

8. Ibid., 263, quote on 333; E. S. Davis to SCP, March 7, 1845, James K. Polk Papers, LOC, Microfilm, Reel 34, Series 2.

9. Elizabeth Fries Ellet, *The Queens of American Society* (New York: Scribners, 1867), 219; Mrs. C. W. Denison, "Mrs. James K. Polk." *Sartain's Union Magazine* VI (January–June 1850): 156; Anson Nelson and Fanny Nelson, *Memorials of Sarah Childress Polk: Wife of the Eleventh President of the United States* (New York: Anson D. F. Randolph and Co., 1892), 92–93.

10. "A Memory of a Trip," *NDA*, March 2, 1889. Invitation to Democratic Inauguration ball sent to Mrs. Sydney Kimmel, Frederick County, MD. "Ball at National Theater,

March 4, 1845. In honor of the President and Vice President," Polk Papers, TSLA; "No Need of Flogging in the Navy," *Naval Journal* 16 (August 1844): 387.

11. James D. Richardson, ed., *Messages and Papers of the Presidents* (Washington, DC: Government Printing Office, 1901), vol. 5, 2226.

12. Elizabeth Fries Ellet, *The Court Circles of the Republic; or, The Beauties and Celebrities of the Nation, Illustrating Life and Society Under Eighteen Presidents; Describing the Social Features of the Successive Administrations from Washington to Grant* (Hartford: Hartford Publishing Co., 1869), 216; receipts, July 1846, Polk Papers, LOC.

13. Ellet, *The Court Circles of the Republic*, 216; E. S. Davis to SCP, March 7, 1845, James K. Polk Papers, LOC, Microfilm, Reel 34, Series 2.

14. Charles Dickens, *American Notes: A Journey* (1842; New York: Fromm, 1985), 124; "Washington News," *NYH*, November 27, 1844; Donald Barr Chidsey, *And Tyler Too* (Nashville: Thomas Nelson, 1978), 121.

15. Sellers, *James K. Polk*, vol. 2, *Continentalist*, 306–7.

16. Nelson and Nelson, *Memorials of Sarah Childress Polk*, 88–89.

17. Ibid.; Seager, *And Tyler Too*, 333.

18. Federal Reserve Bank of Minneapolis, "Consumer Price Index (Estimate) 1800–," https://www.minneapolisfed.org/community/teaching-aids/cpi-calculator-infor mation/consumer-price-index-1800, accessed June 11, 2017; William Seale, *The President's House: A History*, 2nd ed. (Baltimore: Johns Hopkins University Press, 2008), vol. 1, 251; Ester Singleton, *The Story of the White House* (New York: Benjamin Blom, 1907), vol. 1, 304.

19. Jessie Benton Frémont, *Souvenirs of My Time* (Boston: Lothrop Co., 1887), 103; Joanna Rucker to Elizabeth Price, September 9, 1846, Polk Papers, TSLA.

20. Singleton, *The Story of the White House*, vol. 1, 317; Ophelia Polk Hays to SCP, December 12, 1848, Polk Papers, TSLA; Sellers, *James K. Polk*, vol. 2, *Continentalist*, 307; James K. Polk, *Diary of a President*, ed. Milo Quaife (Columbia, TN: James K. Polk Memorial Association, 2005), vol. 1, 321. On the popularity of these events, see Sophia Towson to SCP, n.d., Polk Papers, TSLA.

21. William Woodbridge to Lucy, January 7, 1846, William Woodbridge Papers, Burton Historical Collection, Detroit Public Library; Ellet, *The Court Circles of the Republic*, 382; Polk, *Diary*, vol. 1, 264.

22. Joanna Rucker to Elizabeth Price, January 7, 1846, Polk Papers, TSLA; Benajah Ticknor, Journal, May 23, 1848, Ticknor Collection, Yale University Library.

23. Sellers, *James K. Polk*, vol. 2, *Continentalist*, 308; Polk, *Diary*, vol. 1, 321; Forney, *Anecdotes of Public Men*, 312. On the political nature of the dinners, see, for example, G. M. Dallas to R. Rush, April 25, 1846, Benjamin Rush Papers, 15.

24. Polk, *Diary*, vol. 1, 146; Varina Banks Howell Davis to Margaret K. Howell, January 30, 1846, April 3, 1846, in Jefferson Davis, *The Papers of Jefferson Davis*, vol. 2, *June 1841–July 1846*, ed. Will McIntosh (Baton Rouge: Louisiana State University Press, 1974), 420, 534.

25. Nelson and Nelson, *Memorials of Sarah Childress Polk*, both quotes on 112.

26. William Woodbridge to Lucy, January 7, 1846, William Woodbridge Papers, Burton Historical Collection, Detroit Public Library; Varina Banks Howell Davis to Margaret K. Howell, January 30, 1846, in Davis, *The Papers of Jefferson Davis*, vol. 2, 420; Seale, *The President's House*, vol. 1, 253; Dixon, "Excerpts from the Diary of Elizabeth Dixon of Connecticut, 1845–1847," December 6, 1845; Polk, *Diary*, vol. 4, 402.

27. Frémont, *Souvenirs of My Time*, 103; receipts, January 1846, Polk Papers, LOC; Seale, *The President's House*, 253; John Smith the Younger, "Portraits for the People: The Eastern Heiress," *The National Era*, March 11, 1847; Marie Jenkins Schwartz,

Ties That Bound: Founding First Ladies and Slaves (Chicago: University of Chicago Press, 2017), 271. Robert Seager's assertion that Sarah Polk's "nonalcoholic White House functions did save the taxpayers a few dollars" is based on two faulty assumptions: that because the Polks did not themselves drink, they didn't serve alcohol, and that the "taxpayers" paid for the entertaining expenses of the president, neither of which was true. Equally flawed is his view that Sarah's "four-year tenure in the President's Mansion was generally dubbed a social failure from beginning to end, though it was cheered by the prohibitionists and certain lunatic-fringe ecclesiastical groups as a great triumph of Christian virtue." Seager, *And Tyler Too*, 333, 319.

28. Excerpts Concerning President and Mrs. James K. Polk (Diary of Elizabeth Dixon), December 6, 1845–January 1, 1846, TSLA; Polk, *Diary*, vol. 4, 146. Thanks to Michael David Cohen for this final reference.

29. Seale, *The President's House*, vol. 1, 255–56.

30. "Memorandum of Persons to be employed at the President's House," Polk Papers, LOC. Thanks to Michael David Cohen for this reference. Elizabeth Dowling Taylor, *A Slave in the White House: Paul Jennings and the Madisons* (New York: Palgrave Macmillan, 2012) 152–53; Frémont, *Souvenirs of My Time*, 103; Seale, *The President's House*, vol. 1, 251–53; Schwartz, *Ties That Bound*, 318.

31. Polk, *Diary*, vol. 1, 115.

32. Nelson and Nelson, *Memorials of Sarah Childress Polk*, 90.

33. JKP to Cave Johnson, December 21, 1844, James K. Polk, *Correspondence of James K. Polk*, vol. 8, *September–December 1844* (Knoxville: University of Tennessee Press, 1993), 456.

34. Richard R. Stenberg, "President Polk and California: Additional Documents," *Pacific Historical Review* 10 (1941): 217–19 (Gideon Wells quote on 219); Amy Greenberg, *A Wicked War: Polk, Clay, Lincoln, and the 1846 U.S. Invasion of Mexico* (New York: Vintage, 2012), 69–72.

35. Dixon, "Excerpts from the Diary of Elizabeth Dixon of Connecticut, 1845–1847," December 19, 1845; Benajah Ticknor, Journal, May 23, 1848, Ticknor Collection, Yale University Library.

36. JKP and SCP to Dolley Madison, May 27, 1845, Madison Papers, University of Virginia; Nelson and Nelson, *Memorials of Sarah Childress Polk*, 93.

37. Sellers, *James K. Polk*, vol. 2, *Continentalist*, 192; Nelson and Nelson, *Memorials of Sarah Childress Polk*, 93.

38. SCP to Dolley Madison, July 23, 1845, Dolley Madison to SCP, January 18, 1845, Madison Papers, University of Virginia; Taylor, *A Slave in the White House*, 155–56; Schwartz, *Ties That Bound*, 348.

39. Dolley Madison to SCP, November 6, 1846, April 4, 1845, November 6, 1846, Madison Papers, University of Virginia.

40. Dolley Madison to SCP, July 23, 1845, Madison Papers, University of Virginia; Conover Hunt, "Fashion and Frugality: First Lady Sarah Polk," *White House History* 32 (Fall 2012), online at https://www.whitehousehistory.org/fashion-and-frugality, accessed May 8, 2017.

41. John Morrill Bryan, *Robert Mills: Architect* (New York: AIA Press, 1989), 57; James K. Polk, *Diary of a President*, ed. Milo Quaife (Columbia, TN: James K. Polk Memorial Association, 2005), vol. 3, 175, 323; Polk, *Diary*, vol. 4, 1–3; Elisha Whittlesey to SCP, June 21, 1848, National Archives, entry 468, CS.

42. Margery M. Heffron, *Louisa Catherine: The Other Mrs. Adams*, ed. David M. Michelmore (New Haven, CT: Yale University Press, 2014), 303.

43. Ibid.

44. Ibid.; Caroline O'Reilly Nicholson, "Reminiscences of an Octogenarian," Caroline O'Reilly Nicholson Papers, #547-z, Southern Historical Collection, Wilson Library, University of North Carolina at Chapel Hill, 31; Nelson and Nelson, *Memorials of Sarah Childress Polk*, 16 20.

45. Joanna Rucker to Elizabeth Price, January 7, 1856, Polk Papers, TSLA; Paul H. Bergeron, "All in the Family: President Polk in the White House," *Tennessee Historical Quarterly* 46, no. 1 (1987): 15.

46. Bergeron, "All in the Family," 10–20, quote on 10–11; Nelson and Nelson, *Memorials of Sarah Childress Polk*, 161–62.

47. Joanna Rucker to Elizabeth Childress, July 7, 1846, Polk Papers, TSLA; Joanna Rucker to Elizabeth Price, January 18, 1847, Polk Papers, TSLA; Joanna Rucker to Elizabeth Price, n.d. (probably June 18, 1847), Polk Papers, TSLA. Joanna Rucker's correspondence makes clear what a powerful figure Sarah was in the imagination of her nieces. Joanna Rucker correspondence, Polk Papers, TSLA. See also Mary S. Jetton to SCP, September 25, 1845, Polk Papers, TSLA.

48. Dixon, "Excerpts from the Diary of Elizabeth Dixon of Connecticut, 1845–1847," December 19, 1845; Joanna Rucker to Elizabeth Price, November 29, 1845, Polk Papers, TSLA. Sarah didn't appear to have enough time to write thank-you notes, either. See Mary Taylor to Mrs. Niles, February 23, 1847, Polk Papers, TSLA.

49. Nelson and Nelson, *Memorials of Sarah Childress Polk*, 251–52; Hunt, "Fashion and Frugality: First Lady Sarah Polk."

50. Bergeron, "All in the Family," 11. The christening gown is in the Polk Family Home Collection.

51. Sellers, *James K. Polk*, vol. 2, *Continentalist*, 301; Polk, *Diary*, vol. 2, 345–46.

52. Hunt, "Fashion and Frugality: First Lady Sarah Polk."

53. John Grigg to SCP, March 7, 1845, Polk Papers, TSLA; see also Joshua Lane to SCP, undated, Polk Papers, TSLA.

54. John Rees to SCP, May 28, 1845, Polk Papers, LOC.

55. Septimus Huston to SCP, Washington, June 25, 1845, Polk Papers, LOC; Nathaniel Freeman to SCP, New York, February 2, 1845, Polk Papers, LOC, Microfilm, Reel 39, Series 2; Charlotte J. Hairres to SCP, New York, March 22, 1845, Polk Papers, TSLA.

56. Thomson to SCP, April 10, 1845, TSLA; Sylvia Glover to SCP, March 15, 1845, Polk Papers, LOC, Reel 49; Ann Thomas to SCP, Liberty (VA), n.d., Polk Papers, LOC. See also Ann Nichols to SCP, April 24, 1845, Polk Papers, TSLA; Mary Houston to SCP, March 23, 1845, Polk Papers, LOC.

57. Mary Throckmorton to SCP, April 10 [1845], Prince William County, VA, Polk Papers LOC; C. C. Porter to SCP, September 28, 1845, Polk Papers, LOC.

58. Sylvia Glover to SCP, March 15, 1847, Polk Papers, Microfilm, LOC, Microfilm, Reel 49; Caroline Brewerton to SCP, February 5, 1846, Polk Papers, TSLA. See also M. Lyttle to SCP, November 16, 1847, Polk Papers, LOC; Thomas Childress to SCP, May 17, 1845, Polk Papers, TSLA.

59. Carl Sferrazza Anthony, *First Ladies, The Saga of the Presidents' Wives and Their Power, 1789–1961* (New York: William Morrow, 1990), 140.

60. E. Elliott to SCP, February 20, 1848, Polk Papers, TSLA.

61. JC to SCP, February 20, 1845, Polk Papers, TSLA.

62. JKP to Thomas Childress, October 17, 1845, James K. Polk, *Correspondence of James K. Polk*, vol. 10, *July–December 1845*, ed. Wayne Cutler (Knoxville: University of Tennessee Press, 2004), 242; JKP to Daniel Graham, April 26, 1847, Daniel Graham to JKP, May 4, 1847, James K. Polk, *Correspondence of James K. Polk*, vol. 12,

January–July 1847, ed. Tom Chaffin and Michael David Cohen (Knoxville: University of Tennessee Press, 2013), 200–201, 226; Elizabeth Bancroft to SCP, n.d., Polk Papers, TSLA.

63. Nelson, *Memorials of Sarah Childress Polk*, 5; Joanna Rucker to SCP, October 23, 1847, Polk Papers, TSLA; Mary Louise Polk to SCP, November 5, 1847, Polk Papers, TSLA.

64. Maury, *An Englishwoman in America*, 202; Hunt, "Fashion and Frugality: First Lady Sarah Polk."

65. Frémont, *Souvenirs of My Time*, 100–103.

66. Ellet, *The Court Circles of the Republic*, 217.

67. Cornelia H. Richardson letter to Mrs. Dr. R. Worthington, December 17, 1847, Abraham Lincoln Presidential Library. See also Elizabeth Dixon, "Excerpts from the Diary of Elizabeth Dixon of Connecticut, 1845–1847," December 19, 1845, Connecticut Historical Society, Hartford; receipts, 1845, Polk Papers, LOC.

68. Joanna Rucker to SCP, October 23, 1847, Polk Papers, TSLA; Hunt, "Fashion and Frugality: First Lady Sarah Polk"; Joanna Rucker to SCP, December 1, 1847, Polk Papers, TSLA; Jacob L. Martin to JKP, December 1, 1845, Robert Armstrong to JKP, December 4, 1845, Polk, *Correspondence*, vol. 10, 399, 403; Jacob L. Martin to JKP, September 10, 1847, James K. Polk, *Correspondence of James K. Polk*, vol. 13, *August 1847–March 1848*, ed. Michael David Cohen (Knoxville: University of Tennessee Press, 2017), 156–57.

69. Joanna Rucker to SCP, December 1, 1847, Polk Papers, TSLA; receipts, February 1849, Polk Papers, LOC; Joanna Rucker to Elizabeth Price, April 7, 1845, January 7, 1846 (quote), Polk Papers, TSLA; Mary Louise Polk to SCP, Polk Papers, November 5, 1847; Hunt, "Fashion and Frugality: First Lady Sarah Polk."

70. Dixon, "Excerpts from the Diary of Elizabeth Dixon of Connecticut, 1845–1847," December 6, 1845; Joanna Rucker to Elizabeth Price, October 17, 1845, Polk Papers, TSLA; Seager, *And Tyler Too*, 259, 262, 263; Joanna Rucker to Elizabeth Price, November 29, 1845, Polk Papers, TSLA.

71. Hunt, "Fashion and Frugality: First Lady Sarah Polk"; Seager, *And Tyler Too*, 263; Seale, *The President's House*, vol. 1, 260.

72. Nelson and Nelson, *Memorials of Sarah Childress Polk*, 101–2.

73. Laura Holloway, *The Ladies of the White House* (New York: U.S. Pub. Co., 1870), 445.

74. D. Levy to SCP, November 28, 1845, James K. Polk Papers, LOC, Microfilm, Reel 43, Series 2; Reverend Mr. Bells to SCP, August 29, 1846, Polk Papers, TSLA. Sarah would have appreciated the gesture—at a dollar a dozen, oranges were consistently the most expensive produce she purchased. June 1846 receipts, Polk Papers, LOC; Augustus A. Parker to JKP, August 8, 1845, Polk Papers, LOC, Microfilm, Series 2, Reel 4. Parker wasn't the only American intending to name a daughter after Mrs. Polk without knowing her "Christian name." See also Jesse Chase to JKP, September 22, 1845, Polk, *Correspondence*, vol. 10, 494, and Alex Jones to JKP, April 4, 1845, James K. Polk, *Correspondence of James K. Polk*, vol. 9, *January–June 1845*, ed. Wayne Cutler and Robert G. Hall II (Knoxville: University of Tennessee Press, 1996), 253; Nelson and Nelson, *Memorials of Sarah Childress Polk*, 93–95; *Barre (MA) Patriot*, June 13, 1845, vol. 1, issue 47, p. 3.

75. Seager, *And Tyler Too*, 333; Lydia Howard Sigourney, *Noble Deeds of American Women; with Biographical Sketches of Some of the More Prominent* (Buffalo, NY: G. H. Derby and Co., 1851), 418.

76. Seale, *The President's House*, vol. 1, 256; Gwendolyn Wright, *Building the Dream:*

A Social History of Housing in America (Cambridge, MA: MIT Press, 1981), 111–12; Joanna Rucker to Elizabeth Price, March 1, 1846, Polk Papers, TSLA; Patrick Phillips-Schrock, *The White House: An Illustrated Architectural History* (Jefferson, NC: McFarland, 2013), 44; Dixon, "Excerpts from the Diary of Elizabeth Dixon of Connecticut, 1845–1847"; Charles Sellers, *James K. Polk*, vol. 1, *Jacksonian, 1795–1843* (Princeton, NJ: Princeton University Press, 1957), 111. The piano cost $500, and was made in Baltimore. Lewis Stirn to SCP, Washington, February 13, 1845, Polk Papers, LOC.

77. Nelson and Nelson, *Memorials of Sarah Childress Polk*, 94.

CHAPTER 6. THE POWER OF
AMERICAN WOMEN TO SAVE THEIR COUNTRY

1. James D. Richardson, ed., *Messages and Papers of the Presidents* (Washington, DC: Government Printing Office, 1901), vol. 4, 373–82.

2. Anson Nelson and Fanny Nelson, *Memorials of Sarah Childress Polk: Wife of the Eleventh President of the United States* (New York: Anson D. F. Randolph and Co., 1892), 100.

3. Edmund C. Watmough to SCP, October 24, 1844, Polk Papers, LOC, Microfilm, Reel 29; Edmund C. Watmough, *Scribblings and Sketches: Diplomatic, Piscatory, and Oceanic*, 2nd ed. (Philadelphia: E. Sherman, 1844); Edwin Williams, *New York Annual Register for the Year of Our Lord, 1836* (New York: Edwin Williams, 1836), 475.

4. Watmough, *Scribblings and Sketches*, 120; Catharine Beecher, *A Treatise on Domestic Economy for the Use of Young Ladies at Home and at School* (Boston, 1841), 12, 36. On Beecher's role in formulating and promoting domesticity, see Kathryn Kish Sklar, *Catharine Beecher: A Study in American Domesticity* (New York: Norton, 1973).

5. Lynnea Magnuson, "In the Service of Columbia: Gendered Politics and Manifest Destiny Expansion" (Ph.D. diss., University of Illinois at Urbana-Champaign, 2000); Amy Kaplan, *The Anarchy of Empire in the Making of U.S. Culture* (Cambridge, MA: Harvard University Press, 2002), 23–50.

6. Sklar, *Catharine Beecher*, 169; Catharine Beecher to SCP, September 20, 1845, Polk Family Home Collection.

7. Lyman Beecher, *A Plea for the West*, 2nd ed. (Cincinnati: Truman and Smith, 1835), 10–11.

8. Catharine Beecher to SCP, September 20, 1845, Polk Family Home Collection.

9. Ibid.; Catharine Beecher, *The Duty of American Women to Their Country* (New York: Harper and Bros., 1845), 64.

10. William Seale, *The President's House: A History* (Baltimore: Johns Hopkins University Press, 2008), vol. 1, 244.

11. Alex Jones to SCP, March 29, 1845, Polk Papers, TSLA. On Jones, see James K. Polk, *Correspondence of James K. Polk*, vol. 9, *January–June 1845*, ed. Wayne Cutler and Robert G. Hall II (Knoxville: University of Tennessee Press, 1996), 253; John Rees to SCP, May 28, 1845, Polk Papers, LOC.

12. John Price to SCP, January 31, 1845, Polk Papers, LOC, Microfilm, Reel 33.

13. Joanna Rucker to Elizabeth Price, April 7, 1846, Polk Papers, TSLA; Amy Greenberg, *A Wicked War: Polk, Clay, Lincoln, and the 1846 U.S. Invasion of Mexico* (New York: Vintage, 2012), 76–79, 84–85.

14. On Anglophobia, see Sam W. Haynes, *Unfinished Revolution: The Early American Republic in a British World* (Charlottesville: University of Virginia Press, 2010).

15. John C. Catron to SCP, September 24, 1845, Polk Papers, TSLA.

16. John C. Catron to JKP, September 16, 1845, James K. Polk, *Correspondence of James K. Polk*, vol. 10, *July–December 1845*, ed. Wayne Cutler (Knoxville: University of Tennessee Press, 2004), 237; JKP to John C. Catron, October 4, 1845, Polk, *Correspondence*, vol. 10, 277; William L. Marcy to Zachary Taylor, October 16, 1845, in *Messages of the President of the United States . . . on the Subject of the Mexican War*, House Executive Documents, 30th Congress, 1st Session, No. 60 (Washington, DC: Wendell and Van Benthuysen, 1848), 90–91; James Polk, *Diary of a President*, ed. Milo Quaife (Columbia, TN: James K. Polk Memorial Association, 2005), vol. 1, 171, 189.

17. Gideon Pillow to SCP, January 8, 1846, Polk Papers, LOC, Microfilm, Reel 44, Series 2.

18. Greenberg, *A Wicked War*, 98–104.

19. Richardson, ed., *Messages and Papers of the Presidents*, vol. 4, 442–43; Greenberg, *A Wicked War*, 104

20. Greenberg, *A Wicked War*, 113–22.

21. JC to JKP, June 15, 1846, James K. Polk, *Correspondence of James K. Polk*, vol. 11, *1846*, ed. Wayne Cutler (Knoxville: University of Tennessee Press, 2009), 209.

22. Polk, *Correspondence*, vol. 12, 94n3; Greenberg, *A Wicked War*, 104–7, 192–94.

23. Joanna Rucker to Elizabeth Price, May 30, 1846, Polk Papers, TSLA.

24. Salem Academy Copybook, Polk Family Home; Paul Wells, "Music in the Life of Sarah Childress Polk," *Bulletin of the Society for American Music* 30, no. 1 (2004): 4–5; Seale, *The President's House*, vol. 1, 261.

25. Laura Holloway, *The Ladies of the White House* (New York: U.S. Pub. Co., 1870), 452–53.

26. Ester Singleton, *The Story of the White House* (New York: Benjamin Blom, 1907), vol. 1, 317–18; Joanna Rucker to Elizabeth Price, May 30, 1846, Polk Papers, TSLA.

27. Greenberg, *A Wicked War*, 146–99.

28. Ibid., 137–49.

29. M. Lyttle to JKP, M. Lyttle to SCP, November 16, 1847, Polk Papers, LOC.

30. "Mrs. Polk," *Daily Sentinel and Gazette* (Milwaukee), December 23, 1846.

31. Joanna Rucker to SCP, February 5, 1847, Polk Papers, TSLA.

32. Mary Louise Polk to SCP, November 5, 1847, Polk Papers, TSLA.

33. Ibid.

34. Susanna A. Harney to SCP, January 4, 1848, Polk Papers, TSLA.

35. Anonymous to JKP, April 19, 1847, James K. Polk, *Correspondence of James K. Polk*, vol. 12, *January–July 1847*, ed. Tom Chaffin and Michael David Cohen (Knoxville: University of Tennessee Press, 2013), 183–84.

36. "The War," *Berkshire County Whig* (Pittsfield, MA), May 20, 1847; "First Lady Biography: Sarah Childress Polk," National First Ladies Library, http://www.firstladies.org/biographies/firstladies.aspx?biography=12, accessed June 19, 2015; Greenberg, *A Wicked War*, 72.

37. Nelson and Nelson, *Memorials of Sarah Childress Polk*, 199; Aaron Brown to JKP, June 10, 1846, Polk, *Correspondence*, vol. 11, 202; "Mrs. Polk," *Mississippi Free Trader*, December 27, 1848. See also the two letters addressed to "Mrs. President," John M. Niles to SCP, n.d., Polk Papers, TSLA; Polk, *Diary*, vol. 3, 326.

38. George M. Dallas to Mrs. Dallas, January 15, 1849, Dallas Papers, CS.

39. JKP, Washington, to SCP, New York, November 13, 1848, Polk Papers, LOC.

40. JKP to Robert Armstrong, June 13, 1847, Polk, *Correspondence*, vol. 12, 347–48.

41. Nelson and Nelson, *Memorials of Sarah Childress Polk*, 118.

42. John F. H. Claiborne, *Life and Correspondence of John A. Quitman* (New York: Harper and Bros., 1860), vol. 1, 237; Polk, *Diary*, vol. 2, 74, 456.

43. Nelson and Nelson, *Memorials of Sarah Childress Polk*, 115–16.

44. Polk, *Diary*, vol. 4, 245–46.

45. NYH quoted in the *Portsmouth (NH) Journal*, December 4, 1847.

46. Holloway, *The Ladies of the White House*, 451–52; Nelson and Nelson, *Memorials of Sarah Childress Polk*, 52; George Bancroft to JKP, November 18, 1847, James K. Polk, *Correspondence of James K. Polk*, vol. 13, *August 1847–March 1848*, ed. Michael David Cohen (Knoxville: University of Tennessee Press, 2017), 198–99; George Bancroft to JKP, January 19, 1847, June 3, 1847, Polk, *Correspondence*, vol. 12, 54, 328.

47. Thomas Hart Benton to SCP, Senate Chamber, February 14, 1845, Polk Papers, LOC, Microfilm, Reel 33; Robert B. Campbell to SCP, November 12, 1846, Polk Papers, TSLA.

48. Thomas Richie to SCP, n.d., Polk Papers, LOC. Said letter has disappeared. There is no surviving evidence of correspondence between JKP and Colonel Hiram Paulding. J. H. Wailes to SCP, April 15, 1847, Polk Papers, TSLA.

49. Joanna Rucker to Elizabeth Childress, July 11, 1846, Polk Papers, TSLA; JKP to Vernon K. Stevenson, October 3, 1846, Polk, *Correspondence*, vol. 11, 339–40; Tom Price, "Comfort in My Retirement: Polk Place," *White House History* 33 (Summer 2013): 12–21.

50. JKP to Vernon K. Stevenson, October 3, 1847, Polk, *Correspondence*, vol. 11, 339–40.

51. JKP to John Catron, October 7, 1846, Polk, *Correspondence*, vol. 11, 344–45; JKP to Aaron Brown, November 8, 1846, Polk, *Correspondence*, vol. 11, 388–89; Mary Louise Corse Polk to SCP, October 8, 1848, Polk Papers, TSLA.

52. John M. Bass to JKP, April 10, 1847, Polk, *Correspondence*, vol. 12, 172; Tom Price, "Comfort in My Retirement: Polk Place," 15.

53. JKP to John M. Bass, April 19, 1847, Polk, *Correspondence*, vol. 12, 184; John M. Bass to JKP, April 10, 1847, Polk, *Correspondence*, vol. 12, 172.

54. JKP to SCP, July 4, 1847, Polk, *Correspondence*, vol. 12, 409–10; Wayne Cutler, ed., *North for Union: John Appleton's Journal of a Tour to New England Made by President Polk in June and July 1847* (Nashville: Vanderbilt University Press, 1986), 10–11, 32; James Buchanan to SCP, July 4, 1847, Polk, *Correspondence*, vol. 12, 410; Joanna Rucker to Elizabeth Price, August 18, 1846, Polk Papers, TSLA.

55. JKP to SCP, July 8, 1847, Polk, *Correspondence*, vol. 12, 415.

56. Ibid.; JKP to John Catron, July 10, 1847, Polk, *Correspondence*, vol. 12, 420; JKP to SCP, July 15, 1847, Polk, *Correspondence*, vol. 12, 415; JKP to SCP, July 11, 1847, Polk, *Correspondence*, vol. 12, 417.

57. JKP to SCP, July 12, 1847, Polk, *Correspondence*, vol. 12, 417–18.

58. John Catron to JKP, July 14, 1847, Polk, *Correspondence*, vol. 12, 420; Joanna Rucker to SCP, September 9, 1848, Polk Papers, TSLA.

59. John Catron to SCP, August 14, 1848, James K. Polk Papers, LOC, Microfilm, Reel 53, Series 2.

60. Mary Louise Corse Polk to SCP, October 8, 1848, Polk Papers, TSLA.

61. Matilda Catron to SCP, October 14, 1847, Polk Papers, TSLA.

62. Watch, Pendant, 1925.001.062a-c, October 18, 2016, Polk Family Home Collection, Columbia, Tennessee.

63. Greenberg, *A Wicked War*, 239, 260–61.

64. Catharine Beecher to SCP, September 20, 1845, Polk Family Home Collection; Catharine Beecher, *The Duty of American Women to Their Country* (New York: Harper and Bros., 1845), 64; Amy Greenberg, "Domesticating the Border: Manifest Destiny and the Market in the United States–Mexico Border Region, 1848–1854," in *Land of Necessity: Consumer Culture in the United States–Mexico Borderlands*, ed. Alexis McCrossen (Durham, NC: Duke University Press, 2009), 84–112.

65. "The Mormon Emigrants," *New York Daily Tribune*, March 19, 1849; Duff Green to JKP, January 10, 1847, Polk, *Correspondence*, vol. 13, 149–50.

66. Matthew Restall, *When Montezuma Met Cortés: The True Story of the Meeting That Changed History* (New York: Ecco/HarperCollins, 2018), 346–47; "The Romance of an Historic Picture," *NDA*, January 28, 1883.

67. Nelson and Nelson, *Memorials*, 143; Seale, *The President's House*, vol. 1, 268. Other sources claim that Sarah didn't hang the painting until she moved into Polk Place, where it had a special place of honor. "The Romance of an Historic Picture," *NDA*, January 28, 1883.

CHAPTER 7. THAT FINE MANLY LADY

1. Joanna Rucker to SCP, December 3, 1848, Polk Papers, TSLA.

2. K. Jack Bauer, *Zachary Taylor: Soldier, Planter, Statesman of the Old Southwest* (Baton Rouge: Louisiana State University Press, 1993), 107, 215–39.

3. William Dusinberre, *Slavemaster President: The Double Career of James Polk* (New York: Oxford University Press, 2003), 12.

4. Ibid., 11–22.

5. JKP to JC, August 15, 1846, James K. Polk, *Correspondence of James K. Polk*, vol. 11, *1846*, ed. Wayne Cutler (Knoxville: University of Tennessee Press, 2009), 280–81; JC to SCP, July 26, 1846, Polk Papers, LOC, Microfilm, Reel 46, Series 2; JC to JKP, November 30, 1846, Polk, *Correspondence*, vol. 11, 405; JC to JKP, June 15, 1846, Polk, *Correspondence*, vol. 11, 209. See also JKP to JC, October 10, 1846, Polk, *Correspondence*, vol. 11, 347; Deposition of Jane Polk, January 13, 1898, Case of Dafney Polk, Case Files of Approved Pension Applications of Widows and Other Veterans of the Army and Navy Who Served Mainly in the Civil War and the War with Spain, National Archives, Record Group 15.

6. Deposition of Jane Polk, January 13, 1898, Case of Dafney Polk, Case Files of Approved Pension Applications of Widows and Other Veterans of the Army and Navy Who Served Mainly in the Civil War and the War with Spain, National Archives, Record Group 15; "From Thomas Jefferson to John Wayles Eppes, 30 June 1820," *Founders Online*, National Archives, last modified March 30, 2017, http://founders .archives.gov/documents/Jefferson/98-01-02-1352, accessed May 17, 2017; Dusinberre, *Slavemaster President*, 178–79.

7. Dusinberre, *Slavemaster President*, 52.

8. Ingersoll to Buchanan, June 16, 1847, Ingersoll Papers, CS.

9. James K. Polk, *Diary of a President*, ed. Milo Quaife (Columbia, TN: James K. Polk Memorial Association, 2005), vol. 3, 482–507.

10. George Mifflin Dallas to Mrs. Dallas, June 21, 1848, July 15, 1848, Dallas Papers, CS; Polk, *Diary*, vol. 3, 483.

11. Walter R. Borneman, *Polk: The Man Who Transformed the Presidency and America* (New York: Random House, 2009), 323–28.

12. Ibid., 323–25.

13. JKP to SCP, August 25, 1848, August 27, 1848, James K. Polk Papers, LOC, Microfilm, Reel 53, Series 2; JC to SCP, May 17, 1847, Polk Papers, TSLA.

14. "The Gold Regions of California," *The National Era*, September 28, 1848; *Report of the Woman's Rights Convention, Held at Seneca Falls N.Y., July 19 and 20, 1848* (Rochester, NY: John Dick, 1848), 3; *National Intelligencer*, August 16, 1848; Valerie Palmer-Mehta cites biographies by John Reed Bumgarner and Barbara Bennett Peterson as the sources of this claim. Bumgarner, however, says only, "It has been

suggested that she urged James to go and address the group," without providing citation for the assertion. Peterson provides neither citation nor evidence for her assertion that Sarah "urged President Polk to address the group." Valerie Palmer-Mehta, "Sarah Polk: Ideas of Her Own," in *A Companion to First Ladies*, ed. Katherine A. S. Sibley (Malden, MA: Wiley-Blackwell, 2016), 170; John Reed Bumgarner, *Sarah Childress Polk: A Biography of the Remarkable First Lady* (Jefferson, NC: McFarland, 1997), 95; Barbara Bennett Peterson, *Sarah Childress Polk, First Lady of Tennessee and Washington* (Huntington, NY: Nova History Publications, 2002), 41.

15. Lydia Howard Huntley Sigourney to JKP, February 24, 1848, Polk, *Correspondence*, vol. 13, 346–47.

16. Alfred G. Hall to JKP, August 30, 1845, Polk Papers, LOC, Reel 41, Series 2. A. G. Hall, *Womanhood, causes of its premature decline, respectfully illustrated: being a review of the changes and derangements of the female constitution: a safe and faithful guide to mothers during gestation, before and after confinement: with medical advice of the most salutary and important nature to all females: also, sixty vegetable and domestic recipes with directions: in three parts* (Rochester, NY: E. Shephard, 1845); Janet Farrell Brodie, *Contraception and Abortion in 19th-Century America* (Ithaca, NY: Cornell University Press, 1997), 117–18; Sarah Mytton Maury, *An Englishwoman in America* (London: Thomas Richardson, 1848), 203–4; Helen Lefkowitz Horowitz, *Rereading Sex: Battles over Sexual Knowledge and Suppression in Nineteenth-Century America* (New York: Vintage, 2003).

17. Ellis Lewis to SCP, February 5, 1849, Polk Papers, TSLA; Olin Browder, "Conditions and Limitations in Restraint of Marriage," *Michigan Law Review* 39, no. 8 (1941): 1288–1336; *American Law Reports Annotated* (163), 1165; Burton Alva Konkle, *The Life of Chief Justice Ellis Lewis, 1798–1871: Of the First Elective Supreme Court of Pennsylvania* (Philadelphia: Campion, 1907), 131–32.

18. Ellis Lewis to SCP, February 5, 1949, Polk Papers, TSLA; Mrs E. B. Kinney, "Woman's Champion," in *The Ladies' Wreath: An Illustrated Annual*, ed. Sarah Towne Martyn (New York: Martyn & Miller, 1850), 74.

19. JKP to Lydia Polk Caldwell, April 6, 1846, Polk, *Correspondence*, vol. 11, 122–23; JKP to Lydia Eliza Polk Caldwell, January 31, 1848, James K. Polk, *Correspondence of James K. Polk*, vol. 13, *August 1847–March 1848*, ed. Michael David Cohen (Knoxville: University of Tennessee Press, 2017), 310–11.

20. Elizabeth Blair Lee to Samuel Philips Lee, November 10, 1848, November 12, 1848, Blair-Lee Papers, CS.

21. JKP to SCP, November 11, 1848, November 13, 1848, James K. Polk Papers, LOC, Microfilm, Reel 53, Series 2.

22. Joanna Rucker to SCP, December 8, 1848, Polk Papers, TSLA, Polk Family Home Collection.

23. Vernon K. Stevenson to SCP, February 12, 1849, Polk Papers, TSLA; Mary Childress to SCP, February 11, 1849, Polk Papers, TSLA.

24. Joanna Rucker to SCP, February 7, 1849, Polk Papers, TSLA.

25. Mary Childress to SCP, February 11, 1849, Polk Papers, TSLA; Sarah Polk Rucker to SCP, March 21, 1849, Polk Papers, TSLA. Bettie's birthday has been disputed. Her tombstone lists her date as 1845; other sources claim she was born in 1842.

26. Sarah Polk Rucker to SCP, March 21, 1849, Polk Papers, TSLA; Joanna Rucker to SCP, December 23, 1848, Polk Papers, TSLA.

27. "From *Sartain's Union Magazine* Mrs. James K. Polk," *Pittsfield (MA) Sun*, February 28, 1850.

28. Ibid.; *National Cyclopedia of American Biography*, vol. 9 (1926); Diane Long Hoeveler,

"Denison, Mary Andrews," in *American Women Writers: A Critical Reference Guide from Colonial Times to the Present*, 2nd ed., ed. Taryn Benbow-Pfalzgraf (Detroit: St. James Press, 2000), vol. 1, 279, retrieved from Gale Virtual Reference Library (accessed September 9, 2016); Joanna Rucker to SCP, July 2, 1848, Polk Papers, TSLA.

29. John Allen Kraut and Dixon Ryan Fox, *The Completion of Independence, 1790–1830* (New York: Macmillan, 1948), 368; Hoeveler, "Denison, Mary Andrews," 279.

30. "From *Sartain's Union Magazine* Mrs. James K. Polk," *Pittsfield (MA) Sun*, February 28, 1850.

31. Ibid.

32. Polk, *Diary*, vol. 4, 361–62; Elizabeth Benton Frémont, *Recollections of Elizabeth Benton Frémont* (New York: Frederick H. Hitchcock, 1912), 15; Henry Gilpin to Martin Van Buren, February 14, 1845, Martin Van Buren Papers.

33. Polk, *Diary*, vol. 4, 357–59.

34. Polk, *Diary*, vol. 4, 373.

35. *Nashville Republican Banner*, September 26, 1851.

36. David Potter, *The Impending Crisis, 1848–1861* (New York: Harper and Row, 1976), 122–29.

37. Mrs. Ann S. Stephens, "To Mrs. James K. Polk," *Peterson's Ladies National Magazine* XV (1849): 91.

38. "Example in High Places," *Vermont Chronicle*, March 7, 1849, 38; see also "Mrs. Polk," *The Farmer's Cabinet* (Amherst, NH), vol. 47, issue 32 (March 22, 1849): 1.

39. William Thompson to SCP, February 28, 1849, Polk Papers, TSLA; J. W. Matthews to SCP, February 23, 1849, Polk Papers, TSLA; William L. Helfenstein to JKP, October 8, 1848, Polk, *Correspondence: Transcriptions, April 1848–June 1849* (forthcoming).

40. Anson Nelson and Fanny Nelson, *Memorials of Sarah Childress Polk: Wife of the Eleventh President of the United States* (New York: Anson D. F. Randolph and Co., 1892), 127–35.

41. Ibid., 136.

42. Ibid.

43. Ibid.; Polk, *Diary*, vol. 4, 413.

44. *Nashville Union*, April 3, 1849; Nelson and Nelson, *Memorials of Sarah Childress Polk*, 136, 137; Nathaniel Baxter, "Reminiscences," *American Historical Magazine* (Nashville) VIII (July 1903): 262–70, quote on 270, in CS.

45. Polk, *Diary*, vol. 4, 420.

46. Polk, *Diary*, vol. 4, 425; Bobby L. Lovett, *The African-American History of Nashville, Tennessee, 1780–1930: Elites and Dilemmas* (Fayetteville: University of Arkansas Press, 1999), 17; Nelson and Nelson, *Memorials of Sarah Childress Polk*, 138.

47. Elizabeth Blair Lee to SPL, June 20, 1849, Blair-Lee Papers, CS.

48. JKP to William Marcy, May 9, 1849, Marcy Papers, CS.

49. "Nashville City Cemetery Interments (1846–1979)," Data.Nashville.gov, https://data.nashville.gov/Genealogy/Historic-Nashville-City-Cemetery-Interments-1846-1/iwbm-8it6, accessed February 18, 2018; Nelson and Nelson, *Memorials of Sarah Childress Polk*, 146–50.

50. Paul H. Bergeron, *The Presidency of James K. Polk* (Lawrence: University Press of Kansas, 1987), 234–35, 260; Dusinberre, *Slavemaster President*, 16–17; Nelson and Nelson, *Memorials of Sarah Childress Polk*, 146–50. Matilda, the Polk cook who died, was listed as 110 years old. "Nashville City Cemetery Interments (1846–1979)," Data.Nashville.gov.

51. Nelson and Nelson, *Memorials of Sarah Childress Polk*, 146–50.

52. Elizabeth Blair Lee to SPL, June 20, 1849, Blair-Lee Papers, CS.

53. Nelson and Nelson, *Memorials of Sarah Childress Polk*, 81.

54. "Nashville City Cemetery Interments (1846–1979)," Data.Nashville.gov; Ben Guarino, "James Polk: The Dead President Who Never Rests in Peace," *Washington Post*, March 28, 2017; Peggy McDowell and Richard E. Meyer, *The Revival Styles and American Memorial Art* (Bowling Green, OH: Popular Press, 1994), 53; "Death and Burial," in *James K. Polk: A Biographical Companion*, ed. Mark Eaton Byrnes (Santa Barbara, CA: ABC-Clio, 2001), 51–53; Nelson and Nelson, *Memorials of Sarah Childress Polk*, 11, 153–57.

55. Mary S. Jetton to SCP, September 25, 1845, Polk Papers, TSLA; Nelson and Nelson, *Memorials of Sarah Childress Polk*, 161.

56. Sarah Rucker to SCP, June 21, 1848, Polk Papers, TSLA; Nelson and Nelson, *Memorials of Sarah Childress Polk*, 161.

57. 1850 Census, Census Place: Nashville, Davidson, Tennessee, Roll M432_875, p. 131A, Image 267; "Mrs. James K. Polk," *Macon (GA) Weekly Telegraph*, published as *Georgia Telegraph*, vol. XXIV, issue 28 (February 26, 1850): 2.

58. Advertisement in *New York Evening Post*, vol. XLIX (July 29, 1851): 1. Sadly, this daguerreotype appears to have been lost.

59. Oscar Penn Fitzgerald, *John B. McFerrin: A Biography* (Nashville: M. E. Church, 1888), 243; Jeannette Tillotson Acklen, *Tennessee Records: Tombstone Inscriptions and Manuscripts* (Nashville, 1933), 442, 353, 357. My thanks to the Rutherford County Archives for confirming the two wedding licenses. Joanna sadly reported that one of the few advantages of life back in Tennessee was that she had "ample time for reading & improvement—& I spend most of my time with books." Joanna Rucker to SCP, December 8, 1848, Polk Papers, TSLA.

60. 1850 Census, Census Place: Nashville, Davidson, Tennessee, Roll M432_875, p. 131A, Image 267; receipt, February 18, 1850, Polk Papers, LOC, Microfilm, Reel 63; Nelson and Nelson, *Memorials of Sarah Childress Polk*, 12.

61. Suzanne Lebsock, *Free Women of Petersburg: Status and Culture in a Southern Town* (New York: Norton, 1985), 116–28; Jane Turner Censer, *The Reconstruction of White Womanhood, 1865–1895* (Baton Rouge: Louisiana State University Press, 2003), 88–106.

62. Last Will and Testament of President James K. Polk, 1849, Record Group 21: Records of District Courts of the United States, 1685–2009, Series: Civil Case Files, 1858–1911, National Archives and Records.

63. Dusinberre, *Slavemaster President*, 8.

CHAPTER 8. PROFIT AND LOSS

1. On power relations between white women and their enslaved servants, see Thavolia Glymph, *Out of the House of Bondage: The Transformation of the Plantation Household* (New York: Cambridge University Press, 2008).

2. Elizabeth Fox Genovese, *Within the Plantation Household: Black and White Women of the Old South* (Chapel Hill: University of North Carolina Press, 1988).

3. William Dusinberre, *Slavemaster President: The Double Career of James Polk* (New York: Oxford University Press, 2003), 24, 92.

4. John A. Mairs to JKP, May 24, 1847, James K. Polk, *Correspondence of James K. Polk*, vol. 12, *January–July 1847*, ed. Tom Chaffin and Michael David Cohen (Knoxville: University of Tennessee Press, 2013), 291.

5. Gideon Pillow to JKP, May 1, 1846, James K. Polk, *Correspondence of James K. Polk*, vol. 11, *1846*, ed. Wayne Cutler (Knoxville: University of Tennessee Press, 2009), 150; Dusinberre, *Slavemaster President*, 46.

6. JKP to Gideon Pillow, April 20, 1846, Polk, *Correspondence*, vol. 11, 132.

7. Anson Nelson and Fanny Nelson, *Memorials of Sarah Childress Polk: Wife of the Eleventh President of the United States* (New York: Anson D. F. Randolph and Co., 1892), 99.

8. Frederick Douglass, *Narrative of the Life of Frederick Douglass, an American Slave* (New York: Penguin, 1968), 48–49.

9. Edward E. Baptist, *The Half Has Never Been Told: Slavery and the Making of American Capitalism* (New York: Basic Books, 2014), quotes on xxi, xxiii; Walter Johnson, *River of Dark Dreams: Slavery and Empire in the Cotton Kingdom* (Cambridge, MA: Harvard University Press, 2013), 210–43; Dusinberre, *Slavemaster President*, 92–93, 105, 115. On slave community, see Anthony E. Kaye, *Joining Places: Slave Neighborhoods in the Old South* (Chapel Hill: University of North Carolina Press, 2007).

10. Dusinberre, *Slavemaster President*, 46, 47, 51–53.

11. Isaac Dismukes to JKP, September 27, 1841, James K. Polk, *Correspondence of James K. Polk*, vol. 5, *1939–1841*, ed. Wayne Cutler (Nashville: Vanderbilt University Press, 1979), 762; Dusinberre, *Slavemaster President*, 37.

12. Dusinberre, *Slavemaster President*, 52–54.

13. Ibid., 51–53.

14. Ibid., 39; Thomas Tooke, *A History of Prices and the State of Circulation During the Nine Years 1848–1865* (London: Longman, Orme, Brown, Green and Longmans, 1857), vol. 6, 239–40.

15. John Mairs to SCP, August 19, 1849, James K. Polk Papers, LOC.

16. John Mairs to SCP, September 20, 1849, James K. Polk Papers, LOC. There is no way of determining whether Mairs adopted a different tone with Sarah than with James, as there is no surviving correspondence between the president and the overseer.

17. John Mairs to SCP, March 15, 1850, James K. Polk Papers, LOC; John Spencer Bassett, *The Southern Plantation Overseer as Revealed in His Letters* (Northampton, MA: Smith College, 1925), 180–82; Pickett-Perkins to SCP, December 27, 1852, Polk Papers, LOC; Dusinberre, *Slavemaster President*, 39.

18. Pickett-Perkins and Company to SCP, January 3, 1850, Polk Papers, LOC.

19. Perkins and Company to SCP, March 13, 1858, Perkins and Pickens, March 7, 1855, Polk Papers, LOC.

20. Bassett, *The Southern Plantation Overseer*, 269–71; Dusinberre, *Slavemaster President*, 92; Seth Rockman, "Plantation Goods and the National Economy of Slavery in Antebellum America," manuscript in possession of author. On "Negro Cloth," see Madelyn Shaw, "Slave Cloth and Clothing Slaves: Craftsmanship, Clothing, and Industry," *Journal of Early Southern Decorative Arts* 37 (2016), http://www.mesda journal.org/2012/slave-cloth-clothing-slaves-craftsmanship-commerce-industry/.

21. J. O. Cooper to SCP, September 8, 1857; see also R. B. Hays to SCP, July 29, 1857, Perkins to SCP, July 11, 1857, Polk Papers, LOC; Pickett to SCP, July 7, 1857, and September 10, 1857, Polk Papers, LOC.

22. Bassett, *The Southern Plantation Overseer*, 181; Dusinberre, *Slavemaster President*, 188.

23. Dusinberre, *Slavemaster President*, 101–3.

24. Pickett-Perkins to SCP, March 30, 1855, Polk Papers, LOC.

25. Pickett-Perkins to SCP, April 25, 1855, January 18, 1856, Polk Papers, LOC.

26. Dusinberre, *Slavemaster President*, 53–54.

27. Deposition of Dafney Polk, November 3, 1888, Deposition of Caroline Drain, January 12, 1898, Case of Dafney Polk, Case Files of Approved Pension Applications of Widows and Other Veterans of the Army and Navy Who Served Mainly in the Civil War and the War with Spain, National Archives, Record Group 15; Dusinberre, *Slavemaster President*, 90–91, 94–95.

28. John Mairs to SCP, October 2, 1852, Polk Papers, LOC; Dusinberre, *Slavemaster President*, 96–98.

29. Dusinberre, *Slavemaster President*, 92.

30. Fitzgerald, *John B. McFerrin: A Biography*, 243; Acklen, Tennessee Records, 442, 353, 357.

31. John H. Bills to SCP, January 28, 1852, Polk Papers, LOC; Dusinberre, *Slavemaster President*, 74; Bassett, *The Southern Plantation Overseer*, 197.

32. John Mairs to SCP, January 7, 1856, Polk Papers, LOC; William Dusinberre claims that in 1860, Sarah removed two other runaways, Manuel and Giles, from their wives, Jane and Dafney, but Manuel and Giles were still living at the Polk Plantation in 1863, when they joined the Union army. Dusinberre, *Slavemaster President*, 101–3. Case of Dafney Polk, Case Files of Approved Pension Applications of Widows and Other Veterans of the Army and Navy Who Served Mainly in the Civil War and the War with Spain, National Archives, Record Group 15.

33. John Mairs to SCP, April 15, 1857, January 15, 1858, Polk Papers, LOC; Bassett, *The Southern Plantation Overseer*, 219–20.

34. "Negro Rebellion on Mrs. Polk's Plantation," *Memphis Daily Appeal*, August 5, 1858; "President Polk's Slaves on Trial—A Negro Insurrection," *Chicago Tribune*, January 15, 1859; "Acquitted," *Memphis Daily Appeal*, November 16, 1858; "An Act Authorizing a Change of Venue in the Case of the State Against Giles and Emmanuel, and for Other Purposes," November 25, 1859, Mississippi Legislature, *Laws of the State of Mississippi* (Jackson: E. Barksdale, 1860), 81. Thanks to Lisa Childs for making me take this case seriously.

35. Court case 11675 (Yalobusha Co.), Mississippi Department of Archives and History; "Emmanuel and Giles (slaves) v. State, 36 Miss. R, 627," J. S. Morris, *Mississippi State Cases, Being Criminal Cases Decided in the High Court of Errors and Appeals, and in the Supreme Court, of the State of Mississippi: from the June Term 1818 to the First Monday in January 1872, Inclusive* (Jackson: Published by the compiler, 1872), vol. 2, 1217–20.

36. Ariela J. Gross, *Double Character: Slavery and Mastery in the Antebellum Southern Courtroom* (Princeton, NJ: Princeton University Press, 2000), 5.

37. A. Hutchinson, *Code of Mississippi: Being an Analytic Compilation of the Public and General Statutes of the Territory and State* (Jackson, Mississippi, 1848), 540; Susan B. Carter, Scott Sigmund Gartner, Michael R. Haines, Alan L. Olmstead, Richard Sutch, and Gavin Wright, eds., *Historical Statistics of the United States* (New York: Cambridge University Press, 2006), table Bb212.

38. Deed between Mrs. Sarah Polk and James M. Avent, February 18, 1860, Pontotoc County Deed Records, Book R, 278-279, Mississippi Department of Archives; *Tennessee State Marriages, 1780–2002*, Nashville, TSLA, Microfilm.

39. 1860 Census, Census Place: Nashville Ward 5, Davidson, Tennessee, Roll M653_1246, p. 422, Image 648, Family History Library Film 805246; Deposition of Charlie Avent, January 15, 1898, Case of Dafney Polk, Case Files of Approved Pension Applications of Widows and Other Veterans of the Army and Navy Who Served Mainly in the Civil War and the War with Spain, National Archives, Record Group 15.

40. Lewis Polk Affidavit, June 2, 1887, Deposition of Caroline Nelson, November 3, 1888, Case of Dafney Polk, Case Files of Approved Pension Applications of Widows and Other Veterans of the Army and Navy Who Served Mainly in the Civil War and the War with Spain, National Archives, Record Group 15; MS 1860 Slave Schedule, Yalobusha County (Ancestry.com. *Mississippi, Compiled Census and Census Substitutes Index, 1805–1890* [database online]. Provo, UT: Ancestry.com Operations Inc., 1999), 461.

41. Deed between James M. Avent, Mary Avent, and Sarah Polk to D. C. Topp, Yalo-

busha County Deeds, January 1871, Book 24, p. 356, Mississippi Department of Archives.

42. She paid $12 a year to rent pew 137. Receipt, Polk Papers, LOC, Microfilm, Reel 63; receipts, Polk Papers, LOC, Microfilm, Reel 63. In 1857 she spent over $25 on fabric, including black silk, at L. F. Beech, dealer in English, French and Domestic Dry Goods, but nothing on dresses.

43. Receipt, Polk Papers, LOC, Microfilm, Reel 63; "Visit to Mrs. Polk," *Lebanon (PA) Courier and Semi-Weekly Report,* January 20, 1854. Thanks to Alexis McCrossen for this reference. See also the *Semi-Weekly Standard* (Raleigh, NC), January 21, 1854; Annie S. Gilchrist, *Some Representative Women of Tennessee* (Nashville: McQuiddy Printing Co., 1902), 12.

44. "Congress," *Bangor (ME) Daily Whig & Courier,* Friday, January 4, 1850. Inscriptions in books based on an examination of the library at the Polk Family Home. Richard Chenevix Trench, *On the Study of Words* (New York: Macmillan Co., 1853); Lawrence Levine, *Highbrow/Lowbrow: The Emergence of Cultural Hierarchy in America* (Cambridge, MA: Harvard University Press, 1990).

45. Sheppard M. Ashe, *Monterey Conquered: A Fragment from La Gran Quivira; or, Rome Unmasked. A Poem* (New York: C. Shepard and Co., 1852), v.

46. Ibid., 5.

47. Ibid., 37, 24.

48. SCP to Unknown, 1851, Polk Papers, LOC.

49. SCP to William Polk, March 17, 1852, Polk Papers, PC 75, 2, Correspondence 1850–1853, NCSA.

50. "A Visit to Mrs. James K. Polk," *Jeffersonian Democrat* (Monroe, WI), vol. 1, issue 15 (November 20, 1856): 1.

51. Nelson and Nelson, *Memorials,* 261–262; Jefferson Davis to SCP, March 8, 1856, Papers of Jefferson Davis, Rice University.

52. Nelson and Nelson, *Memorials,* 199.

53. James Buchanan to SCP, September 19, 1859, in John Bassett Moore, ed., *The Works of James Buchanan, Comprising His Speeches, State Papers, and Private Correspondence* (Philadelphia: J. B. Lippincott Co., 1908–11), vol. 10, 331–32.

54. "Mrs. President Polk," *NYH,* June 3, 1879.

55. SCP to James Buchanan, September 28, 1859, Papers of James Buchanan, Historical Society of Pennsylvania, Reel 38, Incoming Correspondence August 1859–December 1859.

56. James Buchanan to SCP, September 19, 1859, in Moore, *The Works of James Buchanan,* vol. 10, 331–32.

57. "Gossip," *Provincial Freeman* (Canada West), January 3, 1857.

58. SCP to James Buchanan, September 28, 1859, Papers of James Buchanan, Historical Society of Pennsylvania, Reel 38, Incoming Correspondence August 1859–December 1859.

CHAPTER 9. NEUTRAL GROUND

1. Many thanks to Tom Price for assistance with Sarah's mourning garb. On mourning conventions, see Karen Halttunen, *Confidence Men and Painted Women: A Study of Middle-Class Culture in America, 1830–1870* (New Haven, CT: Yale University Press, 1982), 136–38.

2. Anson Nelson and Fanny Nelson, *Memorials of Sarah Childress Polk: Wife of the Eleventh President of the United States* (New York: Anson D. F. Randolph and Co.,

1892), 11; 1860 Census, Census Place: Nashville Ward 5, Davidson, Tennessee, Roll M653_1246, p. 422, Image 648, Family History Library Film 805246.

3. Nelson and Nelson, *Memorials of Sarah Childress Polk*, 169–70.

4. Edwin T. Hardison, "In the Toils of War: Andrew Johnson and the Federal Occupation of Tennessee, 1862–1865" (Ph.D. diss., University of Tennessee, 1981), 58.

5. Ibid.; "The Union Ticket," *Nashville Patriot*, July 23, 1861; "House of Representatives," *Nashville Patriot*, October 30, 1861; B. F. Johnson, *Makers of America: Biographies of Leading Men of Thought and Action, the Men Who Constitute the Bone and Sinew of American Prosperity and Life* (Washington, DC: B. F. Johnson, 1915), vol. 1, 567.

6. Bobby L. Lovett, *The African-American History of Nashville, Tennessee, 1780–1930: Elites and Dilemmas* (Fayetteville: University of Arkansas Press, 1999), 44–45; "Colonel William H. Polk," *Nashville Union*, September 9, 1862.

7. Stephen V. Ash, *Middle Tennessee Society Transformed, 1860–1870: War and Peace in the Upper South* (Baton Rouge: Louisiana State University Press, 1988), 2–23; "Rattle and Snap," in *Tennessee Encyclopedia of History and Culture*, http://tennesseeencyclopedia.net/entry.php?rec=1109, accessed September 21, 2017; Glenn Robins, "Leonidas Polk," in *Encyclopedia of the American Civil War: A Political, Social, and Military History*, ed. David S. Heidler and Jeanne T. Heidler (New York: Norton, 2000), 1538.

8. Roy P. Stonesifer Jr., "Gideon Pillow: A Study in Egotism," *Tennessee Historical Quarterly* 25, no. 4 (Winter 1966): 345–49.

9. James McPherson, *Battle Cry of Freedom: The Civil War Era* (New York: Oxford University Press, 1988), 398–404.

10. *The Great Panic: Being Incidents Connected with Two Weeks of the War in Tennessee. By an Eye Witness* (Nashville: Johnson & Whiting, 1862), 19; McPherson, *Battle Cry of Freedom*, 401–3.

11. Walter Durham, *Nashville: The Occupied City, 1862–1863* (Knoxville: University of Tennessee Press, 2008), 3–4.

12. *Boston Post*, May 6, 1861; *Baltimore Sun*, May 7, 1861; Stanley F. Horn, "Nashville During the Civil War," *Tennessee Historical Quarterly* 4, no. 1 (March 1945): 5.

13. Nelson and Nelson, *Memorials of Sarah Childress Polk*, 170; *Clarksville Jefferson*, January 18, 1860, quoted in Ash, *Middle Tennessee Society Transformed*, 66. On the role of women in the Civil War, see Judith Giesberg, "Women," in *A Companion to the U.S. Civil War*, ed. Aaron Sheehan-Dean (New York: Wiley, 2014), vol. 2, 779–94. On female fears of rape during the war, see Crystal Nicole Feimster, *Southern Horrors: Women and the Politics of Rape and Lynching* (Cambridge, MA: Harvard University Press, 2009), 17–22.

14. 1860 Census, Census Place: Nashville Ward 5, Davidson, Tennessee, Roll M653_1246, p. 422, Image 648, Family History Library Film 805246. See the essays in LeeAnn Whites and Alecia Long, eds., *Occupied Women: Gender, Military Occupation, and the American Civil War* (Baton Rouge: Louisiana State University Press, 2009), particularly Lisa Tendrich Frank, "Bedrooms as Battlefields: The Role of Gender Politics in Sherman's March," 33–48.

15. George H. Armistead Jr. "The Void Provisions of a President's Will," *Tennessee Historical Quarterly* 15, no. 2 (1956): 138; Nelson and Nelson, *Memorials of Sarah Childress Polk*, 170. Southern women leveraged their "dependence" in order to gain protection from (and by) the Union army. Stephanie McCurry, *Confederate Reckoning: Power and Politics in the Civil War South* (Cambridge, MA: Harvard University Press, 2010), 97–98.

16. Annie Sehon to Bettie Kimberly, February 8, 1862, Kimberly Family Personal Correspondence, Manuscripts Dept., Southern Historical Collection, University of North Carolina at Chapel Hill, 2; *The Great Panic*, 20–22.

17. Adam Rankin Johnson, *The Partisan Rangers of the Confederate States Army* (Louisville, KY: Geo. G. Fetter Co., 1904), 70–71.

18. Rees W. Porter to Andrew Johnson, March 1, 1862, in *The Papers of Andrew Johnson*, vol. 5, *1861–1862*, ed. Leroy P. Graf, Ralph Haskins, and Patricia P. Clark (Knoxville: University of Tennessee Press, 1979), 168; Ash, *Middle Tennessee Society Transformed*, 85.

19. Horn, "Nashville During the Civil War," 11; Alfred Hudson Guernsey and Henry Mills Alden, *Harper's Pictorial History of the Great Rebellion*, Part 1 (Chicago: McDonnell Bros., 1866), 241; Nelson and Nelson, *Memorials of Sarah Childress Polk*, 170–71.

20. N. G. Markham to Eunice Markham, March 27, 1864, N. G. Markham Papers, Filson Historical Society.

21. William Haines Lytle, *For Honor, Glory and Union: The Mexican and Civil War Letters of Brig. Gen. William Haines Lytle*, ed. Ruth C. Carter (Lexington: University Press of Kentucky, 1999), 148; N. G. Markham to Eunice Markham, Marcy 27, 1864, N. G. Markham Papers, Filson Historical Society; Dan Lee, *Kentuckian in Blue: A Biography of Major General Lovell Harrison Rousseau* (Jefferson, NC: McFarland, 2010), 57; "Mrs. Ex-President Polk," *Galveston Daily News* (Houston), October 25, 1876; Lytle, *For Honor, Glory and Union*, 36.

22. "Mrs. Polk the Traitor," *Daily Cleveland Herald*, April 26, 1862; *Boston Daily Advertiser*, March 27, 1862; *Vermont Chronicle*, April 1, 1862.

23. "From Nashville. The dejected secessionists," *New York Evening Post*, March 7, 1862.

24. Many northerners were concerned that conservative generals treated the southern gentry with kid gloves, so critiquing Sarah's potential loyalty to the Confederacy was also a way to critique the behavior of generals seen as not hard enough on the South. Mark Grimsley, *The Hard Hand of War: Union Military Policy Toward Southern Civilians* (New York: Cambridge University Press, 1995).

25. Elizabeth R. Varon, *Southern Lady, Yankee Spy: The True Story of Elizabeth Van Lew, a Union Agent in the Heart of the Confederacy* (New York: Oxford University Press, 2003), 52–54.

26. *Columbus (GA) Daily Enquirer*, March 29, 1862.

27. John White Geary, *A Politician Goes to War: The Civil War Letters of John White Geary*, ed. William A. Blair (University Park: Penn State University Press, 1995), 125.

28. Mrs. John Trotwood Moore, "The Tennessee Historical Society, 1849–1918," *Tennessee Historical Quarterly* 3, no. 3 (September 1944): 195–225, quote on 207; Nelson and Nelson, *Memorials of Sarah Childress Polk*, 175, 263.

29. "From the Tennessee Capital," *New York Times*, March 5, 1862; Lee, *Kentuckian in Blue*, 57; Nelson and Nelson, *Memorials of Sarah Childress Polk*, 172; Annie Sehon to Bettie Kimberly, February 8, 1862, Kimberly Family Personal Correspondence, Manuscripts Dept., Southern Historical Collection, University of North Carolina at Chapel Hill, 2; Kate S. Carney Diary, May 24, 1862, Call number 139, Manuscripts Dept., Southern Historical Collection, University of North Carolina at Chapel Hill.

30. Lee, *Kentuckian in Blue*, 57; Nelson and Nelson, *Memorials of Sarah Childress Polk*, 172–73.

31. "From the Tennessee Capital," *New York Times*, March 5, 1862; "From the North," *Richmond Times-Dispatch*, March 10, 1862.

32. Nelson and Nelson, *Memorials of Sarah Childress Polk*, 175.

33. Lovett, *The African-American History of Nashville*, 49.

34. Brig. Gen. William Nelson to Major General Don Carlos Buell, July 24, 1862, quoted in Anne Karen Berler, "A Most Unpleasant Part of Your Duties: Military Occupation in Four Southern Cities, 1861–1865" (Ph.D. diss., University of North Carolina at Chapel Hill, 2013), 71, 63–65.

35. William E. Blair, "Johnson in Civil War Nashville," talk for the Richards Civil War Era Center Executive Tour, May 18, 2017, paper in possession of author.

36. William L. Barney, "Hood's Tennessee Campaign," in *The Oxford Encyclopedia of the Civil War* (New York: Oxford University Press, 2011), 165–67.

37. James Birney Shaw, *History of the Tenth Regiment Indiana Volunteer Infantry* (Lafayette, IN: Burt Haywood Co., 1912), 163; Durham, *Nashville: The Occupied City*, 66.

38. Ash, *Middle Tennessee Society Transformed*, 80, 87–89; Chandra Manning, *Troubled Refuge: Struggling for Freedom in the Civil War* (New York: Knopf, 2016), 99–102.

39. Ash, *Middle Tennessee Society Transformed*, 93.

40. Quoted in Berler, "A Most Unpleasant Part of Your Duties," 72–73.

41. *New York Tribune*, August 8, 1862; Edwin T. Hardison, "In the Toils of War: Andrew Johnson and the Federal Occupation of Tennessee, 1862–1865" (Ph.D. diss., University of Tennessee, 1981), 118–19.

42. Hardison, "In the Toils of War," 84–95.

43. Berler, "A Most Unpleasant Part of Your Duties," 85–91; Walter T. Durham, *Reluctant Partners: Nashville and the Union, 1863–1865* (Knoxville: University of Tennessee Press, 20089), 132–36.

44. Horn, "Nashville During the Civil War," 16; Berler, "A Most Unpleasant Part of Your Duties," 91–92.

45. *Boston Post*, May 6, 1861; William E. Blair, *With Malice Toward Some: Treason and Loyalty in the Civil War Era* (Chapel Hill: University of North Carolina Press, 2014), 139–40.

46. SCP to General Miller, August 2, 1864, Miller Papers, Box 2, Folder 12, Stanford University; Andrew Johnson to William L. Utley, October 30, 1863, in *The Papers of Andrew Johnson*, vol. 6, *1862–1864*, ed. Leroy P. Graf and Ralph W. Haskins (Knoxville: University of Tennessee Press, 1983), 444–46.

47. "An Interview with Mrs. Polk," *Nashville Daily Times and True Union*, March 3, 1864.

48. Ibid.

49. Ibid.

50. M. C. Bass to Generals Harding and Barrow, June 24, 1862, Harding-Jackson Papers, 1809–1938, Tennessee Historical Society (Nashville); Durham, *Nashville: The Occupied City*, 176.

51. M. C. Bass to Generals Harding and Barrow, June 24, 1862; Durham, *Nashville: The Occupied City*, 176.

52. *Jackson (MI) Weekly Citizen*, April 23, 1862; "More of the Nashville Ladies," *Daily Morning News* (Savannah, GA), April 14, 1862.

53. Petition 108, Polk Papers, TSLA.

54. SCP to Capt. Goodwin, December 22, 1863, Small Collection, AC No. 77–75, TSLA.

55. SCP to David Tod, April 17, 1862, Polk Correspondence, UT.

56. SCP to Andrew Johnson, February 22, 1855, Andrew Johnson Papers, LOC.

57. 1860 Census, Census Place: Fort Camp, Rutherford, Tennessee, Roll M653_1271, p. 119, Image 241, Family History Library Film 80527; 1860 Census, Census Place: Murfreesboro, Rutherford, Tennessee, Roll M653_1271, p. 162, Image 330, Family History Library Film 805271; Hardison, "In the Toils of War," 115; Kate S. Carney Diary, May 12, 1862, Southern Historical Collection, University of North Carolina at Chapel Hill.

58. "From Rutherford County Citizens," May 22, 1862, in *The Papers of Andrew Johnson*, vol. 5, 410–11; Kate S. Carney Diary, June 8, 1862; SCP to Andrew Johnson, May 17, 1862, Andrew Johnson Papers, LOC; SCP to Andrew Johnson, October 27, 1864, Andrew Johnson Papers, LOC.

59. John Williams Childress, "The Childress Family of Tennessee" (typescript, 1960), Rutherford County Historical Society publication no. 16 (Winter 1981); Annie S. Gilchrist, *Some Representative Women of Tennessee* (Nashville: McQuiddy Printing Co., 1902), 12–14.

60. Lytle, *For Honor, Glory and Union*, 172.

61. SCP to Mrs. Porter, n.d., Polk Papers, TSLA; Naomi Hays to Lucy Polk, July 21, 1863, Polk Papers, PC 75, 7, Correspondence undated, NCSA.

62. Naomi Hays to Lucy Polk, July 21, 1863, Polk Papers, PC 75, 7, Correspondence undated, NCSA.

63. Childress, "The Childress Family of Tennessee."

64. Andrew Johnson to William L. Utley, October 30, 1863, in *The Papers of Andrew Johnson*, vol. 6, 445–46; SCP to David G. Barniby, March 22, 1864, National Archives, Cotton and Captured Property Records, No. 905; SCP to J. G. Parkhurst, March 19, 1864, John G. Parkhurst Papers, Microfilm, 1860–1909, Bentley Historical Library, University of Michigan; SCP to J. G. Parkhurst, March 29, 1864, John G. Parkhurst Papers, Microfilm, 1860–1909, Bentley Historical Library, University of Michigan. On the opportunities for provost marshals to become "petty dictators," see Blair, *With Malice for Some*, 100–127.

65. David G. Barniby (?) to C. A. Fuller, April 4, 1864, National Archives, Cotton and Captured Property Records, No. 905; S. P. Chase to SCP, April 13, 1864, National Archives, entry 57, Letters Sent to Collectors and Assessors of Internal Revenue, State Officers, Banks and Corporations (GS Series); SCP to William Parkhurst, June 15, 1865, John G. Parkhurst Papers, microfilm, 1860–1909, Bentley Historical Library, University of Michigan.

66. McPherson, *Battle Cry of Freedom*, 313, 382.

67. SCP to Andrew Johnson, January 23, 1865 (enclosing Pickett & Joy to SCP, January 5, 1865), National Archives RG 56, Captured Cotton & Abandoned Property, May–June 1865, Treasury Dept., Box 13; Pickett & Joy, November 21, 1864, National Archives, Cotton and Captured Property Records, No. 905.

68. SCP to Andrew Johnson, January 23, 1865 (enclosing Pickett & Joy to SCP, January 5, 1865), National Archives RG 56, Captured Cotton & Abandoned Property, May–June 1865, Treasury Dept., Box 13; Pickett & Joy, November 21, 1864, National Archives, Cotton and Captured Property Records, No. 905.

69. SCP to W. W. Orme, December 20, 1864, National Archives, Cotton and Captured Property Records, No. 2273.

70. Deposition of Jane Polk, January 13, 1898, Case of Dafney Polk, Case Files of Approved Pension Applications of Widows and Other Veterans of the Army and Navy Who Served Mainly in the Civil War and the War with Spain, National Archives, Record Group 15; William Dusinberre, *Slavemaster President: The Double Career of James Polk* (New York: Oxford University Press, 2003), 107–10.

71. Nelson and Nelson, *Memorials of Sarah Childress Polk*, 171.

72. SCP to Andrew Johnson, March 3, 1865, Andrew Johnson Papers, LOC.

73. SCP to Andrew Johnson, June 13, 1865, Andrew Johnson Papers, LOC; Durham, *Reluctant Partners*, 108.

74. SCP to Andrew Johnson, July 28, 1865, in *The Papers of Andrew Johnson*, vol. 8, *May–August 1865*, ed. Paul H. Bergeron (Knoxville: University of Tennessee Press, 1989),

494. The pardon was issued on January 15, 1867. Amnesty Papers (M1003, Roll 48), Tenn., John C. Brown, RG94, National Archives.

75. Deposition of Charlie Avent, January 15, 1898, Case of Dafney Polk, Case Files of Approved Pension Applications of Widows and Other Veterans of the Army and Navy Who Served Mainly in the Civil War and the War with Spain, National Archives, Record Group 15.

76. G. W. Peel testimony, March 1, 1864, Sarah K. Polk, claim no. 14664, Southern Claims Commission, NARA M1407, Davidson, TN; Deposition of Jane Polk, January 13, 1898, Case of Dafney Polk, Case Files of Approved Pension Applications of Widows and Other Veterans of the Army and Navy Who Served Mainly in the Civil War and the War with Spain, National Archives, Record Group 15; Noralee Frankel, *Freedom's Women: Black Women and Families in Civil War Mississippi* (Bloomington: Indiana University Press, 1999), 18; Steven Hahn, *A Nation Under Our Feet: Black Political Struggles in the Rural South from Slavery to the Great Migration* (Cambridge, MA: Harvard University Press, 2003), 91–93; Lovett, *The African-American History of Nashville*, 58–60.

77. Deposition of Jane Polk, January 13, 1898, Case of Dafney Polk, Case Files of Approved Pension Applications of Widows and Other Veterans of the Army and Navy Who Served Mainly in the Civil War and the War with Spain, National Archives, Record Group 15; Frankel, *Freedom's Women*, 16–25.

78. Deposition of Lewis Polk, January 12, 1898, Case of Dafney Polk, Case Files of Approved Pension Applications of Widows and Other Veterans of the Army and Navy Who Served Mainly in the Civil War and the War with Spain, National Archives, Record Group 15; Gideon Pillow to JKP, May 1, 1846, James K. Polk, *Correspondence of James K. Polk*, vol. 11, *1846*, ed. Wayne Cutler (Knoxville: University of Tennessee Press, 2009), 150; 61st Regiment, U.S. Colored Infantry, Company E, Compiled Military Service Records of Volunteer Union Soldiers Who Served the United States Colored Troops: 56th–138th USCT Infantry, 1864–1866, National Archives, Record Group 94, M589 Roll 69; Lovett, *The African-American History of Nashville*, 58–62.

79. Lewis Polk Affidavit, June 2, 1887, Case of Dafney Polk, Case Files of Approved Pension Applications of Widows and Other Veterans of the Army and Navy Who Served Mainly in the Civil War and the War with Spain, National Archives, Record Group 15; Deposition of Lewis Polk, January 12, 1898, Deposition of Dafney Polk, November 3, 1888, Case of Dafney Polk, Case Files of Approved Pension Applications of Widows and Other Veterans of the Army and Navy Who Served Mainly in the Civil War and the War with Spain, National Archives, Record Group 15.

80. "Unknown Smith's Expedition Battle of Tupelo," Broadside, July 22, 1864, Gilder Lehrman Collection, Gilder Lehrman Institute of American History, New York, https://www.gilderlehrman.org/collections/98dbcfba-72ba-43ed-8b67-38971990 5588?back=/mweb/search%3Fneedle%3DGLC06157%2A%2526fields%3D_t30100 1010, accessed October 11, 2017.

81. Ira Berlin, *The Long Emancipation: The Demise of Slavery in the United States* (Cambridge, MA: Harvard University Press, 2015), 174.

82. Lisa Childs, "Polks Serving in 61st Regiment, Co. E, US Colored Infantry, and History Thereof," https://www.ancestry.com/family-tree/tree/73259728/story/0583 ddfb-65a8-4440-950d-7b9c567309c3?pid=&pgn=32798&usePUBJs=true&_phsrc =iuE133, Ancestry.com; Manuel Polk Pension File, U.S. Civil War Pension Index, General Index to Pension Files, 1861–1934, NARA; Deposition of Jane Polk, January 13, 1898, Case of Dafney Polk, Case Files of Approved Pension Applications of Widows and Other Veterans of the Army and Navy Who Served Mainly in the Civil

War and the War with Spain, National Archives, Record Group 15; 1870 Census, Township 24, Yalobusha, Mississippi, Roll M593_754, p. 107B.

83. Many freedpeople returned to their neighborhoods at war's end. Anthony E. Kaye, *Joining Places: Slave Neighborhoods in the Old South* (Chapel Hill: University of North Carolina Press, 2007), 210–14; Frankel, *Freedom's Women*, x–xi, 161–72.

84. Case of Dafney Polk, Case Files of Approved Pension Applications of Widows and Other Veterans of the Army and Navy Who Served Mainly in the Civil War and the War with Spain, National Archives, Record Group 15.

85. Blair, "Johnson in Civil War Nashville."

86. SCP to Mrs. Porter, n.d., Polk Papers, TSLA; Nashville City Cemetery Interments (1846–1979)," Data.Nashville.gov, https://data.nashville.gov/Genealogy/Historic-Nashville-City-Cemetery-Interments-1846-1/iwbm-8it6, accessed February 18, 2018; Manning, *Troubled Refuge*, 99–102.

87. SCP to Andrew Johnson, September 23, 1864, Andrew Johnson Papers, LOC; Employment Rolls and Nonpayment Rolls of Negroes Employed in the Defenses of Nashville, Tennessee, 1862–1863, TSLA; Manning, *Troubled Refuge*, 99–102.

88. M. C. Bass to Generals Harding and Barrow, June 24, 1862, Harding-Jackson Papers, 1809–1938, Tennessee Historical Society; Durham, *Nashville: The Occupied City*, 176; Naomi Hays to Lucy Polk, July 21, 1863, Polk Papers, PC 75, 7, Correspondence undated, NCSA.

89. 1870 Census, Census Place: Nashville Ward 5, Davidson, Tennessee, Roll M593_1523, p. 303A, Image 303131, Family History Library Film 553022; 1870 Census, Census Place: Nashville Ward 5, Davidson, Tennessee, Roll M593_1523, p. 303A, Image 303131, Family History Library Film 553022.

90. "Personal and General," *Daily Arkansas Gazette* (Little Rock), August 21, 1880.

91. "Elias Polk's Death," *St. Louis Post-Dispatch*, January 17, 1887.

92. Ibid.; Geary, *A Politician Goes to War*, 152.

93. Lovett, *The African-American History of Nashville*, 78–79; Jesse Holland, *The Invisibles: The Untold Story of African American Slaves in the White House* (Guilford, CT: Rowman and Littlefield, 2016), 173; "Elias Polk's Death," *St. Louis Post-Dispatch*, January 17, 1887.

94. "Elias Polk's Death," *St. Louis Post-Dispatch*, January 17, 1887; "HERE are the names of some of the more prominent colored men who have declared for Greeley," *Daily Arkansas Gazette*, July 31, 1872; "Andy's Victory," *Daily Evening Bulletin* (San Francisco), February 4, 1875, 19th Century U.S. Newspapers, Gale, https://www.gale.com/c/19th-century-us-newspapers, accessed November 10, 2016. See also *Wisconsin State Register* (Portage), February 6, 1875; *Lowell (MA) Daily Citizen and News*, February 9, 1875. "Mr. Alexander Williams, of Boston, owns a cane which, it is said, he is about to present to General Hancock," *Georgia Weekly Telegraph*, (Macon), August 20, 1880.

95. "Uncle Elias," *Southwestern Christian Advocate*, May 26, 1887; *United States Department of the Interior, Official Register of the United States, Containing a List of Officers and Employees in the Civil, Military and Naval Service, on the First of July, 1881*, vol. 1 (Washington, DC: Government Printing Office, 1881), 10; E. B. Wight, and Special Correspondence of the Inter Ocean, "Washington Chat," *Daily Inter Ocean* (Chicago), December 26, 1886; "Uncle Elias," *Southwestern Christian Advocate*, May 26, 1887. Many Americans saw echoes of Polk in Cleveland. See Allan Nevins, *Grover Cleveland: A Study in Courage* (New York: Dodd, Mead, 1966), 271, 282–83; Denis Tilden Lynch, *Grover Cleveland: A Man Four-Square* (New York: Horace Liveright, 1932), 232.

96. "Personal and General," *Daily Arkansas Gazette*, August 21, 1880; E. B. Wight, and Special Correspondence of the Inter Ocean, "Washington Chat," *Daily Inter Ocean*, December 26, 1886; "Uncle Elias," *Southwestern Christian Advocate*, May 26, 1887; "Multiple News Items," *Milwaukee Daily Journal*, December 31, 1886; "Elias Polk's Death," *St. Louis Post-Dispatch*, January 17, 1887.

97. "President Polk's Body Servant," *St. Louis Globe-Democrat*, January 1, 1887.

98. Nelson and Nelson, *Memorials of Sarah Childress Polk*, 176–77.

99. *New Orleans Times-Picayune*, May 12, 1868; William A. Blair, *Cities of the Dead: Contesting the Memory of the Civil War in the South, 1865–1914* (Chapel Hill: University of North Carolina Press, 2004), 77–105.

100. Drew Gilpin Faust, *Mothers of Invention: Women of the Slaveholding South in the American Civil War* (Chapel Hill: University of North Carolina Press, 1996); McCurry, *Confederate Reckoning;* "Honor for the South," *Confederate Veteran* I (January 1893): 17.

101. LeeAnn Whites, *Gender Matters: Civil War, Reconstruction, and the Making of the New South* (New York: Palgrave Macmillan, 2005), 86–91, quote on 90.

102. Polk Family Home Collection.

103. John Russell Young, *Around the World with General Grant* (New York: American News Company, 1879), vol. 2, 447–48; Polk Family Home Collection.

104. SCP to Andrew Johnson, March 16, 1866, Andrew Johnson Papers, LOC; Henry S. Randall to Andrew Johnson, November 21, 1865, *The Papers of Andrew Johnson*, vol. 9, *September 1865–January 1866*, ed. Paul H. Bergeron (Knoxville: University of Tennessee Press, 1991), 413.

105. Henry S. Randall to Andrew Johnson, November 21, 1865, *The Papers of Andrew Johnson*, vol. 9, 413.

CHAPTER 10. INFLUENCE

1. "An Interview with Mrs. Polk," *Nashville Daily Times and True Union*, March 3, 1864; Laura Holloway, *The Ladies of the White House* (New York: U.S. Pub. Co., 1870), 459, 462; Anson Nelson and Fanny Nelson, *Memorials of Sarah Childress Polk: Wife of the Eleventh President of the United States* (New York: Anson D. F. Randolph and Co., 1892), 184.

2. "President Polk's Widow," *Daily Inter Ocean*, quoted in the *Nashville Republican Banner*, October 31, 1874; William Haines Lytle, *For Honor, Glory and Union: The Mexican and Civil War Letters of Brig. Gen. William Haines Lytle*, ed. Ruth C. Carter (Lexington: University Press of Kentucky, 1999), 148.

3. "President Polk's Widow," *Nashville Republican Banner*, October 31, 1874; Holloway, *The Ladies of the White House*, 458.

4. E. B. Wight, and Special Correspondence of the Inter Ocean, "Washington Chat," *Daily Inter Ocean* (Chicago), December 26, 1886; "President Polk's Widow," *Nashville Republican Banner*, October 31, 1874; Holloway, *The Ladies of the White House*, 458.

5. "Mrs. President Polk," *Cincinnati Daily Enquirer*, December 27, 1869; *Nashville Union and American*, January 2, 1867; "Mrs. James K. Polk," *NYH*, January 2, 1886; "Mrs. Ex-President P.," *Nashville Union and American*, January 2, 1872. Thanks to Alexis McCrossen for her analysis of New Year celebrations in Washington, D.C., and Nashville.

6. Elizabeth Fry Page, "Polk Memorial Hall," *Bob Taylor's Magazine* I, no. 6 (September 1905): 651–59; Holloway, *The Ladies of the White House*, 458; Nelson and Nelson, *Memorials*, 181–87.

7. "Political and General Notes," *Worcester (MA) Daily Spy,* February 23, 1881.

8. "The Grangers Visit Mrs. Ex-President Polk," *NDA,* November 19, 1884.

9. "Mrs. Ex-President Polk," *NDA,* September 5, 1883.

10. SCP to William H. Polk, April 25, 1875, Polk Papers, PC 75, 4, Correspondence 1875–1877, NCSA; SCP to Lucy Tasker Polk, March 31, 1877, Polk Papers, PC 75, 4, Correspondence, 1875–1877, NCSA; "Maj. John W. Childress," *NDA,* October 9, 1884.

11. SCP to William H. Polk, April 25, 1875, Polk Papers, PC 75, 4, Correspondence 1875–1877, NCSA; Nelson and Nelson, *Memorials of Sarah Childress Polk,* 220.

12. SCP to William H. Polk, March 31, 1877, Polk Papers, PC 75, 4, Correspondence 1875–1877, NCSA.

13. SCP to Lucy Tasker Polk, March 31, 1877, Polk Papers, PC 75, 4, Correspondence, 1875–1877, NCSA; SCP to William H. Polk, March 31, 1877, Polk Papers, PC 75, 4, Correspondence 1875–1877, NCSA.

14. SCP to William H. Polk, April 25, 1875, January 28, 1876, May 4, 1876, March 31, 1877, Polk Papers, PC 75, 4, Correspondence 1875–1877, NCSA.

15. J. S. Ingram, *The Centennial Exposition Described and Illustrated: Being a Concise and Graphic Description of This Grand Enterprise Commemorative of the First Centennary of American Independence* (Philadelphia: Hubbard Bros., 1876), 116.

16. Nelson and Nelson, *Memorials of Sarah Childress Polk,* 183; "Mrs. Ex-President Polk," *Galveston Daily News* (Houston), October 25, 1876; "Obituary," *Boston Daily Journal,* August 14, 1891; SCP to William H. Polk, April 25, 1875, Polk Papers, PC 75, 4, Correspondence 1875–1877, NCSA.

17. HR Misc. Doc No. 251, 43rd Cong., 1st Sess. (1874), 2; Judith Giesberg, "The Fortieth Congress, Southern Women, and the Gender Politics of Postwar Occupation," in *Occupied Women: Gender, Military Occupation, and the American Civil War,* ed. LeeAnn Whites and Alecia Long (Baton Rouge: Louisiana State University Press, 2009), 185–94.

18. HR Misc. Doc No. 251, 43rd Cong., 1st Sess. (1874), 1; "Loyalty of the Widow of President Polk," *Critic-Record* (Washington, DC), issue 1761 (April 20, 1874): 4.

19. *Boston Journal,* published as *Boston Evening Journal,* vol. XLIII, issue 14350 (July 18, 1876): 4; "An Act for the Relief of Mrs. James K. Polk of Nashville, Tennessee," August 15, 1876, *The Statutes at Large of the United States of America, from December, 1875, to March, 1877, and Recent Treaties, Postal Conventions, and Executive Proclamations,* vol. XIX (Washington, DC: Government Printing Office, 1877); "Centennial Notes," *Frank Leslie's Illustrated Newspaper* (New York), November 4, 1876.

20. "Editorial Brevities," *Richmond Enquirer,* vol. LXVIII, issue 106 (May 3, 1874): 2.

21. "Death of Ex-Treasurer Polk," *New York Times,* March 1, 1884.

22. Ibid.; "Tennessee's Loss," *NYH,* January 8, 1883. Barbara Bennett Peterson's claim that Sarah's "maternal instinct" was "well rewarded" when the "children cared for by the Polks became outstanding citizens" seems not to extend to Marshall. Peterson, *Sarah Childress Polk, First Lady of Tennessee and Washington* (Huntington, NY: Nova History Publications, 2002), 33; "The Wives of the Presidents," *Boston Herald,* reprinted in the *Wheeling (WV) Register,* published as *Wheeling Sunday Register,* vol. 22, issue 131 (November 30, 1884): 6.

23. Page, "Polk Memorial Hall."

24. "Nashville Reading Club," *NDA,* October 23, 1875; "A Social Event at the Polk Mansion," *Baltimore Sun,* vol. XCVIII, issue 4 (November 20, 1885): 4; "Society," *NDA,* November 20, 1885.

25. "Mrs. James K. Polk," *NYH,* January 2, 1886.

26. "Society" *NDA,* December 6, 1888; SCP to Frances Folsom Cleveland, February 4,

1886, Minnesota Historical Society; "Mrs. James K. Polk, the First Lady in the Land Thirty Five Years Ago—A Visit, and Pleasant Reminiscences of the White House," *Indianapolis Sentinel*, February 21, 1881.

27. "Mr. and Mrs. Cleveland," *Daily Inter Ocean* (Chicago), October 17, 1887; Denis Tilden Lynch, *Grover Cleveland: A Man Four-Square* (New York: Horace Liveright, 1932), 347; "Calling on Mrs. James K. Polk," *New York Tribune*, published as *New-York Tribune*, October 17, 1887, 5.

28. SCP to William H. Polk, April 25, 1875, Polk Papers, PC 75, 4, Correspondence 1875–1877, NCSA.

29. Occie Brooks to S. C. Polk, February 25, 1888, Huntington Library Manuscripts Collection, HM 28835.

30. S. C. Polk to Occie Brooks, February, 1888, Huntington Library Manuscripts Collection, HM 28835.

31. Richard Rush, "Report of Lieut. Richard Rush, U.S. Navy," November 23, 1888, No. 16, Centennial Exposition at Cincinnati, in *Annual Report of the Secretary of the Navy for the Year 1888* (Washington, DC: GPO, 1888), 543.

32. "Mrs Ex prest Polk opened the exposition by signal from Nashville on Obsy time gong. Noon signal rec and clock connected," telegram sent July 4, 1888, received at 11 p.m. from A. B. Clements, Cincinnati, Ohio, to R. L. Pythian, United States Naval Observatory, National Archives RG 78 E-15, USNO Telegrams Received '86–'06; Alexis McCrossen, "Time Balls: Marking Modern Times in Urban America, 1877–1922," *Material Culture Review / Revue de la culture matérielle* (June 2000), https://journals.lib.unb.ca/index.php/MCR/article/view/17860/22101, accessed June 8, 2015.

33. "Cincinnati's Centennial," *NYH*, July 5, 1888; Tom Price, "Comfort in My Retirement: Polk Place," *White House History* 33 (Summer 2013); "Cincinnati's Centennial," *NYH*, July 5, 1888.

34. "An Hour with the Telephone," *NDA*, September 2, 1877.

35. "Cincinnati's Centennial," *NYH*, July 5, 1888.

36. Ibid.

37. U. S. Grant, *Personal Memoirs of U. S. Grant* (New York, 1885), 22–24; William S. McFeely, *Grant: A Biography* (New York: Norton, 1981), 35; Richard Bruce Winders, *Mr. Polk's Army* (College Station: Texas A&M Press, 1997): 202–6; Massachusetts—General Court—House of Representatives, "Documents Relating to the U.S.-Mexican War" (Boston, 1847), 3.

38. "Mrs. James K. Polk, the First Lady in the Land Thirty Five Years Ago—A Visit, and Pleasant Reminiscences of the White House," *Indianapolis Sentinel*, February 21, 1881.

39. Ibid.; *Baltimore Sun*, vol. XCV, issue 153, supplement 2 (November 11, 1884).

40. "News and Other Items," *Portland (ME) Daily Press*, March 12, 1875; "Mrs. President Polk," *NYH*, June 3, 1879; "Forty Years Ago," *St. Louis Globe-Democrat*, issue 168 (November 6, 1884): column F, p. 6. Of course, the United States only gained Alta California in the U.S.-Mexico War. President Polk hoped for Baja California as well, but didn't get it. Amy Greenberg, *A Wicked War: Polk, Clay, Lincoln, and the 1846 U.S. Invasion of Mexico* (New York: Vintage, 2012), 259–60.

41. *The Vedette* 1, no. 9 (June 15, 1880): 7; Wallace E. Davies, "The Mexican War Veterans as an Organized Group," *Mississippi Valley Historical Review* 35, no. 2 (September 1948): 221–38. The Mexican War service pension act was signed into law on January 29, 1887. By the end of that year there were a little more than eight thousand recipients on the pension rolls. The number of recipients reached its peak in 1890 when more than seventeen thousand veterans and more than six thousand widows

were on the rolls. The amount of the pension was eight dollars a month. After the turn of the century, this amount was raised to twelve dollars, later to twenty dollars. On pension abuses, see "Five Separate Pensions," *New York Times,* March 10, 1898; *Philadelphia Record,* March 6, 1898; *The Independent,* January 20, 1898.

42. "Mrs. James K. Polk," *Raleigh (NC) Register,* issue 38 (November 12, 1884): column C.

43. "Mrs. James K. Polk, the First Lady in the Land Thirty Five Years Ago—A Visit, and Pleasant Reminiscences of the White House," *Indianapolis Sentinel,* February 21, 1881.

44. Ibid.

45. Ibid.

46. Elizabeth Fries Ellet, *The Queens of American Society* (New York: Scribners, 1867), 222–23.

47. George Bancroft—J. G. Harris, April 8, 1887, Bancroft Collection, New York Public Library, CS; J. G. Harris to George Bancroft, April 10, 1887, Bancroft Collection, New York Public Library, CS.

48. "Octogenarians in Society," in *Milwaukee Daily Journal,* April 18, 1887.

49. "Mrs. President Polk," *NYH,* June 3, 1879; J. G. Harris to George Bancroft, April 25, 1887, Bancroft Collection, New York Public Library, CS.

50. Nelson and Nelson, *Memorials of Sarah Childress Polk,* 261, 209.

51. J. Henry Hager to Sarah Childress Polk, February 11, 1888, Huntington Library Manuscripts Collection, HM 28834.

52. Ibid.

53. Holloway, *The Ladies of the White House,* 461; William Heth Whitsitt, "Annals of a Scotch-Irish Family: The Whitsitts of Nashville," *American Historical Magazine and Tennessee Historical Society Quarterly* 9 (1904): 240.

54. *Appletons' Cyclopaedia of American Biography,* vol. 5, *Pickering-Sumter,* revised ed., ed. James Grant Wilson and John Fiske (New York: D. Appleton and Co., 1888), 55–56.

55. Gen. Grant Wilson to S. C. Polk, February 23, 1888, Huntington Library Manuscripts Collection, HM 28834; J. W. Weidermeyer to Sarah Childress Polk, February 1, 1888.

56. S. C. Polk to Gen. Grant Wilson, February 27, 1888, Huntington Library Manuscripts Collection, HM 28834. Grant eventually did write an addendum.

57. *Appletons' Cyclopaedia of American Biography,* vol. 5, 50–55.

58. Anson Nelson to J. G. M. Ramsey, July 4, 1877, James Gettys McGready Ramsey Papers, John Hodges Library, UT; E. B. Wight, and Special Correspondence of the Inter Ocean, "Washington Chat," *Daily Inter Ocean* (Chicago), December 26, 1886.

59. Lisa Tetrault, *The Myth of Seneca Falls: Memory and the Women's Suffrage Movement, 1848–1898* (Chapel Hill: University of North Carolina Press, 2003), 86–90; Alison M. Parker, *Purifying America: Women, Cultural Reform, and Pro-Censorship Activism, 1873–1933* (Urbana: University of Illinois Press, 1997), 26–27.

60. Holly Berkley Fletcher, *Gender and the American Temperance Movement of the Nineteenth Century* (New York: Routledge, 2008), 108; Tetrault, *The Myth of Seneca Falls,* 86–90; Karen J. Blair, *The Clubwoman as Feminist: True Womanhood Redefined, 1868–1914* (New York: Holmes & Meier, 1980), 117.

61. Ruth Bordin, *Frances Willard: A Biography* (Chapel Hill: University of North Carolina Press, 1986), 112.

62. Nelson and Nelson, *Memorials of Sarah Childress Polk,* 284; "Mrs. James K. Polk," *Daily Arkansas Gazette* (Little Rock), December 6, 1881.

63. Bordin, *Frances Willard*, 113–14; Fletcher, *Gender and the American Temperance Movement*, 116–17.

64. Bordin, *Frances Willard*, 114; "Mrs. James K. Polk," *Daily Arkansas Gazette*, December 6, 1881; Fletcher, *Gender and the American Temperance Movement*, 116–18.

65. "Mrs. James K. Polk", *NDA*, October 9, 1881.

66. "Mrs. James K. Polk," *News and Observer* (Raleigh, NC), August 14, 1886.

67. On northern visions of sectional reconciliation, see Nina Silber, *The Romance of Reunion: Northerners and the South, 1865–1900* (Chapel Hill: University of North Carolina Press, 1993).

68. Nelson and Nelson, *Memorials of Sarah Childress Polk*, 215–16.

69. Ibid., 214–16.

70. Daughters of the American Revolution, *Lineage Book of the Charter Members of the Daughters of the American Revolution*, vol. 1 (1890–1891) (Harrisburg, PA: Harrisburg Publishing Co., 1895), x; Nelson and Nelson, *Memorials of Sarah Childress Polk*, 266.

71. Sara A. Gordon, *"Make It Yourself": Home Sewing, Gender, and Culture, 1890–1930* (New York: Columbia University Press, 2009), 37–43.

72. E. B. Wight, and Special Correspondence of the Inter Ocean, "Washington Chat," *Daily Inter Ocean* (Chicago), December 26, 1886.

73. SCP to H. Jackson, April 12, 1882, Polk Papers, TSLA.

74. E. B. Wight, and Special Correspondence of the Inter Ocean, "Washington Chat," *Daily Inter Ocean* (Chicago), December 26, 1886.

75. "Forty Years Ago," *St. Louis Globe-Democrat*, issue 168 (November 6, 1884): column F, p. 6.

76. Ibid.; "Belva Lockwood," *New York Times*, May 20, 1917.

77. "Campaigning in Tennessee," *NYH*, October 20, 1886; "Cincinnati's Centennial," *NYH*, July 5, 1888.

78. "The Country's Teachers," *Augusta (GA) Chronicle*, July 19, 1889; Nelson and Nelson, *Memorials of Sarah Childress Polk*, 256; "Mrs. James K. Polk's 86th Birthday," *Trenton (NJ) Evening Times*, published as *Trenton Times*, September 5, 1889.

79. Mrs. John Trotwood Moore, "The Tennessee Historical Society, 1849–1918," *Tennessee Historical Quarterly* 3, no. 3 (September 1944): 201, 216–17, quote on 216; Sarah Polk's will, March 28, 1885, AGS 143–145/Davidson County, Roll 444, Book 31, TSLA.

80. Nelson and Nelson, *Memorials of Sarah Childress Polk*, 268–70.

81. Ibid., 274–75.

82. "Mrs. James K. Polk Dead," *Philadelphia Inquirer*, August 15, 1891; Nelson and Nelson, *Memorials of Sarah Childress Polk*, 276–80; "President Polk's Widow Dead," *New York Tribune*, August 15, 1891.

83. "Mrs. James K. Polk Dies at Nashville," *NYH*, August 15, 1891.

84. "Mrs. Polk's Will Probated," *Birmingham Age-Herald*, October 5, 1891, Polk Papers, TSLA; "President Polk's Widow Dead," *New York Tribune*, published as *New-York Tribune*, August 15, 1891.

85. George H. Armistead Jr., "The Void Provisions of a President's Will," *Tennessee Historical Quarterly* 15, no. 2 (1956): 138.

86. Daniel R. Goodloe to "My Dear Madam" (likely Lucy Polk), May 26, 1892, Polk Papers, PC 75, 7, NCSA.

87. Armistead, "The Void Provisions of a President's Will," 137–38; Harlow N. Higinbotham Journal, undated entry, 1886, Small Manuscript Collections, Rubenstein Library, Duke University; "Harlow Higinbotham," *Chicago Tribune*, April 19, 1919.

88. "President Polk's Widow Dead," *New York Tribune,* published as *New-York Tribune,* August 15, 1891. Marshall actually fled to Texas and died in a U.S. jail.

89. Stephen B. Presser, "The Historical Background of the American Law of Adoption," *Journal of Family Law* 11 (1971–72): 466; William H. Whitmore, *The Law of Adoption* (Boston, 1876), 77.

90. Sallie Fall to Lucy Polk, September 17, 1888, Polk Papers, PC 75, 6, Correspondence 1887–1889, NCSA.

91. Armistead, "The Void Provisions of a President's Will," 139; Naomi Hays to Tasker Polk, undated, Polk Papers, PC 75, 7, Correspondence undated, NCSA.

92. Maria Naomi Hays to Tasker Polk, undated, Polk Papers, PC 75, 7, Correspondence undated, NCSA; "Illustrious Dead," *Nashville Banner,* September 19, 1893; Armistead, "The Void Provisions of a President's Will," 140.

93. Maria Naomi Hays to Tasker Polk, undated, Polk Papers, PC 75, 7, Correspondence undated, NCSA; "Booming," *Nashville American,* April 10, 1897; Armistead, "The Void Provisions of a President's Will," 140. The Polk Papers at the North Carolina State Archives contain a wealth of information about the court cases discussed here, and the disposal of Polk Place.

94. Page, "Polk Memorial Hall."

EPILOGUE: LOVE MAKES MEMORY ETERNAL

1. Caroline Bermeo Newcombe, "The Origin and Civil Law Foundations of the Community Property System, Why California Adopted It and Why Community Property Principles Benefit Women," *University of Maryland Law Journal of Race, Religion, Gender and Class* 11, no. 1 (2011): 1–38.

2. Whitsitt, "Annals of a Scotch-Irish Family: The Whitsitts of Nashville," *American Historical Magazine and Tennessee Historical Society Quarterly* 9 (1904): 240.

3. Anne-Leslie Owens, "John Calvin Brown," *Tennessee Encyclopedia of History and Culture,* http://tennesseeencyclopedia.net/entries/john-calvin-brown/; Annie S. Gilchrist, *Some Representative Women of Tennessee* (Nashville: McQuiddy Printing Co., 1902), 12–16.

4. Owens, "John Calvin Brown"; Anne-Leslie Owens, "Neill Smith Brown," *Tennessee Encyclopedia of History and Culture,* https://tennesseeencyclopedia.net/entries/neill-smith-brown/; Joseph O. Baylen, "A Tennessee Politician in Imperial Russia, 1850–1853," *Tennessee Historical Quarterly* 14 (1955): 227–52.

5. Robert Vincent Remini, *Henry Clay: A Statesman for the Union* (New York: Norton, 1992), 6.

6. "To Old Confederate Veterans and Their Sons," *Confederate Veteran* XXV (July 1917): 338; Chester L. Quarles, *The Ku Klux Klan and Related American Racialist and Anti-semitic Organizations: A History and Analysis* (Jefferson, NC: McFarland, 1999), 32.

7. Tennessee, General Assembly, Senate, Committee on Military Affairs, *Report of Evidence Taken Before the Military Committee in Relation to Outrages Committed by the Ku Klux Klan in Middle and West Tennessee* (Nashville: S. C. Mercer, 1868), 46–47; John Hope Franklin, *Reconstruction After the Civil War,* 2nd ed. (Chicago: University of Chicago Press, 1994), 150–69; Tennessee, General Assembly, *Report of Evidence,* 47; Steven Hahn, *A Nation Under Our Feet: Black Political Struggles in the Rural South from Slavery to the Great Migration* (Cambridge, MA: Harvard University Press, 2003), 265–70; Allen W. Trelease, *White Terror: The Ku Klux Klan Conspiracy and Southern Reconstruction* (Baton Rouge: Louisiana State University Press, 1999), 3–6.

8. Julia C. Brown, "Reconstruction in Yalobusha and Grenada Counties," *Publications of the Mississippi Historical Society* XII (University, MS, 1912): 235–43.

9. Hahn, *A Nation Under Our Feet*, 265–70; David M. Chalmers, *Hooded American-ism: The History of the Ku Klux Klan*, 3rd ed. (Durham, NC: Duke University Press, 1987), 15.

10. Susan Lawrence Davis, *Authentic History, Ku Klux Klan, 1865–1877* (New York: American Library Service, 1924), 21; J. Michael Martinez, *Carpetbaggers, Cavalry, and the Ku Klux Klan: Exposing the Invisible Empire During Reconstruction* (New York: Rowman and Littlefield, 2007), 23. Brown's membership in the Klan, like many things about the Klan, is difficult to prove. His name appears in various histories of the Klan, including Davis's *Authentic History*, but the KKK, not surprisingly, appears in none of his formal biographies. Given that there were only 2,070 people living in Pulaski in 1870, and that the population of Giles County increased precipitously between 1865 and 1870, it seems hard to imagine that John Calvin was not involved at the outset. "Census of Population and Housing: Decennial Censuses," United States Census Bureau, http://www.census.gov/prod/www/abs/decennial/. Writing about his father, John William Childress asserted, "There can be no doubt that he was one of the boys who started the KKK. It was in Pulaski that my father became one of the organizers of the original Ku Klux Klan." Childress, "The Childress Family of Tennessee"; "Judge John W. Childress," *Confederate Veteran* XVI (May 1908): xxxiii.

11. William S. Speer, *Sketches of Prominent Tennesseans: Biographies and Records of Many of the Families Who Have Attained Prominence in Tennessee* (Nashville: Albert B. Tavel, 1888), 27; Childress, "The Childress Family of Tennessee; "Judge John W. Childress," *Confederate Veteran* XVI (May 1908): xxxiii; John William Jones, *The Davis Memorial Volume; or, Our Dead President, Jefferson Davis, and the World's Trib-ute to His Memory* (B. F. Johnson, 1889), 563.

12. "Mrs. President Polk," *NYH*, June 3, 1879; Gilchrist, *Some Representative Women of Tennessee*, 12–16.

13. SCP to Governor J. C. Brown, December 9, 1871, John Calvin Brown Papers, TSLA.

14. "Mrs. President Polk," *NYH*, June 3, 1879.

15. Owens, "John Calvin Brown," *Tennessee Encyclopedia of History and Culture*; Gil-christ, *Some Representative Women of Tennessee*, 12–16.

16. Daughters of the American Revolution, *Lineage Book* (Washington, DC, 1901), vol. 35, 342; Cecilia Elizabeth O'Leary, *To Die For: The Paradox of American Patrio-tism* (Princeton, NJ: Princeton University Press, 1999), 80–81; David W. Blight, *Race and Reunion: The Civil War in American Memory* (Cambridge, MA: Harvard Univer-sity Press, 2001); Caroline E. Janney, *Remembering the Civil War: Reunion and the Limits of Reconciliation* (Chapel Hill: University of North Carolina Press, 2013).

17. Karen L. Cox, *Dixie's Daughters: The United Daughters of the Confederacy and the Preservation of Confederate Culture* (Gainesville: University Press of Florida, 2003), 8–13; Janney, *Remembering the Civil War*, 148–59.

18. "Honor for the South," *Confederate Veteran* I (January 1893): 17; Janney, *Remember-ing the Civil War*, 209–11.

19. LeeAnn Whites, *Gender Matters: Civil War, Reconstruction, and the Making of the New South* (New York: Palgrave Macmillan, 2005), 89–94, quote on 93; Davis, *Authentic History*, 310; Crystal Nicole Feimster, *Southern Horrors: Women and the Politics of Rape and Lynching* (Cambridge, MA: Harvard University Press, 2009), 125–57.

20. "Books Supplied by S. A. Cunningham, Nashville Tennessee," *Confederate Vet-eran* I (December 1893): 381; "Judge John W. Childress," *Confederate Veteran* XVI (May 1908): xxxiii.

21. Mrs. A. A. Campbell, "The United Daughters of the Confederacy: Some of Their Aims and Accomplishments" *Confederate Veteran* XXX (March 1922): 86; Janney, *Remembering the Civil War*, 242–44; Cox, *Dixie's Daughters*, 13–20.

22. Campbell, "The United Daughters of the Confederacy," 86; Janney, *Remembering the Civil War*, 243–44; Cox, *Dixie's Daughters*, 21.

23. Mrs. Alexander B. White, "Mrs. John Calvin Brown," in *Minutes of the Twenty-Fourth Annual Convention of the United Daughters of the Confederacy* (Richmond, VA: Richmond Press, 1918), 529; Janney, *Remembering the Civil War*, 243.

24. Mrs. Alexander B. White, "Mrs. John Calvin Brown," 529.

25. "Mrs. President Polk," *NYH*, June 3, 1879.

Bibliography

UNPUBLISHED DOCUMENTS AND MANUSCRIPTS

Bentley Historical Library, University of Michigan
John G. Parkhurst Papers

Burton Historical Collection, Detroit Public Library
William Woodbridge Papers

Connecticut Historical Society
"Excerpts from the Diary of Elizabeth Dixon of Connecticut, 1845–1847"

Charles Sellers Collection
Blair-Lee Papers
Dallas Papers
Ingersoll Papers
Marcy Papers
Polk Papers
Woodbury Papers

David M. Rubenstein Rare Book and Manuscript Library, Duke University
Campbell Family Papers
Harlow N. Higinbotham Journal

The Filson Historical Society
N. G. Markham Papers, 1854–1905

The Historical Society of Pennsylvania
Papers of James Buchanan

Huntington Library Manuscripts Collection
Gen. Grant Wilson to S. C. Polk
J. Henry Hager to Sarah Childress Polk
J. W. Weidermeyer to Sarah Childress Polk
Occie Brooks to S. C. Polk
S. C. Polk to Gen. Grant Wilson
S. C. Polk to Occie Brooks

Library of Congress
Andrew Johnson Papers
James K. Polk Papers
Martin Van Buren Papers

Mississippi Department of Archives
Pontotoc County Deed Records
Yalobusha County Court Records

National Archives and Records
Bureau of the Census, Census Places: Nashville, Fort Camp, Rutherford, and Davidson, Tennessee, Census Years: 1810, 1850, 1860, 1870
Cotton and Captured Property Records
Letters Sent to Collectors and Assessors of Internal Revenue, State Officers, Banks and Corporations (GS Series)
Record Group 21: Records of District Courts of the United States
USNO Telegrams Received '86–'06

New-York Historical Society
Gulian C. Verplanck Papers

New York Public Library
Bryant-Godwin Papers

North Carolina State Archives
Lucy Williams Polk Papers

The Pennsylvania State University Library, Microfilm
James K. Polk Papers

Polk Family Home Collection
Catharine Beecher to Sarah Childress Polk, September 20, 1845
Salem Academy Copybook
Watch, Pendant, 1925.001.062a-c

Private Collection of Bobby Bennett
Joel Childress to Sarah Childress, April 22, 1818

Rice University
Papers of Jefferson Davis

Rutherford County Historical Society Archives
Division of estate of Joel Childress
Will of Joel Childress

Salem College Archives
Claudia Jack, "Sarah Childress Polk," typescript manuscript
Contents of Salem Academy Library in 1817
Crockett Family Letters
"Rules of the Boarding School at Salem"
Salem Academy Library Contents
Salem Academy Class Schedule 1811

Southern Historical Collection, Wilson Library, University of North Carolina at Chapel Hill
Caroline O'Reilly Nicholson Papers
Kate S. Carney Diary
Kimberly Family Personal Correspondence

Stanford University Libraries
Miller Papers

Tennessee Historical Society
Harding-Jackson Papers

Tennessee State Library and Archives
Deed Book, Registrar's Office, Davidson County, TN
Early Tennessee/North Carolina Land Records, 1783–1927, Record Group 50
Employment Rolls and Nonpayment Rolls of Negroes Employed in the Defenses of Nashville, Tennessee, 1862–1863
Excerpts Concerning President and Mrs. James K. Polk (Diary of Elizabeth Dixon)
Polk Memorial Association Collection of James K. Polk Papers
John Calvin Brown Papers
Register of Deeds: Rutherford County, Sumner County
Sarah Polk Correspondence, 1832–1891
"State vs. Joel Childress." Minutes of the Superior Court of North Carolina Including Mero District (Works Progress Administration transcript, 1938)
Tennessee State Marriages, 1780–2002, Nashville, TN

University of Tennessee
Polk Correspondence

University of Virginia
Madison Papers

Yale University Library
Ticknor Collection

PUBLISHED DOCUMENTS

Massachusetts—General Court—House of Representatives. *Documents Relating to the U.S.-Mexican War*. Boston, 1847.
Mississippi Legislature. *Laws of the State of Mississippi*. Jackson, MS: E. Barksdale, 1860.
Tennessee. General Assembly. Senate. Committee on Military Affairs. *Report of Evidence Taken Before the Military Committee in Relation to Outrages Committed by the Ku Klux Klan in Middle and West Tennessee*. Nashville: S. C. Mercer, 1868.
United States Department of the Interior. *Official Register of the United States, Containing a List of Officers and Employees in the Civil, Military and Naval Service, on the First of July, 1881*. Vol. 1. Washington, DC: Government Printing Office, 1881.

CONGRESSIONAL DOCUMENTS

HR Misc. Doc No. 251, 43rd Cong., 1st Sess. (1874)

NEWSPAPERS, MAGAZINES, AND PERIODICALS

Alexandria (VA) Gazette
American Historical Magazine
Augusta (GA) Chronicle
Baltimore Sun
Bangor (ME) Daily Whig & Courier

Barre (MA) Gazette
Barre (MA) Patriot
Berkshire County Whig (Pittsfield, MA)
Boston Daily Advertiser
Boston Post
Chicago Tribune
Cincinnati Daily Enquirer
Columbus (GA) Daily Enquirer
Confederate Veteran
Critic-Record (Washington, DC)
Daily Arkansas Gazette (Little Rock)
Daily Atlas
Daily Cleveland Herald
Daily Evening Bulletin (San Francisco)
Daily Inter Ocean (Chicago)
Daily Morning News (Savannah, GA)
Daily National Intelligencer
Democratic Banner (Mt. Vernon, OH)
Essex Register (Massachusetts)
Frank Leslie's Illustrated Newspaper (New York)
Galveston Daily News (Houston)
Georgia Weekly Telegraph
Godey's Lady's Book
Hartford Daily Courant
Idaho Statesman (Boise)
Jackson (MI) Weekly Citizen
Jeffersonian Democrat (Monroe, WI)
The Ladies' Wreath: An Illustrated Annual
Lady's Realm, an Illustrated Monthly Magazine
Lebanon (PA) Courier and Semi-Weekly Report
Lowell (MA) Daily Citizen and News
Milwaukee Daily Journal
Mississippi Free Trader
Mississippi State Gazette
Nashville Daily American
Nashville Patriot
Nashville Republican Banner
Nashville Union
Nashville Whig
The Nation
New Orleans Times-Picayune
New York Evening Post
New York Herald
New York Times
News and Observer (Raleigh, NC)
Omaha Daily Herald
Oneida Whig
Pennsylvania Magazine of History and Biography
Peterson's Ladies National Magazine
Pittsfield (MA) Sun
Provincial Freeman (Canada West)

Richmond Enquirer

Richmond Times-Dispatch

Southwestern Christian Advocate (New Orleans)

St. Louis Globe-Democrat

St. Louis Post-Dispatch

The Vedette

Vermont Chronicle

Washington Post

Wisconsin State Register

Worcester (MA) Daily Spy

BOOKS

Abernethy, Thomas Perkins. *Frontier to Plantation in Tennessee: A Study in Frontier Democracy*. Tuscaloosa: University of Alabama Press, 1967.

Acklen, Jeannette Tillotson. *Tennessee Records: Tombstone Inscriptions and Manuscripts*. Nashville, 1933.

Adams Family Correspondence. Ed. L. H. Butterfield, Wendell D. Garrett, and Marjorie Sprague. Cambridge, MA: Harvard University Press, 1963.

Ahlstrom, Sydney E. *A Religious History of the American People*. Vol. 1. Garden City, NY: Doubleday, 1975.

Allgor, Catherine. *Parlor Politics: In Which the Ladies of Washington Help Build a City and a Government*. Charlottesville: University Press of Virginia, 2000.

American State Papers: Indian Affairs. Vols. 1 and 2. Ed. Charles J. Kappler. Washington, DC: Government Printing Office, 1904.

Anthony, Carl Sferrazza. *America's First Families: An Inside View of 200 Years of Private Life in the White House*. New York: Touchstone, 2000.

———. *First Ladies: The Saga of the Presidents' Wives and Their Power, 1789–1961*. New York: William Morrow, 1990.

Appletons' Cyclopaedia of American Biography. Vol. 5, *Pickering-Sumter*. Revised ed. Ed. James Grant Wilson and John Fiske. New York: D. Appleton and Co., 1888.

Ash, Stephen V. *Middle Tennessee Society Transformed, 1860–1870: War and Peace in the Upper South*. Baton Rouge: Louisiana State University Press, 1988.

Ashe, Sheppard M. *Monterey Conquered: A Fragment from La Gran Quivira; or, Rome Unmasked. A Poem*. New York: C. Shepard and Co., 1852.

Baker, Jean. *Mary Todd Lincoln*. New York: Norton, 1987.

Baptist, Edward E. *The Half Has Never Been Told: Slavery and the Making of American Capitalism*. New York: Basic Books, 2014.

Bartlett, Irving H. *John C. Calhoun: A Biography*. New York: Norton, 1993.

Bassett, John Spencer. *The Southern Plantation Overseer as Revealed in His Letters*. Northampton, MA: Smith College, 1925.

Bauer, K. Jack. *Zachary Taylor: Soldier, Planter, Statesman of the Old Southwest*. Baton Rouge: Louisiana State University Press, 1993.

Beecher, Catharine. *A Treatise on Domestic Economy for the Use of Young Ladies at Home and at School*. Boston, 1841.

———. *The Duty of American Women to Their Country*. New York: Harper and Bros., 1845.

Beecher, Lyman. *A Plea for the West*. 2nd ed. Cincinnati: Truman and Smith, 1835.

Beeman, Richard R. *The Evolution of the Southern Backcountry: A Case Study of Lunenburg County, Virginia, 1746–1832*. Philadelphia: University of Pennsylvania Press, 1984.

Beckert, Sven. *Empire of Cotton: A Global History*. New York: Knopf, 2014.

Bergeron, Paul H. *The Presidency of James K. Polk*. Lawrence: University Press of Kansas, 1987.

Berkin, Carol. *Revolutionary Mothers: Women in the Struggle for American Independence*. New York: Knopf, 2005.

Berlin, Ira. *The Long Emancipation: The Demise of Slavery in the United States*. Cambridge, MA: Harvard University Press, 2015.

Blair, Karen J. *The Clubwoman as Feminist: True Womanhood Redefined, 1868–1914*. New York: Holmes & Meier, 1980.

Blair, William E. *Cities of the Dead: Contesting the Memory of the Civil War in the South, 1865–1914*. Chapel Hill: University of North Carolina Press, 2004.

———. *With Malice Toward Some: Treason and Loyalty in the Civil War Era*. Chapel Hill: University of North Carolina Press, 2014.

Blight, David W. *Race and Reunion: The Civil War in American Memory*. Cambridge, MA: Harvard University Press, 2001.

Bordin, Ruth. *Frances Willard: A Biography*. Chapel Hill: University of North Carolina Press, 1986.

Borneman, Walter R. *Polk: The Man Who Transformed the Presidency and America*. New York: Random House, 2009.

Boydston, Jeanne. *Home and Work: Housework, Wages, and the Ideology of Labor in the Early Republic*. New York: Oxford University Press, 1990.

Brodie, Janet Farrell. *Contraception and Abortion in 19th-Century America*. Ithaca, NY: Cornell University Press, 1994.

Bruce, Dickson D., Jr. *Violence and Culture in the Antebellum South*. Austin: University of Texas Press, 2011.

Bryan, John Morrill. *Robert Mills: Architect*. New York: AIA Press, 1989.

Bumgarner, John Reed. *Sarah Childress Polk: A Biography of the Remarkable First Lady*. Jefferson, NC: McFarland, 1997.

Burstein, Andrew. *The Passions of Andrew Jackson*. New York: Knopf, 2003.

Burstein, Andrew, and Nancy Isenberg. *Madison and Jefferson*. New York: Random House, 2010.

Byrnes, Mark Eaton, ed. *James K. Polk: A Biographical Companion*. Santa Barbara, CA: ABC-Clio, 2001.

Caroli, Betty Boyd. *First Ladies: From Martha Washington to Michelle Obama*. New York: Oxford University Press, 2009.

Carson, Barbara G. *Ambitious Appetites: Dining, Behavior, and Patterns of Consumption in Federal Washington*. Washington, DC: AIA Press, 1990.

Carter, Clarence Edwin, ed. *The Territorial Papers of the United States*. Vol. 26, *The Territory of Florida, 1839–1845*. Washington, DC: Government Printing Office, 1962.

Carter, Susan B., et al., eds. *Historical Statistics of the United States*. New York: Cambridge University Press, 2006.

Cashin, Joan. *A Family Venture: Men and Women on the Southern Frontier*. Baltimore: Johns Hopkins University Press, 1994.

Censer, Jane Turner. *The Reconstruction of Womanhood, 1865–1895*. Baton Rouge: Louisiana State University Press, 2003.

Chaffin, Tom. *Met His Every Goal? James K. Polk and the Legends of Manifest Destiny*. Knoxville: University of Tennessee Press, 2014.

———. *Pathfinder: John Charles Frémont and the Course of American Empire*. New York: Hill and Wang, 2002.

Chalmers, David M. *Hooded Americanism: The History of the Ku Klux Klan*. 3rd ed. Durham, NC: Duke University Press, 1987.

Cheathem, Mark Renfred. *Andrew Jackson, Southerner*. Baton Rouge: Louisiana State University Press, 2013.

Chesnut, Mary Boykin. *A Diary from Dixie*. Ed. Ben Ames Williams. Cambridge, MA: Harvard University Press, 1980.

Chidsey, Donald Barr. *And Tyler Too*. Nashville: Thomas Nelson, 1978.

Claiborne, John F. H. *Life and Correspondence of John A. Quitman*. New York: Harper and Bros., 1860.

Claxton, Jimmie Lou Sparkman. *Eighty-Eight Years with Sarah Polk*. New York: Vantage, 1972.

Clay, Henry. *Papers of Henry Clay*. Vol. 9, *The Whig Leader, January 1, 1837–December 31, 1843*. Ed. Robert Seager II and Melba Porter Hay. Lexington: University Press of Kentucky, 1988.

Cohen, Patricia Cline. *The Murder of Helen Jewett: The Life and Death of a Prostitute in Nineteenth-Century New York*. New York: Knopf, 1998.

Cooley, E. *A Description of the Etiquette at Washington City*. Philadelphia: L. B. Clarke, 1829.

Cox, Karen L. *Dixie's Daughters: The United Daughters of the Confederacy and the Preservation of Confederate Culture*. Gainesville: University Press of Florida, 2003.

Cutler, Wayne, ed. *North for Union: John Appleton's Journal of a Tour to New England Made by President Polk in June and July 1847*. Nashville: Vanderbilt University Press. 1986.

Daniel, Susan G. *Rutherford County Tennessee Pioneers*. Murfreesboro, TN: Rutherford County Historical Society, 2003.

Daughters of the American Revolution. *Lineage Book*. Vols. 1–39. Harrisburg, PA: Telegraph Printing Co., 1895–1921.

Davis, Jefferson. *The Papers of Jefferson Davis*. Vol. 2, *June 1841–July 1846*. Ed. Will McIntosh. Baton Rouge: Louisiana State University Press, 1974.

Davis, Susan Lawrence. *Authentic History, Ku Klux Klan, 1865–1877*. New York: American Library Service, 1924.

Day, Charles. *Etiquette*. New York: Wilson and Co., 1843.

Denton, Sally. *Passion and Principle: John and Jessie Frémont, the Couple Whose Power, Politics, and Love Shaped Nineteenth-Century America*. New York: Bloomsbury, 2007.

Detwiler, Donald. *Rutherford County, Tennessee Deaths and Estate Settlements*. Vol. 1, *1804–1849*. Murfreesboro, TN: Rutherford County Historical Society, 2008.

Dickens, Charles. *American Notes: A Journey*. New York: Fromm, 1985. Originally published in 1842.

Dodd, Donald B., and Wynelle S. Dodd. *Historical Statistics of the South, 1790–1970*. Tuscaloosa: University of Alabama Press, 1973.

Douglass, Frederick. *Narrative of the Life of Frederick Douglass, an American Slave*. New York: Penguin, 1968.

Downs, Gregory P. *Declarations of Dependence: The Long Reconstruction of Popular Politics in the South, 1861–1908*. Chapel Hill: University of North Carolina Press, 2011.

Dunaway, Wilma A. *Women, Work, and Family in the Antebellum Mountain South*. New York: Cambridge University Press, 2008.

Durham, Walter T. *Nashville: The Occupied City, 1862–1863*. Knoxville: University of Tennessee Press, 2008.

———. *Reluctant Partners: Nashville and the Union, 1863–65*. Knoxville: University of Tennessee Press, 2008.

Dusinberre, William. *Slavemaster President: The Double Career of James Polk*. New York: Oxford University Press, 2003.

Eaton, Peggy. *The Autobiography of Peggy Eaton*. New York: Charles Scribner's Sons, 1932.

Ellet, Elizabeth Fries. *The Court Circles of the Republic; or, The Beauties and Celebrities of the Nation, Illustrating Life and Society Under Eighteen Presidents; Describing the Social Features of the Successive Administrations from Washington to Grant.* Hartford, CT: Hartford Publishing Co., 1869.

———. *The Queens of American Society.* New York: Scribners, 1867.

Ely, James W., Jr., and Theodore Brown Jr., eds. *Legal Papers of Andrew Jackson.* Knoxville: University of Tennessee Press, 1987.

Faust, Drew Gilpin. *Mothers of Invention: Women of the Slaveholding South in the American Civil War.* Chapel Hill: University of North Carolina Press, 1996.

Feimster, Crystal Nicole. *Southern Horrors: Women and the Politics of Rape and Lynching.* Cambridge, MA: Harvard University Press, 2009.

Fitzgerald, Oscar Penn. *John B. McFerrin: A Biography.* Nashville: M. E. Church, 1888.

Fletcher, Holly Berkley. *Gender and the American Temperance Movement of the Nineteenth Century.* New York: Routledge, 2008.

Forney, John W. *Anecdotes of Public Men.* New York: Harper and Bros., 1873.

Fox-Genovese, Elizabeth. *Within the Plantation Household: Black and White Women of the Old South.* Chapel Hill: University of North Carolina Press, 1988.

Frank, Stephen M. *Life with Father: Parenthood and Masculinity in the Nineteenth-Century North.* Baltimore: Johns Hopkins University Press, 1998.

Frankel, Noralee. *Freedom's Women: Black Women and Families in Civil War Mississippi.* Bloomington: Indiana University Press, 1999.

Franklin, John Hope. *Reconstruction After the Civil War.* 2nd ed. Chicago: University of Chicago Press, 1994.

Frémont, Elizabeth Benton. *Recollections of Elizabeth Benton Frémont.* New York: Frederick H. Hitchcock, 1912.

Frémont, Jessie Benton. *Souvenirs of My Time.* Boston: Lothrop Co., 1887.

Fulcher, Richard Carlton. *1770–1790 Census of the Cumberland Settlements.* Baltimore: Genealogical Publishing Co., 1987.

Gamber, Wendy. *The Boardinghouse in Nineteenth-Century America.* Baltimore: Johns Hopkins University Press, 2007.

Geary, John White. *A Politician Goes to War: The Civil War Letters of John White Geary.* Ed. William A. Blair. University Park: Penn State University Press, 1995.

Gilchrist, Annie S. *Some Representative Women of Tennessee.* Nashville: McQuiddy Printing Co., 1902.

Ginzberg, Lori D. *Untidy Origins: A Story of Woman's Rights in Antebellum New York.* Chapel Hill: University of North Carolina Press, 2005.

———. *Women and the Work of Benevolence: Morality, Politics, and Class in the Nineteenth-Century United States.* New Haven, CT: Yale University Press, 1990.

Glover, Lori. *Southern Sons: Becoming Men in the New Republic.* Baltimore: Johns Hopkins University Press, 2007.

Glymph, Thavolia. *Out of the House of Bondage: The Transformation of the Plantation Household.* New York: Cambridge University Press, 2008.

Good, Cassandra. *Founding Friendships: Friendships Between Men and Women in the Early American Republic.* New York: Oxford University Press, 2015.

Goodman, Dena. *The Republic of Letters: A Cultural History of the French Enlightenment.* Ithaca, NY: Cornell University Press, 1994.

Goodspeed Publishing Company. *History of Tennessee from the Earliest Time to the Present.* Nashville, 1886.

Gordon, John Steele. *An Empire of Wealth: The Epic History of American Economic Power.* New York: HarperCollins, 2004.

Gordon, Sara A. *"Make It Yourself": Home Sewing, Gender, and Culture, 1890–1930*. New York: Columbia University Press, 2009.

Gordon-Reed, Annette. *The Hemingses of Monticello: An American Family*. New York: Norton, 2008.

Grant, U. S. *Personal Memoirs of U.S. Grant*. New York, 1885.

Greenberg, Amy. *A Wicked War: Polk, Clay, Lincoln, and the 1846 U.S. Invasion of Mexico*. New York: Vintage, 2012.

Grimsley, Mark. *The Hard Hand of War: Union Military Policy Toward Southern Civilians*. New York: Cambridge University Press, 1995.

Gross, Ariela J. *Double Character: Slavery and Mastery in the Antebellum Southern Courtroom*. Princeton, NJ: Princeton University Press, 2000.

Guernsey, Alfred Hudson, and Henry Mills Alden. *Harper's Pictorial History of the Great Rebellion*. Chicago: McDonnell Bros., 1866.

Hackel, Heidi Brayman, and Catherine E. Kelly, eds. *Reading Women: Literacy, Authorship, and Culture in the Atlantic World, 1500–1800*. Philadelphia: University of Pennsylvania Press, 2008.

Hahn, Steven. *A Nation Under Our Feet: Black Political Struggles in the Rural South from Slavery to the Great Migration*. Cambridge, MA: Harvard University Press, 2003.

Hallam, John. *The Diary of an Old Lawyer; or, Scenes Behind the Curtain*. Nashville: Southwestern Publishing House, 1895.

Halttunen, Karen. *Confidence Men and Painted Women: A Study of Middle-Class Culture in America, 1830–1870*. New Haven, CT: Yale University Press, 1982.

Haynes, Sam W. *Unfinished Revolution: The Early American Republic in a British World*. Charlottesville: University of Virginia Press, 2010.

Heffron, Margery M. *Louisa Catherine: The Other Mrs. Adams*. Ed. David M. Michelmore. New Haven, CT: Yale University Press, 2014.

Heidler, David S., and Jeanne T. Heidler, eds. *Encyclopedia of the American Civil War: A Political, Social, and Military History*. New York: Norton, 2000.

———. *Henry Clay: The Essential American*. New York: Random House, 2010.

Heller, J. Roderick, III. *Democracy's Lawyer: Felix Grundy of the Old Southwest*. Baton Rouge: Louisiana State University Press, 2010.

Hemphill, Dallett. *Siblings: Brothers and Sisters in American History*. New York: Oxford University Press, 2011.

Henkin, David. *The Postal Age: The Emergence of Modern Communications in Nineteenth-Century America*. Chicago: University of Chicago Press, 2007.

Heyrman, Christine. *Southern Cross: The Beginnings of the Bible Belt*. Chapel Hill: University of North Carolina Press, 1997.

Hickman, George H. *The Life and Public Services of the Hon. James Knox Polk: With a Compendium of His Speeches on Various Public Measures, Also a Sketch of the Life of the Hon. George Mifflin Dallas*. Baltimore: N. Hickman, 1844.

Holland, Jesse. *The Invisibles: The Untold Story of African American Slaves in the White House*. Guilford, CT: Rowman and Littlefield, 2016.

Holloway, Laura. *The Ladies of the White House*. New York: U.S. Pub. Co., 1870.

Hoock, Holger. *Scars of Independence: America's Violent Birth*. New York: Crown, 2017.

Horowitz, Helen Lefkowitz. *Rereading Sex: Battles over Sexual Knowledge and Suppression in Nineteenth-Century America*. New York: Vintage, 2003.

Howe, Daniel Walker. *What Hath God Wrought: The Transformation of America, 1815–1848*. New York: Oxford University Press, 2007.

Huebner, Timothy S. *The Southern Judicial Tradition: State Judges and Sectional Distinctiveness*. Athens: University of Georgia Press, 1999.

Hutchinson, A. *Code of Mississippi: Being an Analytic Compilation of the Public and General Statutes of the Territory and State*. Jackson, MS, 1848.

Ingram, J. S. *The Centennial Exposition Described and Illustrated: Being a Concise and Graphic Description of This Grand Enterprise Commemorative of the First Centenary of American Independence*. Philadelphia: Hubbard Bros., 1876.

Irelan, John Robert. *The Republic; or, The History of the United States of America*. Chicago: Fairbanks and Palmer, 1888.

Isenberg, Nancy. *Sex and Citizenship in Antebellum America*. Chapel Hill: University of North Carolina Press, 1998.

———. *White Trash: The 400-Year Untold History of Class in America*. New York: Viking, 2016.

Jabolonka, Ivan. *History Is a Contemporary Literature: Manifesto for the Social Sciences*. Ithaca, NY: Cornell University Press, 2018.

Jacobs, Harriet Ann. *Incidents in the Life of a Slave Girl*. Boston: Published for the author, 1861.

Janney, Caroline E. *Remembering the Civil War: Reunion and the Limits of Reconciliation*. Chapel Hill: University of North Carolina Press, 2013.

Johnson, Adam Rankin. *The Partisan Rangers of the Confederate States Army*. Louisville, KY: Geo. G. Fetter Co., 1904.

Johnson, Andrew. *The Papers of Andrew Johnson*. Vol. 5, *1861–1862*. Ed. Leroy P. Graf, Ralph Haskins, and Patricia P. Clark. Knoxville: University of Tennessee Press, 1979.

———. *The Papers of Andrew Johnson*. Vol. 6, *1862–1864*. Ed. Leroy P. Graf and Ralph W. Haskins. Knoxville: University of Tennessee Press, 1983.

———. *The Papers of Andrew Johnson*. Vol. 8, *May–August 1865*. Ed. Paul H. Bergeron. Knoxville: University of Tennessee Press, 1989.

———. *The Papers of Andrew Johnson*. Vol. 9, *September 1865–January 1866*. Ed. Paul H. Bergeron. Knoxville: University of Tennessee Press, 1991.

Johnson, B. F. *Makers of America: Biographies of Leading Men of Thought and Action, the Men Who Constitute the Bone and Sinew of American Prosperity and Life*. Vol. 1. Washington, DC: B. F. Johnson, 1915.

Johnson, Walter. *River of Dark Dreams: Slavery and Empire in the Cotton Kingdom*. Cambridge, MA: Harvard University Press, 2013.

Jones, John William. *The Davis Memorial Volume; or, Our Dead President, Jefferson Davis, and the World's Tribute to His Memory*. B. F. Johnson, 1889.

Kale, Steven. *French Salons: High Society and Political Sociability from the Old Regime to the Revolution of 1848*. Baltimore: Johns Hopkins University Press, 2004.

Kaplan, Amy. *The Anarchy of Empire in the Making of U.S. Culture*. Cambridge, MA: Harvard University Press, 2002.

Kaye, Anthony E. *Joining Places: Slave Neighborhoods in the Old South*. Chapel Hill: University of North Carolina Press, 2007.

Kelley, Mary. *Learning to Stand and Speak: Women, Education, and Public Life in America's Republic*. Chapel Hill: University of North Carolina Press, 2006.

Kelly, Catherine E. *Republic of Taste: Art, Politics, and Everyday Life in Early America*. Philadelphia: University of Pennsylvania Press, 2016.

Kerber, Linda. *Women of the Republic: Intellect and Ideology in Revolutionary America*. Chapel Hill: University of North Carolina Press, 1980.

Klepp, Susan E. *Revolutionary Conceptions: Women, Fertility, and Family Limitation in America, 1760–1820*. Chapel Hill: University of North Carolina Press, 2009.

Konkle, Burton Alva. *The Life of Chief Justice Ellis Lewis, 1798–1871: Of the First Elective Supreme Court of Pennsylvania*. Philadelphia: Campion, 1907.

Kraut, John Allen, and Dixon Ryan Fox. *The Completion of Independence, 1790–1830.* New York: Macmillan, 1948.

Lebsock, Suzanne. *The Free Women of Petersburg: Status and Culture in a Southern Town.* New York: Norton, 1985.

Lee, Dan. *Kentuckian in Blue: A Biography of Major General Lovell Harrison Rousseau.* Jefferson, NC: McFarland, 2010.

Levine, Lawrence. *Highbrow/Lowbrow: The Emergence of Cultural Hierarchy in America.* Cambridge, MA: Harvard University Press, 1990.

Littell, John S. *The Clay Minstrel; or, National Songster.* 2nd ed. New York: Greeley and McElrath, 1844.

Lovett, Bobby L. *The African-American History of Nashville, Tennessee, 1780–1930: Elites and Dilemmas.* Fayetteville: University of Arkansas Press, 1999.

Lynch, Denis Tilden. *Grover Cleveland: A Man Four-Square.* New York: Horace Liveright, 1932.

Lytle, William Haines. *For Honor, Glory and Union: The Mexican and Civil War Letters of Brig. Gen. William Haines Lytle.* Ed. Ruth C. Carter. Lexington: University Press of Kentucky, 1999.

Manning, Chandra. *Troubled Refuge: Struggling for Freedom in the Civil War.* New York: Knopf, 2016.

Martinez, J. Michael. *Carpetbaggers, Cavalry, and the Ku Klux Klan: Exposing the Invisible Empire During Reconstruction.* New York: Rowman and Littlefield, 2007.

Maury, Sarah Mytton. *An Englishwoman in America.* London: Thomas Richardson, 1848.

McCrossen, Alexis, ed. *Land of Necessity: Consumer Culture in the United States–Mexico Borderlands.* Durham, NC: Duke University Press, 2009.

McCurry, Stephanie. *Confederate Reckoning: Power and Politics in the Civil War South.* Cambridge, MA: Harvard University Press, 2010.

McDowell, Peggy, and Richard E. Meyer. *The Revival Styles and American Memorial Art.* Bowling Green, OH: Popular Press, 1994.

McFeely, William S. *Grant: A Biography.* New York: Norton, 1981.

McKee, John Miller. *The Great Panic: Being Incidents Connected with Two Weeks of the War in Tennessee. By an Eye Witness.* Nashville: Johnson & Whiting, 1862.

McPherson, James. *Battle Cry of Freedom: The Civil War Era.* New York: Oxford University Press, 1988.

Moore, John Bassett, ed. *The Works of James Buchanan, Comprising His Speeches, State Papers, and Private Correspondence.* Philadelphia, J. B. Lippincott Co., 1908–11.

Morrell, Martha McBride. *"Young Hickory": The Life and Times of President James K. Polk.* New York: G. P. Dutton, 1941.

Morris, Eastin. *The Tennessee Gazetteer; or, Topical Dictionary.* Nashville: W. Hasell Hunt, 1834.

Morris, J. S. *Mississippi State Cases, Being Criminal Cases Decided in the High Court of Errors and Appeals, and in the Supreme Court, of the State of Mississippi: From the June Term 1818 to the First Monday in January 1872, Inclusive.* Jackson, MS: Published by the compiler, 1872.

National Woman Suffrage Association. *Report of the International Council of Women, Assembled by the National Woman Suffrage Association, Washington, D.C., U.S. of America, March 25 to April 1, 1888.* Vol. 1. Washington, DC: Rufus H. Darby, 1888.

Nelson, Anson, and Fanny Nelson. *Memorials of Sarah Childress Polk: Wife of the Eleventh President of the United States.* New York: Anson D. F. Randolph and Co., 1892.

Nevins, Allan. *Grover Cleveland: A Study in Courage.* New York: Dodd, Mead, 1966.

Norton, Mary Beth. *Liberty's Daughters: The Revolutionary Experience of American Women, 1750–1800.* Boston: Little, Brown, 1980.

O'Leary, Cecilia Elizabeth. *To Die For: The Paradox of American Patriotism*. Princeton, NJ: Princeton University Press, 1999.

Parker, Alison M. *Purifying America: Women, Cultural Reform, and Pro-Censorship Activism, 1873–1933*. Urbana: University of Illinois Press, 1997.

Parks, Joseph Howard. *John Bell of Tennessee*. Baton Rouge: Louisiana State University Press, 1950.

Pennsylvania Constitutional Convention. *Convention of the Commonwealth of Pennsylvania to Propose Amendments to the Constitution*. Vol. 2. Harrisburg, PA: Packer, Barrett and Parke, 1837.

Peterson, Barbara Bennett. *Sarah Childress Polk, First Lady of Tennessee and Washington*. Huntington, NY: Nova History Publications, 2002.

Phillips-Schrock, Patrick. *The White House: An Illustrated Architectural History*. Jefferson, NC: McFarland, 2013.

Polk, James K. *Correspondence of James K. Polk*. 13 vols. Ed. Herbert Weaver, Paul H. Bergeron, Wayne Cutler, and Michael David Cohen. Vols. 1–7, Nashville: Vanderbilt University Press; vols. 8–13, Knoxville: University of Tennessee Press, 1969–2017.

———. *Diary of a President*. 4 vols. Ed. Milo Quaife. Columbia, TN: James K. Polk Memorial Association, 2005.

Poore, Ben Perley. *Perley's Reminiscences of Sixty Years in the National Metropolis*. Philadelphia: Hubbard Brothers, 1886.

Potter, David. *The Impending Crisis, 1848–1861*. New York: Harper and Row, 1976.

Putnum, A. W. *History of Middle Tennessee; or, Life and Times of Gen. James Robertson*. Nashville: Printed for the author, 1859.

Quarles, Chester L. *The Ku Klux Klan and Related American Racialist and Antisemitic Organizations: A History and Analysis*. Jefferson, NC: McFarland, 1999.

Ray, Kristopher. *Middle Tennessee, 1775–1825: Progress and Popular Democracy on the Southwestern Frontier*. Knoxville: University of Tennessee Press, 2007.

Remini, Robert Vincent. *Henry Clay: A Statesman for the Union*. New York: Norton, 1992.

Report of the Woman's Rights Convention, Held at Seneca Falls N.Y., July 19 and 20, 1848. Rochester, NY: John Dick, 1848.

Restall, Matthew. *When Montezuma Met Cortés: The True Story of the Meeting That Changed History*. New York: Ecco/HarperCollins, 2018.

Richardson, James D., ed. *Messages and Papers of the Presidents*. Washington, DC: Government Printing Office, 1901.

Rose, Anne C. *Victorian America and the Civil War*. New York: Cambridge University Press, 1992.

Rothman, Adam. *Slave Country: American Expansion and the Origins of the Deep South*. Cambridge, MA: Harvard University Press, 2005.

Rush, Benjamin. *Essays Literary, Moral, and Philosophical*. Philadelphia: Thomas and William Bradford, 1798.

Sargent, Nathan. *Public Men and Events, from the Commencement of Mr. Monroe's Administration, in 1817, to the Close of Mr. Fillmore's Administration in 1853*. Vol. 2. Philadelphia: J. B. Lippincott and Co., 1875.

Saunders, William L., ed. *The Colonial Records of North Carolina*. Vol. 1. Raleigh, NC: P. M. Hale Printer, 1886.

Schneider, Dorothy, and Carl J. Schneider, eds. *First Ladies: A Biographical Dictionary*. 3rd ed. New York: Infobase Publishing, 2010.

Schwartz, Marie Jenkins. *Ties That Bound: Founding First Ladies and Slaves*. Chicago: University of Chicago Press, 2017.

Seager, Robert II. *And Tyler Too: A Biography of John and Julia Gardener Tyler*. New York: McGraw-Hill, 1963.

Seale, William. *The President's House: A History*. 2nd ed. 2 vols. Baltimore: Johns Hopkins University Press, 2008.

Sellers, Charles. *James K. Polk*. Vol. 1, *Jacksonian, 1795–1843*. Princeton, NJ: Princeton University Press, 1957.

———. *James K. Polk*. Vol. 2, *Continentalist, 1843–1846*. Princeton, NJ: Princeton University Press, 1966.

Shaw, James Birney. *History of the Tenth Regiment Indiana Volunteer Infantry*. Lafayette, IN: Burt-Haywood Co., 1912.

Sheldon, Rachel. *Washington Brotherhood: Politics, Social Life, and the Coming of the Civil War*. Chapel Hill: University of North Carolina Press, 2013.

Shire, Laurel Clark. *The Threshold of Manifest Destiny: Gender and National Expansion in Florida*. Philadelphia: University of Pennsylvania Press, 2016.

Sibley, Katherine A. S., ed. *A Companion to First Ladies*. Malden, MA: Wiley-Blackwell, 2016.

Sigourney, Lydia Howard. *Noble Deeds of American Women; with Biographical Sketches of Some of the More Prominent*. Buffalo, NY: G. H. Derby and Co., 1851.

Silber, Nina. *The Romance of Reunion: Northerners and the South, 1865–1900*. Chapel Hill: University of North Carolina Press, 1993.

Silbey, Joel H. *Martin Van Buren and the Emergence of American Popular Politics*. Lanham, MD: Rowman and Littlefield, 2005.

Singleton, Ester. *The Story of the White House*. Vol. 1. New York: Benjamin Blom, 1907.

Sklar, Kathryn Kish. *Catharine Beecher: A Study in American Domesticity*. New York: Norton, 1973.

Smith, Margaret Bayard. *First Forty Years in Washington*. New York: Charles Scribner's Sons, 1906.

Speer, William S. *Sketches of Prominent Tennesseans: Biographies and Records of Many of the Families Who Have Attained Prominence in Tennessee*. Nashville: Albert B. Tavel, 1888.

Taylor, Alan. *American Revolutions: A Continental History*. New York: Norton, 2016.

Taylor, Elizabeth Dowling. *A Slave in the White House: Paul Jennings and the Madisons*. New York: Palgrave Macmillan, 2012.

Tetrault, Lisa. *The Myth of Seneca Falls: Memory and the Women's Suffrage Movement, 1848–1898*. Chapel Hill: University of North Carolina Press, 2003.

Tolbert, Lisa C. *Constructing Townscapes: Space and Society in Antebellum Tennessee*. Chapel Hill: University of North Carolina Press, 1999.

Tooke, Thomas. *A History of Prices and the State of Circulation During the Nine Years 1848–1856*. London: Longman, Orme, Brown, Green and Longmans, 1857.

Trelease, Allen W. *White Terror: The Ku Klux Klan Conspiracy and Southern Reconstruction*. Baton Rouge: Louisiana State University Press, 1999.

Trench, Richard Chenevix. *On the Study of Words*. New York: Macmillan Co., 1853.

Varon, Elizabeth R. *Southern Lady, Yankee Spy: The True Story of Elizabeth Van Lew, a Union Agent in the Heart of the Confederacy*. New York: Oxford University Press, 2003.

———. *We Mean to Be Counted: White Women and Politics in Antebellum Virginia*. Chapel Hill: University of North Carolina Press, 1998.

Walsh, Lorena S. *From Calabar to Carter's Grove: The History of a Virginia Slave Community*. Charlottesville: University Press of Virginia, 1997.

Watmough, Edmund C. *Scribblings and Sketches: Diplomatic, Piscatory, and Oceanic*. 2nd ed. Philadelphia: E. Sherman, 1844.

Wheeler, Leslie, ed. *Loving Warriors: Selected Letters of Lucy Stone and Henry B. Blackwell, 1853–1893*. New York: Dial Press, 1981.

Whites, LeeAnn. *Gender Matters: Civil War, Reconstruction, and the Making of the New South*. New York: Palgrave Macmillan, 2005.

Whitmore, William H. *The Law of Adoption*. Boston, 1876.

Whitton, Mary Ormsbee. *First First Ladies, 1789–1865: A Study of the Wives of the Early Presidents*. New York: Hastings House, 1948.

Willard, Frances E., and Mary A. Livermore, eds. *American Women: Fifteen Hundred Biographies with Over 1,400 Portraits; a Comprehensive Encyclopedia of the Lives and Achievements of American Women During the Nineteenth Century*. Vol. 2. New York: Mast, Crowell & Kirkpatrick, 1897.

Williams, Edwin. *New York Annual Register for the Year of Our Lord, 1836*. New York: Edwin Williams, 1836.

Winders, Richard Bruce. *Mr. Polk's Army*. College Station: Texas A&M Press, 1997.

Wright, Gwendolyn. *Building the Dream: A Social History of Housing in America*. Cambridge, MA: MIT Press, 1981.

Wyatt-Brown, Bertram. *Southern Honor: Ethics and Behavior in the Old South*. New York: Oxford University Press, 1982.

Young, James Sterling. *The Washington Community, 1800–1828*. New York: Columbia University Press, 1966.

Zaeske, Susan. *Signatures of Citizenship: Petitioning, Antislavery, and Women's Political Identity*. Chapel Hill: University of North Carolina Press, 2003.

Zagarri, Rosemarie. *Revolutionary Backlash: Women and Politics in the Early American Republic*. Philadelphia: University of Pennsylvania Press, 2007.

Zboray, Ronald J., and Mary Saracino Zboray. *Voices Without Votes: Women and Politics in Antebellum New England*. Lebanon, NH: University Press of New England, 2010.

JOURNAL ARTICLES

Armistead, George H., Jr. "The Void Provisions of a President's Will." *Tennessee Historical Quarterly* 15, no. 2 (1956): 136–40.

Baylen, Joseph O. "A Tennessee Politician in Imperial Russia, 1850–1853." *Tennessee Historical Quarterly* 14, no. 3 (1955): 227–52.

Bergeron, Paul H. "All in the Family: President Polk in the White House." *Tennessee Historical Quarterly* 46, no. 1 (1987): 10–20.

Browder, Olin. "Conditions and Limitations in Restraint of Marriage." *Michigan Law Review* 39, no. 8 (1941): 1288–336.

Brown, Julia C. "Reconstruction in Yalobusha and Grenada Counties." *Publications of the Mississippi Historical Society* XII (1912): 214–82.

Cain, Mary Cathryn. "The Art and Politics of Looking White: Beauty Practice Among White Women in Antebellum America." *Winterthur Portfolio* 42, no. 1 (Spring 2008): 27–50.

Childress, John Williams. "The Childress Family of Tennessee" (typescript, 1960). Rutherford County Historical Society publication no. 16 (Winter 1981).

Davies, Wallace E. "The Mexican War Veterans as an Organized Group." *Mississippi Valley Historical Review* 35, no. 2 (September 1948): 221–38.

DeFiore, Jayne Crumpler. "COME, and Bring the Ladies: Tennessee Women and the Politics of Opportunity During the Presidential Campaigns of 1840 and 1844." *Tennessee Historical Quarterly* 15 (Winter 1992): 197–212.

Denison, C. W. "Mrs. James K. Polk." *Sartain's Union Magazine* 6 (January–June 1850): 155–56.

Horn, Stanley F. "Nashville During the Civil War." *Tennessee Historical Quarterly* 4, no. 1 (March 1945): 3–22.

Ikard, Robert W. "Surgical Operations on James K. Polk by Ephraim McDowell, or the Search for Polk's Gallstone." *Tennessee Historical Quarterly* 43, no. 2 (1984): 121–31.

Kanon, Tom. "The Kidnapping of Martha Crawley and Settler-Indian Relations Prior to the War of 1812." *Tennessee Historical Quarterly* 64, no. 1 (Spring 2005): 2–23.

McCrossen, Alexis. "Time Balls: Marking Modem Times in Urban America, 1877–1922." *Material Culture Review / Revue de la culture matérielle* (June 2000), https://journals .lib.unb.ca/index.php/MCR/article/view/17860/22101.

Moore, Mrs. John Trotwood. "The Tennessee Historical Society, 1849–1918." *Tennessee Historical Quarterly* 3, no. 3 (September 1944): 195–225.

Newcombe, Caroline Bermeo. "The Origin and Civil Law Foundations of the Community Property System: Why California Adopted It and Why Community Property Principles Benefit Women." *University of Maryland Law Journal of Race, Religion, Gender and Class* 11, no. 1 (2011): 1–38.

Page, Elizabeth Fry. "Polk Memorial Hall." *Bob Taylor's Magazine* 1, no. 6 (September 1905): 651–59.

Polk, James K. "Letters of James K. Polk to Cave Johnson, 1833–1848." *Tennessee Historical Magazine* 1 (September 1915): 209–56.

Presser, Stephen B. "The Historical Background of the American Law of Adoption." *Journal of Family Law* 11 (1971–72): 443–516.

Price, Tom. "Comfort in My Retirement: Polk Place," *White House History* 33 (Summer 2013): 12–21.

Shaw, Madelyn. "Slave Cloth and Clothing Slaves: Craftsmanship, Clothing, and Industry," *Journal of Early Southern Decorative Arts* 37 (2016), http://www.mesdajournal. org/2012/slave-cloth-clothing-slaves-craftsmanship-commerce-industry/.

Smith, Rebecca L. "History of Dilton." Rutherford County Historical Society publication no. 9 (Summer 1977).

Smolenski, John. "From Men of Property to Just Men: Deference, Masculinity, and the Evolution of Political Discourse in Early America." *Early American Studies* 3, no. 2 (2005): 253–85.

Stenberg, Richard R. "President Polk and California: Additional Documents." *Pacific Historical Review* 10 (1941): 217–19.

Stonesifer, Roy P., Jr. "Gideon Pillow: A Study in Egotism." *Tennessee Historical Quarterly* 25, no. 4 (Winter 1966): 340–50.

Watson, Robert P. "The First Lady Reconsidered: Presidential Partner and Political Institution." *Presidential Studies Quarterly* 27, no. 4, Rules of the Game: How to Play the Presidency (Fall 1997): 805–18.

Wells, Paul. "Music in the Life of Sarah Childress Polk." *Bulletin of the Society for American Music* 30, no. 1 (2004): 4–5.

Whitsitt, William Heth. "Annals of a Scotch-Irish Family: The Whitsitts of Nashville." *American Historical Magazine and Tennessee Historical Society Quarterly* 9 (1904): 58–82.

Wolfe, Margaret Ripley. "The Feminine Dimension in the Volunteer State." *Tennessee Historical Quarterly* 55, no. 2 (Summer 1996): 112–29.

Wood, Kristin E. "'One Woman So Dangerous to Public Morals': Gender and Politics in the Eaton Affair." *Journal of the Early Republic* 17 (Summer 1997): 237–75.

DISSERTATIONS

Berler, Anne Karen. "A Most Unpleasant Part of Your Duties: Military Occupation in Four Southern Cities, 1861–1865." Ph.D. diss., University of North Carolina at Chapel Hill, 2013.

Gismondi, Melissa Jean. "Rachel Jackson and the Search for Zion, 1760s–1830s." Ph.D. diss., University of Virginia, 2017.

Hardison, Edwin T. "In the Toils of War: Andrew Johnson and the Federal Occupation of Tennessee, 1862–1865." Ph.D. diss., University of Tennessee, 1981.

Magnuson, Lynnea. "In the Service of Columbia: Gendered Politics and Manifest Destiny Expansion." Ph.D. diss., University of Illinois at Urbana-Champaign, 2000.

Radomsky, Susan. "The Social Life of Politics: Washington's Official Society and the Emergence of a National Political Elite, 1800–1876." Ph.D. diss., University of Chicago, 2005.

ARTICLES IN BOOKS

Baird, Bruce C. "The Social Origins of Dueling in Virginia." In *Lethal Imagination: Violence and Brutality in American History*, ed. Michael Bellesiles, 87–112. New York: NYU Press, 1999.

Barney, William L. "Hood's Tennessee Campaign." In *The Oxford Encyclopedia of the Civil War*, 165–67. New York: Oxford University Press, 2011.

Giesberg, Judith. "The Fortieth Congress, Southern Women, and the Gender Politics of Postwar Occupation." In *Occupied Women: Gender, Military Occupation, and the American Civil War*, ed. LeeAnn Whites and Alecia Long. Baton Rouge: Louisiana State University Press, 2009.

———. "Women." In *A Companion to the U.S. Civil War*, vol. 2, ed. Aaron Sheehan-Dean, 779–94. New York: John Wiley and Sons, 2014.

Hoeveler, Diane Long. "Denison, Mary Andrews." In *American Women Writers: A Critical Reference Guide from Colonial Times to the Present*, 2nd ed., vol. 1, ed. Taryn Benbow-Pfalzgraf. Detroit: St. James Press, 2000.

Hume, David. "Of Essay Writing" (1742). In *The Age of Authors: An Anthology of Eighteenth-Century Print Culture*, ed. Paul Keen. Ontario, Canada: Broadview Press, 2014.

Kelly, Catherine E. "Reading and the Problem of Accomplishment." In *Reading Women: Literacy, Authorship, and Culture in the Atlantic World, 1500–1800*, ed. Heidi Brayman Hackel and Catherine E. Kelly. Philadelphia: University of Pennsylvania Press, 2008.

Lewis, Jan. "Politics and Ambivalence of the Private Sphere: Women in Early Washington, D.C." In *A Republic for the Ages: The United States Capitol and the Political Culture of the Early Republic*, ed. Donald R. Kennon. Charlottesville: University Press of Virginia, 1999.

Palmer-Mehta, Valerie. "Sarah Polk: Ideas of Her Own." In *A Companion to First Ladies*, ed. Katherine A. S. Sibley, 158–75. Malden, MA: Wiley-Blackwell, 2016.

Rush, Richard. "Report of Lieut. Richard Rush, U.S. Navy." November 23, 1888, No. 16, Centennial Exposition at Cincinnati. In *Annual Report of the Secretary of the Navy for the Year 1888*. Washington, DC: Government Printing Office, 1888.

Teute, Frederika J. "Roman Matron on the Banks of Tiber Creek: Margaret Bayard Smith and the Politicization of Spheres in the Nation's Capital." In *A Republic for the Ages: The United States Capitol and the Political Culture of the Early Republic*, ed. Donald R. Kennon. Charlottesville: University Press of Virginia, 1999.

Thacker-Estrada, Elizabeth. "True Women: the Roles and Lives of Antebellum Presidential Wives Sarah Polk, Margaret Taylor, Abigail Fillmore, and Jane Pierce." In *The Presidential Companion: Readings on the First Ladies*, ed. Robert Watson and A. Eksterowicz, 77–101. Columbia: University of South Carolina Press, 2003.

White, Mrs. Alexander B. "Mrs. John Calvin Brown." In *Minutes of the Twenty-Fourth Annual Convention of the United Daughters of the Confederacy,* 528–29. Richmond, VA: Richmond Press, 1918.

Willard, Frances E., and Mary A. Livermore, eds. "Polk, Mrs. Sarah Childress." In *American Women—Fifteen Hundred Biographies with Over 1,400 Portraits: A Comprehensive Encyclopedia of the Lives and Achievements of American Women During the Nineteenth Century,* vol. 2, 577–78. New York: Mast, Crowell & Kirkpatrick, 1897.

UNPUBLISHED PAPERS

Blair, William E. "Johnson in Civil War Nashville." Talk for the Richards Civil War Era Center Executive Tour, May 18, 2017. Paper in possession of author.

Edwards, Rebecca. "Childbearing and U.S. Empire: The Case of the 1850 Oregon Donation Land Act." Unpublished paper presented at the 17th Berkshire Conference on the History of Women, Genders, and Sexualities, June 2, 2017. Paper in possession of author.

Rockman, Seth. "Plantation Goods and the National Economy of Slavery in Antebellum America." Manuscript in possession of author.

ONLINE SOURCES

"Census of Population and Housing: Decennial Censuses." United States Census Bureau. www.census.gov/prod/www/abs/decennial/.

Federal Reserve Bank of Minneapolis. "Consumer Price Index (Estimate) 1800–." www .minneapolisfed.org/community/teaching-aids/cpi-calculator-information /consumer-price-index-1800.

"First Lady Biography: Sarah Childress Polk." National First Ladies Library. www.first ladies.org/biographies/firstladies.aspx?biography=12.

Founders Online. National Archives. https://founders.archives.gov.

Hunt, Conover. "Fashion and Frugality: First Lady Sarah Polk." *White House History* 32. www.whitehousehistory.org/fashion-and-frugality.

"Nashville City Cemetery Interments (1846–1979)." Data.Nashville.gov. https://data .nashville.gov/Genealogy/Historic-Nashville-City-Cemetery-Interments-1846-1 /iwbm-8it6.

Tennessee Encyclopedia of History and Culture. 2017. www.tennesseeencyclopedia.net.

"Unknown Smith's Expedition Battle of Tupelo." Broadside, July 22, 1864. Gilder Lehrman Collection, Gilder Lehrman Institute of American History, New York. www .gilderlehrman.org/collections/98dbcfba-72ba-43ed-8b67-389719905588?back= /mweb/search%3Fneedle%3DGLC06157%2A%2526fields%3D_t301001010.

Wellman, Judith. "The Seneca Falls Convention: Setting the National Stage for Women's Suffrage." *History Now.* Gilder Lehrman Institute of History. http://oa.gilderlehrman .org/history-by-era/first-age-reform/essays/seneca-falls-convention-setting -national-stage-for-women%E2%80%99s-su.

Index

A NOTE ABOUT THE AUTHOR

Amy S. Greenberg is the George Winfree Professor of History and Women's Studies at Penn State University. A leading scholar of the history of nineteenth-century America, she has held fellowships from the Guggenheim Foundation, the National Endowment for the Humanities, and the American Philosophical Society, among others. Her previous books include *A Wicked War* and *Manifest Manhood*.

A NOTE ON THE TYPE

Pierre Simon Fournier *le jeune* (1712–1768), who designed the type used in this book, was both an originator and a collector of types. In 1764 and 1766 he published his *Manuel typographique,* a treatise on the history of French types and printing, on typefounding in all its details, and on what many consider his most important contribution to typography—the measurement of type by the point system.

Composed by North Market Street Graphics
Lancaster, Pennsylvania

Printed and bound by Berryville Graphics
Berryville, Virginia

Designed by Anna B. Knighton